# Executive Roadmap to Fraud

# Prevention and Internal Control

# Executive Roadmap to Fraud

# Prevention and Internal Control

*Creating a Culture of Compliance*

MARTIN T. BIEGELMAN
JOEL T. BARTOW

**WILEY**

John Wiley & Sons, Inc.

Library of Congress Cataloging-in-Publication Data
Biegelman, Martin T.
  Executive roadmap to fraud prevention and internal control : creating a culture of compliance / Martin T. Biegelman, Joel T. Bartow.
    p. cm.
  Includes index.
  ISBN-13: 978-0-471-73927-2 (cloth)
  ISBN-10: 0-471-73927-8 (cloth)
  1. Corporations—Accounting—Corrupt practices—United States. 2. Corporations—Corrupt practices—United States. 3. Accounting fraud—United States. I. Bartow, Joel T., 1958- II. Title.
  HF5686.C7B52 2006
  658.4'73—dc22

                            2005020432

# Dedication

This book is dedicated to our families, who have supported and encouraged us throughout our careers.

# About the Authors

**Martin T. Biegelman,** CFE, is Director of Financial Integrity for Microsoft Corporation in Redmond, Washington. He created and leads a worldwide fraud detection, investigation, and prevention program based within internal audit at Microsoft. In addition to focusing on preventing financial fraud and abuse, he promotes financial integrity and fiscal responsibility in a COSO framework of improved business ethics, effective internal controls, and greater corporate governance.

Mr. Biegelman has more than 30 years of experience in fraud detection and prevention. Previously, he was a Director in the Fraud Investigation Practice at BDO Seidman, LLP, an international accounting and consulting firm. He is also a former federal law enforcement professional, having served as a United States Postal Inspector in a variety of investigative and management assignments. As a federal agent, he was a subject matter expert in fraud detection and prevention.

Mr. Biegelman is a Certified Fraud Examiner (CFE) and in 2004 was elected to the Association of Certified Fraud Examiners' Foundation's Board of Directors. He also serves on the Board of Advisors for the Economic Crime Institute. He is a nationally recognized speaker and instructor on white-collar crime, corruption, security issues, and fraud prevention. He has written numerous articles on fraud-related subjects including corporate crime, fraud prevention, and the Sarbanes-Oxley Act.

Mr. Biegelman holds a Master's degree in public administration from Golden Gate University and a Bachelor of Science degree from Cornell University.

**Joel T. Bartow,** CFE, CPP, is the Director of Fraud Prevention for ClientLogic, an international outsourcing company that has 20,000 employees at more than 50 locations in North America, Europe, the Philippines, and India.

Mr. Bartow served as a Special Agent for the FBI for ten years from 1987 to 1997. During that time, he worked on bank fraud and public corruption cases in Alabama and was a member of the original Russian organized crime squad in New York City, conducting complex money laundering investigations and working directly with the Russian Ministry of Internal Affairs.

After leaving the FBI, Mr. Bartow lived and worked in the former Soviet Union as a police liaison and loss recovery specialist for an American company in Kiev and Moscow. On returning to the United States, he became a partner at The Worldwide Investigative Network, LLC, a fraud consulting and investigations company near Philadelphia.

Mr. Bartow holds a Master of Arts degree in social science and a Bachelor of Arts degree from Lincoln University in Missouri. He is a Certified Fraud Examiner (CFE), a Certified Protection Professional (CPP), and a Certified Business Manager (CBM). He has written several articles for *Fraud Magazine,* a publication of the Association of Certified Fraud Examiners and has also written two crime novels.

Mr. Bartow has 18 years of experience investigating and detecting fraud and corruption in countries all over the world, including Russia, Estonia, Ukraine, Antigua, Switzerland, Greece, Israel, Kenya, Nigeria, and the Philippines, as well as across the United States from Sacramento, California to San Juan, Puerto Rico.

# Contents

# Foreword

Today's business leaders operate in an environment of unprecedented opportunity and complexity. The globalization of business grows apace in nearly every industry. The most competitive companies and best business leaders are seizing this opportunity, with new products and services that are developed, manufactured, and sold in every country of our planet. Partnerships between companies from different regions of the world are commonplace today; in fact, they are expected. The workforces of the best companies reflect the brightest minds from a multitude of cultures and backgrounds. Technological advances have facilitated the advances of global business practices and in many ways have accelerated the speed of change. Capital markets operate around the clock, rewarding the successful and punishing those who fall short. Media and press coverage and scrutiny have never been as pervasive as today. News made in Cairo, Illinois reaches a world audience as quickly as news from Cairo, Egypt. Legal and regulatory regimes vary dramatically from both a regional and national perspective. The largest market, the United States, recently enacted the most sweeping reform of public companies since the 1933 and 1934 Securities Acts. It is accurate to characterize this period as one of the most complex and exciting in the history of capitalism. There is unprecedented opportunity and complexity.

To seize the opportunity and manage the complexity, business leaders are elevating their leadership and improving their management practices. This heightened performance is evident in every facet of the best companies' operations, from R&D and Sales and Marketing all the way through to the Board and the governance of the extended organization. The rewards of global markets for the best companies are unprecedented. However, companies that fail to improve or have lapses in performance face swift and negative consequences to their financial results and company brands.

Nowhere are the negative consequences of inadequate leadership and performance more glaring than when fraud has been perpetrated or internal controls have been compromised. Unfortunately, too many companies have failed to establish a well-architected system of controls and governance. The Sarbanes-Oxley Act is providing a catalyst for change, but in too many instances it is a checklist exercise.

The best global companies today and those of the future will have well-defined and disciplined business practices that are executed uniformly on a global basis. This includes systems of accountability and compliance, regardless of different customs and laws. The Board of Directors and senior management establish codes of conduct and a tone that is well understood and a core part of the company culture. Business processes are defined and established to ensure that accounts are correct, disclosures are complete, and policies are followed. Management does the job of ensuring that prevention and detection systems are established. In short, the best leaders and companies ensure that compliance systems are an integral component of their business. Surprisingly, fraud is often overlooked as a key component of an ongoing compliance environment. The best companies assume that they hire the top people. They set the right tone at the top. They have well-understood and articulated codes of conduct. They are often surprised when individuals in their organizations commit fraud.

The leading companies of the world are taking their compliance programs to the next level by building and staffing fraud units to *prevent* compliance problems. Having been a senior executive at one of the world's premier companies, I can speak first hand about the value and importance of establishing a preventative fraud program as part of a comprehensive compliance environment. Establishing this unit allowed Microsoft to detect and address problems we would not have seen. In addition, the fraud unit leadership became an important part of a management training program to ensure consistent and disciplined business practices worldwide. From a CFO perspective, I was most pleased to see a unit and a program that helped to ensure compliance, but also more than paid for itself!

In this book, the reader will be given a delightful roadmap to fraud prevention and internal controls. Illustrative stories and tips along with practical managerial advice on establishing the right organization, objectives, and practices make this book a must read. There is important contextual information on current practices and requirements from regulatory regimes. Finally, the 14-point management antifraud program will allow every reader to meet challenges and complexities in a global business environment.

Enjoy!

—John Connors

# Preface

In a perfect world, this book would not be needed. All corporate employees, from the Chief Executive Officer, the Chief Financial Officer, and the Board of Directors to the entry-level workers, would have the highest degree of integrity. Fraud and abuse would be nonexistent. There would be no such thing as financial statement fraud, embezzlement, or kickbacks. Unfortunately, we live in an imperfect world in which noncompliance, misfeasance, fraud, and corruption exist. One only needs to read the daily papers or watch the evening news to learn of the latest corporate scandal. Once respected corporate titans now face "perp walks" and prison because of financial impropriety.

Common sense tells us that a business executive or manager only needs to hear: "Never commit fraud of any kind." However, fraud prevention always involves further measures: never condoning fraud in any shape or form, providing fraud awareness and prevention training for employees, instituting strong internal controls, and limiting exposure to fraud through a robust fraud detection, investigation, and prevention program. Nevertheless, it would be naïve to expect that these steps alone would stop all forms of fraud and abuse from occurring. It is a given that corporate crime will always be with us. What is really needed is an ongoing culture of compliance that can take years to build but only a moment to collapse. Corporate executives who are charged with protecting their companies from fraud need a guide to establish an effective program. The passage of the Sarbanes-Oxley Act of 2002, the creation of the Public Company Accounting Oversight Board, and other related developments have forced CEOs and CFOs to understand the protections that need to be in place to prevent corporate fraud.

The authors bring a unique perspective to corporate fraud prevention. We are life-long practitioners in the field, with a combined 50 years of experience in both the public and private sectors detecting and investigating fraud and white-collar crime. Our careers parallel each other. As federal agents with the United States Postal Inspection Service and the Federal Bureau of Investigation, we investigated fraud and corruption including corporate crime, investment fraud, kickback schemes, international fraud scams, insurance and healthcare fraud, organized crime, and violations of the Racketeering and Corrupt Organizations Act (RICO); we also assisted in the prosecutions of hundreds of fraudsters.

We then went into the private sector to conduct investigations on behalf of clients who were victims of corporate fraud and other crimes. We worked cases all over the world for companies large and small, public and private, and we helped business executives understand the importance of fraud prevention. We were subsequently recruited by corporations and given the responsibility of creating and managing worldwide fraud prevention programs using our knowledge, skills, and experience. We are both Certified Fraud Examiners who are still doing this work today.

Fraud is nothing new. History has shown that fraud has long been a part of our society and will continue to be. As Judge Edwin R. Holmes said in the case of *Weiss v. United States* in 1941, "The law does not define fraud; it needs no definition; it is as old as falsehood and as versatile as human ingenuity."[1] What makes the present situation so different is the enormity of the recent corporate scandals and the strong response of both the investing public and the government. Gone are the days of a slap on the wrist to the wrongdoer and then all is forgotten. Today, corporate fraud results in shareholder lawsuits, the implosion of companies, executive prison sentences, and an investor outcry for reform.

In addition, there is a greater focus today than ever before on uncovering and preventing fraud as a result of the loss of billions of dollars in equity and greatly diminished investor confidence in the markets. Financial statement fraud and other internal fraud schemes provide considerable risk to a corporation. The enactment of enhanced reporting requirements and greater public scrutiny of companies have contributed to this new age of enlightenment. The formation of the Corporate Fraud Task Force in July 2002 and the aggressive response of law enforcement and securities regulators

---

[1] *Weiss v. United States*, 122 F.2d 675, 681 (Ct. App. 5th Cir. 1941).

have resulted in zero tolerance for fraud. However, internal fraud is not the only risk that businesses face. External fraud schemes also attack companies and can do significant damage to both finances and reputations.

Although no one expects CEOs, CFOs, and other corporate executives and managers to be experts in fraud prevention, the current climate requires a thorough understanding of the principles of fraud examination and state-of-the art compliance programs. This book is a roadmap to help executives understand fraud and reduce its impact. The late Harvard philosophy professor George Santayana once said that those who do not remember the past are condemned to repeat it. This book looks to the past to gain a better understanding of the nature of fraud and how to prevent it. It relates lessons that can be applied now and in the future to prevent fraud, and it also reviews theories and models that explain how and why fraud happens inside an organization. It then describes the current climate in detail as well as the critical importance of fraud prevention and culminates by providing a roadmap to establishing a culture of compliance. Creating this culture is the only way businesses can position themselves to meet the new environment of tighter regulations, transparency, and accountability. It is a proactive method for actually preventing fraud. Simply reacting to fraud issues as they occur is no longer acceptable.

By setting out the generally accepted standards for fraud prevention along with new recommendations, this book will help executives establish a world-class fraud investigation and prevention program. A discussion of the new attitudes within the United States Department of Justice, the Securities and Exchange Commission, and the New York State Attorney General's Office is also included. Key policy changes and declarations, from the ground-breaking "Thompson Memo" to the landmark "Gatekeepers" speech, are discussed so the reader will clearly understand the implications of fraud and the need for compliance at every turn.

After spending our careers with victims and perpetrators, investigators and prosecutors, in courtrooms and boardrooms, we have great insight into all kinds of fraud and the reasons people commit them. We have many lessons to share as well as numerous case studies and experiences about how to detect, investigate, and prevent fraud. This book is intended to be a primer for corporate executives at both public and private companies who are expected to protect their organizations from fraud and inappropriate behavior. We believe it will provide special insights to executives at medium and smaller size companies who may falsely believe that they are not facing fraud issues or who may not fully understand the relationship between fraud prevention and good corporate compliance. In addition to senior executives, this book will be beneficial for middle and lower level executives and managers to help them understand their roles in fraud prevention. It will also be of value to fraud investigators, prosecutors, academics, students, and anyone with an interest in the world of fraud.

Each chapter starts with an Executive Summary detailing the key points and takeaways from each chapter. Executive Insights and exhibits are used in various chapters to emphasize important concepts and provide case studies. We have designed the book to be user friendly—the reader does not have to be a Certified Fraud Examiner to understand the concepts and procedures described.

In all the years we have been investigating fraud and corruption, we have yet to see any decrease in the problem. We probably never will. However, there have been changes in how fraud is addressed. Tougher laws against corporate wrongdoing have been enacted with greatly increased prison sentences for those convicted. It is not the best of times for fraudsters; it is definitely a good time for guardians of the law. There has never been a better time to be a fraud investigator. Any corporate executive, manager, or employee contemplating a journey to the "dark side" should keep in mind that fraud and noncompliance will be met with the strong arm of the law.

This book will be your roadmap to an understanding of corporate fraud, the implementation of fraud prevention, and the creation of a culture of compliance; it is our honor and privilege to be your guides on this journey.

# Acknowledgments

Writing a book such as this is never an easy task, and we could not have completed it without the wisdom, assistance, and encouragement of others. First, our thanks go to our friend and mentor, Joseph Wells, founder and chairman of the Association of Certified Fraud Examiners, a true fraud prevention visionary. He encouraged us to write this book and helped us along the way.

We acknowledge those who provided ideas, content, and assistance: Carl Pergola, Frank Goldman, Walt Pavlo, Dr. Gary Gordon, John McDermott, Maria Luckas, Dick Carozza, John Gill, Bruce Dean, Thomas Kiernan, Michael Osborne, Karen Popp, George Stamboulidis, Mark Kirsch, Anthony Migliaccio, and Patricia Sweeney.

Although this work is solely ours and does not reflect the views or opinions of Microsoft Corporation or ClientLogic, we would like to thank both companies for allowing us to write the book. Special thanks go to Julie Casteel and Paul Stone at ClientLogic, the driving force behind the formation of the ClientLogic fraud prevention program. Thanks to Mike Boyle, Rod Winters, and Odell Guyton at Microsoft, who were instrumental in the formation of the Financial Integrity Unit and have strongly supported fraud detection and prevention at the company, and to our teams at Microsoft and ClientLogic who ensure that fraud prevention and compliance is built into the very fabric of our work.

We acknowledge those dedicated law enforcement professionals and Certified Fraud Examiners who fight fraud on a daily basis. It is their work that we recognize in this book. They are the ones whose unflagging efforts hold corporate fraudsters accountable while protecting the common good.

A note of thanks goes to our executive editor, Timothy Burgard, for giving us this opportunity and then guiding us through the writing and publishing process.

Special appreciation is due to John Connors for writing our Foreword. As the CFO of Microsoft Corporation, he built a world-class finance organization and led by example in creating a culture of compliance and integrity.

Finally, Martin Biegelman's wife Lynn and son Daniel spent countless hours reviewing the manuscript while providing constructive feedback, suggestions, and ideas for content. Their tireless dedication helped make the difference in completing this book.

# CHAPTER 1

# Fraud's Feeding Frenzy: Overview of Recent Corporate Scandals

## EXECUTIVE SUMMARY

There has been a "feeding frenzy" of corporate fraud over the last few years. Corporate executives who were once respected and trusted revealed themselves as morally corrupt fraudsters. They became rogue employees, too busy stealing from the corporate "piggy bank" to think of the consequences for their employees, shareholders, customers, or themselves. Corporate powerhouses like Enron and WorldCom and their executives were swept up in fraudulent financial accounting and a multitude of other frauds. The government reacted strongly in response to the public outcry after billions of dollars in investments had evaporated. The President promoted the need for corporate responsibility and a promise to arrest any corporate executive with a hand in the corporate "cookie jar." Some indicted CEOs tried to use the "Chutzpah Defense," claiming they were deaf, dumb, and blind when the frauds were going on at their companies. The outcome has been indictments, followed by "perp walks" as well as convictions, and a change in how the government views corporate fraud prevention.

## FRAUD'S FEEDING FRENZY STILL GOING STRONG

In the late 1980s, a federal agent investigated a $95 million swindle in New York City involving mail fraud, bank fraud, money laundering, and a host of other crimes. He and his team made arrest after arrest of the many fraudsters involved in this massive scheme. After the arrest of yet another major player in the fraud, this federal agent commented on the defendants' criminal behavior. He likened it to hungry sharks feeding on their helpless prey and called it a "feeding frenzy of fraud" (J. LaPerla, personal communication). Through the years, the expression has often been used to describe various fraud schemes that made the headlines. This snappy, off-the-cuff description of fraud and the people who commit it tells volumes about the damaging effect it can have. Like unrelenting sharks constantly searching for their next meals, fraudsters never stop their search for new opportunities to commit fraud and economic crime.

Fraud has always been a thorn in the side of honest citizens. The enactment of strong laws and the empowerment of enforcement agents are helpful but certainly do not guarantee an end to fraud, a crime of opportunity that has been with us through the ages. Uninformed people who think that the well-documented corporate wrongdoings in recent years comprised the first such instances of large-scale fraud have much to learn. "Thus, all through the country, thousands of innocent and unsophisticated people, knowing nothing about the ways of these city thieves and robbers, are continuously fleeced and robbed."[1] Does this sound like a description of the many victims of Enron, WorldCom, and other recent corporate frauds? It was said by a congressional sponsor of the United States Mail Fraud Statute[2] well over a century ago. The Mail Fraud Statute, the nation's oldest and premier fraud-fighting mandate, was enacted in 1872 after an epidemic of consumer mail-order frauds. Today, consumer frauds of all types are still prosecuted with the Mail Fraud Statute, as are many corporate frauds, large and small.

## WHAT A DIFFERENCE A FEW YEARS MAKE

Fraud has had a tremendous impact on the corporate landscape of the early 21st century. Companies that were once world class are no more. Their chief executives have either been indicted or convicted or are about to be; millions of investors have lost billions of dollars, and corporate crime remains constantly in the news. Enron, WorldCom, Tyco, Adelphia, HealthSouth, and other companies have dominated the headlines, and their corporate officers have been charged with numerous financial crimes. The list goes on. The feeding frenzy of corporate fraud got so bad that a scorecard needed to be developed to identify and track all the players. MSNBC created its guide to "Corporate Scandals," a Web site listing recent developments in corporate fraud disclosures and prosecutions.[3] More names and details are added continuously.

The many corporate executives who have faced criminal prosecutions over the past few years worked for both well-known and lesser known companies. Although typically the major players have been making the headlines, defendants are coming from all types and sizes of business (e.g., even a bagel business in New Jersey that created fake bagel sales to inflate revenue fraudulently).[4] When it comes to corporate fraud, anyone can be a player. Exhibit 1.1 lists some of the many corporate defendants prosecuted by the Corporate Fraud Task Force.

## PERSONAL PIGGY BANK CONCEPT OF LEADERSHIP

The corporate scandals of the last few years had a common recipe: corporate executives with no integrity, total arrogance, and huge greed, combined with accounting firms that failed to fulfill their responsibility for independent auditing. All these executives showed complete arrogance in their total disregard for shareholders and their belief that they could get away with taking huge amounts of money from their respective companies. In the case of former Tyco CEO Dennis Kozlowski, there are multiple reports of his excessive spending of corporate funds for extravagant parties and personal purchases.[5] Kozlowski received from Tyco a $19 million no-interest loan and $11 million for art, antiques, and furniture for his New York City apartment, including the now infamous $6,000 floral patterned shower curtain. To top it off, Tyco paid half the cost for a $2.1 million junket for friends and family to the Italian island of Sardinia to celebrate the birthday of Kozlowski's wife.[6] Because Kozlowski was

| | |
|---|---|
| Adelphia | Leslie Fay |
| Allfirst | Manhattan Bagel |
| Arthur Andersen | McKesson |
| Biocontrol | Merrill Lynch |
| Cendant | Network Associates |
| Charter Communications | NextCard, Inc. |
| Computer Associates | Nicor Energy |
| Credit Suisse First Boston | Peregrine Systems |
| Dynegy | PurchasePro.com |
| eConnect | Quintus |
| Enron | Qwest |
| Financial Advisory Consultants | Reliant Energy Services, Inc. |
| GenesisIntermedia, Inc. | Rite Aid |
| Golden Bear Golf, Inc. | Symbol Technologies |
| HealthSouth | Targus Group |
| Homestore | US Technologies |
| ImClone | Vari-L Company, Inc. |
| Informix | Waste Management |
| Just for Feet | WorldCom |
| Katun Corporation | Zurich Payroll |
| L90, Inc. | |

**EXHIBIT 1.1** Significant Criminal Cases Prosecuted by the Corporate Fraud Task Force

*Source:* Significant Criminal Cases and Charging Documents, The United States Department of Justice's Corporate Fraud Task Force website, *http://www.usdoj.gov/dag/cftf/cases.htm.*

the CEO, it was easy for him to take as much money out of the company as he wanted. However, he did not escape justice and was subsequently convicted for his criminal behavior.

Kozlowski was not the only corporate titan to take freely from the corporate coffers. Those executives who allow greed to overcome them can easily abuse the power that comes from absolute control. It is a given that former Adelphia CEO John Rigas never thought he would be arrested and convicted for stealing from the corporate cookie jar. Rigas and other Adelphia executives were accused of looting the company of more than $1 billion. They didn't care that the company's assets belonged to shareholders. Even though they felt they were accountable to no one, their accounting fraud was discovered, and federal authorities arrested them.

Former WorldCom CFO Scott Sullivan also thought he had a personal piggy bank on tap. This once well-respected CFO of a telecom powerhouse never thought he would be paraded before the media like a common criminal, but there he was doing the "perp walk" with FBI agents in Manhattan following his arrest for a massive accounting fraud. Soon after, he was helping the government prosecute and convict his boss, former WorldCom CEO Bernard Ebbers.

A culture of noncompliance combined with a lack of accountability and transparency contributed to the wholesale looting of once respected companies by their fraudster CEOs, CFOs, and others. People who commit fraud never think about the consequences, or they believe there will be no consequences. They think the piggy bank is theirs to take, not caring or understanding that investors are the true owners.

---

### EXECUTIVE INSIGHT 1.1: A MILLIONAIRE CEO GETS GREEDY

Rocky Aoki is the founder of the successful Benihana Asian restaurant chain. Aoki started the company in 1964 by introducing the Japanese steakhouse experience with entertaining chefs preparing meals in front of the dining guests. He created outlets all over the United States, and eventually Benihana became a publicly traded company on the NASDAQ, with Aoki as both CEO and Chairman of the Board. The company's slogan of "An Experience at Every Table" says it all about dining at Benihana.[i]

Unfortunately, Aoki had another kind of experience that was anything but positive. In 1993, Aoki participated in an insider trading scheme that would eventually result in his indictment and conviction.[ii] Aoki received insider information from a stock promoter who was also a public relations consultant for Spectrum

Information Technologies. Spectrum was a publicly held corporation in Manhasset, New York.[iii] Spectrum and its corporate officers would later make the headlines with other issues including allegations of "defrauding investors by artificially boosting its stock price" and other frauds.[iv] The Spectrum case is further profiled in Executive Insight 13.1 in Chapter 13.

According to the June 1998 federal indictment of Aoki, in September and October of 1993, Spectrum held secret negotiations with John Sculley, former CEO and Chairman of the Board of Apple Computer, to get him to join Spectrum in a similar executive capacity. During this period, Aoki solicited and received "non-public information concerning Spectrum's negotiations" with Sculley. On October 18, 1993, Spectrum publicly announced that Sculley had accepted the executive positions and would be joining the company. As expected, Spectrum's stock rose from $7.63 to $11.13, a 46 percent jump. Between September 29 and October 15, 1993, Aoki purchased 200,000 shares of Spectrum through three different brokerage accounts. On November 2, 1993, Aoki sold the 200,000 shares for a profit of approximately $590,000.[v]

Aoki then opened a brokerage account for the tipster on or about November 8, 1993 and instructed that 1,000 shares of Spectrum be purchased for that account. Shortly thereafter, Aoki instructed his personal brokerage account to transfer $10,000 to the tipster's account to pay for the 1,000 shares purchased. The tipster then sold the stock.[vi] After the investigation of Aoki became public in May 1998, he resigned as chairman and CEO in the hopes that the impact on Benihana would be lessened by his departure.[vii]

Postal Inspectors on Long Island, New York conducted the investigation that resulted in the June 1998 federal indictment of Aoki for one count of conspiracy and five counts of trading with insider information.[viii] In announcing the indictment, Zachary Carter, then United States Attorney for the Eastern District of New York, stated that "insider trading undermines the public's confidence in the fair operation of our nation's securities markets."[ix]

Although Aoki made a major transgression affecting his life and his company, he realized the error of his ways and took responsibility. He pled guilty on August 23, 1999 to four counts of insider trading and on March 8, 2000 was sentenced to probation and a $500,000 fine.[x] The judge was lenient on Aoki because the plea agreement had mandated a $1 million fine and eight months of home detention.[xi]

John McDermott, the Postal Inspector who had conducted the investigation, commented that Aoki could not resist making a relatively small amount of money compared with his probable net worth. Aoki used the insider information but got caught because he foolishly paid the tipster by wire transfer of the funds from his brokerage account. The wire transfer led right back to Aoki.

---

[i] Benihana, Inc, www.benihana.com.

[ii] Alan Wax and Patricia Hurtado, "Benihana Founder Gets Probation, Reduced Fine," *Newsday*, March 8, 2000, A54.

[iii] *United States v. Rocky Aoki*, defendant, Indictment, United States District Court, Eastern District of New York, CR 98-593.

[iv] James Bernstein, "Feds Charge 3 in Spectrum Fraud, SEC Says Execs Artificially Boosted Stock Price," *Newsday*, December 5, 1997, A77.

[v] *United States v. Rocky Aoki*, defendant, Indictment, United States District Court, Eastern District of New York, CR 98-593.

[vi] Ibid.

[vii] Combined news services, "Benihana Founder Resigns," *Newsday*, May 20, 1998, A47.

[viii] Robert E. Kessler, "Aoki Indicted in Stock Deal, Benihana Founder Allegedly Paid for Insider Information about Spectrum Development," *Newsday*, June 10, 1998, A51.

[ix] Ibid.

[x] Alan Wax and Patricia Hurtado, "Benihana Founder Gets Probation, Reduced Fine," *Newsday*, March 8, 2000, A54.

[xi] Ibid.

## THE ROGUE EMPLOYEE

The corporate frauds discussed so far involve what are called "rogue employees." The rogue employee is any employee, no matter the level, who deviates from hired duties and who is the perpetrator of employee fraud by attacking the company from within, causing financial and reputational damage.[7] Rogue employees have their own agendas, and their interests are not aligned with those of their employers. In fact, they are not really employees of the company. True employees are committed to the company's mission and are part of the team in causing the company to grow to even greater heights and results. Rogue employees are not out for the common good and betterment of the business. They are out to steal, defraud, and line their pockets to the detriment of their employers. The rogue employee typically portrayed in the media has been the CEO, CFO, or other senior executive. Although these positions attract the most media attention, rogue employees can be anywhere in the organization. In many cases, a long-time, lower level employee who stays "below the radar screen" is the culprit. No matter where the rogue employee may be in a company, greater attention to internal controls and fraud prevention is essential in lessening the damaging effects of employee fraud.

## THE CEO'S NEW CHUTZPAH DEFENSE

The recent corporate frauds and resulting prosecutions of responsible corporate executives have provided a new defense posture appropriately named the "Chutzpah Defense." *Chutzpah* is a Yiddish term meaning unbelievable gall, audacity, arrogance, or utter nerve. Corporate executives are taking this word to a new level and applying it to their criminal defense strategies in an attempt to escape criminal convictions and lengthy prison time. You can call this defense what you like—The Deaf, Dumb, and Blind Defense; The Dog Ate My Homework Defense; The Hey, I'm Just the CEO, What Do I Know about What's Going On? Defense; or the popular Chutzpah Defense. This troubling defense strategy is a last-ditch effort to extricate the corporate fraudster from appropriate punishment.

As former federal agents in the pursuit of justice, the authors know full well what capable defense attorneys are obliged to do professionally when representing clients facing criminal charges. However, it is hardly believable that CEOs, CFOs, or other high-level corporate officers would not know what is going on at their companies. If they are so unaware of what is happening, they should not be in those roles. Boiler room scam artists are fond of saying "put some lipstick on this pig and sell it" when trying to push fraudulent securities on unsuspecting investors. That is what some indicted corporate defendants are trying to do with this Chutzpah Defense. Although the deception may work on some, it is generally not working on juries. Recent experience has shown that juries will just not accept the Chutzpah Defense. Corporate executives on trial who have tried this approach to avoid conviction have lost.[8] Juries will just not believe the CEO who claims ignorance of large-scale fraud occurring right under their nose. Pigs, even with lots of lipstick, don't fly.

Bernard Ebbers tried the Chutzpah Defense and lost. During closing arguments the prosecutor called it "The Aw Shucks Defense": Ebbers claimed he had no expert knowledge of accounting and no idea that any fraud was going on at WorldCom. He was just a "good ol' boy," a cheerleader for the company, who left the details to others. Justice prevailed because pleading ignorance about massive fraud when one is the CEO or CFO just does not work. The basic principles of the changes in corporate governance are all about accountability, especially for the corporate executive.

Although it can be argued that acceptance of responsibility for one's actions is on a societal decline of late, judging from the lawsuits filed against McDonald's Corporation blaming their burgers for weight-related problems or their hot coffee for burns, at least there have been changes for the better. Sarbanes-Oxley and improved corporate governance have increased corporate responsibility and accountability. A word to the wise: "The Buck Stops Here" should be written in big letters and displayed on every corporate executive's desk as a reminder to all that the Chutzpah Defense is not an option.

## A SAMPLING OF CORPORATE FRAUDS

Enron's collapse was the first of many publicized corporate scandals and started Congress on the path to enact legislation that would stop corporate fraud. More transgressions and revelations followed. The biotech firm ImClone Systems was probed by congressional investigators for failing to tell investors that one of its drugs had not been approved by the Food and Drug Administration. Adelphia disclosed that it paid billions of dollars in secret loans to its CEO and his family. Arthur Andersen was indicted and convicted on charges of obstruction of justice in the Enron investigation. In May 2005, the Supreme Court overturned the conviction on improper jury instructions, but the damage was done. Merrill

Lynch agreed to pay a $100 million fine to settle charges that the firm's stock research misled investors. These disclosures and others that followed forced Congress to take a new look at corporate reform. There are many similarities in the lessons that can be learned from the fall of these major corporations.

## Enron

More than any other company facing scandal in recent years, Enron stands out as the poster child for corporate greed and fraud. Beginning with Enron's reporting of $638 million in losses on October 16, 2001, the revelations of fraud have been nonstop. The resignation of former CEO Jeffrey Skilling in August 2001 was probably more than a coincidence and a harbinger of things to come. As stated in Skilling's indictment of February 18, 2004, the resignation came with "no forewarning to the public."[9] The reading of the criminal charges tells why he would want to leave as quickly as possible. The indictment of Skilling and other co-conspirators details the feeding frenzy of fraud at Enron. In describing the scheme to defraud, the indictment stated that:

> From 1999 through late 2001, defendants Jeffrey K. Skilling and Richard A. Causey (former Enron Chief Accounting Officer and Executive Vice-President) and their co-conspirators engaged in a wide-ranging scheme to deceive the investing public, the SEC, credit rating agencies, and others about the true performance of Enron's businesses by (1) manipulating Enron's finances so that Enron's publicly reported financial results would falsely appear to meet or exceed analysts' expectations; and (2) making public statements and representations about Enron's financial performance and results that were false and misleading in that they did not fairly and accurately in all material aspects represent Enron's actual financial condition and performance, and omitted to disclose facts necessary to make those statements and representations truthful and accurate.[10]

Early on, there was much criticism of the Enron Task Force for not moving faster in bringing the company's corporate crooks to justice. There was a constant complaint that the prosecutors were dragging their feet and getting nowhere fast. How wrong the critics were. Complex white-collar crime investigations can often take many months and even years to complete before any indictments are brought. A slow and steady but exhaustive collection of evidence cannot be confused with inactivity. Corporate executives need to remember that federal investigators and prosecutors are working behind the scenes interviewing witnesses, subpoenaing documents, quietly "flipping" targets into cooperators, corroborating information, and building a case. This is what happened with the Enron investigation. As United States Assistant Attorney General Christopher Wray said at the time of Skilling's indictment, "the indictment of Enron's CEO shows that we will follow the evidence wherever it leads—even to the top of the corporate ladder."[11]

It appears that former Chairman and CEO Kenneth Lay subscribes to the Chutzpah Defense by using his own variation, the "Mr. Magoo Defense." Mr. Magoo is the bumbling and nearsighted cartoon character who has no clue what is happening around him. Comedian and television host Dennis Miller made a joke about Ken Lay, who was telling everyone who would listen how he was a corporate and financial genius with the ear of presidents, that is, until "the feds" started investigating Enron. Suddenly he became a bumbling Mr. Magoo, who had no idea what was going on inside his own company. He was blind beyond belief to the massive fraud permeating the company he led as founder, chairman, and CEO. Lay repeatedly appeared on television to defend himself and said he knew nothing of Enron's "cooking the books" or other frauds at the company. While the company was heading for bankruptcy, he was publicly encouraging his employees to buy more stock in Enron, claiming it was a great value at the beaten-down price.

Creating a culture of compliance is a common theme of this book. Truly great leaders inspire and mentor their employees to higher standards of accomplishment and integrity. That was clearly missing at Enron. Since the beginning of the probe, more than two dozen company executives have been charged with numerous financial crimes including Skilling, Lay, and former CFO Andrew Fastow. There is no doubt that the "tone at the top" was one of noncompliance and lawlessness that fostered an environment of fraud and corruption at all levels of the company.

## Tyco

Dennis Kozlowski, Tyco's former CEO, was accused with other corporate executives of looting $600 million from the company and defrauding investors through unauthorized loans and bonuses, loans improperly forgiven, and sales of stock that were inflated by fraudulent corporate accounting. Kozlowski joined Tyco in 1975 and rose through the ranks to President, Chief Operating Officer, and then CEO. Over time, he came to typify the corporate lifestyle of excess at every turn. It all came tumbling down when in late May 2002, he learned he was about to be indicted by the Manhattan, New York District Attorney's Office. Kozlowski resigned from Tyco on June 3, 2002, and on June 4, he was arrested.

Tyco's new management commissioned an internal accounting and corporate governance review of the allegations of fraud and abuse by Kozlowski and other former Tyco executives. The review was conducted by New York attorney David Boies with assistance from numerous forensic accountants. The scope of the internal accounting review included 1999 to 2002 reported revenues, profits, cash flow, internal auditing, control procedures (or lack of them), the personal use of corporate assets, the use of corporate assets to pay personal expenses, employee loans and loan forgiveness, and other corporate governance issues. The subsequent report found the company "engaged in a pattern of aggressive accounting which, even when in accordance with Generally Accepted Accounting Principles, was intended to increase reported earnings above what they would have been if more conservative accounting had been employed."[12]

Tyco was successful to a degree in playing the numbers through accounting manipulations. For one, it abused goodwill. Goodwill in accounting terms is a financial advantage that a business gains from the purchase price over fair market value of assets acquired. When a company is purchased, goodwill is the difference between the amount paid over the net asset value. Tyco had a "staggering $26 billion worth of goodwill on its balance sheet."[13] This maneuver greatly increased earnings and cash flow because it allowed Tyco to book additional revenue without associated costs of acquisition. Tyco also did not report acquisitions that it stated were small enough to be considered "immaterial" under Generally Accepted Accounting Principles. "From 1991 through 2001, Tyco spent $8 billion on more than 700 acquisitions that it said were not material. But taken as a group, these 700 deals clearly had a huge impact on Tyco's results."[14] There is no doubt that these accounting moves had a material impact on the revenue and expenses of the company and should have been disclosed.

An important lesson to remember is that no matter how strong the evidence appears to be in a case, there is no such thing as a guaranteed conviction. Dennis Kozlowski's first trial in state court in Manhattan in April 2004 ended in a mistrial. The evidence seemed to be overwhelming, but still the jury could not come to a decision after 12 days of deliberations. After the mistrial, one of the jurors called the case against the defendants "a slam dunk" and stated, "those guys [Kozlowski and Mark Schwartz, Tyco's former CFO] are never going to get acquitted, no matter what they do. The best they can hope for is a hung jury."[15] Despite this juror's view, the jury could not come to an agreement to convict, forcing a retrial of the defendants. At the second trial in June 2005, Kozlowski and Schwartz were found guilty of looting $600 million from the company. It was one of the biggest wins for prosecutors fighting corporate fraud.

## WorldCom

WorldCom was once the second largest long-distance telecommunications company. It was a Wall Street darling that in reality had a culture of noncompliance and criminality at the highest levels of leadership. Former CEO Bernard Ebbers was convicted after trial in March 2005. Former CFO Scott Sullivan pled guilty, as did several other executives who agreed to cooperate against Ebbers. The downfall began in March 2002, when then Vice-President of Internal Audit Cynthia Cooper went to Sullivan with her concerns about the company's accounting. He angrily told her to mind her own business and that everything was fine. Her instincts told her there were big problems, and she kept digging. Ebbers resigned in April 2002 amid questions regarding $408 million in personal loans. A $7.2 billion accounting fraud eventually became a $107 billion bankruptcy filing, the largest in corporate history.

In late May 2002, Cooper and her staff uncovered $500 million in fraudulent computer expenses. Arthur Andersen, WorldCom's auditors, refused to respond to some of Cooper's questions about the auditing. On June 20, 2002, Cooper told WorldCom's Audit Committee that the company was falsifying its accounting. The Audit Committee and Board of Directors are to be credited with acting quickly. A few days later Sullivan was fired, and WorldCom admitted it hid $3.85 billion in expenses, allowing it to post a profit in 2001 instead of a loss. In 1998, *CFO* magazine had named Sullivan one of the country's best CFOs. What *CFO* magazine did not know was that Sullivan had instructed his people to cook the books. WorldCom hid billions of dollars in expenses by transferring them throughout the company's capital expenditures accounts. Cooper exposed this massive fraud and became a famous whistle-blower, recognized as one of *Time* magazine's Persons of the Year for 2002.

Federal prosecutors moved swiftly to prosecute Sullivan and former controller David Myers on 17 criminal counts including conspiracy to commit securities fraud. They were arrested on August 1, 2002, just two days after President Bush signed the Sarbanes-Oxley Act into law. At a Washington, DC, news conference after the arrests, then Attorney General John Ashcroft stated, "With each arrest, indictment and prosecution, we send this clear, unmistakable message: corrupt corporate executives are no better than common thieves."[16]

The subsequent federal indictment issued by a Grand Jury in the Southern District of New York alleged that Sullivan and his co-conspirators "engaged in an illegal scheme to inflate artificially WorldCom's publicly reported earnings by falsely and fraudulently reducing reported line cost expenses."[17] Furthermore, the indictment stated that the "co-conspirators made these false and fraudulent journal entries in WorldCom's general ledger knowing, and intending (1) that such journal entries would ultimately be reflected in WorldCom's financial statements and public filings with the SEC; (2) that WorldCom's financial statements and public filings would falsely overstate WorldCom's earnings; and (3) that the investing public would rely upon such overstated earnings."[18] As often happens, federal prosecutors convinced Sullivan, Myers, and several other executives to testify against an even bigger catch, Ebbers. Ebbers, who steadfastly maintained his innocence and demanded a jury trial, got his wish.

Sullivan was the star government witness against Ebbers at trial. The jury spent eight exhausting days deliberating. It came back on March 15, 2005 with a conviction on all counts, including conspiracy to commit fraud by falsifying WorldCom's financial results; securities fraud by misleading investors and the public about WorldCom's true financial condition; and making false filings that misrepresented WorldCom's financial state with the SEC. Although Ebbers took the stand and claimed he was unaware of the fraud and that Sullivan alone was the mastermind behind it, the jury did not believe him. Leslie Caldwell, the former head of the Enron Task Force, who is knowledgeable about the CEO ignorance defense, stated after the conviction, "There's inherently a lot of suspicion when a highly paid CEO says there were significant things he wasn't aware of. There's a certain cynicism among jurors, who ask 'How'd you get to be CEO?'" On July 13, 2005, Ebbers was sentenced to 25 years in prison for masterminding the fraud at WorldCom. The trial judge rejected his plea for leniency and gave him the harshest sentence yet for corporate fraud.

## Adelphia

John Rigas had it all. At 78 years of age, he was the founder of one of the nation's largest cable companies. He was a son of Greek immigrants who became an entrepreneur and eventually got into the cable subscription business by starting Adelphia Communications Corporation. He built it from the ground up into a public company worth billions of dollars. His two sons were executives in the company. Rigas and his family lived the good life that mega millions in corporate earnings can provide. They had mansions, their own personal golf course, a fleet of luxury cars, and power. Unfortunately, Rigas had a secret that would soon be exposed. He was a corporate fraudster, and Adelphia had become his personal piggy bank.

It all came crashing down for Rigas on July 24, 2002, when United States Postal Inspectors arrested Rigas, his two sons, and two other Adelphia executives and charged them with multiple counts of conspiracy to commit mail fraud, wire fraud, bank fraud, and securities fraud. Rigas and his sons did their obligatory "perp walk" in Manhattan just days before the Sarbanes-Oxley Act was signed into law. Rigas and his sons knew they were about to be arrested and offered to surrender, to avoid the "perp walk." The government refused because they wanted the spectacle of a very public arrest to send a strong message to other corporate crooks. As stated in the criminal complaint, "the defendants and their co-conspirators perpetrated an elaborate and multifaceted scheme to defraud stockholders and creditors of Adelphia, and the public." Another statement found in the criminal complaint describing the defendants' behavior was unusual: "The investigation has revealed probable cause to believe that John J. Rigas, the defendant, together with members of his family, has looted Adelphia on a massive scale, using the company as the Rigas Family's *personal piggy bank* [emphasis added], at the expense of public investors and creditors."[19] The United States Attorney for the Southern District of New York called the crime "one of the most elaborate and extensive frauds ever."

The scheme ran from 1999 through May 2002, but the criminal investigation only began in March 2002, resulting in prosecution by July 2002. When Adelphia filed for bankruptcy protection on June 25, 2002, it listed $18.6 billion in debt. The investigation found that Rigas and his sons had looted the company of more than $1 billion. Among the many financial transgressions they were alleged to have committed are the following:

- Received a million dollars a month in secret cash payments
- Built a $13 million private golf course using Adelphia funds that were not disclosed to the non-Rigas family members of the board of directors or to the public
- Borrowed $2.3 billion from banks with Adelphia guaranteeing loans that were not recorded in the company's books
- Used $252 million to pay margin calls against loans that the family received from various brokerage firms
- Personal use of corporate aircraft and New York City apartments by Rigas family members; Adelphia employees were allegedly instructed not to record personal use of the aircraft in the usage logs.

Rigas, his sons, and one other co-defendant went to trial in New York on March 1, 2004. On July 8, 2004, Rigas and one son, Timothy Rigas, were convicted on all 15 counts. The jury deadlocked on another son, who faces a retrial. A fourth defendant, Adelphia's assistant treasurer, was acquitted. One of the government's star witnesses at trial was cooperating defendant James R. Brown, once Adelphia's Vice-President of Finance. He testified that Adelphia developed a culture of lies. They had kept two sets of books for more than 10 years. One book contained the falsified numbers, and one had the actual numbers, so they would know which ones they had manipulated and by how much. As Brown testified, "we don't want to fool ourselves."[20] Brown was a critical insider witness for the government, and although he spent 18 years at the company and was a loyal employee, the threat of a long prison term turned him into a government cooperator. There are no bonds of loyalty when prison is a reality.

At his sentencing hearing on June 20, 2005, Rigas told the judge, "In my heart and in my conscience, I'll go to my grave really and truly believing that I did nothing but try to improve the conditions of my employees."[21] The judge did not buy Rigas' story and sentenced him to a "life sentence" of 15 years in prison. For the now 80-year-old Rigas, the only way he can get out of jail is if prison doctors determine he has less than three months to live. Rigas' son, Timothy, received 20 years in prison.[22]

## THE PRESIDENT'S DRIVE FOR CORPORATE RESPONSIBILITY

In 2002, President George W. Bush saw corporate fraud as such an enormous problem that he made corporate responsibility a core element of his administration, along with the war on terrorism. Early on in the emerging corporate scandals, President Bush set out an aggressive agenda to fight corporate fraud including:

- Exposing and punishing acts of corruption
- Holding corporate officers and directors accountable
- Protecting small investors, pension holders, and workers
- Moving corporate accounting out of the shadows
- Developing a stronger, more independent corporate audit system
- Providing better information to investors.[23]

On March 7, 2002, the President announced his "Ten-Point Plan to Improve Corporate Responsibility and Protect America's Shareholders."

It was based on three principles: information accuracy and accessibility, management accountability, and auditor independence. The Ten-Point Plan declares that:

1. Each investor should have quarterly access to the information needed to judge a firm's financial performance, condition, and risks.
2. Each investor should have prompt access to critical information.
3. CEOs should personally vouch for the veracity, timeliness, and fairness of their companies' disclosures, including their financial statements.
4. CEOs or other officers should not be allowed to profit from erroneous financial statements.
5. CEOs or other officers who clearly abuse their power should lose their right to serve in any corporate leadership positions.
6. Corporate leaders should be required to tell the public promptly whenever they buy or sell company stock for personal gain.
7. Investors should have complete confidence in the independence and integrity of companies' auditors.
8. An independent regulatory board should ensure that the accounting profession is held to the highest ethical standards.
9. The authors of accounting standards must be responsive to the needs of investors.
10. Firms' accounting systems should be compared with best practices, not simply against the minimum standards.[24]

These tenets were to form the basis of the Sarbanes-Oxley Act of 2002.

President Bush went further to demonstrate to the investing public that he meant business. On July 6, 2002, he called on Congress to legislate new powers and statutes to stop corporate fraud and bring to justice those wrongdoers who violated the public and corporate trust. On the same date, he created the Corporate Fraud Task Force, headed by then Deputy Attorney General Larry Thompson, to coordinate the investigation and prosecution of financial accounting fraud and other corporate frauds. The full force of federal law enforcement would be brought to bear on corporate wrongdoers. Although some may argue that it should not have taken massive corporate implosions and billions of dollars in losses to get the government to act, "better late than never" was the refrain of the day.

Congress and the President did act. On July 30, 2002, President Bush signed the Sarbanes-Oxley Act into law. This law has great implications for public companies. Sarbanes-Oxley will not make fraud disappear, but its strong language and stiff penalties could deter corporate executives who are tempted to stray. Sarbanes-Oxley is not yet a household name outside corporate America, accounting firms, and government prosecutors' and regulators' offices, but with a little time and some more well-publicized prosecutions, it soon will be. In the offices and boardrooms of public companies, Sarbanes-Oxley and its requirements, safeguards, and sanctions are discussed daily. Just as the Racketeer Influenced and Corrupt Organizations Act (RICO) has struck fear into organized crime for more than 30 years, Sarbanes-Oxley will do the same for corporate crooks, if not now, then surely in the years to come.

## FIGHTING FRAUD IS GUARANTEED EMPLOYMENT

Investigators beginning a career or assignment in fraud detection are commonly told never to worry about being out of a job because investigating fraud provides job security. The message is that fraud is an evil that will always be present in our society and that anyone smart enough to enter the field of fraud detection and prevention will find full and long-term employment. Sad as it may seem, fraud will always take place wherever there is opportunity. The feeding frenzy of fraud will not abate unless fraud prevention is embraced and instituted at all levels of a company, especially in the executive suite.

## ENDNOTES

1. Attributed to an unnamed Congressional sponsor of the *Mail Fraud Statute,* enacted in 1872.
2. *The Mail Fraud Statute, U.S. Code* 18 (2005), § 1341.
3. "Corporate Scandals Front Page," MSNBC, www.msnbc.com/id/3032230.
4. *United States v. Allan Boren and Eric Cano,* defendants, First Superseding Indictment filed February 2001, Cr. No. 01-730(A)-GAF, United States District Court for the Central District of California, 5-6.

5. Mark Maremont and Colleen DeBaise, "Prosecutor Says Two Executives Used Tyco as 'Piggy Bank,'" *The Wall Street Journal,* March 17, 2004, C1.

6. Colleen DeBaise, "Newest 'Tyco Gone Wild' Video Is Out, and Jurors See $6,000 Shower Curtain," *The Wall Street Journal,* November 26, 2003, C1.

7. Timothy L. Mohr, "Employee Fraud and Rogue Employees-Prevention and Detection," a professional project submitted to the faculty of Utica College, Utica, NY, December 2002.

8. The acquittal of former HealthSouth CEO Richard Scrushy in June 2005 is an exception. Although the evidence against Scrushy appeared to be formidable, the jury felt otherwise. There are some who attribute the acquittal to the "homefield advantage" of having the case tried in Birmingham, AL, where Scrushy is very popular, as well as the excellent work of the defense team in impeaching many of the prosecution witnesses.

9. *United States v. Jeffrey K. Skilling and Richard A. Causey,* defendants, Superseding Indictment filed February 18, 2004, Cr. No. H-04-25, United States District Court, Southern District of Texas, Houston Division at 3.

10. Ibid., 5.

11. "Ex-Enron CEO Named in 42-Count Indictment," MSNBC.com, February 19, 2004, www.msnbc.msn.com/id/4311642.

12. Summary of Findings of Accounting and Governance Review prepared for Tyco International, Ltd. by Boies, Schiller & Flexner, December 30, 2002.

13. Anthony Bianco, William Symonds, Nanette Byrnes, and David Polek, "The Rise and Fall of Dennis Kozlowski," *Business Week,* December 23, 2002, 64-77.

14. Ibid.

15. Christopher Mumma and Thomas Becker, "Jurors Expect Conviction in Tyco Retrial," *The Seattle Times,* April 7, 2004, E4.

16. Carrie Johnson and Ben White, "WorldCom Arrests Made," *Washington Post,* August 2, 2002, A1.

17. *United States v. Scott D. Sullivan,* First Superseding Indictment, S1 02 Cr. 114 (BSJ), United States District Court for the Southern District of New York, 9.

18. Ibid., 10.

19. *United States v. John J. Rigas, Timothy J. Rigas, Michael J. Rigas, James R. Brown, and Michael C. Mulcahey,* defendants, criminal complaint unsealed on July 24, 2002, United States District Court, Southern District of New York, sworn to by United States Postal Inspector Thomas F.X. Feeney.
20. Peter Grant, "Adelphia Insider Tells of Culture of Lies at Firm," *The Wall Street Journal,* May 19, 2003, C1.
21. "Adelphia Founder Gets 15-Year Term; Son Gets 20," MSNBC.com, June 20, 2005, www.msnbc.msn.com/id/8291040/.
22. Ibid.
23. "Corporate Responsibility," The White House web site, www. whitehouse.gov/infocus/corporateresponsibility.
24. Ibid.

# Fraud Theory and Prevention

**EXECUTIVE SUMMARY**

The Association of Certified Fraud Examiners (ACFE) reports that the average organization loses 6 percent of its annual revenue to fraud and abuse. That statistic alone should be reason enough to embrace fraud prevention. Even if that number is off somewhat, the losses to businesses are staggering. Why do people commit fraud? There are many theories. One centers on the elements of motive, opportunity, and rationalization. Can fraud be prevented? Lessening or removing opportunity is one way to fight fraud. This can be accomplished by improved internal controls and accountability. If people know they will be held responsible for acts of fraud, then likely perpetrators will often not commit the crime. Understanding the importance of fraud prevention is critical for a business organization in this new era of improved corporate governance.

# FRAUD 101

What is fraud? Before one can completely understand fraud prevention, one must know what fraud is. Webster's dictionary defines fraud as "an instance or act of trickery or deceit especially when involving misrepresentation; an intentional misrepresentation, concealment, or nondisclosure for the purpose of inducing another in reliance upon it to part with some valuable thing belonging to him or to surrender a legal right."[1] *Black's Law Dictionary* defines fraud as "the knowing misrepresentation of the truth or concealment of a material fact to induce another to act to his or her detriment and a misrepresentation made recklessly without belief in its truth to induce another to act."[2] The Mail Fraud Statute, the first federal statute enacted to protect Americans from fraud and scams, defines fraud as "any scheme or artifice to defraud, or for obtaining money or property by means of false or fraudulent pretenses, representations, or promises."[3] The word *artifice* was included in the original wording of the Mail Fraud Statute in 1872 and means trickery or guile, both of which are very descriptive of fraud.

The Association of Certified Fraud Examiners uses the term "occupational fraud and abuse" and defines it as "the use of one's occupation for personal enrichment through the deliberate misuse or misapplication of the employing organization's resources or assets."[4] When boiled down to its essence, fraud is all about stealing, cheating, lying, and lack of integrity. However, the best definition might be something reformed fraudster Barry Minkow once said, "Fraud is nothing more than the skin of a truth stuffed with a lie."[5] Minkow was a teenager in Southern California in the 1980s who founded and built a multimillion-dollar carpet cleaning business. Unfortunately, he succumbed to the "dark side" and engaged in fraud. He decided to take his company public and conspired to defraud investors in a $26 million Initial Public Offering (IPO) fraud. He went to jail for seven years and now lectures and writes about the consequences of fraud. Proving that it takes one to know one, his definition says it all about fraud.

## CORPORATE FRAUD

The term "corporate fraud" has been defined by the Department of Justice to include the following illegal conduct:

> 1. *Falsification of corporate financial information* (including, for example, false/fraudulent accounting entries, bogus trades, and other transactions designed to artificially inflate revenue, fraudulently overstating assets, earnings and profits or understating/concealing liabilities and losses, and false transactions designed to evade regulatory oversight);
> 2. *Self-dealing by corporate insiders* (including, for example, insider trading, kickbacks, misuse of corporate property for personal gain, and individual tax violations related to any such self-dealing);
> 3. *Fraud in connection with an otherwise legitimately operated mutual or hedge fund* (including, for example, late trading, certain market-timing schemes, falsification of net asset values, and other fraudulent or abusive trading practices by, within, or involving a mutual or hedge fund); and
> 4. *Obstruction of justice, perjury, witness tampering, or other obstructive behavior* relating to categories 1 to 3 above.[6]

Whether it is a boiler room scam promising a luxurious, seven-day, all expenses paid cruise to the Bahamas that turns out to be a cruise to nowhere, or a "cooking the books" accounting scheme at a major corporation, fraud is the skin of a truth, stuffed with a lie. All fraud appears on the surface to be forthright, but as one peels away the layers, the inner deceit, corruption, and lies are exposed.

As young federal agents, the authors wanted to arrest every fraudster they could find. Although a fair number of them were arrested, it was easy to see that there were not enough law enforcement officers to arrest all the criminals out there. Also, even if there were enough resources to put every schemer in jail, the damaging effects of fraud would not be reversed, nor would lost assets or reputations be restored. It became apparent that detecting fraud early, or, better yet, stopping it from occurring, was far more effective. However, stopping fraud's feeding frenzy is easier said than done.

Preventing fraud is often much harder than it would appear. Human nature and greed guarantee that society and corporations will always face the issue of fraud. It may be noble to try to stop all fraud, but the reality is that it will always be present, although much can be done to limit its effects. The key to preventing fraud is first to understand that fraud exists and then limit its potential for harm. To do this, the detection of fraud is paramount, along with exceptional fraud prevention programs.

## THE ACFE 2004 REPORT TO THE NATION ON OCCUPATIONAL FRAUD AND ABUSE

The ACFE is the world's premier provider of antifraud training and education. The organization has over 33,000 members worldwide who fight and prevent fraud in the public and private sectors. A number of them are Certified Fraud Examiners (CFE). CFEs are certified specialists in the detection, investigation, and prevention of fraud. They have a unique set of skills and experiences to resolve allegations of fraud. The ACFE's goal is to reduce business fraud worldwide and inspire public confidence in the value and integrity of the fraud detection and prevention profession. The ACFE also conducts studies and issues reports on occupational fraud to examine the effects of occupational fraud and abuse on individuals and organizations.

The ACFE's *2004 Report to the Nation*[7] covers 508 cases of occupational fraud in the United States, with a total of over $761 million in losses. Participants in the study included CFEs with direct involvement in the actual detection and investigation of the fraud. The study found some very interesting and ominous trends for fraud:

- The typical United States organization loses 6 percent of its annual revenues to fraud. Applied to the Gross Domestic Annual Product for 2003, that equates to approximately $660 billion in total losses. Although this number may seem high, even a loss of one percent translates into a significant shortfall for a company. Thus, any reduction in the amount of fraud and abuse that occurs in a business will result in additional gains for the bottom line.
- The study found that occupational frauds are more likely to be detected through an employee tip than through internal audits or internal controls. This finding clearly supports the key Sarbanes-Oxley requirement for audit committees to establish confidential

reporting mechanisms. This requirement will be covered in more detail in Chapters 3 and 12.

- The establishment of confidential reporting mechanisms can dramatically reduce fraud losses. The median loss for organizations that had a confidential and/or anonymous reporting hotline was $56,500. The study further found that organizations without established reporting processes had median losses that were more than double those with established reporting procedures.

- Tips about fraud are reported not only by employees but also by those outside the company with connections and knowledge. The study found that 60 percent of tips came from employees of the subject company, 20 percent came from customers, and 16 percent came from vendors. Thus, it is imperative to publicize the existence of a hotline and other confidential reporting mechanisms to ensure that all possible allegations are investigated.

- Although internal controls have long been established as an effective way to reduce fraud and abuse, all too often they are not robust enough to be effective in detecting and stopping fraud. The study found that internal controls ranked fourth behind "by accident" in how frauds were discovered.

- There is a false impression that small companies are better protected from fraud than larger companies. Small companies were defined as those with fewer than 100 employees. The median loss experienced by small companies was $98,000. That was higher than the median loss suffered by all but the very largest businesses. A small company may not be able to survive a large fraud loss and needs to be at least as proactive in fraud prevention as larger companies. The key message is that all companies, no matter the size, need to have effective fraud detection and prevention programs in place.

- The fraud loss amount is directly related to the position of the perpetrator. Common sense and history tell us that a CFO can do far more financial damage to a company than someone in the mailroom. The study found that frauds perpetrated by owners and executives resulted in a median loss of $900,000. This was six times higher than the losses resulting from managers and 14 times higher than losses caused by lower level employees.

- The study also found that most occupational fraudsters were first-time offenders. (The authors of this book had the same experience—the vast majority of the people they arrested were first-time fraud offenders.) Only 12 percent of the subjects in the study had a previous conviction for fraud. Instituting a process for conducting background checks will eliminate some offenders from an organization but clearly will not be enough to stop all fraud and abuse. An important point to remember is that just because fraudsters have not been arrested before does not mean they have not been committing fraud for some time. Fraud is often hard to expose, so it is common for fraudsters to be involved in long-term schemes without being detected.

■ Detecting fraud does not automatically mean that an organization will be able to make good on the losses. The study found that once fraud is detected, a company is unlikely to recover its losses. The median recovery in the study was only 20 percent of the original loss. Approximately 40 percent of organizations victimized by fraud did not recover anything.

The *2004 Report to the Nation*, like its predecessor reports in 1996 and 2002, shows that the 6 percent figure for loss of total revenue to occupational fraud has remained the same; the actual losses have increased, however. The report classified occupational fraud into three major categories:

1. Asset misappropriation, which involves theft or misuse of an organization's assets such as billing schemes, payroll schemes, and expense reimbursement schemes. These types of fraud will be discussed in Chapter 7.
2. Corruption, including conflicts of interest in which the employee's motivations may not be aligned with the best interests of the employer. Typical examples include kickbacks, bid-rigging, and hidden business interests in vendors. These types of fraud will also be discussed in Chapter 7.
3. Fraudulent financial statements, including overstating revenues and understating liabilities and expenses. These types of fraud will be discussed in Chapter 6.

Although asset misappropriation schemes were by far the most common (more than 90 percent), they had the lowest median loss, of just $93,000. Fraudulent financial schemes occurred only 7.9 percent of the time but had the highest median losses, of $1,000,000.[8] Typically, companies can recover from asset misappropriation schemes, but financial statement frauds can have devastating effects on an organization, as can be seen with Enron, WorldCom, and others.

## FRAUD PREVENTION

The ACFE's *Fraud Examiners Manual* states that "Fraud prevention requires a system of rules, which, in their aggregate, minimize the likelihood of fraud occurring while maximizing the possibility of detecting any fraudulent activity that may transpire. The potential of being caught most often persuades likely perpetrators not to commit the fraud. Because of this principle, the existence of a thorough control system is essential to fraud prevention."[9] The key words here are in the last two sentences. The "potential of being caught" and "the existence of a thorough control system" are critical to any effective fraud prevention program. It is about being proactive rather than reactive. As the important elements of a fraud prevention program are discussed within a company, repetition and reinforcement are necessary because they are so critical to the success of a program.

Fraud prevention is much more than just a good business practice; it is a requirement today. Companies face a number of risks, each of which is huge and potentially devastating. Among these risks, the issue of vicarious liability stands out. Corporations and other organizations can be held liable for criminal acts committed as a matter of organizational policy. They may also be held liable for the criminal acts of their employees if those acts are performed in the course and scope of their employment for the purpose of benefiting the corporation. An organization can be held liable for something an employee does on behalf of the organization even if the employee is not authorized to perform that act.

The financial risks from fraud losses, shareholders' lawsuits, federal prosecution, fines, and convictions for fraud are all good reasons to institute a strong fraud prevention program. Risk to reputations and the emotional toll of fraud should also be considered. As hard as it is to believe now, Arthur Andersen once had a sterling reputation among accounting firms. If Arthur Andersen, the founder, were alive today, he would be devastated to see what has happened to the company that he spent the better part of his life building into an accounting and consulting powerhouse. The sad fact is that it takes just a handful of employees to destroy a company of many thousand innocent individuals. The emotional toll of fraud is the impact on the employees and families who had nothing to do with their company's fraud but who suffer the consequences. The personal devastation to the Enron employees who believed in their company and were deceived like all the other shareholders is but one example. These employees saw their jobs, life savings, and retirement plans disappear, all because of corporate fraud and executives with no integrity.

## PERP WALKS AS A FORM OF FRAUD PREVENTION

We have recently seen numerous "perp," or perpetrator, walks as corporate executives are arrested for fraud. Perp walks have come to be expected in high-profile cases. They are the very public parading of a high-profile person charged with a serious crime before television cameras by law enforcement officers, for the express purpose of publicizing the defendant's arrest and sending a strong message to other such criminals that this is what will soon happen to them.

Perp walks are nothing new. They have long been used by law enforcement to publicize arrests. They were often called "conga lines" because they resembled the rhythmic line dance with defendants handcuffed and led by law enforcement officers in a twisting formation from the street to the courthouse. By the early 1990s, law enforcement officers in some jurisdictions were being criticized by judges and prosecutors for conducting perp walks, as the defendants had only been charged with a crime and were deemed innocent until proved guilty. The belief was that the very public displays could prejudice potential jurors. Federal judges, United States Attorneys' Offices, and federal law enforcement agencies issued edicts against them.

In reality, perp walks were a simplistic form of fraud prevention. The public display of fraudsters was thought to send a strong message. It was hoped that parading fraudsters to court and plastering their faces all over newspapers and television would deter others from committing such crimes. It was also used to turn co-conspirators into informants and witnesses in order to avoid being perp-walked themselves. The authors remember suspects in cases saying that they would cooperate in criminal investigations as long as there was a promise not to expose them to the media. Perp walks are back with a vengeance as the government is using old as well as some new weapons to prosecute and prevent corporate crime. Perp walks show defendants that although they were once captains of industry with billions of dollars, now the whole world can see they are just common criminals. Although perp walks are useful for publicizing and sending a strong message about committing fraud, they are only a small piece of the business of fraud prevention.

In the mind of federal agents and prosecutors, nothing stops fraud better than the arrest of corporate fraudsters resulting in criminal prosecutions. Law enforcement knows all too well the damaging effects of corporate fraud in recent years. The pursuit of justice requires that corporate crooks be held accountable for their criminal acts. The knock on the front door at six o'clock in the morning by two beefy federal agents in suits with an arrest warrant in one hand and handcuffs in the other will bring even the most powerful and arrogant corporate executive to tears. Getting arrested, cuffed, fingerprinted, photographed, and taken to court are traumatic experiences. Federal authorities know this and use it to their advantage.

## ELIOT SPITZER AS A CORPORATE FRAUD PREVENTION HERO

New York State Attorney General Eliot Spitzer, Wall Street's corporate cop, has made headlines over the last few years with his highly publicized probes, prosecutions, and billion-dollar settlements involving brokerage firms and mutual funds that defrauded and misled investors. The subjects of his investigations read like a "Who's Who" of the investment world. Credit Suisse First Boston, Merrill Lynch, and Salomon Smith Barney were accused of issuing fraudulent research reports and paid fines totaling hundreds of millions of dollars to settle their cases. Spitzer's office obtained the conviction of the Vice Chairman and Chief Mutual Fund Officer of Fred Alger Management, Inc., a prominent mutual fund. Additional investigations have involved other top mutual funds. Inquiries into the financial and insurance companies AIG, Marsh & McLennan, and Ace have proved that no industry or practice is beyond the reach of investigation and prosecution.

Spitzer and his team of investigators and prosecutors have become the de facto fraud detection and prevention arm of a number of firms because those firms could not do the job themselves. These companies obviously had fraud prevention programs that did not work and did not protect their firms, their employees, or their shareholders from the devastating charges and resultant publicity. The fraud prevention basics were not in place. Spitzer laments that corporate executives do not necessarily learn from the mistakes or prosecutions of others and often fail to comprehend the importance of a culture of compliance. As he stated in an interview from 2004,

> *A large part of it is the culture you find inside a company. One of the frustrating issues has been the lack of self-regulation, the lack of internal self-discipline in many companies that have permitted improper behavior to continue. I've observed before that one of the frustrations for me is that not once in the course of everything we have done has a corporate executive stopped these practices before we've found them. And I look forward to the day when that happens. We need to breed a new culture of responsibility inside the company so that competitive pressure doesn't drive companies to the lowest common denominator, which is too often what is happening. We need to say, forget the once in every five years that a major CEO is fired because of this type of impropriety. Day-to-day think about growing a culture of responsibility inside a company so we'll do better on a regular basis.*[10]

Spitzer has announced his intention to leave his position as Attorney General and run for governor of New York State in 2006. This "champion of the people" will have left a strong legacy for protecting the average investor. The good work of his office will no doubt continue, as the public has come to expect this high level of enforcement. New York is the nation's financial center and will always be faced with the threat of fraud. Corporate wrongdoers should expect no lessening of the aggressive approach from this office as well as an equally strong attack from the New York County District Attorney and the United States Attorneys in New York and Brooklyn.

## EDWIN SUTHERLAND AND WHITE COLLAR CRIME

The term "white collar crime" was coined in 1949 by a criminologist from Indiana University named Edwin H. Sutherland. He defined white-collar crime as "a crime committed by a person of respectability and high social status in the course of his occupation."[11] Sutherland rejected the common belief at the time that attributed theft and fraud to either abject poverty or genetics. Sutherland's "white collar criminal" was described as a person who learned how to commit crimes, much like a person learns other things. The longer the person committed crimes, the better they got at committing crimes. Sutherland attributed the reason for the theft to criminal rationalizations, motives, and other learned attitudes.

## DR. DONALD CRESSEY AND THE FRAUD TRIANGLE

Although it is common knowledge that people and corporations commit fraud, what is often not understood is why they do it. Understanding the motive behind fraud is important in preventing it. Dr. Donald Cressey, a famed teacher and pioneer in fraud research and an important fraud expert developed the Fraud Triangle Theory

**EXHIBIT 2.1**  The Fraud Triangle

*Source:* Reprinted with permission from the Association of Certified Fraud Examiners, Austin, Texas © 2005.

(Exhibit 2.1) to explain why people commit fraud. Dr. Cressey came to the conclusion that the propensity for fraud occurred when three critical elements came together: motive, opportunity, and rationalization. Each of these three elements is necessary and interrelated in order for a person to actually commit a fraud. The absence of any one of them would not allow a person to commit a fraud. Every corporate executive needs to understand the Fraud Triangle and why employees commit various kinds of fraud.

## MOTIVE

Motive is the reason people commit fraud. It is the element that causes a person to act or react and often implies an emotion or desire.[12] It is the driving force behind a person changing from a law-abiding citizen to one who commits a felony. There are many motivations to commit fraud; most of them are greed related. They include living beyond one's means, an immediate financial need, debts, poor credit, a drug or gambling addiction, and family pressure, to name a few. In the movie *Wall Street*, the character Gordon Gekko was fond of saying "Greed is Good." [13] Greed epitomized Wall Street in the 1980s. Just as greed led many down the path to insider trading and other financial crimes, it is a motivating force in all kinds of frauds, especially the corporate frauds seen over the last few years.

Although greed is the usual motive, sometimes revenge and ego play a role. An employee may feel anger and hostility against a company for some perceived wrong and may try to get back at the company by defrauding it. Although the argument goes that this is revenge, when this behavior results in money in the pocket, it boils down to greed, pure and simple. Sometimes the motive is a desire to beat the system. People may think they are smarter than anyone else, and they believe that no one can stop them. Pressure to perform is often a motive for fraud. Sometimes the perpetrator has committed fraud to help improve the bottom-line financial results. Emotional instability is also a motivating factor, but this is seen far less than the other motives for fraud.

An excellent example of greed as a motive is a case involving a multimillionaire industrialist from New York. He owned businesses all over the country. He lived in a mansion in one of Long Island's most exclusive communities. He gave large donations and endowments to universities, museums, hospitals, and other charitable organizations. Most amazing of all, he served several presidents in a variety of diplomatic and economic assignments in his lifetime. He was well respected, and reference materials include pages of his accolades and achievements. Compared with all the good this man did throughout a lifetime, the one stain on his career is his conviction for fraud. Unfortunately, he conspired with others to submit a fraudulent insurance claim on one of his many businesses.

Why would this otherwise good man do something that was so contrary to the rest of his life? What was his motive? The answer that comes to mind is simply greed. His path to a courtroom and a sentencing before a federal judge started with an insurance claim for damage at a factory. The problem was that the type of damage that occurred was not covered by the policy. The damage was in the hundreds of thousands of dollars. Rather than just let it go and view it as a business loss, this industrialist decided to take the advice of his public adjuster and falsify the claim by changing the cause of damage to one that was covered by the policy. Payoffs were made to insurance adjusters to go along with the fraudulent claim. The kickbacks that were paid took almost half of the proceeds from the insurance claim.

This insurance fraud might have gone undiscovered if not for the fact that greed overtook the insurance adjusters involved. They continued to engage in staged and inflated insurance claims with dozens of other insureds and insurance adjusters in settling bogus insurance claims. When federal agents eventually discovered their crimes, the adjusters admitted their long involvement in insurance fraud, the many phony claims they had submitted to numerous insurance companies, and the many co-conspirators with whom they had worked. Again proving that there is no honor among thieves, they gave up the name of the industrialist. After a short investigation, the industrialist admitted his involvement and pled guilty to charges of fraud.

## OPPORTUNITY

Opportunity is the favorable circumstance that allows a fraud to occur. The amount of opportunity that a person has to commit fraud is usually determined by his or her position of authority in the company and access to assets and records. Poor internal controls contribute to opportunity and fraud. An employee who can both open a new vendor account and also pay that vendor provides an example of weak internal controls and a good opportunity for fraud. Blank check stock that is not properly inventoried and locked is another example of opportunity. Strong separation of duties along with oversight lessens the opportunity to commit and succeed at fraud. Of the three Fraud Triangle elements, opportunity is the one area in which fraud prevention can excel. Removing or lessening the opportunity to commit fraud and abuse is important in any fraud prevention program but is absolutely critical for a corporate fraud prevention program.

Scammers commit the frauds they do because they have the opportunity. A mailroom employee may not be able to conspire with a vendor to create a contract that provides no service but yields a kickback to the employee, yet, a mail clerk could steal incoming mail containing highly confidential proprietary information and sell it to a competitor in a foreign country. It all depends on the opportunity and how it is limited.

## RATIONALIZATION

The third element of the Fraud Triangle is rationalization. Rationalization is how the fraudster justifies inappropriate actions. It is "the provision of reasons to explain to oneself or others behavior for which one's real motives are different and unknown or unconscious."[14] When the elements of need and opportunity come together, the fraudster is convinced that what occurred is not bad or wrong. Fraudsters often think of themselves as honest. It was borrowing from the company and not stealing. Rather than consider themselves as criminals who just defrauded their company, they make themselves into victims. They may say: *I was only borrowing the money, I'll pay it back someday; This is not much money, the company is rich and won't really miss it; Everybody does it; They owe it to me; I'll stop once I get over this financial hump; It's for a good purpose; The company mistreats me.* Rationalization is another way of saying the end justifies the means.

In their careers as federal agents, the present authors arrested hundreds of fraudsters. None of these criminals ever expected to get caught. They all thought that they would get away with their crimes. They rationalized what they did and came to believe they were invulnerable. If they didn't rationalize their actions, their consciences would take over.

## DR. W. STEVE ALBRECHT'S FRAUD SCALE

In the 1980s, Dr. W. Steve Albrecht of Brigham Young University studied and analyzed frauds. His findings showed that the persons most likely to commit fraud in the workplace were living beyond their means and had personal or gambling debts, a desire to have personal status, or pressure to have status from family or peers. Those employees who believed they were underpaid or underappreciated were also more likely to steal from their workplace. The desire to give free merchandise to friends and family was also mentioned as a motivator.

Dr. Albrecht explained the motivations to commit fraud by creating a Fraud Scale. Similar to Cressey's Fraud Triangle, Albrecht's Fraud Scale theorizes that even if opportunity and situational needs are present, some employees will never commit fraud. According to Albrecht, the motivation to commit fraud depends on how strong each of the three factors is in each particular employee. It is a complex combination of the degrees to which the three factors of opportunity, motive, and rationalization exist in each situation. Thus, Albrecht believes that fraud is much harder to predict than Cressey believed.

## FRAUD THEORIES

In addition to the traditional theories of fraud just described, the authors have designed some theories of their own. Over their many years as fraud investigators, they have seen more than their share of schemes, scam, cons, and frauds. Some were simple, such as credit card fraud and loan scams. Others were complex financial crimes such as insider trading and securities fraud. Some were so well thought out and successful that they were repeated time after time. Although some of these new theories may seem light-hearted and even whimsical at first, they speak volumes about how and why fraud is perpetrated and is all too often successful.

## Tip of the Iceberg Theory of Fraud

When first discovered, very few frauds yield their true extent, along with the actual amount of the loss. Often the fraud first seen is just a small part of the actual deceit, like most of an iceberg is hidden below the surface. As an investigator conducts the investigation, interviews people, reviews supporting documentation, and takes other related steps in the process, a much larger fraud is usually revealed. Corporate fraud is no different.

An excellent example of the "Tip of the Iceberg Theory of Fraud" is an insurance fraud case investigated by the Postal Inspection Service, the IRS, and the FBI in the 1990s in New York. The case started with an anonymous tip to an insurance company that homeowner property claims were fraudulently inflated. One of the first claims investigated was for $8,000, rather small in terms of insurance fraud that would be authorized for federal prosecution. The federal agents on the case believed that more than one fraudulent claim was involved and kept digging. Their hard work paid off. By the end of the case several years later, more than 200 defendants had been arrested and convicted, and more than $500 million in staged and inflated commercial and homeowner property claims had been uncovered.

## Potato Chip Theory of Fraud

Committing fraud and getting away with it can become addictive. Once one succeeds at an embezzlement scheme or payment of a bribe to a foreign government official to secure a contract and gets away with it, it gets harder and harder to stop that activity. This may be characterized as the "Potato Chip Theory of Fraud." Just as a person is unable to eat only one potato chip, once employees start committing fraud, they cannot stop. Assuming they do not get caught, they will commit fraud after fraud, even branching out to new frauds to get money and other things of value. An excellent example is a longtime employee of a corporation who was investigated for allegedly receiving kickbacks from a vendor. Applying the Potato Chip Theory of Fraud, other avenues of possible fraud were investigated. Knowing that expense reporting fraud is very common, a review of this employee's travel and entertainment reports found personal expenses fraudulently claimed as business expenses. Thus, two different frauds against the company were discovered.

Greed and success in not getting caught become addictive, yet if fraudulent behavior continues, the perpetrator will eventually be found out. Criminals make mistakes no matter how smart they think they are. They can get bolder and bolder each time they are not discovered. Experience has taught us that they eventually make fatal mistakes leading to detection. However, employees involved in fraud can do great damage until they are caught. The longer a fraud continues, no matter the employee level, the greater the potential financial and reputational damage.

## Rotten Apple Theory of Fraud

It has often been said that one rotten apple can infect an entire barrel. This can be applied to unchecked fraud in an organization or group. True leaders can inspire their employees to reach new heights of personal growth and career development. They can be role models who help create a new generation of corporate leaders. Employees want to emulate the leaders they see at their companies. Executives and managers who lead by example in compliance and integrity lessen the risk of fraud by their employees.

Unfortunately, the opposite also applies. Poor leaders who lack character and integrity, and who turn to fraud and abuse, can damage the people they lead. In a twist on imitation being the sincerest form of flattery, there are examples of employees who turn to fraud because their managers were doing it and getting away with it. This is also called the "Culture of Noncompliance Theory" because when there is no culture of compliance, a breakdown of rules, policies, and accountability occurs.

A manager committed thousands of dollars fraud by charging personal expenses on his corporate credit card. He did this on a continuing basis, and his subordinate saw that he did it. The employee copied the fraudulent behavior of his boss. When discovered, the subordinate unsuccessfully claimed that he was just doing what his superior did and should not be fired. This strategy did not work, and both were fired.

Another variation of the "Rotten Apple Theory of Fraud" is seen when a manager fails to provide adequate supervision of a team, leaving the team members with no direction. When oversight is lacking, successful fraud is easier to commit. Expense reporting fraud is much more common in groups in which it is known that managers do not thoroughly review the submitted payment requests. Although these kinds of managers do not personally commit the fraud, they promote it by not being alert and fully engaged. "Trust but verify" should be an ongoing policy.

## Low-Hanging Fruit Theory of Fraud

Although priority attention should be given to high-risk fraud such as financial misstatement and accounting issues, one must not forget about the lower risk but high occurrence frauds such as procurement frauds. It is often thought that fraudsters are cunning, imaginative, and brilliant in devising and executing their many schemes, but this presumption is often a misconception. Investigators, at times, give these violators too much credit for thoroughly thinking through their fraudulent activity and subsequent actions.

The reason that so much fraud is eventually discovered is simply that most fraudsters make mistakes that lead to their discovery. If the "low-hanging frauds" are not given appropriate attention, the fraudster employees will continue their crimes until discovered. This could be months or years, and by that time, more damage will have been done. Executives should ensure that their fraud investigation units do not overlook these low-hanging frauds, as they will solve several problems. First, they are usually simple frauds that do not take a significant amount of investigative time. Second, by stopping this fraudulent activity, there is an immediate benefit by removing a bad employee while sending a strong message about the company's commitment to fraud prevention. Third, the fraudster employee is removed before he or she is able to commit much more complex and serious frauds.

## Addition by Subtraction Theory of Fraud

One of the best ways to reduce fraud is by removing the source of the problem. When a company terminates an employee who has committed fraud, a risk is removed and that improves the company. This theory refers to the benefits that an organization receives when it takes a proactive approach to fraud detection and investigation. As simple as that may sound in theory, it is often hard to do in practice. It requires a business to take a zero tolerance and hard-core approach to fraudulent behavior by its employees, partners, and vendors. In a case involving embezzlement by a relatively low-level employee, the evidence was overwhelming that the fraud did indeed occur. In addition, the employee admitted his involvement when confronted with the evidence found by investigators.

When the manager was provided with the evidence, he commented that he was sorry he had to terminate the employee because that worker had the potential to be a high-level executive one day. What the manager failed to realize was the "Addition by Subtraction Theory of Fraud." The company is best served when a dishonest employee is removed before he or she moves up the corporate ladder, where far more damage can be done. If a business is going to have a zero tolerance for fraud, it must apply to all employees. As soon as a high-level executive who commits any kind of fraud is not held accountable, the entire program has lost credibility.

### Fraudster as Employee Theory of Fraud

The employee who turns to the "dark side" and commits fraud against the company should not be considered an employee. Good employees are critical to the operation of a business. As stated previously, they are ideally concerned about the future of the business, working hard to ensure its growth and future, maintaining integrity, and bettering the company. Fraudsters masquerading as employees use their positions to find weaknesses in the internal controls and exploit them to commit fraud. These people are not out to better the company, other employees, shareholders, customers, or partners. They are only out to line their pockets with ill-gotten gains and they have ceased to be employees—they have gone into business for themselves. Executives need to understand this concept when dealing with employees who commit fraud.

## ENDNOTES

1. *Webster's Third New International Dictionary,* 1986 ed., s.v. "fraud."
2. Bryan Garner, ed., *Black's Law Dictionary,* 7th ed., s.v. "fraud."
3. *Mail Fraud Statute, U.S. Code* 18 (2005), § 1341.
4. Association of Certified Fraud Examiners, *2004 Report to the Nation on Occupational Fraud and Abuse* (Austin, TX: ACFE, 2004), 1.
5. Adam Zagorin, "Scambuster, Inc," *Time,* January 31, 2005, 47.
6. "Second Year Report to the President," *Corporate Fraud Task Force,* July 20, 2004, 3.2, www.usdoj.gov/dag/cftf/2nd_yr_fraud_report.pdf.
7. Association of Certified Fraud Examiners, *2004 Report to the Nation on Occupational Fraud and Abuse* (Austin, TX: ACFE, 2004), 1.
8. Ibid.
9. Association of Certified Fraud Examiners. *Fraud Examiners Manual,* (Austin, TX: ACFE, 2006), 4.601.
10. Dick Carozza, "Rapid Reformer: An Interview with Eliot Spitzer, New York State Attorney General," *Fraud Magazine,* 19, no. 1 (January/February 2005), 53.
11. Edwin H. Sutherland, *White Collar Crime* (New York: Holt, Rinehart and Winston, 1949), 9.
12. *Webster's Third New International Dictionary,* 1986 ed., s.v. "motive."
13. *Wall Street,* DVD, directed by Oliver Stone (1987; Beverly Hills: Twentieth Century Fox, 2003).
14. *Webster's Third New International Dictionary,* 1986 ed., s.v. "rationalization."

# CHAPTER 3

# The Path to Greater Corporate Compliance, Accountability, and Ethical Conduct: COSO to Sarbanes-Oxley

## EXECUTIVE SUMMARY

The path to greater corporate compliance, accountability, and ethical conduct did not spring up overnight. It has been evolving and improving over the last 20 years. It began in 1985 with the Committee of Sponsoring Organizations (COSO) and a framework of compliance, continued in 1991 with the Federal Sentencing Guidelines for Organizations, and then exploded into corporate suites and boardrooms with the enactment of the Sarbanes-Oxley Act of 2002. Transparency, fairness, and honesty became key words for corporate governance, government oversight, and investor protection. If corporate executives could not be trusted to protect employees and shareholders, then government would step in. New laws and compliance requirements resulted from the many corporate scandals, and although some may be onerous to businesses, they are the result of fraudulent conduct of the highest magnitude and impact.

Looking back at the corporate road that is littered with the many companies that have been devastated as a result of systemic and unimpeded fraud, it is hard to understand how this could have happened. Fraud is not new. Fraud scandals have hit businesses time and again. Consider these examples of business frauds over the last 75 years:

- Ivar Kreuger, known as the Swedish Match King, cornered the world market in matches in the 1920s. No one would imagine that one of the world's richest men would perpetrate a scam—but by the early 1930s, his investors, both corporate and individual, had lost hundreds of millions of dollars. Kreuger created a fraudulent maze of dozens of shell companies, accounting trickery that inflated his company's earnings and stock price, phony bond offerings, and wholesale deception. For the man who graced the cover of *Time* magazine the week the American stock market crashed on October 29, 1929, the end came by suicide in 1932 once the accounting fraud was discovered.[1]

- Equity Funding Corporation of America was once a major financial services company that began in 1960 and went public in 1964. Until the discovery of a massive accounting and investment fraud in 1973, the company was considered a Wall Street success story. The Equity Funding scam defrauded thousands of investors who thought they were investing their retirement savings in supposedly safe and secure insurance policies, as well as those who bought the stock thinking it was a sound investment. Instead, the company created 64,000 phony policies to falsely increase revenue and profits, forged death certificates for phony policy holders and collected the proceeds through reinsurance companies, counterfeited $25 million in corporate bonds to use as collateral for loans, and ultimately committed over $800 million in fraud. It was learned that Equity Funding had been "cooking the books" since 1964, but auditors never caught on. In fact, some of the auditors were in on the scam and were also prosecuted.[2]

- Ivan Boesky and Michael Milken personified the "Age of Greed" on Wall Street in the 1980s. Boesky, a "corporate raider extraordinaire," and Milken, the "junk bond king," teamed up to create a litany of financial schemes that plagued Wall Street for years and resulted in numerous prosecutions. They were implicated in insider trading schemes that led to charges of mail fraud and multiple securities violations. Boesky, the model for the Gordon Gekko character in the movie *Wall Street*, became a federal informant in 1986 to "nail" Milken and others. Both Boesky and Milken went to jail for their crimes, but Wall Street did not learn its lesson.[3]

All these frauds sadly illustrate that it has taken a long time for the corporate world to understand the importance of not just saying that corporate executives and businesses need to be ethical and honest, but to take steps to ensure they truly are. The path to greater corporate compliance, accountability, and ethical conduct did not open up overnight. It took the implosions of once respected companies because of billion dollar frauds to put real teeth into compliance programs.

## WHAT IS CORPORATE GOVERNANCE?

There has been a great deal of discussion about corporate governance and its importance. Corporate governance is a system of checks and balances between management and all other interested parties with the aim of producing an effective, efficient, and law-abiding corporation. It is how a company defines itself to its shareholders, analysts, employees, partners, customers, government regulators, and others in terms of compliance and accountability. In fact, the degree of compliance with best practices separates good companies from great companies. General Electric (GE) is an excellent example of a great company with superior corporate governance. As GE Chairman of the Board and CEO Jeffrey R. Immelt states about corporate governance on the company Web site, "Sound principles of corporate governance are critical to obtaining and retaining the trust of investors." Immelt goes on to say that:

- ■ "We should talk externally the way we run GE internally."
- ■ "We should try to satisfy the spirit, not just the letter, of the new corporate governance requirements."
- ■ "We should act promptly to implement changes in governance, and not wait for 'formal' effective dates in the law which may be many months in the future."[4]

Today, corporate governance involves all aspects of a company's operations including the roles of management and the board of directors, the qualifications and independence of the board, ethics, conflicts of interest and enforced codes of conduct, reporting of fraud and other business practice issues, corporate citizenship, succession planning, and shareholder rights. These words or ones very similar can be seen on the Web sites and in the annual reports of companies large and small because of the many changes in corporate accountability and responsibility.

## TRANSPARENCY IS THE NAME OF THE GAME

Corporate governance is about promoting fairness, honesty, and transparency. Transparency has become a key word in improved corporate governance and is reflected throughout Sarbanes-Oxley and the other key compliance initiatives. It is a term "that has been adopted by the business community to describe the obligation to disclose basic financial information."[5] Transparency is the quality or state of being open, easily detected, or seen through. *Black's Law Dictionary* defines it as a "lack of guile in attempts to hide damaging information especially in financial disclosures where organizations interact with the public."[6] Transparency is a critical element in allowing investors and government regulators to know exactly what is going on behind the corporate veil. If investors knew about the off-book transactions, the self-dealings, the hidden loans, and the looting at Enron and Adelphia, there is no doubt that most people would never have invested their hard-earned money there. It is imperative that all financial transactions be transparent, with no possibility of financial shenanigans, undisclosed deals, or conflicts of interest. Transparency reassures shareholders, corporate employees, and the public that they have a level playing field in which to invest and hopefully makes it harder for corporate crooks to "cook the books."

## A CULTURE OF COMPLIANCE

A culture of compliance takes time to develop. It can be a long journey to reach the highest levels of ethical standards and compliance requirements. All the positive changes in legislation, initiatives, and policies have taken many years to unfold, and each is built on the previous ones, with the purpose of improving corporate governance. It can be argued that this journey to greater compliance started with the creation of COSO in 1985, continued with the United States Sentencing Guidelines for Organizational Crime in 1991, and went right through to the enactment of the Sarbanes-Oxley Act of 2002 and the subsequent enhanced accounting and auditing standards. In a culture of compliance, an organization's one-time initiative changes into a cultural mind-set that is built into the structure of the company.

As William H. Donaldson, former Chairman of the Securities and Exchange Commission (SEC), stated in a speech to the National Press Club on July 30, 2003, "If companies view the new laws as opportunities—opportunities to improve internal controls, improve the performance of the board, and improve their public reporting—they will ultimately be better run, more transparent, and therefore more attractive to investors."[7] Many new laws and compliance requirements have changed the way businesses operate. Today's informed executives and, in fact, all employees must be aware of them and their impact on a culture of compliance. Executive Insight 3.1 provides a timeline of the various corporate compliance initiatives and milestones since 1985.

---

### EXECUTIVE INSIGHT 3.1: TIMELINE OF CORPORATE COMPLIANCE INITIATIVES AND MILESTONES

| Year | Compliance Initiatives and Milestones | Impact |
|------|----------------------------------------|--------|
| 1985 | Committee of Sponsoring Organizations (COSO) | "Voluntary private sector organization dedicated to improving the quality of financial reporting through business ethics, effective internal controls and corporate governance[i]" |

| Year | Compliance Initiatives and Milestones | Impact |
|------|----------------------------------------|--------|
| 1987 | Report of the National Commission on Fraudulent Financial Reporting (The Treadway Commission) | "Studied the financial reporting system in the U.S. to identify causal factors that can lead to fraudulent financial reporting and steps to reduce its incidence[ii]" |
| 1991 | United States Sentencing Guidelines for Organizational Crime | Guidelines to hold organizations accountable by applying "just punishment" for criminal actions and "deterrence" incentives to detect and prevent crime[iii] |
| 1992 | Internal Control— Integrated Framework (COSO Report) | Established "common definition" for internal controls and "a standard against which businesses can assess their control systems and how to improve them[iv]" |
| 1996 | Statement on Auditing Standards (SAS) 82, "Consideration of Fraud in a Financial Statement Audit" | Provided guidance to auditors for detecting fraud when conducting audits. Replaced the previously used term "errors and irregularities" with "fraud" for the first time.[v] |

| Year | Compliance Initiatives and Milestones | Impact |
|---|---|---|
| 1998 | Arthur Levitt's the "Numbers Game" Speech | Prophetic speech by former SEC chairman foretelling the coming doom in the financial markets by exposing the deception being played with earnings management |
| 1999 | National Commission on Fraudulent Financial Reporting, 1987–1997 | "Research project" to guide efforts to "combat the problem of financial statement fraud and to provide a better understanding of financial statement fraud cases[vi]" |
| 2002 | Sarbanes-Oxley Act | Public Company Accounting Reform and Investor Protection Act of 2002—landmark legislation with most significant changes to U.S. securities laws in 60 years |
| 2002 | Statement on Auditing Standards (SAS) 99, "Consideration of Fraud in a Financial Statement Audit" | Auditing standard that superseded earlier SAS 82 and gave auditors the "responsibility to plan and perform the audit to obtain reasonable assurance about whether the financial statements are free of material misstatement, whether caused by error or fraud[vii]" |

| Year | Compliance Initiatives and Milestones | Impact |
|------|----------------------------------------|--------|
| 2003 | "Principles of Federal Prosecution of Business Organizations" (the Thompson Memo) | Provided Department of Justice prosecutors with groundbreaking guidance when deciding to seek charges against a business organization |
| 2003 | SEC's Final Rule for Section 404 of Sarbanes-Oxley | SEC's adoption of rules for Section 404 requiring management's assessment and reporting of internal control over financial reporting and attestation by external auditor |
| 2003 | New York Stock Exchange & NASDAQ Listing Requirements | New listing requirements for issuers of securities including independence of directors and enhanced corporate governance |
| 2004 | PCAOB Auditing Standard No. 2: An Audit of Internal Control over Financial Reporting Performed in Conjunction with an Audit of Financial Statements | Provides increased responsibilities for external auditors beyond those required by SAS 99 including requiring auditors to evaluate antifraud programs and controls as part of the audit of internal control over financial reporting |

| Year | Compliance Initiatives and Milestones | Impact |
|------|----------------------------------------|--------|
| 2004 | Stephen Cutler's "Gatekeepers" Speech | Seminal speech by former SEC Director of Enforcement in which he reinforced the critical role of gatekeepers— those people who are responsible for monitoring and oversight of others in the financial markets |
| 2004 | United States Sentencing Commission's Amendments to the Federal Sentencing Guidelines | Introduced seven updated amendments to strengthen corporate compliance and ethics programs of business organizations to mitigate punishment for a criminal offense |

[i] The Committee of Sponsoring Organizations of the Treadway Commission, www.coso.org.

[ii] National Commission on Fraudulent Financial Reporting, *Report of the National Commission on Fraudulent Financial Reporting,* (October, 1987), 1, ("The Treadway Report"), www.coso.org/publications/NCFFR_Part_1.htm.

[iii] Supplemental Report on Sentencing Guidelines for Organizations, (August 30, 1991), 6, www.ussc.gov/corp/OrgGL83091.PDF.

[iv] The Committee of Sponsoring Organizations of the Treadway Commission, *Internal Control-Integrated Framework,* (1992), www.coso.org/publications/executive_summary_integrated_framework.htm.

[v] Association of Certified Fraud Examiners, *Fraud Examiners Manual,* 3rd ed., (Austin, 2001), 1.203.

[vi] The Committee of Sponsoring Organizations of the Treadway Commission, *Fraudulent Financial Reporting: 1987–1997: An Analysis of U.S. Public Companies,* (1999), http://www.coso.org/publications/executive_summary_fraudulent_financial_reporting.htm.

[vii] Statement on Auditing Standards 99, "Consideration of Fraud in a Financial Statement Audit," The American Institute of Certified Public Accountants, www.aicpa.org.

## COSO NOT COSTCO

If a corporate executive does not know the difference between COSO and Costco (the international chain of membership discount warehouses) something is terribly lacking. COSO is the Committee of Sponsoring Organizations, a voluntary, private sector organization dedicated to improving the quality of financial reporting through business ethics, effective internal controls, and corporate governance. COSO's extensive studies and intuitive recommendations over the years provide great insight into the problem and prevention of corporate fraud. In today's compliance-driven environment, a thorough understanding of a COSO framework is a prerequisite to an effective culture of fraud prevention.

COSO was formed in 1985 by the major accounting and finance professional organizations including the American Accounting Association, the American Institute of Certified Public Accountants, Financial Executives International, The Institute of Internal Auditors, and the Institute of Management Accountants. COSO sponsored the National Commission on Fraudulent Financial Reporting that studied the financial reporting system in the United States "to identify causal factors that can lead to fraudulent financial reporting and steps to reduce its incidence."[8] The first Chairman of the National Commission was James C. Treadway, Jr., Executive Vice-President and General Counsel, Paine Webber, Incorporated, and a former SEC Commissioner. Thus the National Commission is commonly referred to as the Treadway Commission (The Commission).

The Commission reviewed numerous instances of fraudulent financial reporting, including 119 enforcement actions against public companies or associated individuals, and 42 cases against independent public accountants or their firms brought by the SEC from 1981 to 1986.[9] The Commission defined fraudulent reporting as "intentional or reckless conduct, whether by act or omission, that results in materially misleading financial statements."[10] Many different factors were considered including the distortion of corporate records, falsified transactions, misapplication of accounting principles, and other related intentional misconduct. The Commission did not include in its study other internal frauds such as asset misappropriation or corruption schemes. The study found that opportunities for fraudulent financial reporting exist when certain circumstances are present including:

- "The absence of a strong and engaged board of directors or audit committee that vigilantly oversees the financial reporting process
- Weak or non-existent internal accounting controls
- Unusual or complex financial transactions
- Accounting estimates requiring subjective judgment by company management
- Ineffective internal audit staffs resulting from inadequate staff size, staff expertise or limited audit scope."[11]

The Commission's key recommendations fall into several categories including the tone at the top as set by senior management; the quality of internal accounting and audit functions; the roles of the board of directors and the audit committee; the independence of external auditors; and enforcement enhancements. The findings and recommendations of the Commission are as relevant today as in 1987. Some of the key recommendations are as follows:

- The top management of a public company must "identify, understand, and assess the factors" that may result in financial statement fraud.
- Internal controls must provide a "reasonable assurance" that fraudulent financial reporting will in the best case be prevented or in the worst case be quickly detected.
- "Public companies should develop and enforce written codes of corporate conduct" to "foster a strong and ethical climate" and ensure compliance with the code.
- An effective and objective internal audit function "staffed with an adequate number of qualified personnel" must be in place.
- The audit committee should be "composed solely of independent directors" and "have adequate resources and authority to discharge their responsibilities."
- The audit committee should provide "vigilant and effective" oversight of the company's financial reporting process and internal controls.
- There should be an evaluation of the independence of the company's public accountant by the audit committee.

- The SEC should require the CEO and/or the CFO to include signed management reports in annual reports to shareholders.
- The SEC should require the chairperson of the audit committee to provide a signed letter in the company's annual report detailing the "committee's responsibilities and activities" in the past year.
- "Public accounting firms should recognize" and address the inherent pressures that can potentially affect audit quality and independence.
- The SEC should seek new "statutory authority to bar or suspend corporate officers and directors involved in fraudulent financial reporting."
- There should be an increased emphasis on criminal prosecutions and the SEC should devote greater resources to detecting and preventing fraudulent financial reporting.[12]

COSO believes that internal controls are an important component of a robust fraud prevention program. However, internal controls can only provide reasonable, not absolute, assurance and should be geared to the achievement of objectives. In 1992, COSO issued a landmark report on internal controls entitled *Internal Control—Integrated Framework* that is the basis for establishing an effective internal control system. If adopted by a company, this system would promote (1) efficient and effective operations, (2) accurate financial reporting, and (3) compliance with laws and regulations. The report outlined the five essential elements of an effective internal control program:

1. The **control environment,** which is the basis for the system by providing fundamental discipline and structure
2. **Risk assessment,** which involves the identification and analysis by management of risks to achieving, predetermined objectives
3. **Control activities** or policies, procedures, and practices to ensure that management objectives and risk mitigation are achieved
4. **Information and communication** by management so that all employees are aware of their control responsibilities and their requirement to support them
5. **Monitoring,** which encompasses external oversight of internal controls by management and independent auditors outside the process to determine the quality of the program and compliance.[13]

A COSO framework is the standard for many corporations in the United States, and there is no reason the same framework could not be universally used worldwide. However, the voluntary COSO framework didn't stop many corporations from collapsing. Enron had controls in place, but they were overridden by senior management. Arthur Andersen, its auditor, developed Enron's risk assessment framework, but Enron did not follow it. Enron's "push the envelope" environment, emanating from the highest levels of the company, contributed to its demise.

As a follow-up to the original 1987 report, the Treadway Commission studied more fraudulent financial statement fraud occurring during the period 1987 to 1997. The result was a research report entitled *Fraudulent Financial Reporting 1987–1997: An Analysis of U.S. Public Companies*. One concern was whether there had been any lessening of the problem of fraudulent financial reporting in the years since the previous report. Nearly 300 companies facing allegations of fraudulent financial reporting were identified, and from that number, 200 companies were randomly selected for detailed analysis. The Summary of Findings from the report includes the following:

- Most companies that committed financial statement fraud were relatively small, with most well below $100 million in total assets, and most were not listed on the New York or American Stock Exchanges.
- Senior executives were frequently involved in the fraud, with 83 percent of CEOs and CFOs associated in some way.
- Financial pressures were in play in the period before the occurrence of the financial statement fraud that may have contributed to the fraud.
- Most audit committees met only once a year, some companies had no audit committees, and most had no accounting or finance expertise.
- Insiders and "gray" directors (nonindependent outsiders with special ties to the company) dominated boards.
- The dollar amounts of the frauds were high in comparison with the relatively small size of the companies involved.
- The average fraud continued for almost two years before discovery.

- Overstating revenues and assets was the most common technique involved.
- Both large and small audit firms were associated with the companies committing the frauds, with no significance as to size.
- External auditors were implicated in 29 percent of the frauds as being either complicit or negligent.
- There were severe consequences for the companies committing fraud, including bankruptcy, delisting, and SEC actions. Few executives either admitted wrongdoing or ever served any prison time.[14]

## FEDERAL SENTENCING GUIDELINES FOR ORGANIZATIONAL CRIME

The disparity in federal sentencing of defendants for all crimes was an issue among prosecutors, defendants, defense attorneys, judges, and the public. The prison term, or lack of one, that a defendant received in one federal jurisdiction would vary greatly for a similar act by a different defendant in another. After years of complaints about the system, The Sentencing Reform Act of 1984 changed the way federal sentencing was conducted. The Act created the United States Sentencing Commission (USSC) as an independent agency of the Judicial Branch. The USSC was directed to develop guidelines and policy for federal courts to follow when sentencing offenders convicted of federal crimes. The Sentencing Guidelines for individuals who committed any type of federal crime was enacted and made effective as of November 1, 1987.[15]

The next step for the USSC was dealing with organizational crime. Organizations, like individuals, can commit crimes and also be charged with and convicted of criminal conduct. Although organizations cannot be sentenced to prison for their crimes, there are penalties if a guilty verdict is delivered. The resulting convictions and fines can put a company out of business. In 1991, the USSC issued guidelines for the criminal sentencing of corporations as well as recommended guidelines for corporate compliance programs. The guidelines were an attempt to lessen the harshest aspects of federal sentencing for crimes if an organization could demonstrate that it instituted an appropriate compliance program prior to being charged. There was a substantial reduction in fines for corporations that have vigorous fraud prevention and detection programs in place prior to the offense and that self-report the crimes. To receive any mitigating credit under the guidelines, the organization must have reported the criminal activity promptly to appropriate authorities.

A robust fraud prevention program at the time had to consider and implement the following seven steps for compliance with the Federal Sentencing Guidelines for Organizational Crimes:

- **Established compliance standards:** policies and procedures reasonably capable of reducing the prospect of criminal activity that must be followed by all employees
- **Setting the tone at the top:** oversight by high-level management to ensure compliance
- **Use of due care not to delegate to individuals who might engage in illegal activities:** instituting background checks and management oversight to lessen the chance that employees who either have criminal histories or a propensity to engage in illegal activities will be placed in positions of authority
- **Effective communication of standards to all employees:** requiring participation in training programs and creating and communicating codes of conduct through employee handbooks and in new employee orientation
- **Reasonable steps to achieve compliance:** utilizing monitoring and auditing systems to detect criminal and other improper activity, as well as creating reporting systems for whistle-blowers to report such conduct
- **Consistent enforcement and discipline:** the creation of an appropriate disciplinary mechanism, consistent and fair, incremental to the conduct alleged and made known to all employees
- **Reasonable steps in response to reports of compliance concerns:** identifying internal control lapses and deficiencies and taking all reasonable steps to respond to the offense appropriately, including making modifications to the program to prevent and detect violation of law.[16]

The Sentencing Guidelines for Organizational Crime were a good beginning, but it would take many more years before they would be dramatically improved as a result of the changing landscape of corporate fraud.

## SAS 82

For too long, accountants and auditors felt no responsibility to uncover fraud. Their excuse was that it was not their job. With the growing importance of effective compliance stemming from COSO and the United States Sentencing Guidelines, fraud mitigation became a consideration but not always a priority for every company. By the mid-1990s, the accounting and auditing profession determined that it needed to take stronger measures to detect and prevent fraud in business in the wake of growing criticism that it was not doing enough to stop fraud. It now had to catch up and take more vigorous action against fraudulent financial reporting. In November 1996, the Auditing Standards Board of the American Institute of Certified Public Accountants (AICPA) issued SAS 82, "Consideration of Fraud in a Financial Statement Audit." SAS 82 provided new guidance to auditors for detecting fraud when conducting audits. In previously issued guidance for auditors, fraud had not been defined, and instead the term "errors and irregularities" was used. Moreover, auditors were not responsible for finding "intentional misstatements concealed by collusion."[17]

The new standard stated that an auditor now "has a responsibility to plan and perform the audit to obtain reasonable assurance about whether the financial statements are free of material misstatement, whether caused by error *or fraud* [emphasis added]."[18] SAS 82 stated that "The primary factor that distinguishes fraud from error is whether the underlying action in financial statements is intentional or unintentional."[19] Under SAS 82, financial statement fraud includes the falsification, manipulation, or alteration of accounting records and supporting documents; deliberate misapplication of accounting principles to defraud; and submission or omission of misleading financial transactions or other significant information.

SAS 82 required the auditor to plan and perform an audit in order to determine whether the financial statements are free of material misstatements. The auditor was required to assess 41 risk factors related to fraudulent financial reporting and misappropriation of assets. The risk factors fell into three main categories; some of the more important ones are as follows:

- Risk Factors Relating to Management's Characteristics and Influence
  - Performance-related compensation plans
  - Management's desire to keep the stock price high
  - Need for credit and financing
  - Management's desire to reduce tax liability
  - Corporate values or ethics not being effectively communicated
  - Domination of one person or group of persons in management
  - Lack of control monitoring
  - Ineffective accounting, information technology, or internal auditing staff
  - Nonfinancial management's excessive involvement in accounting and finance activities
  - High turnover of management
  - Strained relations between management and employees
  - History of fraudulent behavior
- Risk Factors Relating to Industry Conditions
  - New accounting or statutory regulations
  - High degree of market competition with declining margins
  - Rapidly changing industry, such as technology
- Risk Factors Relating to Operational Characteristics and Financial Stability
  - Cash flow problems while also reporting earnings or growth in earnings
  - Pressure or need to obtain additional capital financing
  - Assets, liabilities, revenues, or expenses based largely on estimates
  - Significant related-party transactions not in the ordinary course of business
  - Significant, unusual, or highly complex transactions
  - Significant bank accounts or a subsidiary branch in tax-haven jurisdictions
  - Overly complex operational structure or unusual legal entities
  - Difficulty in determining the individual(s) who controls the entity

- Especially high vulnerability to changes in interest rates
- Unusually high dependence on debt or marginal ability to meet payment requirements
- Unrealistically aggressive sales or profitability incentive programs
- Threat of imminent bankruptcy
- Poor, deteriorating financial position when management has personally guaranteed significant debts of the entity.[20]

Auditors needed to assess the total risk from fraud facing a company and design the audit to encompass the fraud risk as well as other business risks. Risks involving the misappropriation of assets related to their susceptibility to such fraud and whether appropriate controls were in place to mitigate the risk were now considered. When conducting the audit, the auditor needed to consider possible fraud involving revenue recognition, inventory, and cash flow, among many others. SAS 82 stated that, "The auditor is not required to plan the audit to discover information that is indicative of financial stress of employees or adverse relationships between the entity and its employees."[21]

SAS 82 only required that when a material fraud was discovered, the auditor should consider the implications and discuss with appropriate management. Although evidence that a fraud may exist would be communicated, the presence of a fraud risk that did not meet the evidence of fraud threshold might not be communicated. SAS 82 did prescribe that the audit committee or its equivalent be advised of any fraud involving senior management, but it would have been rare for an auditor under SAS 82 to go above the management structure to report serious fraud issues to either the audit committee or outside counsel. The problem was that senior management was often involved in financial statement fraud and other corporate scams. SAS 82 was meant to provide guidance to auditors on how to consider the possibility of fraud when conducting an audit and evaluating the results when conducting financial statement audits; it was not a guide to the many other frauds affecting companies.[22] It was never meant to make auditors into fraud examiners. In fact, there was no requirement that auditors be trained in fraud examination and detection. SAS 82 provided an excuse for auditors when fraud under their noses went undetected. Many in the profession wanted nothing to do with ferreting out corporate crime.

In a survey conducted in 1999 asking auditing partners and managers how they felt about SAS 82 and acting as "detectives" when conducting audits, some expected results emerged. More than 61 percent disagreed that they should be responsible for looking for fraud when conducting audits. Almost 76 percent felt they should not act as Certified Fraud Examiners or detectives when performing an audit. Although the survey response rate was fewer than 200 people, the feelings were common at the time.[23] SAS 82 was a good beginning, but it was clearly not enough. Implementing SAS 82 did not detect or stop the many corporate frauds of recent years, and it was certainly no substitute for an effective fraud prevention program. It is fair to question why auditors did not find the financial fraud that permeated so many companies. After all, they were supposed to be trained and *independent* auditors. SAS 82 lacked a strong fraud detection role for an independent auditor; this lack would eventually be corrected but only after much effort.

## ARTHUR LEVITT AND THE "NUMBERS GAME"

Although July 30, 2002 may mark the birth of the new age of corporate enlightenment and governance, with the signing of the Sarbanes-Oxley Act into law, September 28, 1998 may very well be its conception. On that day, Arthur Levitt, the former Chairman of the SEC, gave a powerful and prophetic speech at the New York University Center for Law and Business in New York City. The speech was aptly called the "Numbers Game," and Levitt spoke like a modern-day Nostradamus foretelling the coming doom in the financial markets. Levitt used this speech as a forum to discuss what he felt was a deception being played with earnings management. He called it "a game that, if not addressed soon, will have adverse consequences for America's financial reporting system," and "a game that runs counter to the very principles behind our market's strength and success."[24] Coming fully three years before the Enron collapse, few listened to Levitt as the bubble continued to grow.

Levitt warned that there was "erosion in the quality of earnings, and therefore the quality of financial reporting." He saw fraud as a possible end result because of pressure from management to meet or beat the numbers expected by Wall Street. The audience was told that there was a distinct possibility of executives who would cross into the "gray area" by "cutting corners" rather than be totally honest to investors about financial performance. Although he did not use the "F" word of fraud or the term "cooking the books," Levitt implied that the integrity of the markets was being called into question. He stated, "Managing may be giving way to manipulation; integrity may be losing out to illusion."[25] He was telling us the about the future, but not all in the corporate suites were listening.

Levitt gave a brief history lesson on how financial shenanigans result in investor panic and financial ruin. He expressed his concern about the need for improving accounting and disclosure rules, the need for independence and oversight of external auditors, and the importance of a company's board of directors and audit committee. He mentioned the critical importance of transparency and accurate reporting. All these issues became core elements of the Sarbanes-Oxley legislation. There is no doubt that when the congressional framers of Sarbanes-Oxley sat down to build the act's content, they read what Levitt had said. He also made a point of saying that the serious issues he was discussing would not be solved by government alone and that it would take the dedicated involvement of investors, financial analysts, and, of course, corporate executives. Of the three, investors were the most naïve and the least concerned at the time to have any impact on financial reporting.

Levitt said the SEC was seeing five accounting "gimmicks" of "accounting hocus-pocus" that were proving problematic:

- "Big Bath Restructuring Charges": when companies overstate restructuring charges or make other large charges that have a tendency to "clean up" the balance sheets with a "big bath." Restructuring involves significant changes in the financial structure, ownership, or operations of a company to ultimately increase value through various practices such as mergers and acquisitions, leveraged buyouts, divestitures, and recapitalization.[26] Inappropriate one-time charges for restructuring can inflate earnings going forward. Levitt cautioned that all involved parties including management, employees, investors, vendors, and others need to fully understand the effects of any restructuring and ensure accurate and transparent financial reporting.

■ "Creative Acquisition Accounting": classification of acquisition costs as "in-process research and development" so they can be "written off as one-time charges removing any future earnings drag."

■ "Cookie Jar Reserves": unrealistic estimates of liabilities such as sales returns, loan losses, or warranty costs that tend to stockpile accruals in "cookie jars" to be used in times of financial instability. Large, one-time losses to earnings can be problematic for financial reporting and can lead to scandal and prison.

■ "Immaterial Misapplication of Accounting Principles": Levitt said that materiality helps build flexibility into financial reporting and that "some items may be so insignificant that they are not worth measuring and reporting with exact precision." However, he argued that some companies "fib" (again, as close to using the F-word that he would say in this speech) by intentionally including errors that pump up the bottom line. He added, "In markets where missing an earnings projection by a penny can result in a loss of millions of dollars in market capitalization, I have a hard time accepting that some of these so-called non-events simply don't matter."

■ "Premature Recognition of Revenue": the manipulation of revenue is one of the most serious accounting issues faced today. Recognizing revenue before the contract is signed, sealed, and delivered, when the customer still has the option to return the goods or refuse the services, is an easy way to commit fraud and abuse. Levitt recognized it as a problem in 1998 and maintained that some unnamed companies recognized revenue before a transaction was complete or a product had been delivered. He stated that this attempt to "boost earnings" was like a "bottle of fine wine" that one "wouldn't pop the cork on. . .before it was ready."

Levitt ended his visionary speech by outlining an action plan to improve the transparency of financial statements and reporting. The program included recommendations for an improved accounting framework, improved outside auditing of the financial reporting process, strengthening the audit committee process, and the need for a culture change. Levitt stated that, "For corporate managers, remember, the integrity of the numbers in the financial reporting system is directly related to the long-term interests of a corporation. While the temptations are great, and the pressure strong, illusions in numbers are only that—ephemeral, and ultimately self-destructive."[27] Few were listening in 1998, but they are now.

## THE SARBANES-OXLEY ACT OF 2002

The fall of the stock market in 2000 was quickly followed by daily revelations of corporate fraud and indiscretions. The constant reporting of corporate scandals reinforced the belief that some corporate titans personified greed and lack of accountability, while lining their pockets at the expense of the average investor. Investors lost faith in the financial markets. They came to believe the market was rigged and no one was there to protect their interests and their hard-earned money. Something needed to be done to restore faith and trust in Wall Street and punish the many corporate fraudsters.

Congress responded in July 2002 by passing landmark legislation, The Public Company Accounting Reform and Investor Protection Act of 2002, commonly called the Sarbanes-Oxley Act. Sarbanes-Oxley is named for its Congressional sponsors, Senator Paul Sarbanes (D-Maryland) and Representative Michael Oxley (R-Ohio). In support of his measure, Senator Sarbanes said "the problems originally laid bare by the collapse of Enron are by no means unique to one company, one industry, or even one profession." He added that "something needs to be done to restore confidence in the world's greatest marketplace."[28]

Many were uncertain the bill would become law. Previous efforts to curb corporate crime had languished in Congress because of opposition from the accounting profession and from politicians. But WorldCom's $3.8 billion accounting fraud and collapse in June 2002 spurred Congress to pass the Sarbanes-Oxley Act with overwhelming bipartisan support in the House and Senate. President Bush signed the Act into law on July 30, 2002. "Every corporate official," he said at the signing, "who has chosen to commit a crime can expect to face the consequences."[29]

The legislation strengthens corporate accountability and governance of public companies; affects their officers and directors; improves auditor integrity and independence; greatly empowers audit committees; addresses conflicts of interests by stock analysts; and most importantly, protects employees, pension holders, and investors from fraud.

The Act is comprehensive and ground-breaking. It consists of 11 titles covering the public company accounting oversight board, auditor independence, corporate responsibility, enhanced financial disclosures, and analyst conflicts of interest. It also includes the Corporate and Criminal Fraud Accountability Act (Title VIII), the White-Collar Crime Penalty Enhancements Act of 2002 (Title IX), and the Corporate Fraud Accountability Act of 2002 (Title XI). The Act covers areas of great importance to companies, shareholders, and the government, including concerns that had not been addressed before.

This section covers the salient points of the Act but is by no means an exhaustive overview of all its aspects. For such an overview, the reader is invited to read the text of the Sarbanes-Oxley Act of 2002 (www.aicpa.org/sarbanes/index.asp) to gain a detailed understanding. An overview of the key sections of the Sarbanes-Oxley Act can be found in Appendix A.

### Implications for Independent Auditors

The Act creates a strong and independent Public Company Accounting Oversight Board (PCAOB) to oversee the audit of public companies that are subject to securities laws. More information on the formation of the PCAOB and its implications can be found in Chapter 4. The PCAOB protects the interests of investors in the preparation of accurate and independent audit reports. The Act requires that the PCAOB have five members appointed from among prominent individuals of integrity and reputation who have a demonstrated commitment to the interests of investors and the public. The members cannot currently be connected with any public accounting firm. Each member must have financial expertise and understand generally accepted accounting principles, internal controls, financial statements, and audit committee functions. Two of the members must be or have been Certified Public Accountants (CPAs), and the remaining three must not be and cannot have been CPAs. The chair may be held by one of the CPA members, provided that the person was not engaged as a practicing CPA for five years.

The PCAOB will oversee the accounting industry, subject to SEC supervision through a number of actions including:

- Registering public accounting firms that prepare audit reports for issuers
- Establishing or adopting, or both, by rule, auditing, quality control, ethics, independence, and other standards relating to the preparation of audit reports for issuers
- Conducting inspections of public accounting firms
- Conducting investigations and disciplinary proceedings and imposing appropriate sanctions on public accounting firms
- Performing such other duties or functions as the PCAOB (or the SEC, by rule or order) determines are necessary or appropriate to promote high professional standards and improve the quality of audit services offered by public accounting firms
- Enforcing compliance with the Act, the rules of PCAOB, professional standards, and the securities laws relating to the preparation and issuance of audit reports.

## Auditor Independence

The Act promotes auditor independence by prohibiting an auditor from providing a number of nonaudit services when performing an audit for a public company audit client including the following:

- Bookkeeping or other services related to the accounting records or financial statements of the audit client
- Financial information systems design and implementation
- Appraisal or valuation services, fairness opinions, or contribution-in-kind reports
- Actuarial services
- Internal audit outsourcing services

- Management functions or human resources
- Broker or dealer, investment advisor, or investment banking services
- Legal services and expert services unrelated to the audit
- Any other service that PCAOB determines, by regulation, is not permissible.

The Act allows a registered public accounting firm to engage in any nonaudit service, including tax services, which are not described previously only if the activity is approved in advance by the audit committee of the issuer. "Registered" means a public accounting firm registered with the PCAOB in accordance with Sarbanes-Oxley. "Issuer" means an issuer of securities as defined in Section 3 of the Securities Exchange Act of 1934 whose securities are registered under the Securities Exchange Act. Additionally, the audit firm must rotate its lead audit partner and the audit partner responsible for reviewing the audit so that neither role is performed by the same accountant for more than five consecutive years. Furthermore, the Act requires that an accounting firm may not provide audit services for a public company if the company's CEO, CFO, Controller, Chief Accounting Officer, or others serving in an equivalent position were employed by the accounting firm and participated in any capacity in the audit of the issuer during the one-year period before the start of audit services.

In January 2003, the SEC adopted amendments to strengthen the provisions of the Act by now requiring that the top two partners on an audit engagement must take five years off after five years of service to an audit client. The new rule also extends the rotation requirement to certain other significant audit partners, who will now be subject to a seven-year rotation with a two-year time-out period. The Act requires auditors to retain their audit-related documents for five years. The SEC rule goes beyond the Act's language and now requires auditors to retain their audit files and work papers for a minimum of seven years after they file the audit with the SEC. The definition of relevant documents that must be retained has been expanded to include "those documents that record the audit or review procedures performed, the evidence obtained, and the conclusions reached by the auditor."

## Corporate Responsibility: Implications for Audit Committees

The Act intends to improve corporate responsibility by increasing the independence of the audit committee. Audit committee members cannot be affiliated with the issuers except in this oversight role and cannot accept any consulting or advisory work or any other compensation from the issuer. Each member of the audit committee shall be a member of the board of directors of the issuer and shall be independent. Auditors must report to the audit committee of a client and not to management. The audit committee will be responsible for the appointment, compensation, and oversight of the work of the auditor, as well as resolution of any disagreements or disputes between the company and the auditor.

The company must also disclose whether the audit committee has at least one member who is a "financial expert." The Act defines a financial expert as a person who, through education and experience as a public accountant or auditor, or from serving as a principal financial officer, comptroller, or principal accounting officer of an issuer, or from a position involving the performance of similar functions, has:

- An understanding of generally accepted accounting principles and financial statements
- Experience in the preparation or auditing of financial statements for generally comparable companies
- Experience with internal accounting controls
- An understanding of audit committee functions.

Previously, many audit committees did not have "financial experts" among the members. The belief is that by having individuals who are knowledgeable and experienced in financial matters, corporate indiscretions and deceptions will be discovered and reported. The SEC has ruled that the expert's name must be disclosed and whether the expert is independent of management. A company that does not have such an expert will be required to disclose this and must explain why it has no such expert.

Each public accounting firm is required to report, on a timely basis, to the audit committee on all critical accounting policies and practices used in the financial statements. This report must include all alternative treatments of financial information within generally accepted accounting principles that have been discussed with management, the ramifications of the use of such treatments, and the treatments preferred by the accounting firm. In addition, the auditors must provide any material written communications between the firm and company management, such as management letters or schedules of unadjusted differences.

## Complaints and Whistle-Blower Protection

Sarbanes-Oxley requires each publicly traded company to create a reporting system for employees to report misconduct. Although the Act does not specifically mention whistle-blowers, the implication is clear. Thanks to Sherron Watkins, formerly of Enron, and Cynthia Cooper, formerly of WorldCom, whistle-blowers have gained new respectability and the gratitude of the investing public. *Time* magazine recognized these women as the 2002 Persons of the Year for their commitment to disclosing corporate fraud.

Each audit committee must establish procedures for receiving, retaining, and responding to complaints received by the issuers including the confidential, anonymous submission of questionable accounting, internal accounting controls, or auditing matters. Generally, these will be in the form of hotlines to receive confidential calls and provide the information to the company for appropriate action. Hotlines can help employees feel safe from retaliation.

The Act provides enhanced whistle-blower protection for employees of publicly traded companies who are discharged, demoted, suspended, threatened, harassed, or discriminated against after disclosing evidence of fraud and assisting in investigations to stop fraud. A whistle-blower who has been retaliated against may seek relief through the United States Department of Labor and the district courts. What many people do not realize is that there is now a criminal consequence for someone who retaliates against a whistle-blower. The Act makes retaliation a federal offense punishable by up to 10 years in prison.

## Improving Corporate Governance: Implications for Public Companies

**CEO and CFO Certifications**    Sarbanes-Oxley enhances corporate governance and accountability by requiring both the CEO and CFO of a public company to certify the disclosures they make in periodic reports. This puts the responsibility directly onto the key officers of a company to ensure that their financial statements and other disclosures filed with the SEC are truthful. Executives can no longer ask "Who, me?" or say "I didn't know."

In required certifications, CEOs and CFOs must certify that:

- They have reviewed the report.
- To the best of their knowledge, the report contains no untrue material fact and does not omit a material fact that would make the statements misleading.
- To the best of their knowledge, the financial statements and other financial information in the report fairly presents, in all material respects, the financial condition and results of operations of the company.
- They are responsible for establishing and maintaining internal controls.
- They have designed internal controls to ensure that material information relating to the company is made known to other officers in the company.
- They have evaluated the effectiveness of the internal controls within their company prior to the issuance of the report.
- They have presented in the report their conclusions about the effectiveness of their internal controls.
- They have disclosed to their auditors and the audit committee all significant deficiencies in the design or operation of internal controls that could adversely affect the company's ability to record, process, and report financial data, and they have identified any material weaknesses in internal controls.
- They have disclosed whether or not there were significant changes in internal controls or other factors that might significantly affect internal controls subsequent to the date of their evaluation, including any corrective actions taken.

■ They have disclosed any fraud, whether material or not, that involves management or other employees who have a significant role in the company's internal controls.

Ignorance of the law is no excuse. Certifying officers who violate this section of the act will face criminal prosecution and be guaranteed a "perp walk" in front of the media's cameras. A violation of this certification process is a felony punishable by up to 20 years in prison if the violation is knowing and willful.

**Insider Trading**  A common concern is that corporate executives under investigation will falsely reassure investors and employees about the health of the company while quietly dumping large amounts of their stock. Sarbanes-Oxley addresses this by dramatically shortening the deadline for insiders to report any trading in their company's securities. Officers and directors of a publicly traded company previously had up to 40 days to report their trades of company stock, but they now have two business days. The trades must also be posted on the company's Web site. There is also a prohibition on insider trades during pension fund blackout periods. Any profits realized by an officer or director in violation of this section may be recovered by the company.

**Disgorgement**  Under the Act, if a company is required to restate its financial statement as a result of misconduct, the CEO and CFO must reimburse the company for any bonuses or other compensation received during the 12-month period following the first public issuance or filing with the SEC of the financial document. This is a new concept for chief executives but one that should have occurred long ago. Having to surrender ill-gotten gains or even legally permissible gains that were not obtained with transparency is a new phenomenon in corporate America.

**Ban on Personal Loans to Officers and Directors**  The Act bans personal loans from public companies to their executive officers and directors that they do not make in the ordinary course of business. John Rigas, former CEO of Adelphia, Dennis Kozlowski, former CEO of Tyco, and others took large personal loans without the knowledge or approval of their company boards. Corrupt executives who use their companies as personal piggy banks will now face civil and criminal penalties.

**Code of Ethics**    The cornerstone of an effective fraud prevention program and a culture of compliance is a strong value system based on integrity. These values can best be reflected in a code of ethics or conduct to ensure that employees know what is expected of them and then make the right decisions. This is especially true for executives and officers. Sarbanes-Oxley requires that public companies have a code of ethics for its senior financial officers. It must then disclose whether it has adopted a code of ethics; if it has not, it must disclose the reasons for not doing so.

**Enhanced Financial Disclosures**    The Act enhances financial disclosures in a number of other ways. A company must file a report on its internal controls with its annual reports. The report must confirm management's responsibility for establishing and maintaining adequate internal control structures and procedures for reporting, as well as evaluating the effectiveness of these controls and procedures. The issuer's public accountants must attest to and report on the management assessment as part of the audit engagement. These are the requirements of Section 404 that have been dreaded by so many companies.

The Act also improves on the timely reporting of potentially derogatory information. Each annual report filed with the SEC containing financial statements will be required to include all material correcting adjustments. Each annual and quarterly financial report shall disclose all material off-balance sheet transactions and other relationships that may have a material effect on the financial condition of the company. Enron used off-balance sheet transactions to hide debt that contributed to the massive fraud at the Houston energy company.

### Protecting Investors and Ending Conflicts of Interest: Implications for Securities Analysts

There have been continuing investigations as to whether the nation's largest securities firms misled investors with sham research. Jack Grubman, once Salomon Smith Barney's star stock analyst, was accused of misleading investors with overly optimistic and sometimes false stock research. He has agreed to pay a $15 million fine for his actions and will be barred for life from the securities industry.[30] The

New York State Attorney General investigated this questionable stock research and subpoenaed e-mails of other analysts. The e-mails show that while some analysts were giving rosy projections to the public for some stocks, they were privately calling them dogs. For example, while Merrill Lynch promoted a particular Internet company in public, they were disparaging it in internal e-mails.[31]

As a result of the Wall Street scandals, there has been a concerted effort to reel in stock analysts. Sarbanes-Oxley addresses the widespread lack of faith in securities analysts and their research reports. It provides tougher guidelines for stock research and analysts to ensure honest and unbiased evaluations. Analysts will need to disclose conflicts of interest that may cloud their judgment as well as compensation arrangements based on winning business for their employers.

### Obligation to Report Violations of Securities Law: Implications for Attorneys

Exactly when the attorney-client privilege ends and the best interests of the public begin has long been debated. Sarbanes-Oxley addresses that conundrum by enacting new rules of professional responsibility for attorneys representing public companies. Under the Act, an attorney appearing and practicing before the SEC is required to report evidence of a material violation of the securities laws or a breach of fiduciary responsibility by a company or its agents to the company's CEO or general counsel. If the CEO and/or general counsel do not properly respond to the disclosure, the outside attorney must report the matter to the company's audit committee, independent directors, or board of directors. If there is no response, the attorney must tell the SEC.

The SEC approved this provision of the Act but has delayed a proposal that would require attorneys to resign and report alleged fraud to the SEC if the corporation does not act on the evidence. This was in response to an outcry from the country's attorneys that this so-called report out or noisy withdrawal would damage attorney-client confidentiality and privilege. The SEC is considering an alternative proposal that shifts the responsibility of reporting an attorney's resignation to the client company.

The New York County District Attorney's Office obtained e-mails written by outside attorneys representing Tyco. The district attorney indicted Tyco's former chairman and CEO, Dennis Kozlowski, and its former general counsel, Mark Belnick, on a multitude of criminal charges relating to defrauding the company including grand larceny, securities fraud, and falsifying business records. The e-mails show that Tyco's attorneys were aware that Kozlowski used corporate funds for personal use and had concerns about the company's financial reports. One outside attorney wrote to Belnick that, "There are payments to a woman whom the folks in finance describe to be Dennis' girlfriend." The payments to the woman totaled $100,000 and were called a "loan."[32]

The attorney called the payments "an embarrassing fact" and recommended that the information be disclosed to the SEC. Belnick responded in an e-mail that the information did not need to be disclosed. In another e-mail to Belnick, another outside attorney stated that the company's financial reports suggest "something funny which is likely apparent if any decent accountant looks at this." The attorneys later argued that the attorney-client privilege protects them from disclosing this information to law enforcement and regulatory agencies. Although the outside attorneys may have been following the letter of the law at the time, Sarbanes-Oxley now requires that outside attorneys must take appropriate action when they discover evidence of wrongdoing.

Proving that it is sometimes hard to hold attorneys responsible for fraud committed by corporate executives, Belnick was acquitted of all charges in July 2004 after a jury trial in Manhattan.

## Civil and Criminal Penalties

The Act creates a number of new criminal statutes and amends others to add some strong teeth to enforcement actions. These include the following:

**Destruction, Alteration, or Falsification of Records in Federal Investigations and Bankruptcy.** The destruction, alteration, or falsification of records or documents with the intent to impede, obstruct, or influence a federal investigation is a new statute punishable by a fine, imprisonment of up to 20 years, or both. An accountant who conducts an audit of an issuer of securities is now required to maintain all audit or review work papers for a period of five years from the end of the fiscal period in which the audit or review was concluded. This new statute provides a fine, a maximum term of imprisonment of 10 years, or both, for anyone who knowingly and willfully violates it.

**Securities Fraud.** This new statute provides criminal penalties for defrauding shareholders of a publicly traded company. It complements existing securities law and provides a fine, a maximum term of imprisonment of 25 years, or both. The statute of limitations for securities fraud is increased to two years after the discovery of the facts constituting the violation or five years after such violation.

**White-Collar Crime Penalty Enhancements.** Criminal penalties are increased under Title IX of the Act, which is called the "White-Collar Crime Penalty Enhancement Act of 2002." There is increased jail time for a number of existing criminal statutes including the workhorse of fraud prosecution, the Mail Fraud Statute. Sarbanes-Oxley increases the criminal penalties for mail fraud as well as wire fraud to 20 years in prison. There are also increased penalties for violations of the Employee Retirement Security Income Act (ERISA) of 1974, tampering with or impeding an official investigation, and retaliation against informants and whistle-blowers.

**Failure of Corporate Officers to Certify Financial Reports.** There is also a new criminal statute relating to the certification of periodic financial reports filed by a company with the SEC. If the CEO or CFO falsely certifies any statement regarding the financial condition and results of operations of the company, he or she can face up to 20 years in prison and/or a $5 million fine.

**Amendment to the Federal Sentencing Guidelines.** The Act orders the U.S. Sentencing Commission to review and amend its sentencing guidelines for securities fraud, obstruction of justice, and extensive criminal fraud. As a result of Sarbanes-Oxley, there are harsher sentences in fraud cases with large numbers of victims and large dollar losses, cases involving officers and directors of public companies, destruction of evidence, and falsely certifying financial statements.[33]

The USSC has increased penalties for corporate crimes that affect a large number of victims or endanger the financial viability of publicly traded companies. A corporate officer who defrauds more than 250 employees or investors of more than $1 million will now face a sentence of 121 to 151 months in prison. This is more than double the previous sentencing guidelines. The penalty for obstruction of justice by destroying documents or records related to an investigation has also been increased from 18 months in prison to 30 to 37 months in prison.

Shortly after the enactment of Sarbanes-Oxley, a criminal defense attorney commented that he was amazed at the Act's comprehensiveness, strong language, and multiple ways that fraudsters can be prosecuted for corporate wrongdoing. The attorney was also impressed with the increased protection for whistle-blowers and the legal remedies available in case of retaliation. He said he saw his practice growing significantly as a result of increased work from representing clients who violate the Act's provisions as well as whistle-blowers who will need representation in lawsuits.

## ENDNOTES

1. Joseph T. Wells, *Frankensteins of Fraud* (Austin, TX: Obsidian Publishing Company, 2000).
2. Raymond L. Dirks and Leonard Gross, *The Great Wall Street Scandal* (New York: McGraw Hill, 1974).
3. Martin T. Biegelman, *Protecting with Distinction: A Postal Inspection Service History of the Mail Fraud Statute* (Washington, DC: U.S. Postal Inspection Service, 1999).
4. "Jeff Immelt on Corporate Governance," GE Corporate Governance, www.ge.com/en/company/investor/corp_governance.htm.
5. Don Tapscott, "Transparency as a Business Imperative," *Association Management,* April 2005, 17.
6. Bryan Garner, ed. *Black's Law Dictionary,* 8th ed, s.v. "transparency."
7. William H. Donaldson, "Speech by SEC Chairman: Remarks to the National Press Club" (speech, Washington, DC, July 30, 2003), www.sec.gov/news/speech/spch073003whd.htm.

8. National Commission on Fraudulent Financial Reporting, *Report of the National Commission on Fraudulent Financial Reporting,* October, 1987, 1 ("The Treadway Report"), www.coso.org/publications/NCFFR_Part_1.htm.
9. Ibid., 23.
10. Ibid., 1.
11. Ibid., 24.
12. Ibid., 17–78.
13. The Committee of Sponsoring Organizations of the Treadway Commission, *Internal Control—Integrated Framework* (1992), www.coso.org/publications/executive_summary_integrated_framework.htm.
14. Mark S. Beasley, Joseph V. Carcello, and Dana R. Hermanson, *Fraudulent Financial Reporting 1987-1997, An Analysis of U.S. Public Companies* (Committee of Sponsoring Organizations of the Treadway Commission, 1999), www.coso.org/publications/FFR_1987_1997.PDF.
15. *Sentencing Reform Act, U.S. Code* 28 (2003) § 991.
16. *United States Sentencing Commission Guidelines Manual,* Ch. 8, Sentencing of Organizations, November 1, 1991, www.ussc.gov/1994guid/chap8.htm.
17. Association of Certified Fraud Examiners. *Fraud Examiners Manual,* 3rd ed. (Austin, TX: 2001), 1.203.
18. Ibid, 1.204.
19. Donald Fogel, "SAS 82: Providing Guidance in the Hunt for Fraud," *The White Paper,* (September/October 1998), 28.
20. Association of Certified Fraud Examiners. *Fraud Examiners Manual,* 3rd ed. (Austin, TX: ACFE, 2001), 1.205-1.206.
21. Donald Fogel, "SAS 82: Providing Guidance in the Hunt for Fraud," *The White Paper,* September/October 1998, 38.
22. SAS 82 content reprinted with permission from the *Fraud Examiners Manual,* 3rd ed. (Austin, TX: ACFE, 2001), 1.203-1.207, and the Association of Certified Fraud Examiners, Austin, Texas (c) 2005.
23. Barbara R. Farrell and Joseph R. Franco, "The Role of the Auditor in the Prevention and Detection of Business Fraud: SAS No. 82." *Western Criminology Review* 2, no. 1 (1999), http://wcr.sonoma.edu/v2nl/v2nl.html.

24. Arthur Levitt, "The 'Numbers Game'" (speech, New York University Center for Law and Business, New York, September 28, 1998), www.sec.gov/news/speecharchive/1998/spch220.txt.

25. Ibid.

26. Ian Giddy, *Corporate Financial Restructuring*, www.stern.nyu.edu/~igiddy/restructuring.html.

27. Arthur Levitt, "The 'Numbers Game'" (speech, New York University Center for Law and Business, New York, September 28, 1998), www.sec.gov/news/speecharchive/1998/spch220.txt.

28. Eric Winig, "Government Meddling Won't Stop Cheats," *Washington Business Journal*, July 12, 2002.

29. Elisabeth Bumiller, "Bush Signs Bill Aimed at Fraud in Corporations," *New York Times*, July 31, 2002. A2.

30. "The Securities and Exchange Commission, New York Attorney General's Office, NASD and the New York Stock Exchange Permanently Bar Jack Grubman and Require $15 Million Payment," Securities and Exchange Commission, www.sec.gov/news/press/2003-55.htm, April 28, 2003.

31. Eliot Spitzer, interview, *60 Minutes,* CBS, May 25, 2003, transcript available at: www.cbsnews.com/stories/2003/05/23/60minutes/main555310.shtml (comments made by New York Attorney General Eliot Spitzer during segment entitled "The Sheriff of Wall Street).

32. Laurie P. Cohen and Mark Maremont, "E-Mails Show Tyco's Lawyers Had Concerns," *Wall Street Journal,* December 27, 2002, C1.

33. Martin T. Biegelman, "Sarbanes-Oxley Act: Stopping U.S. Corporate Crooks from Cooking the Books," *The White Paper,* March/April 2003, reprinted with permission from the Association of Certified Fraud Examiners, Austin, Texas © 2005.

# The Path to Greater Corporate Compliance, Accountability, and Ethical Conduct: SAS 99 to the Sarbanes-Oxley Influence on Private and Nonprofit Organizations

## EXECUTIVE SUMMARY

Improved corporate compliance and stricter enforcement did not end with the enactment of Sarbanes-Oxley. The American Institute of Certified Public Accountants released their Statement on Auditing Standards (SAS) 99, an auditing standard that now requires greater involvement of external auditors in developing reasonable assurance that an entity's financial statements are free of material misstatements whether by fraud or error. The government gave strong guidance to federal prosecutors in its historic "Thompson Memo" of how and when to bring criminal charges against an organization. In the process, the government sent a chilling message to corporations that cross the line. The Securities and Exchange Commission (SEC) drove home the important role of "gatekeepers" in protecting the interests of the investing public and the government. The government greatly enhanced prison sentences for fraud so that a fraud conviction could now bring a life sentence. Other compliance enhancements followed, all leading the way toward the creation of a culture of compliance.

## THE SAS 99 FIX

After several tries and the inability to detect massive financial statement frauds, the accounting industry may have finally gotten it right. In December 2002, the new SAS 99, Consideration of Fraud in a Financial Statement Audit, superseded the earlier SAS 82 and gave auditors better tools and guidance for effectiveness in uncovering fraud. Auditors now have "a responsibility to plan and perform the audit to obtain reasonable assurance about whether the financial statements are free of material misstatement, whether caused by error or fraud."[1] Quite simply, SAS 99 now requires auditors to look for fraud throughout the audit process. SAS 99 provides auditors with guidance on detecting fraud through the following content:

- Description and characteristics of fraud
- The importance of exercising professional skepticism
- Discussion among engagement personnel regarding the risks of material misstatement because of fraud
- Obtaining the information to identify risks of material misstatement because of fraud
  - Inquiring of management and others within the entity about the risks of fraud
  - Considering the results of the analytical procedures performed in planning the audit
  - Considering fraud risk factors
- Identifying risks that may result in a material misstatement because of fraud
- Assessing the identified risks after taking into account an evaluation of the entity's programs and controls
- Responding to the results of the assessment
  - A response that has an overall effect on how the audit is conducted, that is, a response involving more general considerations apart from the specific procedures otherwise planned
  - A response to identified risks that involves the nature, timing, and extent of the auditing procedures to be performed
  - A response regarding the performance of certain procedures to further address the risk of material misstatement because of fraud involving management override of controls
- Evaluating audit evidence

- Communicating about fraud to management, the audit committee, and others
- Documenting the auditor's consideration of fraud.[2]


## Fraud According to SAS 99

SAS 99 incorporates fraud theory and practice in developing reasonable assurance that an entity's financial statements are free of material misstatements whether by fraud or error. SAS 99 defines fraud as "an intentional act that results in a material misstatement in financial statements that are the subject of an audit."[3] Cressey's Fraud Triangle is incorporated into SAS 99 with a discussion of the three conditions that are generally present for fraud to occur: incentive or pressure (motive), opportunity, and rationalization or attitude. Furthermore, two types of financial misstatements are defined under SAS 99, misstatements arising from fraudulent financial reporting and misstatements arising from misappropriation of assets, often referred to as defalcation or theft. The fraud risk factors related to fraudulent financial reporting are given in Appendix B, and the fraud risk factors related to misappropriation of assets are given in Appendix C.

Misstatements arising from fraudulent financial reporting are considered intentional misstatements or omissions of information from financial statements with the intent to deceive. SAS 99 explains that fraudulent financial reporting can be accomplished by:

- Manipulation, falsification, or alteration of accounting records or supporting documents from which financial statements are prepared
- Misrepresentation in or intentional omission from the financial statements of events, transactions, or other significant information
- Intentional misapplication of accounting principles relating to amounts, classification, manner of presentation, or disclosure.

SAS 99 takes into consideration that financial schemes, such as manipulating accounting records and management override, are often perpetrated by a company's management. As a result, auditors are urged to be aware of this possibility in addition to collusion among employees engaging in a fraud and the falsification of documentation that is presented for review. As an example, SAS 99 details how the common management override of internal controls can be accomplished by:

- Recording fictitious journal entries, particularly those recorded close to the end of an accounting period in order to manipulate operating results
- Intentionally biasing assumptions and judgments used to estimate account balances
- Altering records and terms related to significant and unusual transactions.

## Exercising Professional Skepticism

SAS 99 requires auditors to apply professional skepticism when doing their audits to ensure that the truth is found. This requires a questioning mind at all times and critical assessments of the statements and documentation provided by the entity. The auditor must also conduct the audit with the idea in mind that a fraud may be present and without bias by past experiences or beliefs in the honesty and integrity of management. Many of the auditors involved in corporate frauds failed to exercise the due care or skepticism that might have detected the accounting deception early on.

## Discussion among Engagement Personnel

SAS 99 requires that auditors exchange ideas or "brainstorm" either before or during an audit about how an entity's financial statements might be fraudulently misstated, how fraud may be concealed, and how assets could be misappropriated. The various elements of the Fraud Triangle should be discussed as to the fraud risks that might be in play at the company. The key members of the audit team must be involved in this brainstorming with consideration given to involving other experts in fraud detection as the need arises. Communication among team members is critical throughout the audit to ensure that all fraud risks are considered in evaluating the existence of material misstatements.

## Obtaining, Identifying, and Assessing Fraud Risks

When beginning an engagement, auditors must make inquiries of management to learn about the organization's business and the potential risks of material misstatement because of fraud. This inquiry should include questioning whether:

- Management has an understanding of fraud and fraud risks facing the entity
- Management has knowledge of allegations of fraud either through identified parties or whistle-blower hotlines
- The organization has implemented programs and controls to detect, deter, and prevent fraud and how it monitors the programs and controls
- Organizations with multiple locations and business segments are appropriately monitoring the fraud risk at each location or business segment and whether, as a result, there is significantly more risk involved
- Management communicates to employees its policies on ethical standards and business practices.

Auditors should inquire of management whether the audit committee has been briefed on how the entity's internal controls help detect and prevent fraud. In addition to discussions with management, auditors should also speak with the audit committee about their understanding of fraud risks and whether the audit committee has any knowledge of allegations of fraud. Auditors should also ask the entity's internal audit function about their views on fraud risk and whether there have been instances of fraud. If so, auditors should inquire about the response to these allegations by the internal audit group and management's response to any findings emanating from a fraud investigation. In addition, inquiries should be made of any other appropriate employees such as fraud investigators and legal compliance personnel who might have knowledge of fraud within the entity. Auditors must always remember that fraudsters within a company will not willingly reveal their involvement in fraudulent activities and thus, there is the need for independent verification and corroboration.

In determining the entity's fraud risk, the motive/incentive/pressure to commit fraud, the opportunity that exists to commit fraud, and the rationalization/attitude to justify the fraudulent actions must all be considered by the auditors. Analytical procedures to identify unusual or suspect transactions must also be considered. Examples of such analytical procedures might include reviewing sales volume over production capacity for fictitious sales. Trend analysis of revenues and sales returns may disclose channel stuffing and side agreements for customers to return merchandise, resulting in revenue recognition issues. Channel stuffing is an illegal practice by a company to inflate its sales and earnings numbers at the end of a fiscal year by offering distributors and other channel partners more products than they might be able to reasonably sell.

SAS 99 requires auditors to consider a number of issues involving fraud risk, including the following:

- The *type* of risk that may exist and whether it involves fraudulent financial reporting or misappropriation of assets
- The *significance* of the risk identified and whether it could lead to a material misstatement
- The *likelihood* that the risk will result in a material misstatement
- The *pervasiveness* of risk as to whether it permeates the entire financial statement or is confined to a particular transaction or account.

To assess any identified fraud risks, auditors must have a thorough understanding of an entity's internal controls that have been designed and are in place. The program and controls must be evaluated to determine whether they are sufficient to mitigate the risk of material misstatement fraud.

The auditors must recognize the possibility of other fraud risks for misstatement being present in the entity, including the following:

- *Revenue recognition.* Material misstatements are common because of premature revenue recognition, recording fictitious revenues, and improperly shifting revenues to a later period.
- *Management overrides.* Overrides by management are also common and should be considered a potential risk. Today there is

greater scrutiny of management overrides such as phony journal entries. Fraudsters have favored manual entries and now auditors are looking closely at them.

- *Inventory quantities.* Falsifying inventory numbers is another fraud risk. Auditors should consider identifying the location of inventory and conducting a physical inventory count if there is an indication of manipulation. The examination may include the contents of boxes, the manner in which the goods are stacked, and the quality of the contents. Fraudsters have been known to stack empty boxes, as well as boxes containing damaged or discontinued stock to deceive auditors checking inventory.

- *Management estimates.* The fraud risk may involve specific transactions including acquisitions, restructurings, or disposals of business segments or significant accrued liabilities such as pension and other postretirement benefit obligations.

- *Manipulation of journal entries.* Material misstatements often involve recording inappropriate or unauthorized journal entries throughout the year or at year-end, as well as making adjustments to financial statements that are not reflected in formal journal entries.

### Evaluating Audit Evidence

Under SAS 99, auditors may identify risks that need further examination in order to determine the full extent of a possible fraud, including the following:

- Discrepancies in Accounting Records
  - Transactions that are not recorded in a complete or timely manner or are improperly recorded as to amount, accounting period, classification, or entity policy
  - Unsupported or unauthorized balances or transactions
  - Last-minute adjustments that significantly affect financial results
  - Evidence of employees' access to systems and records inconsistent with that necessary to perform their authorized duties
  - Tips or complaints to the auditor about alleged fraud

■ Conflicting or Missing Evidential Matter
  - Missing documents
  - Documents that appear to have been altered
  - Unavailability of documents other than photocopies or electronically transmitted documents when original documents are expected to exist
  - Significant unexplained items on reconciliations
  - Inconsistent, vague, or implausible responses from management or employees arising from inquiries or analytical procedures
  - Unusual discrepancies between the entity's records and confirmation replies
  - Missing inventory or physical assets of significant magnitude
  - Unavailable or missing electronic evidence, inconsistent with the entity's record retention practices or policies
  - Inability to produce evidence of key systems development and program change testing and implementation activities for current-year system changes and deployments.
■ Problematic or Unusual Relationships between the Auditor and Management
  - Denial of access to records, facilities, certain employees, customers, vendors, or others from whom audit evidence might be sought
  - Undue time pressures imposed by management to resolve complex or contentious issues
  - Complaints by management about the conduct of the audit or management intimidation of audit team members, particularly in connection with the auditor's critical assessment of audit evidence or in the resolution of potential disagreements with management
  - Unusual delays by the entity in providing requested information
  - Unwillingness to facilitate auditor access to key electronic files for testing through the use of computer-assisted audit techniques
  - Denial of access to key IT operations staff and facilities, including security, operations, and systems development personnel
  - An unwillingness to add or revise disclosures in the financial statements to make them more complete and transparent.

If, after conducting a thorough audit, the auditor believes there is the likelihood of misstatements that could be material to the entity's financial statements, the auditor should:

■ Attempt to obtain additional evidence to determine whether material fraud has occurred or is likely to have occurred, and if so, the effect on the financial statements
■ Consider the implications for other aspects of the audit that may require additional testing
■ Discuss the matter with an appropriate level of management that is at least one level above those involved as well as with senior management and the audit committee
■ If appropriate, suggest that the entity consult with legal counsel.

### Communicating and Documenting the Risk of Fraud

As an element of SAS 99, when auditors find evidence of fraud, they must communicate it to the appropriate level of management. Any fraud that is discovered involving senior management, as well as fraud related to material misstatements, must be disclosed to the audit committee. Risks of fraud should also be communicated to other appropriate parties because of their potential to result in fraud at some future time. For a record of the auditor's consideration of fraud, the following should be documented:

■ The discussion(s) among engagement personnel when planning the audit as to the susceptibility of the organization's financial statements to material misstatements resulting from fraud, how and when the discussion(s) took place, the audit team members who participated, and what was discussed
■ The specific procedures performed to identify and assess the risks of material misstatement because of fraud as well as a description of the auditor's response to those risks
■ The specific risks of material misstatement that were identified and the auditor's response to those risks
■ The results of procedures performed to address the risk of management override of controls

- Any other conditions or analytical relationships that caused the auditor to believe that additional audit procedures were required
- The nature of the communications about fraud made to management, the audit committee, and others.[4]

## THE THOMPSON MEMO

On January 20, 2003, former Deputy Attorney General Larry Thompson took the fight against corporate fraud to a higher level. On that date, he issued a landmark memorandum entitled "Principles of Federal Prosecution of Business Organizations" and sent it to all United States Attorneys' Offices. It contained a revised set of principles to guide Department of Justice prosecutors when they were deciding to seek charges against a business organization.

The Thompson Memo is a roadmap for federal prosecutors in the investigation and prosecution of corporate fraud. Every vigilant executive must be aware of the strategy contained in this groundbreaking memo. It provides a unique window into the government's strategy on corporate fraud prosecution. Mr. Thompson's own words should help businesses focus on protection of their employees and investors from fraud, and themselves from prosecution. Additionally, by understanding how the government thinks about prosecuting businesses, organizations can implement robust compliance and fraud prevention programs to lessen their culpability. As Mr. Thompson states, "the main focus of the revisions is increased emphasis on and scrutiny of the authenticity of a corporation's cooperation. Too often business organizations, while purporting to cooperate with a Department of Justice investigation, in fact take steps to impede the quick and effective exposure of the complete scope of wrongdoing under investigation. The revision makes clear that such conduct should weigh in favor of a corporate prosecution. The revisions also address the efficacy of the corporate governance mechanisms in place within a corporation, to ensure that these measures are truly effective rather than mere paper programs."[5]

These guidelines for federal prosecutions of business organizations apply not only to public companies but also to other types of businesses including partnerships, sole proprietorships, government entities, and unincorporated associations. Every corporate executive and general counsel should be familiar with this government strategy memo. In fact, it should be read and reread by every CEO and CFO as a reminder of the consequences for a culture of noncompliance.

## THE FINAL RULE OF THE SEC FOR SECTION 404 OF SARBANES-OXLEY

Sarbanes-Oxley's Section 404 requires that the SEC adopt rules requiring companies subject to the reporting requirements under the Securities Exchange Act of 1934 to include in the company's annual reports a report from management on the company's internal control over financial reporting. Section 404 requires an annual evaluation and report by management on the effectiveness of internal controls and procedures for financial reporting, as well as a report by the independent auditor attesting to management's assertions.[6] In August 2003, the SEC issued its final rule entitled *Management's Report on Internal Control over Financial Reporting and Certification of Disclosure in Exchange Act Periodic Reports*. The SEC's rule defines internal controls and procedures for financial reporting to mean "controls that pertain to the preparation of financial statements for external purposes that are fairly presented in conformity with generally accepted accounting principles."[7]

As stated in the rule, "The assessment of a company's internal control over financial reporting must be based on procedures sufficient both to evaluate its design and to test its operating effectiveness. Controls subject to such assessment include...controls related to the prevention, identification, and detection of fraud." The final SEC rules require that a company's annual report contain an internal control report from management that includes the following:

- A statement of management's responsibility for establishing and maintaining adequate internal control over the company's financial reporting.
- A statement identifying the framework used by management to conduct the required evaluation of the effectiveness of the company's internal control over financial reporting (ICFR).

- Management's assessment of the effectiveness of the company's ICFR as of the end of the company's most recent fiscal year, including a statement as to whether or not the company's ICFR is effective. The assessment must include a disclosure of any "material weaknesses" in the company's ICFR identified by management. A "material weakness" is defined as "a reportable condition in which the design or operation of one or more of the internal control components does not reduce to a relatively low level the risk that misstatements caused by errors or fraud in amounts that would be material in relation to the financial statements being audited may occur and not be detected within a timely period by employees in the normal course of performing their assigned function."[8] Management is not permitted to conclude that the company's ICFR is effective if there are one or more material weaknesses in the company's ICFR.
- A statement that the registered public accounting firm that audited the financial statements included in the annual report has issued an attestation report on management's assessment of the company's ICFR reporting as well as the actual attestation report of the accounting firm that audited the company's financial statements.[9]

A common complaint from companies is the cost of implementing Section 404. Some large companies feel they are wasting money, whereas some small companies are postponing public offerings because of Section 404 costs and compliance requirements. There is no doubt that businesses have spent a great deal of money thus far. Financial Executives International (FEI) surveyed 217 public companies with average revenues of $5 billion to measure compliance costs. The study was released in March 2005 and found that compliance with Section 404 averaged $4.36 million per company for first-year compliance. These costs included internal costs and auditor fees. The $4.36 million cost was an increase of 39 percent from FEI's earlier survey in July 2004.[10] The findings mirror another survey from Oversight Systems in December 2004 in which 222 financial executives were surveyed, and 54 percent found that their Section 404 compliance costs were more than expected.[11]

In the FEI survey, 55 percent of companies believe that Section 404 provides more confidence in financial reporting. Interestingly, 83 percent of companies with revenues over $25 billion also feel the same way. Unfortunately, 94 percent of respondents felt that the cost of compliance exceeds the benefits.[12] The Oversight Systems survey had similar findings. It found that 57 percent of executives surveyed believed that compliance was a good investment for shareholders. Seventy-nine percent reported a stronger internal control program as a result of Section 404, and 74 percent believed that their companies benefited from Sarbanes-Oxley compliance. Thirty-three percent believed that Sarbanes-Oxley created a cost burden for their companies, and 25 percent said that the cost of complying outweighs the benefits.[13] Thirty-eight percent stated that Congress overreacted to the unethical and illegal behavior of a few corporate executives. Clearly there are conflicting messages coming from these executives, but the bottom line is that compliance, while costly, is a necessity.

## NEW YORK STOCK EXCHANGE AND NASDAQ LISTING REQUIREMENTS

In October 2002, the SEC began implementation of Section 301 of Sarbanes-Oxley, which requires all audit committee members to be independent and establishes procedures for processing complaints and anonymous employee submissions regarding the company's accounting, accounting controls, or auditing matters. The SEC understood that good corporate governance and market integrity could only be effective through appropriate oversight of the financial reporting process by an entity's audit committee. Board members are accountable to shareholders and others. They must ensure compliance and provide independent review and oversight of the financial reporting process, internal controls, and independent auditors.

By April 2003, the SEC adopted a new rule that "directed the national securities exchanges and national securities associations to prohibit the listing of any security of an issuer that is not in compliance with the audit committee requirements mandated by the Sarbanes-Oxley Act of 2002." The SEC required compliance by the earlier of their first annual meeting after January 15, 2004 or October 31, 2004. Foreign private issuers will have additional time to comply with the new audit committee standards but still must comply.[14] Both the New York Stock Exchange (NYSE) and the NASDAQ corporate governance rule changes were finalized in November 2003.

The NYSE listing requirements include the following:

- Listed companies must have a majority of independent directors. An independent director is one who has no material relationship with the listed company either directly or as a partner, shareholder, or officer of an organization that has a relationship with the company.
- Nonmanagement directors must meet at regularly scheduled executive sessions without management.
- Listed companies must have a nominating/corporate governance committee composed entirely of independent directors.
- Listed companies must have a compensation committee composed entirely of independent directors.
- Listed companies must have a effective audit committee with the following requirements:
  - A minimum of three members
  - Independent status
  - A written charter
  - Mandatory maintenance of an internal audit function to provide management and the audit committee with ongoing assessments of the company's risk management processes and system of internal controls.
- Listed companies must adopt and disclose corporate governance guidelines.
- Listed companies must adopt and disclose a code of business conduct and ethics for directors, officers, and employees and must promptly disclose any waivers of the code for directors or executive officers.
- Listed foreign private issuers must disclose any significant ways in which their corporate governance practices differ from those required of domestic companies under NYSE listing standards.
- Each listed CEO must certify to the NYSE each year that he or she is not aware of any violations by the company of NYSE corporate governance listing standards.
- The NYSE may issue a public reprimand letter to any listed company that violates a NYSE listing standard.

The complete NYSE corporate governance rules can be found at www.nyse.com/pdfs/section303A_final_rules.pdf.

The NASDAQ listing requirements include the following:

- A majority of independent directors are required on the board.
- Regularly convened (at least twice per year) executive sessions of the independent directors must be held.
- A company's audit committee or a comparable body of the board of directors must review and approve all related-party transactions.
- A director is not considered independent if during the previous three years he or she has received any payments (including political contributions) in excess of $60,000 other than for board service. This prohibition also covers the receipt of payments by a nonemployee who is an immediate family member of the director.
- An audit committee member may not receive any compensation except for board or committee service.
- A director is not considered independent if he or she has been employed by the company (or a parent or subsidiary) within the previous three years, or if an immediate family member is employed as an executive officer of the company (or a parent company or subsidiary) or has been so employed within the previous three years.
- Rules now include not-for-profit entities. This means a director is prohibited from being considered independent if the company makes payments to any other entity, including a not-for-profit entity, in which the director is an executive officer and the payments exceed the greater of $200,000 or five percent of the recipient's gross revenues. This rule also expands to cover situations in which an immediate family member of the director is an executive officer of the entity receiving payments.
- Current partners of the company's outside auditor and their immediate family members cannot be considered independent for three years. Additionally, any former partner or employee of a company's outside auditor who worked on a company's audit will not be considered independent for three years.
- A director is not considered independent if, during the previous three years, the director or an immediate family member was employed as an executive of another company in which any executives of the

listed company serve on the compensation committee of the company of which the director is an executive.

- In case of investment companies, a director is not considered independent if he or she is an "interested person" under the Investment Company Act.
- Independent directors must approve director nominations, either by independent nominating committee or by a majority of the independent directors.
- A charter is required describing the role of the nominating committee or, alternatively, a board resolution describing the role of the independent directors, in the nomination process.
- Independent director approval of CEO compensation is required, either by an independent compensation committee or by a majority of the independent directors in a meeting in executive session.
- Other executive officer compensation must also have independent approval, either by an independent compensation committee or by a majority of the independent directors in a meeting at which the CEO may be present.
- Audit committees will have the sole authority to appoint, determine funding for, and oversee the outside auditors.
- Audit committees must approve, in advance, the provision by the auditor of all permissible nonaudit services.
- Audit committees are required to have authority to engage and determine funding for independent counsel and other advisors.
- Audit committees must establish procedures for the receipt, retention, and confidential and anonymous treatment of complaints received by the company regarding accounting, internal accounting controls, or auditing.
- All audit committee members must be able to read and understand financial statements at the time of their appointment.
- Exceptions to the audit committee requirements are eliminated for Small Business Filers.
- Effective July 31, 2005, only foreign private issuers are eligible for exemptions under the new rules.
- Issuers must adopt a code of conduct for all directors and employees and make it publicly available.
- Waivers to the code of conduct for executive officers and directors can only be granted by the issuer's board and must be disclosed.

The complete NASDAQ corporate governance rules can be found at www.nasdaq.com/about/CorpGovSummary.pdf. The American Stock Exchange has a similar corporate governance policy for listed companies and that can be found at www.amex.com.

## THE PCAOB AND AUDITING STANDARD NO. 2

The Public Company Accounting Oversight Board (PCAOB) was created by the Sarbanes-Oxley legislation to be a strong and independent oversight body of the auditing of public companies by external auditors. The PCAOB is a private sector, nonprofit corporation set up to protect the interests of investors and ensure the preparation and release of accurate and independent audit reports. Several sections of Sarbanes-Oxley pertain to the PCAOB including the following:

- Section 102: prohibits accounting firms that are not registered with the PCAOB from preparing or issuing audit reports on United States public companies and from participating in such audits
- Section 103: directs the PCAOB to establish auditing and related attestation, quality control, ethics, and independence standards and rules to be used by registered public accounting companies in the preparation and issuance of audit reports
- Section 104: requires the PCAOB to conduct a continuing program of inspections of registered public accounting firms
- Section 105: grants the PCAOB broad investigative and disciplinary authority over registered public accounting firms and persons associated with such firms.

The PCAOB has a strong enforcement role to prevent violations of Sarbanes-Oxley. To assist their mission, they have established the PCAOB Center for Enforcement Tips, Complaints and Other Information. Individuals can file a complaint or provide tips on potential violations by a public accounting firm, its employees or others, or provide any information that might be relevant to the work of the PCAOB. There are several ways to contact the PCAOB hotline, including their Web site at www.pcaobus.org/Enforcement/Tips/tips.aspx, via e-mail, by letter, or by telephone. This hotline will take action on any information received including the referral of other violations out of their jurisdiction to appropriate law enforcement agencies.

On March 9, 2004, the PCAOB adopted Auditing Standard No. 2, *An Audit of Internal Control over Financial Reporting Performed in Conjunction with an Audit of Financial Statements.* Standard No. 2 provides increased responsibilities for external auditors beyond those required by SAS 99. Although SAS 99 provides detailed guidance on a fraud risk assessment, it only requires an auditor to gain an understanding of management's fraud prevention and detection programs and controls. Standard No. 2 actually requires auditors to evaluate antifraud programs and controls as part of the audit of internal control over financial reporting. It requires an integrated audit of the financial statements and an audit of internal control over financial reporting. It requires external auditors to test a company's internal controls themselves and not rely on any work performed by the company. It states that the costs of internal control must be appropriate to the expected benefits reaped from improved controls. It also requires auditors to evaluate the fraud-related activities of the internal audit department. The detailed content of Auditing Standard No. 2 is too voluminous to include here, but some of the key provisions of Auditing Standard No. 2 are as follows:

- Evaluating management's assessment
- Obtaining an understanding of internal control over financial reporting including performing walkthroughs
- Identifying significant account and relevant assertions
- Testing and evaluating the effectiveness of the design of controls
- Testing operating effectiveness
- Timing of testing
- Using the work of others
- Evaluating the results of testing
- Identifying significant deficiencies
- Forming an opinion and reporting
- No disclosure of significant deficiencies
- Material weaknesses resulting in adverse opinion on internal control
- Testing controls intended to prevent or detect fraud.[15]

## Fraud Considerations in an Audit of Internal Control over Financial Reporting

As Standard No. 2 advises, "Strong internal controls also provide better opportunities to detect and deter fraud. For example, many frauds resulting in financial statement restatement relied upon the ability of management to exploit weaknesses in internal control."[16] It goes on to say, "For this reason, Auditing Standard No. 2 specifically addresses and emphasizes the importance of controls over possible fraud and requires the auditor to test controls specifically intended to prevent or detect fraud that is reasonably possible to result in material misstatement of financial statements."[17]

Auditors must now evaluate all controls specifically intended to address fraud risks that may have a likelihood of having a material impact on the company's financial statements. These controls may be part of the COSO framework of control environment, risk assessment, control activities, information and communication, and monitoring. Some of the controls that must be evaluated include the following:

- Poor or lack of controls over misappropriation of assets that could result in a material misstatement
- The company's risk assessment processes
- Code of ethics and conduct provisions, especially those related to conflicts of interest, related party transactions, illegal acts, and the monitoring of the code by management and the board
- Adequacy of the internal audit function and whether internal audit reports directly to the audit committee, as well as the audit committee's involvement and interaction with internal audit
- Adequacy of the company's procedures for responding to complaints and accepting confidential submissions of questionable accounting and auditing matters.

Auditors are now required to identify, inquire about, and evaluate fraud of any magnitude on the part of senior management of a company. Senior management includes the principal executive and financial officers signing the Sarbanes-Oxley 302 certifications as well as any other members of management who play a significant role in the company's financial reporting process.

## STEPHEN CUTLER'S "GATEKEEPERS SPEECH"

In September 2004, Stephen M. Cutler, former SEC Director of Enforcement, delivered a landmark speech entitled "The Themes of Sarbanes-Oxley as Reflected in the Commission's Enforcement Program." The speech was presented to the UCLA School of Law in Los Angeles and has become known as the "Gatekeepers Speech." Cutler tackled the importance of gatekeepers, those people who are responsible for monitoring and oversight of others in the financial markets. They are the people in important positions to whom the investing public, the government, and others look for truth and honesty in financial reporting. They must be beyond reproach and accountable for their actions.

Cutler started the speech with an interesting quote regarding the impact of fraud and corruption on corporations. He said, "The public corporation is currently under severe attack because of the many revelations of improper corporate activity. It is not simple to assess the cause of this misconduct. Since it has taken so many forms, the one-dimensional explanation that...such conduct is a way of life, is simply not acceptable."[18] Although the quote sounded like a reference to the current corporate scandals, Cutler surprised the audience when he told them it was actually said in 1974 by then SEC Enforcement Director Stanley Sporkin, who was describing the many disclosures of bribes paid to foreign government officials that led to enactment of the Foreign Corrupt Practices Act. Cutler warned that history repeats itself time and again unless a culture change occurs in the securities markets.

Cutler outlined three ongoing themes that he believed were needed in order to prevent history from repeating itself:

- The critical role of gatekeepers in maintaining fair and honest markets
- The requirement for integrity in the investigative process to detect, investigate, and prosecute securities law violations
- The need for greater personal responsibility and accountability from corporate executives and strong civil and criminal penalties when they cross the line.

Cutler defined gatekeepers as "[t]he sentries of the marketplace: the auditors who sign off on companies' financial data; the lawyers who advise companies on disclosure standards and other securities law requirements; the research analysts who warn investors away from unsound companies; and the boards of directors responsible for oversight of company management. They're paramount in ensuring that our markets are clean. And Congress recognized that when it enacted Sarbanes-Oxley."[19]

Cutler recalled the many criminal prosecutions and civil enforcement actions taken against corporations and corporate executives, independent directors, in-house counsel gone astray, research analysts, financial services firms, and others who failed in their important roles as gatekeepers. He stressed that holding gatekeepers responsible for their actions was key to preventing continued corporate fraud and abuse. He cited his intention to go after outside counsel who assist their companies or clients in covering up evidence of fraud, independent directors who are anything but, external auditors who have not lived up to their required role, and others who fail in their roles as gatekeepers.

## ENHANCED SENTENCING GUIDELINES: LESS CARROT AND MORE STICK

With the continuous tweaking of compliance programs, it only makes sense that the Federal Sentencing Guidelines for Organizations would be reworked and strengthened. Previously, the United States Sentencing Commission (USSC) recommended seven minimum requirements for an effective program to prevent and deter violations of law that encompassed self-reporting and acceptance of responsibility. Effective November 1, 2004, the USSC enhanced the guidelines by emphasizing effective compliance and ethics programs in order to mitigate punishment for a criminal offense. Now organizations must promote an organizational culture that encourages ethical conduct and a commitment to compliance with the law. It places the responsibility directly on the chief executives and directors to ensure compliance. Organizations must now have adequate resources, authority, training programs, reporting mechanisms, risk assessment, and periodic evaluation to ensure that fraud prevention and compliance are paramount.

The 2004 guidelines still have seven requirements, but they are now significantly enhanced, as follows:

- Standards and Procedures
  - The organization shall establish standards and procedures to prevent and detect criminal conduct and ensure compliance with the law. In other words, an organization's code of conduct must be robust and embed ethical conduct as an integral component of the ethics and compliance program.
- Organizational Leadership and a Culture of Compliance
  - The organization's governing authority shall be knowledgeable about the content and operation of the compliance and ethics program. (This would normally be the CEO, CFO, and the Board of Directors.)
  - They shall exercise reasonable oversight with respect to the implementation and effectiveness of the compliance and ethics program.
  - Specific individual(s) within the highest levels of the organization shall be assigned overall responsibility for the compliance and ethics program.
  - Specific individual(s) within the organization shall be delegated day-to-day operational responsibility for the compliance and ethics program. The individual(s) with operational responsibility shall report periodically to high-level personnel and, as appropriate, to the governing authority on the effectiveness of the compliance and ethics program.
  - To carry out such operational responsibility, such individual(s) shall be given adequate resources, appropriate authority, and direct access to the governing authority of the organization.
- Reasonable Efforts to Exclude Prohibited Persons
  - The organization shall use reasonable efforts not to include within the substantial authority personnel whom the organization knew, or should have known through the exercise of due diligence, have engaged in illegal activities or other conduct inconsistent with an effective compliance and ethics program.

- Training and Communication
  - The organization shall take reasonable steps to communicate periodically and in a practical manner its standards and procedures, and other aspects of the compliance and ethics program by conducting effective training programs and otherwise disseminating information appropriate to such individuals' respective roles and responsibilities.
  - Training shall be provided to members of the governing authority, other high-level leadership, employees, and, as appropriate, the organization's agents.
- Monitoring, Auditing, and Evaluating Program Effectiveness
  - The organization shall take reasonable steps to ensure that the organization's compliance and ethics program is followed, including monitoring and auditing to detect criminal conduct.
  - The organization shall take reasonable steps to evaluate the effectiveness of the organization's compliance and ethics program.
  - The organization shall take reasonable steps to have and publicize a system, which may include mechanisms that allow for anonymity or confidentiality, where the organization's employees and agents may report or seek guidance regarding potential or actual criminal conduct without fear of retaliation, such as hotlines.
- Performance Incentives and Disciplinary Action
  - The organization's compliance and ethics program shall be promoted and enforced consistently within the organization through appropriate incentives to perform in accordance with the compliance and ethics program.
  - The organization's compliance and ethics program shall be promoted and enforced consistently within the organization through appropriate disciplinary measures for engaging in criminal conduct and for failing to take reasonable steps to prevent or detect criminal conduct.
- Remedial Action
  - After criminal conduct has been detected, the organization shall take reasonable steps to respond appropriately to the criminal conduct and to prevent further similar conduct, including making any necessary modifications to the organization's compliance and ethics program.

- The organization shall periodically assess the risk of criminal conduct and shall take appropriate steps to design, implement, or modify each compliance requirement to reduce the risk of criminal conduct identified through this process.[20]

In addition to the preceding seven requirements, there are others that must be implemented by an organization. An organization must incorporate and adhere to industry practices and standards of compliance as required by government regulation. Unless this is followed, an organization is not considered to have an effective compliance and ethics program. Waivers of attorney-client privilege and work-product protections are not a prerequisite to a reduction in culpability score unless they are needed to provide information known to the organization. The Department of Justice will consider waivers of attorney-client privilege and work-product protections as elements of timely cooperation and will consider such actions when making decisions in prosecution determinations. Courts are required to order probation if the organization failed to have an effective compliance program in place when one was required and can upwardly depart from the guidelines if a compliance program is not in place. Organizations must remember that the only way to avoid or at least lessen the impact of prosecution is through self-reporting, cooperation with the government, acceptance of responsibility, and an effective compliance and ethics program.

## HOW SARBANES-OXLEY IS INFLUENCING PRIVATE AND NONPROFIT ORGANIZATIONS

Although Sarbanes Oxley focuses on public companies, many private and nonprofit organizations are voluntarily adopting aspects of what has become the new standard for business transparency. Voluntary compliance can improve a private company's reputation for accountability and integrity that may translate to greater business development and growth. It may make it easier to obtain credit and funding to expand, go public, or be an acquisition target. Compliance with Sarbanes-Oxley makes good business sense, especially in enhancing fraud prevention and detection. After all, it was not just the shareholders of public corporations who were victims of fraud's feeding frenzy. A prime example was United Way under William Aramony, who in 1992 was caught using his nonprofit organization as a personal slush fund.

### William Aramony and United Way: "I Took at the Office"

For most of his 20-year career as head of United Way, William Aramony seemed to be a consummate professional. He moved the organization forward and increased donations. At some point he became a different man and started using charity money for his own purposes. The board of directors was not paying attention, and the other executives of United Way were either too loyal to Aramony or too afraid to challenge him.

The former president and CEO of United Way set his girlfriend up in a Manhattan condo paid for by funds laundered from United Way through Partnership Umbrella, Inc. Aramony was 59 years old and married. His girlfriend was seventeen and fresh out of a Florida trailer park, seeing the big city with her new "sugar daddy." Aramony bought the condo in New York with the help of United Way CFO Thomas Merlo, who also routed roughly $80,000 directly to Aramony's girlfriend, Lori Villasor. The lavish spending didn't stop there. There was another $70,000 to decorate the condo, limo service bills, an Egyptian cruise down the Nile River, a car, flights on the Concorde, credit cards, trips to Las Vegas, and braces for Lori's teeth.[21]

Aramony was prosecuted and convicted of 25 counts of mail fraud, money laundering, and tax violations. He served 84 months in prison and was released in October 2001. During the trial it was discovered that prior to his affair with Lori Villasor, Aramony had been in a sexual relationship with Lori's older sister, Lisa Villasor. Ethical leaders put the needs of the many ahead of their own. William Aramony was not an ethical leader.

### Lessons Learned

In the past, board members for charities were not selected for their financial oversight expertise. When there was a hint of a scandal, the first impulse was to cover it up. William Aramony's fraud hurt the United Way's incoming donations for several years. Beyond the criminal provisions that apply directly to everyone, Sarbanes-Oxley's corporate governance requirements for publicly traded companies are effective practices from which private companies can benefit.

Board members from some nonprofit organizations, private companies, and universities are now pressuring their organizations to voluntarily comply with the Sarbanes-Oxley standard. Many believe that private companies and nonprofits will soon be subjected to "copycat laws" from either Congress or individual states. Both California and New York, for example, have legislation pending that would extend Sarbanes-Oxley requirements to private companies and nonprofit organizations in those states. To increase their comfort level, public companies that are subject to Sarbanes-Oxley may require their private business partners to improve internal controls. Businesses that are considering an Initial Public Offering (IPO) are better off becoming Sarbanes-Oxley compliant before they are required to do so, so that they understand the costs and the work associated with compliance. Robert Half International conducted a survey of 1,400 CFOs from private companies and found that 58 percent said they were adopting some new accounting practices based on the new regulations. Of the respondents, 44 percent are having the CEO and CFO attest to the financial statement's accuracy. Many respondents felt that Sarbanes-Oxley regulations promote better management for any company, public or private.[22]

A survey of 9,000 CEOs and CFOs by Foley & Lardner LLP in 2004 found similar figures, with 60 percent of the executives from private companies admitting to self-imposed corporate governance reforms and 44 percent attesting to the accuracy of financial statements.[23] As a practical matter, many nonprofits and public companies cannot afford the cost nor do they have the personnel to comply with all aspects of Sarbanes-Oxley. Some best practices, however, can be implemented even within very small organizations to help ensure compliance with the spirit of Sarbanes-Oxley, which has become the standard of excellence in business transparency. Such voluntary compliance can put the company in a better position to borrow capital or to do business with the federal government. A small nonprofit organization might consider creating an independent audit committee from some of the current board members and seek a financial expert specifically to sit on the audit committee. Management should adopt a code of ethics to ensure an ethical company from the top down including all senior officers and directors. They should establish an anonymous reporting system to receive business conduct violations including allegations of fraud from employees and others.

At the very least, a nonprofit organization should establish a policy to guide employees regarding record retention, handling, and disposing of documents, specifically documents that may relate to matters within the jurisdiction of the federal government. Nonprofits should seriously consider adopting some form of policy of disclosure of misconduct or mishandling of funds, to ensure that funds are properly handled and that any certifications or reports made to donors are correct and are true representations of the finances and operations of the organization.

## ENDNOTES

1. Statement on Auditing Standards 99, "Consideration of Fraud in a Financial Statement Audit," The American Institute of Certified Public Accountants, www.aicpa.org.
2. Ibid.
3. Ibid.
4. Ibid. Various content from SAS 99 reprinted with permission from the AICPA; Copyright © 2002 by the American Institute of Certified Public Accountants.
5. Larry D. Thompson, "Principles of Federal Prosecution of Business Organizations," United States Department of Justice, January 20, 2003, www.usdoj.gov/dag/cftf/corporate_guidelines. htm. The full text of the memorandum is available online, and the authors highly recommend that it be read in full.
6. *Sarbanes-Oxley Act, U.S. Code* 15 (2005), § 7262.
7. Securities and Exchange Commission, "Final Rule: Management's Reports on Internal Control over Financial Reporting and Certification of Disclosure in Exchange Act Periodic Reports," www.sec.gov/rules/final/33-8238.htm.
8. Codification of Statements on Auditing Standards (AU §325), "Communication of Internal Control Related Matters Noted in

an Audit," American Institute of Certified Public Accountants, 434, http://www.aicpa.org/download/members/div/auditstd/AU-00325.PDF

9. Securities and Exchange Commission, "Final Rule: Management's Reports on Internal Control Over Financial Reporting and Certification of Disclosure in Exchange Act Periodic Reports," www.sec.gov/rules/final/33-8238.htm.

10. Financial Executives International, "Sarbanes-Oxley Compliance Costs Exceed Estimate," March 21, 2005, www.fei.org/404_survey_3_21_05.cfm

11. Oversight Systems, "Financial Executives Call Sarbanes-Oxley Compliance a 'Good Investment' According to Oversight Survey," December 14, 2004, www.oversightsystems.com/news_events/release_041212.html.

12. Financial Executives International, "Sarbanes-Oxley Compliance Costs Exceed Estimate," March 21, 2005, www.fei.org/404_survey_3_21_05.cfm

13. Oversight Systems, "Financial Executives Call Sarbanes-Oxley Compliance a 'Good Investment' According to Oversight Survey," December 14, 2004, www.oversightsystems.com/news_events/release_041212.html

14. Securities and Exchange Commission, "Standards Relating to Listed Company Audit Committees," April 10, 2003, www.sec.gov/rules/final/33-8220.htm.

15. Public Company Accounting Oversight Board, "Auditing Standard No. 2—An Audit of Internal Control Over Financial Reporting Performed in Conjunction with an Audit of Financial Statements," March 9, 2004, 11-24, www.pcaobus.org/Rules_of_the_Board/Documents/Rules_of_the_Board/Auditing_Standard_2.pdf.

16. Ibid., 4.

17. Ibid., 24.

18. Stephen M. Cutler, "The Themes of Sarbanes-Oxley as Reflected in the Commission's Enforcement Program" (speech, UCLA School of Law, Los Angeles, CA, September 20, 2004), www.sec.gov/news/speech/spch09202004smc.htm.

19. Ibid.

20. United States Sentencing Commission, Federal Sentencing Guidelines Manual, www.ussc.gov/2004guid/CHAP8.pdf, 476-81.

21. Barbara Kellerman, *Bad Leadership* (Boston: Harvard Business School Press, 2004), 163.

22. Robert Half International, "The Impact of Sarbanes-Oxley on Private Business," July 2003, www.roberthalf.com.

23. Mondaq LTD, "The Impact of Sarbanes Oxley on Private Companies," Mondaq Business Briefing, September 2004, www.mondaq.com.

# Internal Controls and Antifraud Programs

**EXECUTIVE SUMMARY**

The best way to ensure a culture of compliance is through an appropriately designed internal control and antifraud program. The American Institute of Certified Public Accountants' Management Antifraud Programs and Controls is an exceptional 14-step program that any organization can implement to mitigate fraud. The steps include creating a culture of honesty and high ethics, evaluating antifraud processes and controls, and developing an appropriate oversight process. A key component of any program is a proper code of conduct or ethics policy that can help set a tone of honesty and integrity in an organization. The code must be well communicated to all employees. Before fraud risks can be mitigated, the risks must be identified and properly quantified as to their likelihood and potential financial impact. These two factors will help determine the method of risk mitigation. There are several methods in use to conduct a risk assessment. Some methods for charting the likelihood and impact of fraud are more effective than others.

## INTERNAL CONTROLS AND THE FINANCE FUNCTION

The accounting concept of internal controls refers to a company's system of checks and balances used to prevent loss and ensure accurate financial reporting. Internal controls are the basis of the finance function. As Sarbanes-Oxley increased the requirements for internal controls and mandated executives to attest to their validity, companies have been scrambling to become compliant.

Corporate America is finally realizing the importance of a strong and independent finance division and the internal audit department in particular. In the past, the financial watchdogs of a company were too often lured or pushed across the line that divides the finance function from operations. Some CFOs were unable to say no to aggressive CEOs, and others were unable to say no to the money. That has all changed in the post-Sarbanes-Oxley environment. Properly designed, staffed, and empowered finance organizations protect their company, their employees, their shareholders, and their future as a viable, growing entity. The state-of-the-art finance function and fraud prevention go together like Batman and Robin.

### The Role of the Compliance Officer

The compliance officer is a corporate manager in charge of overseeing and managing compliance with all manner of regulatory issues. The goal of the compliance officer is to demonstrate sincere, ongoing efforts to comply with all applicable laws and revise current policies and procedures to enhance this compliance effort. In light of the substantial adverse consequences that could result from noncompliance, this is a critical position. In many companies the compliance officer is responsible for designing compliance training programs, as well as establishing a compliance committee comprised of representatives of various departments.

## EXECUTIVE INSIGHT 5.1: BOEING RAMPS UP ITS ETHICS AND COMPLIANCE PROGRAMS

It has not been the best of times at aerospace giant Boeing. Like other major companies, Boeing has faced a number of scandals in recent years that brought into question its ethical conduct at the highest levels of the company. Take for instance the following examples of ethical lapses:

- In the summer of 2003, the Pentagon canceled $1 billion in Air Force rocket orders after Boeing was found to be in possession of rival Lockheed Martin Corporation's proprietary documents.[i]
- Former CEO Philip M. Condit resigned as chairman and CEO in December 2003 after "allegations of questionable conduct by a Boeing executive involved in negotiating an $18 billion deal with the Pentagon."[ii] Others would also be pulled into this serious issue.
- In February 2005, former Boeing CFO Michael Sears was sentenced to four months in prison for his part in illegally negotiating employment at Boeing for an Air Force contracting officer who oversaw government contracts including those for Boeing.[iii] Sears pled guilty to a federal charge of aiding and abetting illegal employment negotiations.[iv] Sears entered into an agreement to hire Darleen Druyun at a $250,000-a-year salary while she was still working as the Air Force's deputy acquisitions chief. During this time, Druyun was reviewing Boeing's bid for a $20 million Air Force contract.[v] Druyan subsequently left the government to join Boeing.
- Druyun was also charged by federal prosecutors and, in April 2004, pled guilty to a conspiracy charge for violating federal conflict of interest rules for entering into job negotiations with Boeing.[vi] In October 2004, she was sentenced to nine months in prison after admitting that she "improperly steered billions in contracts to Boeing."[vii]

■ The CEO who replaced Condit, Harry Stonecipher, was ousted by the board of directors in March 2005 after an investigation into his affair with a female executive at Boeing.[viii] An internal investigation found that a "series of explicit and graphic e-mails exchanged during the affair would have embarrassed the company if made public."[ix]

As a result of these many ethical lapses, "Boeing agreed to an Air Force demand as part of a broader settlement" to hire a special compliance officer to be an independent monitor to ensure compliance with ethical standards.[x]

Boeing announced on its Web site in April 2005 that the Air Force had lifted the 20-month suspension to bid for government launch contracts after the company "demonstrated that enhanced internal controls had been put in place."[xi] Boeing agreed to "maintain improvements to its ethics and compliance programs that it adopted as a result of internal initiatives and the recommendations of four independent reviews."[xii]

Boeing hired former United States Senator Warren Rudman to lead the external review that recommended improvements in management involvement; hiring and employment practices; procurement integrity; employee training; and internal investigation procedures.[xiii]

Boeing will hire an ethics watchdog with the title of Special Compliance Officer (SCO) who will serve as an independent monitor to ensure Boeing's compliance with the government agreement as well as improved ethical standards. The SCO will be located within the company's Office of Internal Governance.[xiv]

---

[i] Andy Pasztor, "Boeing Co. Hires an Ethics Watchdog," *Wall Street Journal*, May 4, 2004, A3.

[ii] Stanley Holmes, "Boeing: What Really Happened," *Business Week*, December 15, 2003, 33.

[iii] Matthew Barakat, "Boeing Ex-CFO to be Sent to Prison," *Seattle Times*, February 19, 2005, E1.

[iv] Ibid.

[v] Ibid.

[vi] Alan Bjerla, "Ex-Boeing Exec Pleads Guilty to Conspiracy," *Seattle Times*, April 21, 2004, C1.

[vii] Andy Pasztor and Jonathan Karp, "How U.S. Defense Aide Known for Her Integrity Wound Up in Disgrace," *Wall Street Journal*, December 9, 2004, A1.

[viii] Dominic Gates, "Boeing Exec Who Had Affair with CEO Quits," *Seattle Times*, March 19, 2005, E4.

[ix] Ibid.

[x] Andy Pasztor, "Boeing Co. Hires an Ethics Watchdog," *Wall Street Journal*, May 4, 2004, A3.

[xi] "Boeing in the News: Boeing Gets OK to Bid on USAF Launches," *Boeing Frontiers*, Vol. 3, Issue 11, April 2005, www.boeing.com/news/frontiers/archive/2005/april/i_bitn.html.

[xii] Ibid.

[xiii] Ibid.

[xiv] Ibid.

## Due Diligence and Background Checks

Chapter 13 is entirely devoted to background checks, but the topic is mentioned here because such checks should become part of the internal controls mind-set. No one should consider making any major business decision without due diligence. The following story is a perfect example.

One of the authors met a man who represented himself as facilitator for setting up business overseas and wanted to "help" the author's company grow. This man was always talking about his days in Special Forces, so much so that the author decided to check his background. It turned out that the man had a military history, but he had had more dealings with the JAG Corps than with Special Forces. The military had sued the man for fraud in excess of $300,000. The man was using an alias, and his new company had been incorporated for only a few months.

## Standard Controls

All executives know the standard controls that need to be followed, but fraud cases still pop up every year in which one of the following issues is a contributing factor to the fraud:

- Poor separation of duties
- Use of inexperienced accountants
- Lack of well-defined roles
- Lack of coordination with internal audit
- Lack of a formal process for merger and acquisitions, or not following the process in place
- Manual workarounds in accounting.

## Code of Ethics

The FBI has a simple ethics policy: "Don't embarrass the Bureau!" When Louis Freeh became Director in 1993, the FBI began to teach new agents about "the book, the bell, and the candle" to deal with questionable ethical situations. The book reminds the agent to think, "Is this conduct legal?" The bell reminds the agent to be alert for the little mental alarm going off, telling the agent that this doesn't feel right. The candle reminds the agent to ask, "What would your mother think if this came to light?"

A code of ethics provides a moral compass for employees by defining the company's position on ethical issues and promoting integrity. To be effective, management has to embody the code of ethics, and all employees have to be informed and committed. Some companies have separate codes of conduct especially for vendors or for the procurement function as well as for finance.

## MANAGEMENT ANTIFRAUD PROGRAMS AND CONTROLS: THE 14-POINT PROGRAM

In 2002, the Fraud Task Force of the American Institute of Certified Public Accountants (AICPA) commissioned a study to provide guidance to help prevent and detect fraud. The AICPA, the Association of Certified Fraud Examiners, the Institute of Internal Auditors, and other professional organizations sponsored the study. The resulting *Management Antifraud Programs and Controls* was released in November 2002 as an exhibit to SAS 99.[1] The overall message of this document is those organizations that take proactive steps to prevent and deter fraud will preserve their financial integrity, their reputation, and their future.

The study found that an organization must take three fundamental actions to mitigate fraud. They include creating a culture of honesty and high ethics, evaluating antifraud processes and controls, and developing an appropriate oversight process. The following are some of the highlights from the document, which should be the cornerstone of any fraud prevention program. There are 3 main headings and 14 subheadings.

## Creating a Culture of Honesty and High Ethics

It is the organization's responsibility to create a culture of honesty and high ethics and to communicate clearly acceptable behavior and expectations for each employee. Creating a culture of honesty and high ethics should include the following:

**1. Setting the Tone at the Top**   Directors and officers of corporations set the "tone at the top" for ethical behavior within any organization. Research in moral development strongly suggests that honesty can best be reinforced when a proper example is set (the tone at the top). The management of an entity cannot act one way and expect others in the entity to behave differently.

**2. Creating a Positive Workplace Environment**   Research indicates that less wrongdoing occurs when employees have positive feelings about work. Factors that detract from a positive work environment and that may increase the risk of fraud include the following:

- Top management that does not seem to care about or wish to reward appropriate behavior
- Negative feedback and lack of recognition for job performance
- Perceived inequities in the organization
- Autocratic rather than participative management
- Low organizational loyalty or feelings of ownership
- Unreasonable budget expectations or other financial targets

- Fear of delivering "bad news" to supervisors and/or management
- Less-than-competitive compensation
- Poor training and promotion opportunities
- Lack of clear organizational responsibilities
- Poor communication practices or methods within the organization.

**3. Hiring and Promoting Appropriate Employees**   The threshold at which dishonest behavior starts will vary among individuals. If an entity is to be successful in preventing fraud, it must have effective policies that minimize the chance of hiring or promoting individuals with low levels of honesty, especially for positions of trust. Proactive hiring and promotion procedures may include:

- Conducting background investigations on individuals being considered for employment or for promotion to a position of trust. Some organizations also have considered follow-up investigations, particularly for employees in positions of trust, on a periodic basis (for example, every five years) or as circumstances dictate.
- Thoroughly checking a candidate's education, employment history, and personal references.
- Periodic training of all employees about the entity's values and code of conduct.
- Incorporating into regular performance reviews an evaluation of how each individual has contributed to the creation of an appropriate workplace environment in line with the entity's values and code of conduct.

**4. Training**   New employees should be given training at the time of hiring covering the entity's values and its code of conduct. This training should explicitly cover expectations of all employees regarding (1) their duty to communicate certain matters; (2) a list of the types of matters, including actual or suspected fraud, to be communicated along with specific examples; and (3) information on how to communicate those matters. Such training should include an element of "fraud awareness," the tone of which should be positive but nonetheless stress that fraud can be costly (and detrimental in other ways) to the entity and its employees. In addition to training at the time of hiring, employees should receive refresher training periodically thereafter.

**5. Confirmation** Management needs to articulate clearly that all employees will be held accountable to act within the entity's code of conduct. All employees within senior management and the finance function, as well as other employees in areas that might be exposed to unethical behavior (for example, procurement, sales, and marketing) should be required to sign a code of conduct statement annually, at a minimum.

**6. Discipline** The way an entity reacts to incidents of alleged or suspected fraud will send a strong deterrent message throughout the entity, helping to reduce the number of future occurrences. The following actions should be taken in response to an alleged incident of fraud:

- A thorough investigation of the incident should be conducted.
- Appropriate and consistent actions should be taken against violators.
- Relevant controls should be assessed and improved.
- Communication and training should occur to reinforce the entity's values, code of conduct, and expectations.

Expectations about the consequences of committing fraud must be clearly communicated throughout the entity. If a violation occurs and an employee is disciplined, it can be helpful to communicate that fact, on a no-name basis. Seeing that other people have been disciplined for wrongdoing can be an effective deterrent, increasing the perceived likelihood of violators being caught and punished. It can also demonstrate that the entity is committed to an environment of high ethical standards and integrity.

## Evaluating Antifraud Processes and Controls

Neither fraudulent financial reporting nor misappropriation of assets can occur without a perceived opportunity to commit and conceal the act. Organizations should be proactive in reducing fraud opportunities by (1) identifying and measuring for fraud risks, (2) taking steps to mitigate identified risks, and (3) implementing and monitoring appropriate preventive and detective internal controls and other deterrent measures.

**7. Identifying and Measuring Fraud Risks** Management has the primary responsibility for establishing and monitoring all aspects of the entity's fraud risk assessment and prevention activities. Fraud risks are often considered part of an enterprise-wide risk management program, although they may be addressed separately. The fraud risk assessment process should consider the vulnerability of the entity to fraudulent activity (fraudulent financial reporting, misappropriation of assets, and corruption) and whether any of those exposures could result in a material misstatement of the financial statements or material loss to the organization. In identifying fraud risks, organizations should consider the organizational, industry, and country-specific characteristics that influence the risk of fraud. The topic of fraud risk assessment is addressed in more detail later in this chapter.

**8. Mitigating Fraud Risks** It may be possible to reduce or eliminate certain fraud risks by making changes to the entity's activities and processes. An entity may choose to sell certain segments of its operations, cease doing business in certain locations, or reorganize its business processes to eliminate unacceptable risks. For example, the risk of misappropriation of funds may be reduced by implementing a central lockbox at a bank to receive payments instead of receiving money at the entity's various locations. The risk of corruption may be reduced by closely monitoring the entity's procurement process. The risk of financial statement fraud may be reduced by implementing shared services centers to provide accounting services to multiple segments, affiliates, or geographic locations of an entity's operations. A shared services center may be less vulnerable to influence by local operations managers and may be able to implement more extensive fraud detection measures cost-effectively.

**9. Implementing and Monitoring Appropriate Internal Controls** Once a fraud risk assessment has taken place, the entity can identify the processes, controls, and other procedures that are needed to mitigate the identified risks. Effective internal controls include a secure information system and appropriate monitoring activities. In particular, management should evaluate whether appropriate internal controls have been implemented in any areas management has identified as posing a higher risk of fraudulent activity, as well as controls over the entity's financial reporting process.

## Developing an Appropriate Oversight Process

Oversight can take many forms and can be performed by many individuals within and outside the entity, under the overall oversight of the Audit Committee (or Board of Directors when no Audit Committee exists).

**10. Audit Committee**   The Audit Committee should evaluate management's identification of fraud risks, implementation of antifraud measures, and creation of the appropriate tone at the top. Active oversight by the audit committee can help reinforce management's commitment to creating the proper antifraud culture. The Audit Committee has the responsibility to oversee the activities of senior management and to consider the risk of fraudulent financial reporting involving the override of internal controls or collusion.

**11. Management**   Management is responsible for overseeing the activities carried out by employees, and typically does so by implementing and monitoring processes and controls, such as those discussed previously. However, management also may initiate, participate in, or direct the commission and concealment of a fraudulent act. Accordingly, the Audit Committee (or the Board of Directors when no Audit Committee exists) has the responsibility to oversee the activities of senior management and to consider the risk of fraudulent financial reporting involving the override of internal controls or collusion.

**12. Internal Auditors**   An effective internal audit team can be extremely helpful in performing aspects of the oversight function. Their knowledge about the entity may enable them to identify indicators that suggest fraud has been committed. Internal auditors also have the opportunity to evaluate fraud risks and controls and to recommend action to mitigate risks and improve controls. Internal audit should have a reporting line to the audit committee in addition to the CFO or other executive leadership.

Internal audits can be both a detection and a deterrence measure. Internal auditors can assist in the deterrence of fraud by examining and evaluating the adequacy and the effectiveness of the system of internal control, commensurate with the extent of the potential exposure or risk in the various segments of the organization's operations.

In carrying out this responsibility, internal auditors should, for example, determine whether:

- The organizational environment fosters control consciousness.
- Realistic organizational goals and objectives are set.
- Written policies (for example, a code of conduct) exist that describe prohibited activities and the action required whenever violations are discovered.
- Appropriate authorization policies for transactions are established and maintained.
- Policies, practices, procedures, reports, and other mechanisms are developed to monitor activities and safeguard assets, particularly in high-risk areas.
- Communication channels provide management with adequate and reliable information.
- Recommendations need to be made for the establishment or enhancement of cost-effective controls to deter fraud.

**13. Independent Auditors**   Independent auditors can assist management and the Board of Directors (or Audit Committee) by providing an assessment of the entity's process for identifying, assessing, and responding to the risks of fraud. The Board of Directors (or the Audit Committee) should have an open and candid dialogue with the independent auditors regarding management's risk assessment process and the system of internal control. Such a dialogue should include a discussion of the susceptibility of the entity to fraudulent financial reporting and the entity's exposure to misappropriation of assets.

**14. Certified Fraud Examiners**   Certified Fraud Examiners may assist the Audit Committee and Board of Directors with aspects of the oversight process either directly or as part of a team of internal auditors or independent auditors. Certified Fraud Examiners can provide extensive knowledge and experience about fraud that may not be available elsewhere within a corporation. They can provide more objective input into management's evaluation of the risk of fraud (especially fraud involving senior management, such as financial statement fraud) and the development of appropriate antifraud controls that are less vulnerable to management override. They can assist the Audit Committee and Board of Directors in evaluating the fraud risk assessment and fraud prevention measures implemented by management. Certified Fraud Examiners also conduct examinations to resolve allegations or suspicions of fraud, reporting either to an appropriate level of management or to the Audit Committee or Board of Directors, depending on the nature of the issue and the level of personnel involved.[2]

The Association of Certified Fraud Examiners, of which both authors are members, has developed a Fraud Prevention Check-Up, which is a good place to start a fraud risk assessment.[3] It is a series of questions about processes that may or may not be in place at a particular company. The answers are awarded points. Beware! Only a score of 100 is passing. The idea is to get leaders thinking about what processes need to be in place.

---

### EXECUTIVE INSIGHT 5.2: ACFE FRAUD PREVENTION CHECK-UP

How vulnerable is your company to fraud? Do you have adequate controls in place to prevent it? Find out by using the Association of Certified Fraud Examiners' (ACFE) *Fraud Prevention Check-Up,* a simple yet powerful test of your company's fraud health. Test fraud prevention processes designed to help you identify major gaps and fix them before it is too late. The ACFE Fraud Prevention Check-Up can pinpoint opportunities to save an organization from financial and reputational risk.

#### Before You Take the ACFE Fraud Prevention Check-Up

- Let your entity's general counsel or outside legal counsel know you plan to take the test. They may want to have you use the test under their direction, to protect your entity's legal rights.
- Do not take the check-up if you plan to ignore the results. If it shows you have poor fraud prevention processes, you need to fix them. Failing to act could cause legal problems.

## Who Should Perform the ACFE Fraud Prevention Check-Up?

- The check-up should ideally be a collaboration between objective, independent fraud specialists (such as Certified Fraud Examiners) and people within the entity who have extensive knowledge about its operations.
- Internal auditors bring extensive knowledge and a valuable perspective to such an evaluation. At the same time, the perspective of an independent and objective outsider is also important, as are the deep knowledge and experience of fraud that full-time fraud specialists provide.
- It is helpful to interview senior members of management as part of the evaluation process. But it is also valuable to interview employees at other levels of the entity, since they may sometimes provide a "reality check" that challenges the rosier view management might present, e.g., about management's commitment to ethical business practices.

## How Many Points Should Be Awarded for Each Answer?

- The number of points available is given at the bottom of each question. You can award zero points if your entity has not implemented the recommended processes for that area. You can give the maximum number of points if you have implemented those processes and have had them tested in the past year and found them to be operating effectively. Award no more than half the available points if the recommended process is in place but has not been tested in the past year.
- The purpose of the check-up is to identify major gaps in your fraud prevention processes, as indicated by low point scores in particular areas. Even if you score 80 points out of 100, the missing 20 could be crucial in fraud prevention measures that leave you exposed to major fraud. So there is no passing grade other than 100 points.

### The ACFE Fraud Prevention Check-Up

Entity: _____

Date of Check-Up:_____

RESULTS

1. *Fraud risk oversight*
   - To what extent has the entity established a process for oversight of fraud risks by the board of directors or others charged with governance (e.g., an audit committee)?
   *Score: From 0 (process not in place) to 20 points (process fully implemented, tested within the past year, and working effectively).*

2. *Fraud risk ownership*
   - To what extent has the entity created "ownership" of fraud risks by identifying a member of senior management as having responsibility for managing all fraud risks within the entity and by explicitly communicating to business unit managers that they are responsible for managing fraud risks with in their part of the entity?
   *Score: From 0 (process not in place) to 10 points (process fully implemented, tested within the past year, and working effectively).*

3. *Fraud risk assessment*
   - To what extent has the entity implemented an ongoing process for regular identification of the significant fraud risks to which the entity is exposed? *Score: From 0 (process not in place) to 10 points (process fully implemented, tested within the past year and working effectively).*

4. *Fraud risk tolerance and risk management policy*
   - To what extent has the entity identified and had approved by the board of directors its tolerance for different types of fraud risks? For example, some fraud risks may constitute a tolerable cost of doing business, while others may pose a catastrophic risk of financial or reputational damage to the entity. The entity will likely have a different tolerance for these risks.
   - To what extent has the entity identified and had approved by the board of directors a policy on how the entity will manage its fraud risks? Such a policy should identify the risk owner responsible for managing fraud risks, what risks will be rejected (e.g., by declining certain business opportunities), what risks will be transferred to others through insurance or by contract, and what steps will be taken to manage the fraud risks that are retained. *Score: From 0 (process not in place) to 10 points (process fully implemented, tested within the past year, and working effectively).*

5. *Process level antifraud controls/ reengineering*

■ To what extent has the entity implemented measures, where possible, to eliminate or reduce through process reengineering each of the significant fraud risks identified in its risk assessment? Basic controls include segregation of duties relating to authorization, custody of assets, and recording or reporting of transactions. In some cases it may be more cost effective to reengineer business processes to reduce fraud risks rather than layer on additional controls over existing processes. For example, some fraud risks relating to receipt of funds can be eliminated or greatly reduced by centralizing that function or outsourcing it to a bank's lockbox processing facility, where stronger controls can be more affordable.

■ To what extent has the entity implemented measures at the process level designed to prevent, deter, and detect each of the significant fraud risks identified in its risk assessment? For example, the risk of sales representatives falsifying sales to earn sales commissions can be reduced through effective monitoring by their sales manager, with approval required for sales above a certain threshold.

*Score: From 0 (process not in place) to 10 points (process fully implemented, tested within the past year, and working effectively).*

6. *Environmental level antifraud controls*
  - Major frauds usually involve senior members of management who are able to override process-level controls through their high level of authority. Preventing major frauds therefore requires a very strong emphasis on creating a workplace environment that promotes ethical behavior, deters wrongdoing, and encourages all employees to communicate any known or suspected wrongdoing to the appropriate person. Senior managers may be unable to perpetrate certain fraud schemes if employees decline to aid and abet them in committing a crime. Although "soft" controls to promote appropriate workplace behavior are more difficult to implement and evaluate than traditional "hard" controls, they appear to be the best defense against fraud involving senior management.
  - To what extent has the entity implemented a process to promote ethical behavior, deter wrongdoing, and facilitate two-way communication on difficult issues? Such a process typically includes:
  - Having a senior member of management who is responsible for the entity's processes to promote ethical behavior, deter wrongdoing, and communicate appropriately on difficult issues. In large public companies, this may be a

full-time position as ethics officer or compliance officer. In smaller companies, this will be an additional responsibility held by an existing member of management.

- A code of conduct for employees at all levels, based on the entity's core values, which gives clear guidance on what behavior and actions are permitted and which ones are prohibited. The code should identify how employees should seek additional advice when faced with uncertain ethical decisions and how they should communicate concerns about known or potential wrongdoing affecting the entity.
- Training for all personal upon hiring and regularly thereafter concerning the code of conduct, seeking advice, and communicating potential wrongdoing.
- Communication systems to enable employees to seek advice where necessary prior to making difficult ethical decisions and to express concern about known or potential wrongdoing affecting the entity. Advice systems may include an ethics or compliance telephone help line or e-mail to an ethics or compliance office/officer. The same or similar systems may be used to enable employees (and sometimes vendors, customers, and others)

to communicate concerns about known or potential wrongdoing affecting the entity. Provisions should be made to enable such communications to be made anonymously, though strenuous efforts should be made to create an environment in which callers feel sufficiently confident to express their concerns openly. Open communication makes it easier for the entity to resolve the issues raised, but protecting callers from retribution is an important concern.

- A process for promptly investigating where appropriate and resolving expressions of concern regarding known or potential wrongdoing, then communicating the resolution to those who expressed the concern. The entity should have a plan that sets out what actions will be taken and by whom to investigate and resolve different types of concerns. Some issues will be best addressed by human resources personnel, some by general counsel, some by internal auditors, and some may require investigation by fraud specialists. Having a prearranged plan will greatly speed and ease the response and will ensure appropriate persons are notified where significant potential issues are involved (e.g., legal counsel, board of directors, audit committee, independent auditors, regulators, etc.)

- Monitoring of compliance with the code of conduct and participation in the related training. Monitoring may include requiring at least annual confirmation of compliance and auditing of such confirmations to test their completeness and accuracy.
- Regular measurement of the extent to which the entity's ethics/compliance and fraud prevention goals are being achieved. Such measurement typically includes surveys of a statistically meaningful sample of employees. Surveys of employees' attitudes towards the entity's ethics/compliance activities and the extent to which employees believe management acts in accordance with the code of conduct provide valuable insight into how well those items are functioning.
- Incorporation of ethics/compliance and fraud prevention goals into the performance measures against which managers are evaluated and that are used to determine performance related compensation.

*Score: From 0 (process not in place) to 10 points (process fully implemented, tested within the past year, and working effectively).*

7. *Proactive fraud detection*

   ▪ To what extent has the entity established a process to detect, investigate, and resolve potentially significant fraud? Such a process should typically include proactive fraud detection tests that are specially designed to detect the significant potential frauds identified in the entity's fraud risk assessment. Other measures can include audit "hooks" embedded in the entity's transaction processing systems that can flag suspicious transactions for investigation and/or approval prior to completion of processing. Leading edge fraud detection methods include computerized e-mail monitoring (where legally permitted) to identify use of certain phrases that might indicate planned or ongoing wrongdoing.
   
   *Score: From 0 (process not in place) to 10 points (process fully implemented, tested within the past year, and working effectively).*

   **TOTAL SCORE** (out of a possible 100 points)

## Interpreting the Entity's Score

A brief fraud prevention check-up provides a broad idea of the entity's performance with respect to fraud prevention. The scoring necessarily involves broad judgments, while more extensive evaluations would have greater measurement data to draw upon.

Therefore, the important information to take from the check-up is the identification of particular areas for improvement in the entity's fraud prevention processes. The precise numerical score is less important and is only presented to help communicate an overall impression.

The desirable score for an entity of any size is 100 points, since the recommended processes are scalable to the size of the entity. Most entities should expect to fall significantly short of 100 points in an initial fraud prevention check-up. That is not currently considered to be a material weakness in internal controls that represents a reportable condition under securities regulations. However, significant gaps in fraud prevention measures should be closed promptly in order to reduce fraud losses and reduce the risk of future disaster.

Source: Reprinted with permission from the Association of Certified Fraud Examiners, Austin, Texas © 2005.

## THE FRAUD RISK ASSESSMENT PROCESS

Management must conduct periodic assessments of the risk of fraud at all levels and document the results. In most cases, companies predict the risk of fraud based on recent past events and current conditions. Although an outside audit can identify control gaps, only an honest inside assessment can truly gauge a company's risk of fraud. The decision of what control activities should be implemented means little if the decision is not based on a complete assessment of risk. There are three types of risk to consider when one is conducting risk assessments:

1. **Financial Reporting Risk** is the risk that there could be fraud on the financial statement or misconduct by senior management. Although this is a relatively low-occurrence fraud, it is devastating for a company. The Board, the Audit Committee, and the Internal Auditor are responsible for reducing the Financial Reporting Risk at their company in conjunction with the CEO and CFO.

2. **Operational Risk** is the risk that the organization itself will commit fraud by action or omission, such as not paying taxes or cheating customers. Again, this is fraud that involves senior management, so the Board, the Audit Committee, and the Internal Auditor are responsible for controlling Operational Risk.
3. **Compliance Risk** is the risk of corruption, internal asset misappropriation, and external fraud anywhere in the company. This is where the job of assessment becomes complicated. There are multiple ways for a company or organization to be defrauded by its own employees or outsiders. The response to compliance risk is much more complex than the other types of risk since there are many more factors to be considered and many more ways a company can experience a loss (see Exhibit 5.1).

The fraud risk assessment is the process through which management identifies the risks of fraud it faces as an organization. The

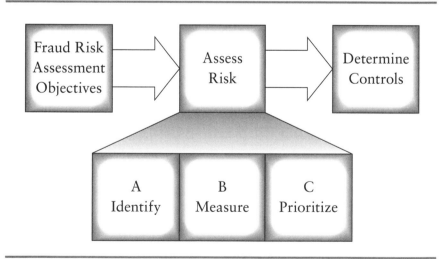

**EXHIBIT 5.1**   Fraud Risk Assessment Objectives
*Source:* David McNamee, "Assessing Risk Assessment," www.mc2consulting.com

exercise involves identifying the fraud risks, analyzing their likelihood, and determining the impact. This assessment looks at frauds that have affected the business in the recent past, that are common to their industry, and that are located in specific geographic locations (countries, cities) that may increase the risk of fraud.

Fraud risk assessments are not compliance audits, rather they look for areas in which the company could be exposed to criminal activity that could result in a financial loss, a loss of reputation, or any other liability. The fraud risk assessment looks at all business units, departments, and geographic areas of the company to determine the risk of specific frauds. This process can be as formal as a company wishes, but it is usually best to keep things simple. There has been a long debate between scientists and social scientists as to whether risk can actually be measured objectively.

The use of a cigar box as a petty cash drawer is a theft risk. Theft is very likely from this unsecured box, but the impact is limited to the amount of petty cash in the box at any one time (usually less than $100). The risk management solution would be to use a lock box, which is inexpensive and simple. The fraud risk posed by payroll accounts is much greater, and the risk management will be more complicated and expensive.[4] The goal is to determine:

- The areas where fraud is possible (risks)
- The probability of a fraud (likelihood)
- The cost of the fraud (impact)
- The proper countermeasure and its cost (risk management)
- Various methods are being used to rate the likelihood and impact of a fraud risk: the Quad Method, the Staggered Box Method, and the "Chessboard" Method. They are described in the text that follows.

### The Quad Method

This method rates the probability of a certain type of fraud on a scale of 1 to 10, with 1 being highly unlikely, 5 being neutral, and 10 being highly probable. After the probability of a certain fraud has been determined, the risk is classified as to materiality and the impact each type of fraud would have on the company on a scale of 1 to 10, with 1 being no factor, and 10 being devastating to the company. The results are then charted using an X- and Y-axis graph. The X- and Y-axis graph is then split into quads, which will later be used to prioritize our mitigation efforts.

The risk assessment looks at each type of fraud and determines how likely the fraud is to occur at a company and how significant it would be if it did occur. At least five areas or business cycles need to be assessed for fraud risk:

### Sales and Collection
- Orders from customers
- Invoices to customers
- Collecting receivables
- Allowances, returns, and write-offs.

### Purchasing and Payment
- Processing purchase orders and invoices from vendors
- Receiving and recording goods and documenting services performed
- Processing and recording cash disbursements and returns.

### Inventory and Warehousing
- Processing purchase requisitions
- Receiving materials and goods
- Storing materials and goods
- Processing goods for shipment.

### Payroll and Expenses
- Timekeeping
- Processing payroll checks or direct deposits
- Reimbursing expenses and travel.

### Financial Statement Reporting
- Reconciling accounts
- Preparing and reviewing accruals and other journal entries
- Analyzing operating reports and financial statements.

Using the X- and Y-axis graph system, frauds will be classified into four categories. Any fraud that has a high probability and a high significance of material effect on the company (Quad 1) must be addressed with processes and procedures that proactively prevent this type of fraud. Frauds that have high materiality but relatively low probability (Quad 2) are contained and controlled with detection and monitoring (data mining and fraud screening). Frauds that fall into Quad 3 could be mitigated with insurance, whereas those in Quad 4 need less attention (see Exhibit 5.2).

Fraud risks that need to be addressed include the following: theft from checking, wire transfer, escrow, or other open accounts; theft from accounts payable via fictitious vendors or fraudulent invoices; theft from payroll by ghost employees or falsified hours; theft of receivables (checks or cash); theft by expensing bogus or personal

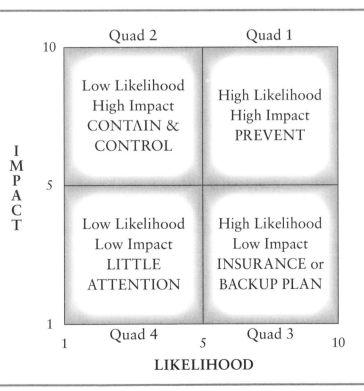

**EXHIBIT 5.2** Quad Method
*Source:* Michael Cangemi and Tommie Singleton, *Managing the Audit Function,* 3rd ed. (Hoboken, NJ: John Wiley & Sons, 2003), 71.

expenses to the company; theft of inventory (warehouse and retail center); and theft of cash from deposits, or refunds, or by skimming.

Exhibit 5.3 shows the following hypothetical examples of frauds with their X and Y values charted.

1. Theft of inventory (likelihood 6, impact 3)
2. Thefts from petty cash (likelihood 5, impact 1)
3. Falsifying inventory (likelihood 6, impact 6)
4. Payments to fictitious vendors (likelihood 5, impact 5)
5. Theft of proprietary customer data like credit card numbers (likelihood 6, impact 7)
6. Kickbacks (likelihood 5, impact 9)
7. Ghost employees (likelihood 2, impact 2)
8. Check fraud (likelihood 8, impact 9).

Not all risk managers are comfortable with these simple quadrants to prioritize mitigation, and with good reason. In Exhibit 5.3, the

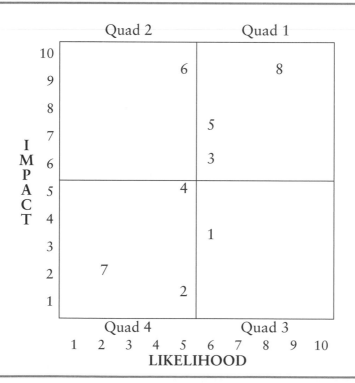

**EXHIBIT 5.3**   Quad Method

frauds represented by the numbers 3 and 4 are not so far apart that one should give the first a priority of 1 and the other a priority of 4. Critics of the quad method would also question whether the fraud represented by number 6 is really a lower priority than the fraud represented by number 3.

## The Staggered Box Method

To correct the problem with the quad method, the quadrants are replaced with a staggered chart of 25 squares shaded in four different degrees (Exhibit 5.4). There are still four levels of risk (black, dark gray, light gray, and white), but they are not represented by perfect squares.

Starting from the upper left box, the system staggers down every two squares. Using this method, the frauds represented by the numbers 3 and 4 are together in priority 2, whereas before they were in Quads 1 and 4, respectively. Furthermore, the fraud represented by

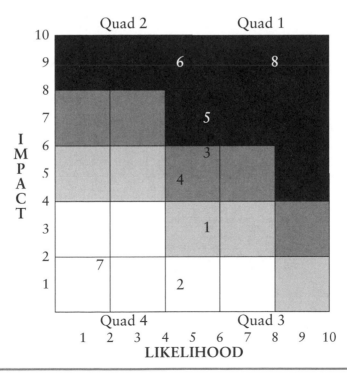

**EXHIBIT 5.4** Staggered Box Method

the number 6 is now in priority 1. The staggered grid of 25 boxes has solved the concerns raised about the quad method.

There is still a problem with the 25-box method, however: that of how much weight to give the impact of a particular fraud. There is no real objective difference between a rating of 4 for impact and a 5 for impact. How probable is a 1 compared with a 2? The solution to this problem is to make the progression between steps geometric rather than arithmetic. If one rates the impact of a fraud in dollars and increases each step by the power of ten, one can rate the impact of each fraud as a $1,000 fraud, a $10,000 fraud, or a $100,000 fraud—and isn't impact all about dollars anyway? A geometric progression stagger method is now described.

### The "Chessboard" Method

To understand the Chessboard method, assume the following:
Let $i$ = impact of the fraud. Then
- $1i = \$10$
- $2i = \$100$
- $3i = \$1,000$
- $4i = \$10,000$
- $5i = \$100,000$
- $6i = \$1$ million
- $7i = \$10$ million
- $8i = \$100$ million.

Let $f$ = frequency of the fraud (again in geometric progression $\times$ 10). Then
- $1f$ = one time in 300 years
- $2f$ = one time in 30 years
- $3f$ = one time in 3 years
- $4f$ = one time in 100 days
- $5f$ = one time in 10 days
- $6f$ = one time per day
- $7f$ = ten times per day
- $8f$ = 100 times per day.

One can now calculate the Annual Loss Expectancy (ALE) of each type of fraud with a "chessboard" chart of 64 squares.

| | | Frequency *(f)* | | | | | | |
|---|---|---|---|---|---|---|---|---|
| | 1 | 2 | 3 | 4 | 5 | 6 | 7 | 8 |
| **1** | | | | | $300 | $3K | $30K | $300K |
| **2** | | | | $300 | $3K | $30K | $300K | $3M |
| **3** | | | $300 | $3K | $30K | $300K | $3M | $30M |
| **4** | | $300 | $3K | $30K | $300K | $3M | $30M | $300M |
| **5** | $300 | $3K | $30K | $300K | $3M | $30M | $300M | |
| **6** | $3K | $30K | $300K | $3M | $30M | $300M | | |
| **7** | $30K | $300K | $3M | $30M | $300M | | | |
| **8** | $300K | $3M | $30M | $300M | | | | |

(Row axis label: Impact *(i)*. In row 1, the $300K cell is circled; in row 5, the $300K cell is circled.)

**EXHIBIT 5.5**

*Source:* James F. Broder, *Risk Analysis and the Security Survey,* 2nd ed. (Boston: Butterworth Heinemann, 2000) 24.

As can be seen in Exhibit 5.5, a $10 fraud (8*f*) that happens 100 times a day (1*i*) would cost the company $300,000—the same as a $100,000 fraud (5*i*) that happens once every 100 days (4*f*). Because these two problems cost the company the same amount ($300,000), they should be addressed as equally important. This makes the risk estimation (assessment) process much easier to document. If a company gets about 100 credit card frauds per day on its Web site, and they average $100 per instance, it is a $3 million a year problem (2*i*, 8*f*), just like a one time $3 million fraud. They deserve the same ranking on the mitigation strategy. There is much less chance of incorrectly assessing the fraud risk posed by a particular type of fraud using the geometric progression model that is called the "chessboard" method of fraud risk assessment.

Once the fraud risks have been assessed, the decision is made about how to respond to the risk:

- Avoid the risk: discontinue the practice that creates the risk.
- Transfer the risk: get insurance.
- Accept the risk: do nothing until the fraud happens.
- Control the risk: put controls in place to reduce the risk to an acceptable level.

## TRAINING AS A CRITICAL INTERNAL CONTROL FUNCTION

This chapter closes with a note on training, which is very important. No matter what internal controls are put in place, those controls will only be as good as the training each employee receives. Controls work only if they are followed, and they are followed only if employees are properly trained. Training is covered in more detail in Chapter 14.

## ENDNOTES

1. Statement on Auditing Standard 99, "Consideration of Fraud in a Financial Statement Audit," The American Institute of Certified Public Accountants, www.aicpa.org.
2. Management Antifraud Programs and Controls is reprinted with permission from the AICPA; Copyright © 2002 by the American Institute of Certified Public Accountants.
3. Fraud Prevention Check-Up, Association of Certified Fraud Examiners, www.cfenet.com/services/FrdPrevCheckUp.asp.
4. Charles A. Sennewald, *Effective Security Management,* 3rd ed. (Boston: Butterworth-Heinemann, 1988), 180.

# CHAPTER 6

# Financial Statement Fraud

**EXECUTIVE SUMMARY**

Financial statement fraud can be fatal to a company. One way to prevent it is to understand what motivates executives to do it. Barry Minkow, who was convicted of fraud as CEO of ZZZZ Best, said that he began to feel that his worth as a person was tied to the performance of his stock. Joseph Wells, founder of the Association of Certified Fraud Examiners, has said that the only thing that will deter fraudsters is the real perception that they will be caught if they commit the crime. Only personal accountability, as required by Sarbanes-Oxley, will prevent corporate fraud. Threats of sanctions against a company or potential reputational damage are not sufficient deterrents. Numerous red flags and elements of financial statement fraud should be understood to lessen the possibility of its occurrence. It is always important to remember the corruption equation in preventing fraud. Corruption comes from power without sufficient accountability.

Corporate fraud has three separate areas that all need to be addressed. The first thing that comes to mind when one mentions corporate fraud or Sarbanes-Oxley are typically the public scandals of Enron, Worldcom, and Arthur Andersen. "Cooking the books," as they call it, actually refers to financial statement fraud. Financial statement frauds make up only about 8 percent of all internal fraud, as opposed to "traditional fraud," which involves asset misappropriations like embezzlement, or procurement fraud. Traditional fraud can attack the company internally or externally. Although most traditional fraud attacks will be internal, fraud programs must also address the ingenious fraudster who poses as a customer or vendor. There are three main types of fraud:

1. Financial statement fraud
2. Internal traditional fraud (asset misappropriation and corruption)
3. External traditional fraud

Each of these frauds is discussed in this book, and it is important to address all of them in a fraud prevention program. Many books on Sarbanes-Oxley only address financial statement fraud. Most books on stopping fraud in a business do not address how to protect the company from customers who are fraudsters. This book addresses the basics of all three. Although it will not discuss every internal and external fraud scheme, a number of the most common frauds are covered.

## RECURRING THEMES IN FINANCIAL STATEMENT FRAUD

An old joke featured two young accountants applying for a job. The deciding question for the candidates was, "What is 2 + 2?" The losing candidate answered "4." The winning candidate answered, "What do you want it to be?" That joke is no longer as funny as it used to be.

Financial statement fraud cases contain the following recurring themes:

- Pressure on senior management to meet financial goals
- Autocratic senior management
- Aggressive accounting practices

- Weak internal controls
- No whistle-blowers.

Sarbanes-Oxley was passed as a result of the flood of financial statement fraud, but any fraud prevention program in a company has to include efforts to prevent all types of fraud. The rest of this chapter addresses financial statement fraud, with the succeeding chapters addressing internal asset misappropriation and external fraud, respectively.

## COOKING THE BOOKS

In financial statement fraud cases, the CEO, CFO, Controller, or others may engage in any of several manipulations to improve the financial statement:

- Overstatement of inventory, which is the most frequent area of fraudulent asset valuation
- Overstating assets and income by using timing differences
  - Holding the books open to record January sales as December sales
  - Holding December liabilities until January
  - Shifting future expenses to the current period as a special charge
- Failure to record write-offs as required—reversing bad debt into income
- Capitalizing expenses
- Concealing liabilities—it is difficult for an auditor to audit something that is not listed on the books
- Boosting income with one-time gains
- Recording revenue before it is realized or revenue that may never be collected
- Creating fictitious revenues, that is, bogus sales with phony invoices, which result in a boost to assets and income or bribing companies into buying by using "boomcrang" deals—a boomerang might be an agreement for company A to invest in company B if company B agrees to purchase products from company A.[1]

There are obvious risks to a company when the choice is made to manipulate the figures in order to achieve earnings estimates:

- Loss of a stock's market value
- Lawsuits
- Loss of reputation
- Criminal prosecution
- Bankruptcy

---

### EXECUTIVE INSIGHT 6.1: A $300 MILLION FRAUD IS NOTHING TO SNEEZE AT

Fortune 100 companies are not the only ones that commit massive accounting frauds. American Tissue may not be well known by name, but many consumers use American Tissue products on a daily basis. This public company was once the fourth largest United States manufacturer of toilet paper, paper towels, napkins, pulp, and office paper products. It had almost 5,000 employees in offices and mills in the United States and Mexico.

In March 2003, the United States Attorney in Brooklyn, New York charged seven former executives including the CEO and CFO of American Tissue, Inc. for defrauding investors and creditors of over $300 million. American Tissue filed for bankruptcy protection in September 2001 as a result of the wholesale looting of the company. The defendants recorded fraudulent sales and created phony documentation to inflate American Tissue's revenues and ensure a continuing line of credit from banks and other lenders. The CEO also diverted tens of millions of dollars to two other corporations he controlled. The charges filed by the government included securities fraud, bank fraud, and obstruction of justice.[i]

The SEC also charged the company and three former executives with fraudulently overstating revenue, earnings, and assets in 2000 and 2001. The diversion of money and equipment had probably been going on for many years. American Tissue's external auditor, Arthur Andersen, also assisted in the conspiracy as

American Tissue was about to collapse in the bankruptcy filing. A senior Andersen auditor ordered other Andersen employees to shred incriminating American Tissue documents and delete e-mails.[ii]

In a related civil suit, the former American Tissue executives were alleged to have used their public company as if it was a personal piggy bank. They received almost $24 million in loans with no interest or repayment schedule. Another $2.3 million was provided to family and friends, and fraudulent transactions were hidden by using more than 4,000 phony checks and invoices. The CEO and another executive at first blamed the CFO and Arthur Andersen for the sloppy record keeping.[iii] The federal investigation by Postal Inspectors and the FBI in New York proved that was not the case.

The former CEO was convicted on all counts after a ten-week trial. The company's former CFO pled guilty and testified for the government, as did other former employees. Brooklyn United States Attorney Roslyn Mauskoff commented on the conviction by stating, "This massive corporate fraud was a classic case of greed, lies, and obstruction. Today's conviction demonstrates our commitment, as part of the President's Corporate Fraud Task Force, to investigating and prosecuting corporate fraud to the full extent of the law."[iv]

As in other trials of CEOs, the defendant used the "Mr. Magoo Defense." His defense attorneys contended that the CEO "was essentially a talented technician who knew little about business finances, and that the frauds were created by others in the company, who were interested in profits."[v] One defense attorney further added that his client was a refugee from Iran and "didn't understand our business ways; he's from another country.... He doesn't have a college degree in accounting or an MBA."[vi] The prosecutor said it best by telling the jury that the CEO controlled every aspect of the operation and "oversaw a sinkhole of fraud."[vii] The prosecutor then added, "Sometimes you have to wonder, with all the fraudulent activity going at that time, how they had any time to make tissue."[viii]

American Tissue was also alleged to have defrauded its employees by "deducting money from workers' salaries for medical insurance and 401(k) retirement plans but never making the required payments."[ix] A union president in northern New Hampshire, where one of American Tissue's mills was once located, blamed the CEO for "destroying people's lives, their retirements, their savings plans" and said that the government needs "to deal with him like the criminal he is."[x]

[i] First Year Report to the President, Corporate Fraud Task Force, July 22, 2003, www.usdoj.gov/dag/cftf/first_year_report.pdf; Second Year Report to the President, Corporate Fraud Task Force, July 20, 2004, www.usdoj.gov/dag/cftf/2nd_yr_fraud_report.pdf.

[ii] "Former Andersen Auditor Arrested, Charged with Obstruction of Justice," *Accountingweb.com*, March 12, 2003, www.accountingweb.com.

[iii] "Suit Targets American Tissue's Memphis Mill," *Memphis Business Journal* online, September 18, 2003, http://memphis.bizjournals.com/memphis/stories/2002/09/16/daily28.html.

[iv] Press release issued by the United States Attorney's Office, Eastern District of New York, April 13, 2005, www.usdoj.gov/usao/nye/pr/2005apr13a.htm.

[v] Robert E. Kessler, "Convicted on All Counts," *Newsday*, April 14, 2005, A46.

[vi] Ibid.

[vii] Frank Eltman, "Former CEO Convicted of Fraud Scheme in American Tissue Case," *Newsday*, April 13, 2005, http://library.newsday.com.

[viii] Ibid.

[ix] James T. Madore, "Hurt Paper-Mill Towns See Rays of Justice in Indictments," *Newsday.com*, March 18, 2003, A63.

[x] Ibid.

## WHY DO THEY TAKE THE RISK?

The potential results of financial statement fraud are disastrous, so why do so many companies take the risk? The motive is often in the incentives. When huge bonuses are tied to meeting projections, the manager who would receive that bonus loses sight of the potential for disaster. At the point that an executive is considering fudging the numbers to ensure a bonus, the primary question in the executive's mind is, "What is the likelihood that anyone will catch this?" Pressure to meet high estimates could put executives in fear of their jobs if projections are not met. The emphasis on results in the short term creates an environment in which failure is seen as unforgivable. If the perception of detection is low, the idea of fraud becomes a viable option in the mind of the executive.

Some CEOs run their companies in a highly autocratic manner. If such a CEO is reasonably sure that no one will ask questions, there is a low likelihood that anyone will catch questionable practices. Autocratic CEOs often feel like they are deserving of perks and luxuries. CEOs who make millions of dollars a year can begin to feel superhuman and think they can get away with anything. No one seemed to be able to say no to Dennis Kozlowski. When he turned around some poorly performing operations, Kozlowski moved into the limelight. As the CEO of Tyco International in 1997, he was making over $8 million a year, but it wasn't enough. By 1999, Kozlowski was making $170 million a year, but it wasn't enough. He allegedly stole another $430 million through illicit stock sales.[2] These are the actions of a man who thought he was above question, above detection. For an example of how U.S. companies compensate their CEOs compared with average employee salaries, see Exhibit 6.1.

Since many companies offer bonuses and stock options based on financial statement measures, executives and managers are motivated to report more favorable financial results. This creates an environment that encourages financial shenanigans.[3]

Convicted fraudster Barry Minkow explained it best: "...I would get letters from people telling me how great I was and what a business genius I was.... What people thought about me *became the prize* and an end in itself...my worth as a person was tied up in the performance of my stock."[4] Minkow went on to say that he cared more about what other people thought of him than he did about what was right.[5]

**EXHIBIT 6.1**  Average CEO Salary versus Employee Salary

| Country | |
| --- | --- |
| United States | 531 times greater |
| Great Britain | 35 times greater |
| Japan | 20 times greater |

*Source:* Citizen Works, "Crack Down on Corporate Crime," www.citizensworks.org/corp/reforms.php, 12.

A corporate Board of Directors has the responsibility to be independent from the CEO. If a company's Board were truly independent, CEO pay would be representative of how well the company did each year. However, senior executives seem to get ever higher salaries and bonuses, even for substandard performance. If a board cannot reduce a CEO's pay for bad years, it is probably a rubber stamp board. This is a red flag for investors.

## THE NEW AND IMPROVED TYCO

In 2003, Tyco had a new board of directors and new executives as a result of the fraud allegations against its CEO and others. One of the first things addressed was compensation. Tyco learned a hard lesson: The structure of incentives had to reflect corporate goals. The new compensation structure included the following:

- Capped bonuses, even for good years
- Capped stock option equity awards
- Limited severance packages for senior executives up to 299 percent of their annual base pay plus bonus.[6]

## THE PERCEPTION OF DETECTION

In almost every instance of creative corporate accounting, one or more persons in the organization sees signs of trouble. The misdeeds can take on a life their own, with the coverup becoming more of a job than the initial misdeed.

As Joseph Wells, founder of the Association of Certified Fraud Examiners, has said many times, the only thing that will deter potential fraudsters is the perception that their actions will be detected. It has little to do with what the potential repercussions are: jail, financial scandal, or bankruptcy. Simply put, people who think they will get caught don't commit fraud.[7] Those who do not understand this principle think that Sarbanes-Oxley is too strict or that government regulation is not the answer.

## Karpov and Lott's Enforcement Effect of Reputation

Jonathan Karpov, a finance professor at the University of Washington Business School, believes that recognizing the financial value of a law-abiding reputation is the best way to prevent future financial reporting scandals, not tighter government controls.

Karpov and John Lott, from the University of Pennsylvania's Wharton Business School, cite the "enforcement effect" of reputation, which will do more than expensive and possibly harmful government regulation to encourage companies to audit themselves honestly.

Karpov and Lott studied 132 cases of actual and alleged corporate fraud from 1978 to 1987 and found that the average company involved in the frauds lost over $60 million in stock valuation drop. This was 20 times any fines, penalties, restitution, and legal costs. Karpov argues that this research shows that reputational costs far outweigh legal penalties.[8]

Although one would hope that all companies would strive to be honest in their financial reporting for the sake of their corporate reputation, this does not appear to be the case. Fear of financial scandal did not prevent Enron executives from choosing to "cook their books," so why would the results of Enron's fraud discourage future financial statement frauds?

## Accountability Is the Word

Actually, there is a formula for corruption: Power without Accountability breeds Corruption. The authors call it the CPA formula (see Exhibit 6.2).

$$C = P - A$$

Corruption = Power − Accountability

**EXHIBIT 6.2**   The CPA Formula

When an executive has absolute power to make a decision and there is no accountability, corruption is sure to follow. Thus anything that increases accountability, such as Sarbanes-Oxley, will reduce corruption and fraud.

The lack of accountability from years of government deregulation of business has taken its toll. In fact, the latest flood of financial statement frauds followed relaxation of regulations against corporate fraud or "tort reform" in the late 1990s. Two laws actually provided incentives for supporting players to turn a blind eye to the frauds being committed inside their own companies:

- The Private Securities Litigation Reform Act (PSLRA) of 1995
- The Securities Litigation Uniform Standards (SLUSA) of 1998.

These laws significantly limited the ability of defrauded investors to seek restitution from those who aided and abetted the financial fraud. The laws increased the standards of evidence required, limited discovery, and reduced damages.[9] When corporate insiders are not going to be held accountable, the likelihood of fraud increases.

## Clinard and Yeager

This idea that fear of sanctions is not a deterrent is supported by the research on corporate crime conducted by Marshall Clinard and Peter Yeager, which is appropriately titled *Corporate Crime* (published in 1980). Clinard and Yeager's work is required reading for the Certified Fraud Examiner or anyone interested in why corporate fraud occurs. In their research, Clinard and Yeager analyzed 477 corporations that had engaged in illegal behavior of all kinds, finding that only 10 percent of the corporations even received sanctions for their behavior.[10]

According to Clinard and Yeager's findings, the discipline of the market is not a sufficient force to dissuade corporate crime. Consumers are often unaware that corporations have engaged in illegal activity. Therefore, the illegal activity rarely results in decreased patronage, significant reputational damage, or organized boycotts.

Not all firms suffer the way Enron and Arthur Andersen did. Some firms are able to control the damage and survive, or even prosper.

A prime example of such a company is Citigroup. It had record quarterly profits in 2004 at the same time regulators were considering charges against top Citi officials for failure to supervise analysts and investment bankers. The Securities and Exchange Commission (SEC) and the Justice Department were examining whether Citigroup Asset Management overcharged mutual fund investors for record keeping. British authorities were investigating Citi's government bond desk in London for selling European debt in August and then quickly buying it back at a much lower price. Enron creditors were suing Citi for failure to say what they knew about the state of Enron's finances, and the SEC was looking at Citi's accounting in Argentina, where it wrote off $2 billion in bad loans.[11] Bad headlines and questionable accounting did not result in sufficient damage to Citi's reputation to impact its stock price or profits.

Of those companies who are caught and exposed for committing financial fraud, the financial impact of the negative publicity can be devastating, but how many more companies would continue to get away with or attempt financial statement fraud in the future without the regulations imposed by Sarbanes Oxley? Sarbanes-Oxley lets executives know that someone will check on them. They see detection of fraud as a real possibility; thus Sarbanes-Oxley acts as a deterrent.

## IS SARBANES-OXLEY WORKING TO REDUCE FINANCIAL STATEMENT FRAUD?

One of the worst abuses cited in the pre-Sarbanes-Oxley era of corporate fraud was that big auditing firms were also in the business of consulting with their clients on how to use aggressive, gray-area accounting tactics to make the bottom line look better. The independence of the auditor was lost. Has Sarbanes-Oxley restored the independence of the auditor? According to the responses to a 2004 survey of public company executives by Foley & Lardner LLP, it appears so.

- "There are signs that our relationship [with our auditor] is becoming more adversarial."
- "Our outside auditor has turned into a regulator and not a business advisor, as in the past."
- "[Our auditor] is less likely to offer constructive advice, being much more cognizant of their audit role."[12]

In looking at these responses, it is clear that auditing firms take Sarbanes-Oxley regulations seriously, and their clients are aware of the new rules of engagement. Auditors are clearly less likely to ignore creative accounting that skews the financial statement. How can this be a bad thing for investors? Two-thirds (67 percent) of the business executives responding to the Foley & Lardner survey felt that corporate governance and public disclosure reforms were too strict.[13]

In 2004, the CEO of Unisys, Larry Weinbach, accused Congress of overreacting when it passed Sarbanes-Oxley. "Congress was shooting from the hip in response to mistakes some businesses made in not living up to financial transparency. Congress felt it had to do something and did not realize the full ramifications."[14] Although Mr. Weinbach is entitled to his opinion, the authors would not characterize the fall of Arthur Andersen, Enron, and WorldCom as "mistakes that some businesses made in not living up to financial transparency."

It is interesting to note that since the 1970s, federal law has required companies to have internal controls regarding off-the-book payments and auditors to test the controls. The Foreign Corrupt Practices Act has provisions that require these controls. The uproar over Sarbanes-Oxley's controversial section 404 is because executives and auditors must now certify that the controls are effective. The fact that some executives are uncomfortable means that they were probably ignoring federally mandated controls for the past 30 years.[15]

## THE GREED FACTOR

Perhaps all this greed is the result of the increasing emphasis that began to be placed on practical arts like finance, marketing, and business management in the past 25 years. In the 1980s, the "me" generation scoffed at a liberal arts education as outdated. The glory was in big business, high finance, and material gain. CEOs were heroes to be emulated. Today, CEOs are depicted in the media as less than heroic.

In 2003, Diane L. Coutu argued in the *Harvard Business Review* that this backlash against corporate executives is just another form of pandering to the public by the media. The pandering allows many to see themselves as victims of greedy corporate America. Coutu argues that strong egotists are needed to make their companies grow. Replacing them with modest men may soothe the rage, but the economy may suffer for it.[16]

As Scott Green points out in his *Manager's Guide to the Sarbanes-Oxley Act,* it would be wise for any CEO to avoid any hint of unfair dealing. The Board of Directors should adopt a policy to automatically investigate any sale of company stock by management if it preceded the release of bad news. Such a policy, according to Green, would cause senior managers to ensure that they consider all legal and ethical requirements before they sell stock.[17]

Why stop at investigation? Why not force managers who sell stock just before a price drop to pay the money back? The *Financial Times* reported in July 2002 that some 200 executives from the largest 25 U.S. companies to file for bankruptcy in 2001 and the first half of 2002 walked away with over $3 billion in earnings from such precollapse stock sales.[18] The vast majority of these funds is never repaid. It is the SEC's responsibility to the shareholders to make sure that these funds are returned, but the SEC's record is not very good.[19]

If a company already has a strong ethics policy and an anonymous tip line and conducts appropriate background checks, the question might be "What next?" Maintain controls! Beyond the fundamental steps listed earlier, elimination of control weaknesses is the next place to look. This is an ongoing process, as turbulent growth creates new opportunities for fraud. Sloppiness and lack of oversight create an environment that encourages unethical employees to steal when motive and rationalization meet an opportunity created by weak controls. During periods of growth, the management staff may be overloaded and might resort to short cuts. In their 1999 *Business Fraud Survey,* the Institute of Management and Administration/Institute of Internal Auditors found that 63 percent of survey participants recommended strict monitoring of basic internal controls as the best way to enhance fraud detection.[20]

## EXECUTIVE INSIGHT 6.2: SYMBOL TECHNOLOGIES: AN OLD FRAUD AND A NEW APPROACH

The nightmare started with an anonymous letter to the SEC alleging revenue recognition irregularities at New York Stock Exchange-listed company Symbol Technologies. What helped end the irregularities was the change in culture at the company and an agreement to cooperate with the government to expose the fraud and corruption. The ensuing investigation found a smorgasbord of fraud including questionable revenue recognition, bogus transactions, and fraudulent journal entries. Ultimately, this fraud would result in indictments and convictions of corporate executives, a huge corporate fine, corporate reforms, and a former CEO on the run. As an indication of the extent of the conspiracy, the former head of the Postal Inspection Service in New York said that this fraud was a "textbook example of a company cooking the books," but "what is somewhat unique was the amount of cooks in the kitchen."[xi]

Symbol Technologies is the world's leading manufacturer and distributor of wireless and mobile computing equipment, bar code scanners, and related products. It is a public company headquartered in Holtsville, New York, with 5,400 employee and revenues of more than $1.7 billion. In April 2001, the SEC received an anonymous letter alleging fraudulent revenue recognition practices around two specific financial transactions and saying that "these two transactions are just the tip of the iceberg of how Symbol management continues to manipulate and improperly handle business accounting."[xii]

The SEC started a criminal investigation along with the Postal Inspection Service and the Internal Revenue Service. Symbol also started an internal investigation. Unfortunately, several Symbol executives, including the former Senior Vice-President for Finance allegedly "engaged in conduct designed to interfere with and obstruct the internal investigation."[xiii] Symbol discovered this conduct in September 2002 and fired the Senior Vice-President. What made this case somewhat unique was the total cooperation of Symbol after the company had fired the executive. Symbol provided the government investigators with the results of internal interviews with hundreds of current and former employees, customers, and others, as well as over one-half million pages of documents and thousands of e-mails and voicemails.[xiv]

Symbol also waived the attorney-client privilege to assist the government's investigations further and identified numerous witnesses that could help determine the extent of the fraud scheme.[xv] This level of transparency and cooperation by a corporation under investigation was extraordinary and would generally not have been seen prior to Sarbanes-Oxley. Symbol realized that the only way to continue as a business was to sever all ties to those executives engaged in corporate fraud and assist the government in exposing and punishing the fraudsters.

The investigation determined that Symbol was "cooking the books" between 1999 and 2002 to inflate corporate earnings fraudulently by $200 million to meet Wall Street's earning estimates. Among the accounting crimes charged by the government were "false and prematurely recognized revenue, a complex dance of manipulation of accounting entries to fabricate higher revenues and lower costs, referred to by the conspirators as 'tango adjustments,' phony classification of expenses, and the creation of 'cookie jar' reserves."[xvi] The "tango adjustments" refer to the systematic overstatement of quarterly revenues and earnings and the subsequent understatement of expenses by a complex "dance," nicknamed the tango, to match analyst's projections for Symbol fraudulently. The fraudsters also used "channel stuffing" to overstate quarterly revenue and created "cookie jar reserves" to manipulate financial reserves.

In June 2004, the government indicted Symbol's former President and CEO, former Senior Vice-President and CFO, and five other top executives. In addition, the former General Counsel was indicted and pled guilty to orchestrating "a scheme by which he and other senior executives fraudulently exploited the company's stock option plans to enrich themselves and illegally minimize their tax obligations."[xvii]

The other corporate executives and directors pled guilty and are cooperating with the government's investigations. In their guilty pleas, the former Chief Accounting Officer and former Vice-President of Worldwide Sales and Finance "admitted to participating in a scheme in which Symbol's senior management defrauded the investing public by materially misrepresenting Symbol's quarterly and annual revenues, expenses, and earnings through the use of sales transactions and fraudulent accounting entries in order to ensure that Symbol consistently reported that it had met or exceeded projected quarterly revenue and earnings."[xviii]

The company has formally accepted responsibility for the fraudulent conduct of its former executives, agreed to continued cooperation with the government, and adopted significant corporate reforms including appointment of a new management team, restructuring of the Board of Directors to ensure appropriate oversight, appointment of an independent examiner to monitor internal controls and financial reporting practices, retention of a new audit firm, and mandated training and education programs on corporate governance.

Symbol also agreed to pay $139 million to compensate victims of the fraud, to settle a private class action suit, and to contribute to the Postal Inspection Service's Consumer Fraud Fund, which provides investigative resources for corporate fraud investigations. By doing all of this, Symbol escaped being charged criminally as a corporation. Throughout the investigation, Symbol has advised shareholders and the public of the investigation through ongoing press releases. In a statement of October 8, 2003, the then interim chairman and CEO stated, "There previously existed in the Company an atmosphere and culture that, we believe, allowed for and fostered a working environment that, ultimately, led to the difficulties we're now working so hard to correct."[xix]

As a postscript to justice delayed, former CEO Tomo Razmilovic resigned from Symbol in February 2002 and moved to Europe. He received a generous severance package of millions of dollars. Although aware that he was indicted, he has claimed innocence and refuses to return to the United States to face justice. He is currently living in Sweden, but as a Swedish national by marriage, he is protected from extradition to the United States.

[xi] Mark Harrington, "8 Charged in Fraud at Symbol," *Newsday*, June 4, 2004, A7.

[xii] "Former Senior Executives at Symbol Technologies Indicted in Massive Corporate Fraud Scheme—Corporation Has Purged Executives Responsible for the Fraud, Implemented Significant Corporate Reforms, Agreed to Cooperate with the Government's Investigations and Pay $139 Million," Press release issued by the United States Attorney's Office, Eastern District of New York, June 3, 2004, www.usdoj.gov/usao/nye/pr/2004jun3.htm.

[xiii] Ibid.

[xiv] Ibid.

[xv] Ibid.

[xvi] Ibid.

[xvii] Second Year Report to the President, Corporate Fraud Task Force, July 20, 2004, www.usdoj.gov/dag/cftf/2nd_yr_fraud_report.pdf., 3.11.

[xviii] First Year Report to the President, Corporate Fraud Task Force, July 22, 2003, www.usdoj.gov/dag/cftf/first_year_report.pdf, 3.15.

[xix] "Symbol Technologies Report Unaudited Results for 2003's First and Second Quarters and Unaudited Results for Period of Financial Restatement, 1998 through 2002," Press release issued by Symbol Technologies, October 8, 2003, www.symbol.com/news/pressreleases/unaudited_2003_1_and_2_q.html.

## RED FLAGS OF FINANCIAL STATEMENT FRAUD

Joseph Wells provides some questions to ask when one is looking for red flags that may signal financial statement fraud:

- Does management display significant disregard for regulations or controls?
- Has management restricted the auditor's access to documents or personnel?
- Has management set unrealistic financial goals?
- Does one person or small group dominate management?[21]

Scott Green in his *Manager's Guide to the Sarbanes-Oxley Act,* lists more red flags for financial statement fraud:

- Aggressive revenue recognition policies
- Frequent changes in accounting policies regarding bad debt reserves, depreciation, and amortization expenses or comprehensive income
- Unsupported topside entries affecting income
- Underfunded defined pension plans
- Management compensation that is seriously out of line with company performance.[22]

### Michael Young's Six Elements of Financial Statement Fraud

Michael Young, in his book *Accounting Irregularities and Financial Fraud,* explains financial statement fraud as a symptom of our real-time world. There is an insatiable desire for financial information. There are cable television stations dedicated completely to financial news. People expect the latest financial statistics to be available on the television or computer screen.

Young goes on to point out that the financial reporting system used by U.S. companies today was designed in the 1930s. Financial information then was designed to be communicated on paper. Speed was not a concern. Financial information was a periodic report to the public so they could make their investments accordingly. Then, according to Young, analysts began to make projections to fill the void of financial news. Analysts' projections and expectations are the result of the real-time world's demand for up-to-the-minute financial information. These projections are up to the minute, but they might not be right![23]

These analysts' projections can have a huge impact on the stock price of companies. Because investors expect companies to meet projected earnings, there is great pressure to meet these estimates. Every division of the company is made aware of what it must bring in.

The market volatility during "earnings season" shows what potential for disaster this system has created. Some executives see failure to meet projections as unfathomable because much of their personal earnings is tied to the stock price of their companies.

Picture a fictitious, publicly traded manufacturing company, called Willoughby Manufacturing. Profits have been good for the past four years and are growing steadily. The stock price has grown, and several Wall Street analysts have begun reporting on the company. The publicity on television and in the newspapers has caused the stock to rise even higher. There are projections that this quarter will be a record profit.

Unbeknownst to the investment community, there is a problem. The market for the goods manufactured by this company has begun to level off. The Wall Street projections are not realistic, but the price of the company's stock is now tied to this projection. Investors are "counting their chickens" in shares of Willoughby that will never hatch.

The managers at Willoughby can either accept the bad news or put the pressure on all managers to meet sales projections. Willoughby's CEO chooses pressure. Each division is expected to meet unrealistic sales quotas. One division president, called Peter, is already afraid for his job. Peter knows that he can never get to the quota by the end of the quarter. Rather than risk his job by failing to meet quota, Peter books sales in this quarter that will not really be earned until next quarter. By then, sales will probably be better, he hopes.

Thanks to creative accounting in several divisions, Willoughby Manufacturing has met market projections for the quarter and set a record. The projections for the next quarter are for continued growth; however, three divisions have already booked sales that are in the pipeline to the last quarter. Three divisions are now already behind on meeting an unrealistic projection for the next quarter. There is no way out. Eventually someone higher up will find out, the auditor or the CFO. Some CFOs might choose a cover-up rather than public disclosure of the irregularity in the timing of transactions, which could kill the stock price. Michael Young cites six elements in our story:

1. It doesn't start out as dishonesty.
2. It starts with pressure.
3. It starts small.
4. It starts in gray areas of accounting.
5. The fraud grows over time.
6. There is no way out.[24]

## Lessons Learned

The lessons for corporations regarding financial reporting are simple:

- Book profits for real transactions that have been completed.
- Profit is what a company earns for taking a risk, not what a company gets by taking advantage.
- Booking profits too soon is building a pyramid scheme on sand; it cannot last.[25]

## WHEN BAD AUDITS HAPPEN TO GOOD ACCOUNTANTS

Sarbanes-Oxley restricts auditors from providing certain nonaudit services when performing an audit while greatly empowering the audit committee. Audit committees are now eager to avoid possible conflicts. At the end of 2004, the Public Company Accounting Oversight Board (PCAOB) proposed stricter controls on audit firms that also provide certain tax services to the same client. It is hoped that having separate accounting firms performing the tax and audit functions will stop the conflict of interest that had been in place prior to Sarbanes-Oxley.

### Ambiguity and Bias

As already discussed, the practice of allowing accounting firms to consult on accounting services with their audit clients was a conflict of interest that hindered the objectivity of the auditors. Sarbanes-Oxley has created a more adversarial relationship between the company and the audit firm. However, even with the elimination of consulting services, and the protections of Sarbanes-Oxley, the audit system is not perfect. Ambiguity and bias contributed as much to the industry problems as did fraud.

One might argue that ambiguity still has a firm hold on the accounting and auditing profession, but it was not always that way. Around the time of the American Civil War, auditors looked for fraud or errors by reviewing nearly every transaction in the books.

There were no noncash transactions. By 1900, business had become too complex and fast paced for an auditor to check each and every transaction. Auditors were now considered more like financial advisors helping clients sort out complex tax laws. Fraud prevention was assumed to be located in controls such as the separation of duties, a proper approval structure, and having a monthly statement close.[26]

It made good business sense to keep clients happy. If an auditing firm rejected a client's interpretation of the accounting rules, two things could happen: the client backed down and endured the pain, or the client found a new audit firm to hire. The longer the client retained the audit firm, the less likely the audit firm would risk a confrontation. This could lead to bias. Bias is inevitable whenever information can be interpreted in various ways.

Psychological research shows that desires powerfully influence how information is processed, even when one tries to be objective and impartial. When people are motivated to reach a particular conclusion, they usually do.[27]

### MicroStrategy Becomes MicroTragedy

Few auditors want to be the messenger breaking the news to a client that earnings will have to be restated. Such an event can be disastrous. Take the example of MicroStrategy, a data mining software maker. In 2000, MicroStrategy became "MicroTragedy" when it had to restate its 1998 and 1999 earnings. The first problem was that rather than spreading earnings out over the length of multiyear consulting contracts, MicroStrategy booked the profits right away. Another problem was the October 1999 announcement of a $52 million licensing agreement with NCR Corporation, whereby MicroStrategy "invested" in NCR, and NCR would purchase products from MicroStrategy—a "boomerang!"[28]

The restatement of MicroStrategy earnings turned a reported $12 million profit into a $34 million dollar loss. The shares of MicroStrategy plummeted from $333 per share in March 2000 to $22 in May 2000, and MicroStrategy was hit with three lawsuits.[29] Avoiding such immediate adverse consequences is a human defense mechanism that can lead to an auditor deciding to "go with the flow."

## Going with the Flow

Going with the flow sometimes includes looking the other way when related-party transactions are used to create earnings. This is what happened at Enron. The real accounting scandal at Enron was a failure to disclose the full details of Special Purpose Entities (SPEs). Enron sold assets to SPEs and booked a profit on the sales. Later, Enron bought back the assets at a higher price. These were really loans from the SPEs to Enron, and the assets never actually changed hands. Enron officers were partners in the SPEs and made money from these short-term loans, which was a conflict of interest.[30] Arthur Andersen went along for the ride. They decided not to question the financial genius of Ken Lay, a corporate giant, who had the ear of more than one U.S. president. They went with the flow.

## Where Were the Stock Analysts?

According to Joseph Wells, fraud is very difficult to find in many audit situations because it is often committed by insiders who are more familiar with the accounting system(s) than the auditors are.[31] Because of the limited time auditors spend looking at the records, they just see a snapshot in time. They do not monitor the books on a day-to-day basis.

Some of the burden belongs with the stock analysts. Analysts took WorldCom's reported income as proof that it was doing well. If those analysts had analyzed the free cash flows of WorldCom, they would have seen that capital expenditures were false, designed to hide the operating costs.[32]

Other questions that analysts should ask include:

- Is the company negotiating financing based on its receivables?
- Have receivables increased significantly but not sales?
- Has cash decreased compared with sales and receivables?
- Are shipping costs consistent with sales?[33]

Perhaps a question that is as valid as "Where were the auditors?" is "Where were the investment analysts?" Here are some more instances that might signal the need for closer review:

- High-growth companies entering a low-growth phase; there may be a temptation to mask the decline
- Companies that are always under the Wall Street microscope; any bad news could tank the stock
- Companies that are not followed by most analysts
- New businesses, which have to decide how to measure key transactions
- Complex ownerships or financial structures, which can make related-party transactions less transparent.[34]

There have been numerous instances in which analysts have been not just sloppy or negligent, but downright corrupt. Several investigations since 2000 have shown that the stock analysis done by several large firms was neither independent nor unbiased.

In 2002, investment giant Merrill Lynch paid a $100 million dollar fine after an internal e-mail was discovered showing that analysts were publicly recommending stocks that they knew were not good investments. These were, of course, the stocks of companies from which Merrill wanted to win investment business.[35]

Conflict of interest cases also surfaced at the investment firms Goldman Sachs, Morgan Stanley, and Citigroup Global Markets. In October 2002, New York State Attorney General Eliot Spitzer filed suit against five clients of Citigroup for granting investment business to Citibank in exchange for favorable stock ratings by Citigroup analysts.[36]

How is it that bias has invaded the advice of stock analysts? In 1975, Congress removed the fixed rate on commissions for analysts, allowing the market to dictate commission rates. Of course, competition for the business of middle-class Americans entering the stock market for the first time drove commissions lower. Lower commissions forced many Wall Street brokerage companies to rely more and more on investment banking deals to maintain themselves in the manner to which they had become accustomed.

Jack Grubman from Salomon Smith Barney, the investment banking arm of Citigroup, had become one of the top dealmakers. Grubman generated tens of millions of dollars in fees from companies that benefited from Grubman's market research. In 1998, Citi rewarded Grubman with a contract that would pay him $20 million over a five-year period.[37]

In 2000, Grubman was pushing the stocks of WorldCom and Global Crossing, which were expanding with billions of dollars worth of bonds issued by Citigroup. These telecom giants made money from broadband and cable lines, the rates for which were in free fall. With the rates dropping, someone should have questioned whether WorldCom and Global Crossing would still be able to pay their debts. Grubman did not seem to be concerned.[38] This is the perfect example of why Karpov and Lott's Enforcement Effect of [a good] Reputation is so hard to accept. When business executives and star analysts lose touch with reality, they cannot be thinking of their company's good reputation.

## ENDNOTES

1. Joseph T. Wells, "So That's Why It's Called a Pyramid Scheme," *Journal of Accountancy,* 190 (October 2000), 91; and Howard Schilit, *Financial Shenanigans,* 2nd ed. (New York: McGraw Hill, 2002), 62.
2. Scott Green, *Manager's Guide to the Sarbanes-Oxley Act* (New York: John Wiley & Sons, 2004), 93.
3. Howard Schilit, *Financial Shenanigans,* 2nd ed. (New York: McGraw Hill, 2002), 29.
4. Barry Minkow, *Cleaning Up* (Nashville: Nelson Current, 2005), 155.
5. Ibid., 215.
6. Eric Pillmore, "How We're Fixing Up Tyco," *Harvard Business Review* 81, no. 12 (December 2003), 96.
7. Joseph Wells, "The S&L Scandal, the Biggest Crime of All Time?" *The White Paper* (May/June 1990), 2.
8. Robyn Eifertsen, "Regulations Not Best Prevention against Fraud," *University Week* (University of Washington) 19, no. 20 (March 14, 2002).

9. Citizen Works, "Crack Down on Corporate Crime," www. citizenworks.org/corp/reforms.php, 8.

10. Marshall Clinard and Peter Yeager, *Corporate Crime* (New York: Free Press, 1980).

11. Mara Der Hovanesian, Paula Dwyer, and Stanley Reed, "Can Chuck Prince Clean Up Citi?" *Business Week*, October 2, 2004, 11.

12. Thomas E. Hartman, "The Cost of Being Public in the Era of Sarbanes-Oxley," www.foley.com/news, 5/21/2004.

13. Ibid.

14. Mark Tran, "USA: Corporate Governance Law 'Too Strict,'" *CorpWatch*, www.corpwatch.org/article.php?id=11374.

15. David Henry, Amy Borrus, Louis Lavelle, Diane Brady, Michael Arndt, and Joseph Weber, "Death, Taxes & Sarbanes-Oxley?" *Business Week*, January 17, 2005, 28.

16. Diane L. Coutu, "I Was Greedy Too," *Harvard Business Review* (February 2003, vol. 81, no. 2), 38–44.

17. Scott Green, *Manager's Guide to the Sarbanes-Oxley Act,* (New York: John Wiley & Sons, 2004), 136.

18. "The Barons of Bankruptcy," *Financial Times*, July 31, 2002.

19. Citizen Works, "Crack Down on Corporate Crime," www. citizenworks.org/corp/reforms.php, 2.

20. Joseph W. Koletar, *Fraud Exposed* (New York: John Wiley & Sons), 106.

21. Joseph T. Wells, "Why Employees Commit Fraud," *Journal of Accountancy* 191 (February 2001), 89.

22. Scott Green, *Manager's Guide to the Sarbanes-Oxley Act,* (New York: John Wiley & Sons, 2004), 123.

23. Michael R. Young, *Accounting Irregularities and Financial Fraud*, 2nd ed. (New York: Aspen Publishers, 2002), 306–309.

24. Ibid., 11–13.

25. Jerry Fleming, *Profit at Any Cost?* (Grand Rapids, MI: Baker Books, 2003), 28, 52.

26. Joseph T. Wells, "Accountancy and White Collar Crime," *Annals of the American Academy of Political and Social Science* (January 1993, vol. 525), 83–94.

27. Max H. Bazerman, George Loewenstein, and Don A. Moore, "Why Good Accountants Do Bad Audits," *Harvard Business Review* 80, no. 11 (November 2002), 97–102.

28. Howard Schilit, *Financial Shenanigans,* 2nd ed. (New York: McGraw Hill, 2002), 44.
29. H. David Sherman and S. David Young, "Tread Lightly through These Accounting Minefields," *Harvard Business Review* 79, no. 7 (July-August 2001), 129–35.
30. William A. Sahlman, "Expensing Options Solves Nothing," *Harvard Business Review* 80, no. 12 (December 2002), 91–96.
31. Joseph T. Wells, "Follow the Likely Perp," *Journal of Accountancy* 191 (March 2001), 91.
32. William A. Sahlman, "Expensing Options Solves Nothing," *Harvard Business Review* 80, no. 12 (December 2002), 91–96.
33. Joseph T. Wells, "Follow the Likely Perp," *Journal of Accountancy* 191 (March 2001), 91.
34. H. David Sherman and S. David Young, "Tread Lightly through These Accounting Minefields," *Harvard Business Review* 79, no. 7 (July-August 2001), 129–35.
35. Joshua Kurlantzick, "Word on the Street," *Entrepreneur,* January 2005, 55.
36. Ibid.
37. Charles Gasparino, *Blood on the Street* (New York: Free Press, 2005), 96.
38. Ibid., 7.

# Internal Fraud:
# Protecting a Company

**EXECUTIVE SUMMARY FOR CHAPTER 7**

Financial statement fraud is not the only kind of fraud that can damage a company. According to the Association of Certified Fraud Examiners' *2004 Report to the Nation on Occupational Fraud and Abuse*, 92 percent of all frauds perpetrated against companies are asset misappropriation. The three types of cash misappropriation are larceny, skimming, and fraudulent disbursements. These are frauds committed by employees and others such as contractors. Check fraud, although still a concern, is not the problem it used to be, because of technological advances that have improved prevention. Corruption schemes involving bribery, kickbacks, and bid-rigging continue to be a problem and are more common than most people realize. Executives need to recognize that a security program protecting the physical security aspects of an organization is not a substitute for a separate and dynamic fraud prevention program.

## FRAUDULENT DISBURSEMENTS AND ASSET MISAPPROPRIATION

After Sarbanes-Oxley, many internal audit departments increased their testing aimed at finding financial statement fraud, but one cannot ignore the other type of occupational fraud and abuse, internal asset misappropriation (see Exhibit 7.1).

There are various schemes and methods to misappropriate assets, and some tend to show up more frequently than others. In its *2004 Report to the Nation*, the Association of Certified Fraud Examiners classifies the different types of asset misappropriations, which are involved in about 92 percent of all internal frauds (and which are also the lowest in median cost, about $93,000 per incident).

- The two types of asset misappropriations are cash and noncash (goods).
- Only 20 percent are noncash misappropriations.
- The three types of cash misappropriation are larceny, skimming, and fraudulent disbursements.
- There are several types of fraudulent disbursements (see Exhibit 7.2).

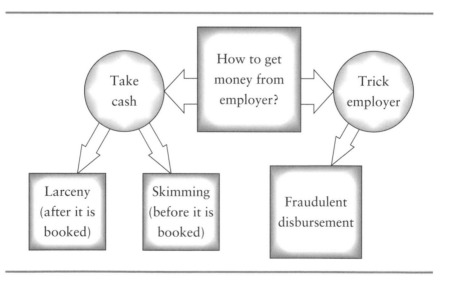

**EXHIBIT 7.1**   Employee Fraud
*Source:* Peterson and Zikmund, "10 Truths You Need to Know about Fraud," *Strategic Finance*, May 2004, 29.

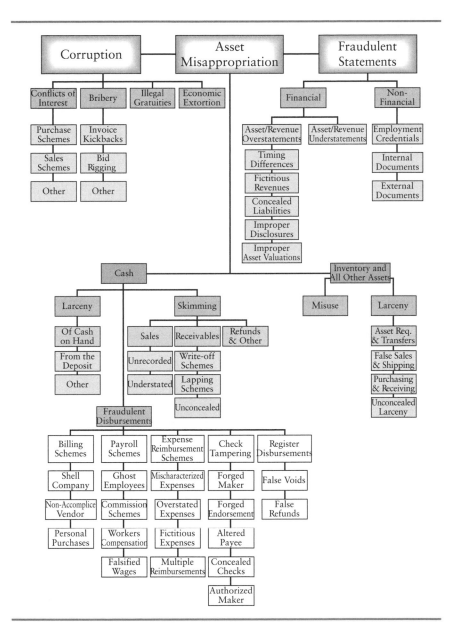

**EXHIBIT 7.2** Uniform Occupational Fraud Classification System
*Source:* Reprinted with permission from the Association of Certified Fraud Examiners, Austin, Texas ©2005.

Fraudulent disbursements constitute an important area in which to conduct a fraud risk assessment. Employees may attempt fraudulent disbursements in various ways, so there are numerous controls to be considered. Of all fraudulent disbursements, more than half are billing schemes.[1]

## FALSE BILLING SCHEMES

### Invoicing through Shell Companies

Although sometimes a legitimate business need exists for shell companies, they are often created for the sole purpose of committing fraud or masking the true owner of funds. Some shells are actually incorporated in the United States. (Delaware and Nevada are popular because of low cost and ease of incorporation.) Other shell companies are incorporated offshore to take advantage of privacy laws. The shell can be nothing more than a fake name and a post office box used to collect proceeds from false billings, or as elaborate as multiple companies in several different countries. It is a good idea to check out any vendor thoroughly, especially one using a post office box address.

Not all fraudsters are street smart. Some employees submit fake invoices for nonexistent companies and use their home addresses or the maiden names of wives and mothers. A comparison of employee addresses with a list of vendor addresses will catch these novice fraudsters.

Once a shell company has been established and the fraudster has opened a bank account in the name of the shell, invoices are created by various means. The invoices are usually for services, as these are harder to track than goods. Often the fraudster has approval power, or a supervisor who simply rubber-stamps everything. Invoices that have not been folded have probably not been mailed, but rather placed into the system from someone inside.

Accounts payable staff should be on the lookout for unfolded invoices and for the following:

- Vendors that have received payments at two different addresses
- More than one vendor with the same address
- Vendors that have the same address as an employee
- Vendors using post office box addresses or commercial mail receiving agencies.

## The Pass-Through Scheme

More ingenious fraudsters do not invoice for nonexistent goods or services. Instead, they use the shell company to purchase actual goods at regular prices. They then resell these goods to their companies at inflated prices. This is known as a pass-through scheme. The fraudster is usually someone in charge of purchasing for the victim company. A practice of putting big-ticket items out for bid can stop this, as competitive bids will be lower than the pass-through company's price.

## Personal Purchases with Company Money

This fraud can easily start when a manager purchases software, for example. The manager asks how to get a certain program and is told to put in a formal request under the office supply budget. The manager is able to approve the purchase, as the amount is only a few hundred dollars. The software arrives, and a clerk brings it directly to the manager. The manager has ordered, approved, and received goods. There is no separation of duties. At this point the manager realizes that anything can be purchased within reason, be it for personal or business use. Only conscience and the fear of being caught control the manager's actions. This is how most internal frauds start. An employee finds an area without strong controls and takes advantage of it. This is the "opportunity" mentioned in Donald Cressey's Fraud Triangle Theory.

**EXECUTIVE INSIGHT 7.1 EXPENSE REPORTING FRAUD: DO WHAT I SAY, NOT WHAT I DO**

Expense reporting fraud is one of the most common asset misappropriation frauds, and experience has shown that employees at all levels of an organization can be involved. In addition, it has often been said that anyone can fall victim to a fraud, including expense fraud. It is particularly embarrassing when the victim is a corporate governance center at a respected institution of higher learning. This story involves Florencio López-de-Silanes, who was a renowned professor of finance and economics as well as the Director of the International Institute of Corporate Governance at the prestigious Yale School of Management. López-de-Silanes advised organizations and governments around the world on corporate governance best practices. He was a founding member of the Blue Ribbon Panel on Corporate Governance in Russia and the Committee on Best Corporate Practices in Mexico. He received his undergraduate degree and a doctorate from Harvard University as well as numerous achievements and honors throughout his career.[i]

Officials at Yale started an investigation in September 2004 and "uncovered alleged evidence that he double-billed for hotels, flights and similar travel expenses" that totaled almost $150,000 since 2001.[ii] In December 2004, Yale's senior faculty was told that the investigation "found a pattern of financial impropriety and was negotiating with Mr. López-de-Silanes' attorney to avoid the messy process of removing his tenure."[iii] In January 2005, it was decided that López-de-Silanes would leave Yale because of "financial misconduct and irregularities."[iv] In a statement issued by López-de-Silanes' attorney, the professor said, "I deeply regret any unintended harm. I can offer no excuse except the intensity of my focus on work. I am leaving Yale because it is the right thing to do for the Institute and all concerned."[v] Subsequently, the Yale School of Management Web site advised that López-de-Silanes was on a leave of absence for Spring 2005 and had resigned effective June 30, 2005.

Jack Siegel, author of *Avoiding Trouble While Doing Good: A Guide for the Non-Profit Director and Officer*, commented on his Web blog that Yale set a very bad example in handling the situation and in the process undermined the university's credibility as a provider of corporate governance training. Siegel said with respect to corporate governance, "the talisman is transparency" and that was not the case here. He added, "As a consequence, we don't know the facts, including the exact amount involved, the amount of intentional behavior on Mr. López-de-Silanes' part, or the extent of the weaknesses in Yale's accounting system. If there was blatant wrongdoing, there should not have been negotiation." Siegel also questioned what kind of example this would provide to Yale students who may find themselves in fiduciary roles later in life.[vi]

There are a few lessons to be learned here. One, travel and expense reporting fraud and abuse are widespread and can be found in any organization. Proactive detection and prevention are always required. Second, any organization, especially a high-profile one, must always remember that its actions will be scrutinized. Any decisions that are suspect will open the organization to adverse publicity. A good rule to remember is how the final action will look if it is published on page one of the *Wall Street Journal*. As an ironic touch to this story, the Yale School of Management's Web site at the time advised that López-de-Silanes had been working on a research paper entitled "Theft Technologies."[vii]

---

[i] Yale School of Management faculty page at their Web site page, mba.yale.edu/faculty/professors/lopez.shtml.

[ii] Joann S. Lublin, "Travel Expenses Prompt Yale to Force Out Institute Chief," *Wall Street Journal*, January 10, 2005, B1.

[iii] Ibid.

[iv] The Associated Press, "Governance Expert Resigns over Finances," MSNBC.com, January 10, 2005, www.msnbc.msn.com/id/6809368.

[v] Ibid.

[vi] Jack Siegel, "Tunneling through Expense Account Reimbursements at Yale: "Do What I Say, Not What I Do," charitygovernance.blogs.com/charity_governance/2005/01/tunneling_throu_1.html.

[vii] Yale School of Management faculty page at their Web site, mba.yale.edu/faculty/professors/lopez.shtml.

## PAYROLL SCHEMES

These schemes can take many forms, from a person lying on a time card to entering nonexistent or ghost employees on the payroll. The company cuts the ghost employee a paycheck, which is intercepted by the fraudster and cashed. Use of direct deposit only makes the fraudster's work easier. The best way to discover ghost employees is to check periodically to determine whether more than one check is going to a single address or to a single bank account. Looking for two employees with the same Social Security number is also a way to find ghosts. Lack of segregation of duties or the absence of review makes it easier for the fraudster to slip ghosts into the system. Ghost employees will often have no withholding for insurance or taxes.

### Check Tampering

This could be internal or external. Anyone who has seen the movie *Catch Me If You Can* starring Tom Hanks and Leonardo Di Caprio, about the life and crimes of Frank Abagnale, has an idea of how the world of check fraud used to be. With the onset of wire transfers and Positive Pay, the check forger or "paperhanger" is a dying threat to the corporate world, unless one is in the business of cashing checks. Positive Pay is a service provided by a bank to its commercial customers, whereby the customer company provides an electronic file to the bank that lists the date, payee, and amount of all checks written each period. If a check that is not on the list is presented for payment, the bank must get approval before honoring the check. Positive Pay is highly regarded, as more than 50 percent of all check tampering schemes are "forged maker" schemes.[2] This means that a fraudster has obtained a blank check and forged the signature of the official signatory. It includes the use of photocopy forgeries. The fraudster often presents these checks for cashing at casinos or check cashing services. Positive Pay prevents the funds from being withdrawn from a company's bank account because these checks will not be on the list prepared for the bank. In his book *The Art of the Steal,* Frank Abagnale writes, "I feel that positive pay is the greatest concept available to deal with the problems of forgery or fraud."[3] That is a high-level endorsement. (See Exhibit 7.3 for the different types of check schemes.)

**EXHIBIT 7.3** Types of Check Schemes by Percentage

| | |
|---|---|
| Forged Maker | 50 |
| Alteration to Payee | 20 |
| Authorized Maker | 15 |
| Forged Endorsement | 11 |
| Concealed Checks | 4 |

*Source:* Joseph T. Wells, *Occupational Fraud and Abuse* (Austin, TX): Obsidian Publishing, 1997), 159.

There are two types of check fraud that occur when a valid check is intercepted by an inside fraudster. Alteration to payee occurs when the fraudster changes the payee and then converts the check to his or her own use. The other type of check fraud occurs when the check is intercepted and the endorsement forged. The inside fraudster poses as the payee and converts the check.

Authorized maker schemes take place when those with signature authority write checks to themselves. Concealed checks are bogus checks slipped in with valid checks for the official signatory to sign.

To prevent check interception schemes, checks should be mailed directly to the third party as soon as they are prepared. Employees and contractors should not be allowed to collect checks in person. Electronic funds transfers are good in that they reduce the number of persons with access to negotiable documents.

For a fraudster, checks have some very big drawbacks; they leave behind an audit trail, handwriting evidence, and fingerprints which can be detected for months or even years after a transaction. Passing counterfeit checks also involves face-to-face transactions and false identification, which are more risky and difficult than making long-distance orders with stolen credit card numbers. For these reasons, credit card fraud has become a more popular, easier, and safer way to make a dishonest living. Some paperhangers still use the "Bust Out" strategy (described in Chapter 9), which involves becoming a trusted customer by placing small orders before eventually placing a very large one, paying with a bad check, and leaving. This "one-time hit" strategy is the norm.

Another type of employee check fraud commonly seen is the "stop payment scam." This usually occurs when an employee is leaving a company, and the last paycheck is being mailed. The employee will wait until the paycheck has been mailed, ask that payment be stopped, and then request that a new check be issued and mailed to a new address. The former employee will then attempt to cash both checks and move on.

### Payroll Debit Cards

Along with Positive Pay, Payroll debit cards are an excellent way to curb check fraud. Controllers or treasurers never have to sign checks again. Once an employee has been issued a card, payday is as easy as electronic payments into the accounts. The employee does not have to have a checking account. The payroll debit card is like a prepaid credit card. The American love affair with plastic is well documented. Employees without bank accounts who were used to cashing paychecks will save the 2 to 3 percent check cashing fee imposed by check cashing services, plus employees do not have to walk around with large amounts of cash. According to *INC.* magazine, some 30 million American workers do not have checking accounts.[4]

The Association of Certified Fraud Examiners (ACFE) Fraud Examiners Manual lists some red flags that may signal check tampering in a company:

- Voided checks: these should be verified against the physical copies of the checks.
- Missing checks: they indicate lax control over check stock. Stop payment on all missing checks.
- Checks, other than paychecks, payable to any employee: these should be reviewed.
- Altered or dual endorsements: these may mean fraud.[5]

## BRIBERY, KICKBACKS, AND BID-RIGGING

In many parts of the world, a bribe is a normal business transaction. The bribe is put on the books as a facilitation fee, and everyone is happy. The bribe buys influence and is sometimes the cost of doing business. However, if the bribe involves a government official or is made without knowledge of the company for which the payer works, this transaction becomes at the least unethical and probably illegal.

Bribery is often defined as *giving* something of *value* with the *intent* to *influence* an *official act*. Notice the key words in italics. "Official act" is the original terminology used when describing bribes paid to political figures. Commercial bribery would involve payments to influence a person in a position to make business decisions that can benefit the bribe payer.

Bribery includes three different types of schemes:

1. Straight Bribery: company A makes a one-time payment to a particular person at company B (without the knowledge or consent of company B) to influence the decision of that person in a way favorable to company A. Company A is willing to pay, and the bribe-taker pockets the money. An example is a bank that bribes the decision-maker at a company to steer the company's banking business to that bank.

2. Kickbacks: company A overcharges or submits bogus invoices to company B. There is an accomplice inside company B who helps cover the fraud in exchange for part of the proceeds being kicked back to the accomplice on a continuing basis. An example is a quality inspector who approves substandard work or equipment for a cut of the profits.

3. Bid-Rigging: company A is bidding on a large contract with company B. The person at company B in charge of the bid solicitation offers to help company A win the contract in exchange for a percentage of the profit from the contract. Once the agreement has been made, the bribe-taker can specify items in the contract that only company A can provide, or make sure that company A's bid is the lowest by passing on inside information. One bribe-taker even went as far as submitting bogus bids from nonexistent companies, all higher than the company that had agreed to pay him a bribe. Once the contract is awarded to company A, the inside bribe-taker protects the relationship and continues to receive a portion of the profit on a continuing basis. An example is a company bribing the bid solicitor to overlook the fact that the company has no references, work history, or other required qualifications. The bid solicitor helps the company falsify the proper documents in exchange for a cut of the contract.

Corruption is a term that usually surfaces when bribes are involved, but corruption is more than just bribery. Corruption is using one's position in government or in business to personal advantage. This would include insider trading and graft. A simple formula for the development of corruption was discussed in the last chapter (see Exhibit 7.4).

Corruption equals Power minus Accountability. In other words, when someone has absolute power to make a decision and there is no accountability, corruption is sure to follow. Anything that increases accountability, like Sarbanes-Oxley, will reduce corruption. Again, it is the belief that one will be caught that prevents the deed.

Red flags for corruption include the following:

- A company paying more than the best price available
- Very specific requirements that tend to favor one bidder
- Projects that are broken into two contracts to keep them under a review limit or approval authority
- Very narrow time window for companies to submit bids
- A too-successful bidder who is consistently winning bids
- Social contact between the bid solicitors and bidders
- Lower quality goods from a new vendor
- A company procurement officer living beyond his/her means.

There are various ways to make a bribe payment to avoid detection. Many bribes take the form of expensive gifts, trips, drugs, or sexual favors. Of course the most preferred bribe is cash. When very large sums are involved, cash is not always practical. Cash transactions of more than $10,000 should generate reporting documents. One of the favored methods to get cash to the bribe-taker is for the bribe-taker to apply for a loan. The company paying the bribe then makes the loan payments for the bribe-taker. A variation on this idea

$$C = P - A$$

Corruption = Power − Accountability

**EXHIBIT 7.4**

would be the bribe-payer making payments to the bribe-taker's credit card(s). In some cases, the bribe-payer simply hands over a credit card as the bribe and then pays the bills, which are sent directly to the bribe-payer. A bribe might take the form of a house sold at a fraction of market value, or the spouse of the bribe-taker being employed by the bribe-paying company at a high salary or no-show job.

Every industry has its rotten apples. At Home Box Office (HBO), the director of print services was sentenced in 2004 to five years of probation for soliciting more than $400,000 in kickbacks from vendors in exchange for awarding them HBO ad business. She used some of that money to pay for a lavish wedding at the Plaza Hotel in Manhattan.[6]

---

### EXECUTIVE INSIGHT 7.2 FRANK GRUTTADAURIA: THE ROGUE EMPLOYEE

Rogue employees can cause great financial and reputational damage to an organization. It is unusual for a rogue employee to disclose a fraud personally through pangs of guilt and a change in personal rationalization. However, this is exactly what happened in the case of rogue employee Frank Gruttadauria. In January 2002, Gruttadauria sent a letter to the Cleveland office of the FBI identifying himself as Managing Director of the brokerage firm Lehman Brothers in Cleveland. In the confession letter, Gruttadauria stated, "During the course of the past 15 years, I have caused misappropriation through various methods which resulted in other violations. It has occurred at brokerage firms Lehman Brothers, SG Cowen Securities Corp., Cowen & Co., Hambrecht & Quist, Inc. and LF Rothschild, Inc."[viii]

The FBI started an investigation, as did Lehman Brothers. It was discovered that Gruttadauria maintained a "stand-alone" computer that was not connected to Lehman's computer network. This computer allowed Gruttadauria to create phony customer account statements that he caused to be mailed to customers. A comparison of Lehman's actual client statements and the doctored statements in Gruttadauria's computer found 110 instances in which statements that were "mailed to said customers contained grossly inflated values totaling approximately $289 million, while the actual account values of the same Lehman Brothers' customer accounts on the same date were only approximately $12 million."[ix]

Gruttadauria had stolen millions of dollars for years, and no one was the wiser. He worked at SG Cowen prior to working at Lehman Brothers and committed the same fraud there. The FBI initially estimated that he cooked his client's books by as much as $300 million.[x] Soon an arrest warrant was issued for Gruttadauria, and after a nationwide search, he surrendered to authorities on February 9, 2002. The continuing investigation found that Gruttadauria was operating a Ponzi scheme, taking money from one investor and paying it to another. He moved money out of the accounts of his richest investors without their knowledge to cover withdrawal requests from other clients.[xi] He did this to avoid detection while he was cleaning out his clients' accounts. He diverted client statements to a post office box he opened and then sent clients phony statements showing inflated balances. When he fled, he created phony identities to avoid detection by law enforcement.

On February 21, 2002, the Securities and Exchange Commission (SEC) charged Gruttadauria and two companies he controlled, DH Strategic Partners and JYM Trading Trust, with a massive fraud against more than 50 customers over a 15-year period. In August 2002, Gruttadauria pled guilty to securities fraud, mail fraud, identity theft, and making false statements to a bank. He was subsequently sentenced to seven years in prison.

Gruttadauria's last employer, Lehman Brothers, may have missed the red flags. He produced almost $6 million in commissions in 1999 compared with the industry average of $485,500. He also earned almost $3 million in compensation.[xii] In his letter to the FBI, Gruttadauria said, "The various firms' greed and lack of attention on a senior level contributed greatly" to his committing the fraud and "I hardly believe that I could have done this without detection for so long."[xiii]

Defrauded investors also felt that Gruttadauria was not the only one to blame for the fraud. They blamed the brokerage firms that employed Gruttadauria for not doing enough to detect and stop the fraud. Greater attention to internal controls, compliance, and fraud prevention programs may have caught this fraud earlier. Gruttadauria's free reign at the brokerage firms where he worked may have contributed to the fraud going undetected for so long. He created phony account statements, used post office boxes to send out client statements, and had a personal computer not connected to the company network but no compliance programs ever detected this as possible fraud.

Defrauded investors sued Lehman Brothers and SG Cowen for the return of their defrauded investments. A prosecutor in Cuyahoga County, Ohio, threatened to hold Lehman Brothers and SG Cowen criminally liable under a theory of "willful blindness" for not discovering and stopping the fraud. As a result, Lehman Brothers and SG Cowen agreed in January 2004 to pay $1.74 million and $4.5 million, respectively, to the county prosecutor to settle the case and avoid criminal charges.[xiv] Both companies also settled civil proceedings with the SEC but did not admit to any wrongdoing. Lehman Brothers agreed to pay $2.5 million to the SEC, and SG Cowen agreed to pay $5 million.[xv]

---

[viii] *United States Securities and Exchange Commission, Plaintiff, v. Frank D. Gruttadauria, DH Strategic Partners Inc., JYM Trading Trust*, defendants, United States District Court, Northern District of Ohio, filed February 21, 2002, 1:02CV324, 6.

[ix] *United States v. Frank D. Gruttadauria*, defendant, criminal complaint, United States District Court, Northern District of Ohio, sworn to by FBI Special Agent William Henterly, Jr. on January 2, 2002, 3.

[x] Susanne Craig and Charles Gasparino, "Lehman's Gruttadauria Planned Run With Aliases, French Francs," *Wall Street Journal*, February 12, 2002, C8.

[xi] Teresa Dixon Murray, John Caniglia, and Bill Lubinger, "Mr. Coffee Co-Founder, Forbes Lose Millions," *Cleveland Plain Dealer*, February 7, 2002, A1.

[xii] Charles Gasparino and Susanne Craig, "Disappearing Act: A Lehman Broker Vanishes, Leaving Losses and Questions," *Wall Street Journal*, February 8, 2002, A1.

[xiii] Ibid.

[xiv] "Firms Agree to Pay for Broker's Fund," *Wall Street Journal*, January 8, 2004, C7.

[xv] Ann Davis and Susanne Clark, "Cowen, Lehman Are to Settle Case of Broker's Fraud," *Wall Street Journal*, January 6, 2004, C6.

## FRAUD PREVENTION VERSUS SECURITY

Finding a practical application for the knowledge presented in books is not always easy for many business executives. One major problem in the corporate response to internal fraud is that managers often confuse fraud prevention and examination with security guard/access control functions. There are really three separate concepts: Internal controls are set in place to provide reasonable assurance that there are no errors or irregularities on the financial statement. Fraud prevention is the proactive and examination is the reactive mitigation of all types of fraud including asset misappropriation by employees and fraud by customers. Security functions prevent theft and damage by employees or outsiders and protect company assets and employees. All three of these are separate functions and are best handled by different specialists. A sound fraud prevention program goes beyond compliance with Sarbanes-Oxley and should not be thought of as providing good "security." To illustrate this point, the authors offer the following short story.

### Hey, the Rats Are Stealing My Cheese!

Millions of business executives enjoyed the wisdom of the mice in Dr. Spencer Johnson's creative book *Who Moved My Cheese?* The following story uses the same cheese analogy to illustrate how most business managers think of fraud prevention. *Hey, the Rats Are Stealing My Cheese!* explains what every fraud prevention professional wants business executives to know, that fraud prevention is not security and security is not fraud prevention.

For the purposes of the story, Cheese is any valuable commodity. The mice are workers and security guards at the Cheese Company. In exchange for a measured amount of money each week, some mice transport and keep track of the Cheese, and one team of mice guards the Cheese from rats. Rats (fraudsters) are unwilling to work for a living and would rather find creative ways to get Cheese without working for it. The business manager of the Cheese Company does not know much about keeping out rats, but he has the mice working for him. He thinks he has nothing to worry about. The board of directors and the shareholders know that there are mice on duty looking out for rats.

At first, the mice just had to walk the perimeter of the company, sniffing for signs of rats—holes, scratches, or missing Cheese. When the mice found holes that had been dug by rats, they set traps. Eventually, the rats learned how to avoid the traps. The mice began to take more proactive measures. Sweet poisons were placed around the facility just in case a rat was able to enter.

On occasion, rats were able to enter the facility, but they were lured by the sweet poison and died. The business manager praised the ingenuity of the mice in protecting the company from rats. The head mouse was given a plaque and a bonus. However, the word eventually got out about the poison. Soon the rats learned to resist the sweet smell of the poison and were able to steal large amounts of Cheese. The business manager called in the mice and told them to find the rats.

One mouse, Sharp, was a little sharper than the other mice. He was given the task of tracking down the rats that had broken in and stolen the Cheese. Sharp began to interview all the mice that worked in the area where the hole had been dug. Although none of the mice interviewed said they knew anything, one mouse was a little odd in his responses. Sharp decided to do a background check on the odd mouse. A record check was ordered. It cost some money, but a great deal can be learned from such things.

Sharp was shocked to learn that the odd mouse was, in reality, a small rat! After a long interrogation, and after being confronted by the records, the rat confessed. The hole had not been dug in from outside, rather the rat/mouse had dug the hole from the inside out to his rat friends.

After calling the city exterminators, who showed up with their uniforms and handcuffs, to come and pick up the rat, Sharp set out on a mission to check all the mice in the company. They could not afford to have any more rats working for them. The business manager saw that the cost of the checks would be less than the cost of losing Cheese to rat employees.

The business manager paid for security cameras to watch for any holes being dug from the inside or the outside of the building. One mouse watched the TV monitor of the security cameras. There would be no more theft of Cheese!

Several weeks passed without any Cheese being stolen. The business manager told everyone that the cost of the security equipment and the background checks had been worth the price, as there was no longer a theft problem. The business manager got a bonus and shook hands with everyone.

The rats were not about to give up their quest for free Cheese. They did research to determine how the Cheese Company did business. The rats learned that customers were sent Cheese in exchange for a magic 16-digit number and an expiration date. With such information, the rats could have Cheese mailed directly to their nests. The rats set out to find some magic numbers.

There were some rats that lived in a hotel, where travelers stayed overnight. The travelers gave magic numbers to the hotel clerks. These hotel clerks had lots of magic numbers. One night, some rats snuck into the hotel office and copied down a list of magic numbers and expiration dates. Armed with these magic numbers, the rats began calling the Cheese Company to order Cheese. Thousands of pounds of Cheese were shipped to hundreds of rats before the company that issued the magic numbers called the Cheese Company. The man at the magic number company told the business manager at the Cheese Company that he would not be paid for all the Cheese that had been shipped to rats using stolen magic numbers. The company had lost even more Cheese than ever.

"How could this happen?" demanded the business manager of the head mouse.

"I don't know, but we will find a way to stop it," the head mouse said.

"I have already allowed you to spend all kinds of money for equipment to prevent this," the business manager said angrily.

"We did not expect this," the head mouse said. "The rats keep changing their tactics!"

"You get that security mouse, Sharp, to figure out how to stop this! I need to know all the names and addresses on all the rat orders and how much was lost. Then call the city exterminators, with their uniforms and handcuffs, and work with them to find these rats!"

"Yes, sir!" answered the head mouse, but he did not know anything about how city exterminators worked. The head mouse was a little scared to work with city exterminators. The city exterminators wore uniforms, and when they showed up, everyone knew there was trouble. The head mouse knew nothing about magic numbers or how the rats could have gotten them. He did not know whether the numbers had been stolen from the Cheese Company's customer database or somewhere else. The head mouse called Sharp and told him to handle the assignment.

Sharp knew how to watch for rats breaking into the warehouse and how to ask for background checks, and even how to make it harder for the rats to get to the Cheese. However, Sharp did not know anything about magic numbers or city exterminators or how they worked. Sharp told the business manager that the company needed to create a new unit. The mice were not exterminators. The business manager needed to find a Certified Rat Exterminator (a CRE). This CRE would not work with or report to the security mice. The CRE would check security policies and procedures and give recommendations on how to improve security, but the day-to-day functions of the security mice would not be the responsibility of the CRE. A CRE would only look for tricky rats, which the city exterminators didn't have time to try to find. Although the city exterminators did go after rats, it usually had to be a pretty big rat before they would get interested.

Everyone knows that city exterminators are more concerned with gang-related pests like ants and termites. City exterminators are also good at taking out the occasional assassin bug or poisonous spiders, which cause pain and suffering, but a CRE only does rats. The new CRE would report directly to the Chief Financial Officer of the Cheese Company. The CRE would have to set up denial tables to keep track of the addresses used by rats. Any order that was being sent to a known rat nest would be held. The CRE had lots of experience dealing with rats and knew how rats thought.

The CRE set up all kinds of tables and data mining to find rats that were using magic numbers without permission. When the CRE showed his plan to the CFO and the business manager, there was great debate on the cost of these measures.

"We have already spent a lot of money on security!" the business manager said.

"This is not security," said the CRE. "This is a proactive approach to stop rats with stolen magic numbers from getting free Cheese. This is something your customers have come to expect. I would like to look at all our transactions. There are rats everywhere, and if we do not go looking for them, they will just keep stealing."

"How can you be so sure that you will find rats? We are already doing background checks for rats in the workplace."

"We can use tables and data to find activity that does not fit normal business activity. This activity is most likely rat activity," the CRE said. "We will lower the amount of chargebacks to our clients' magic number merchant accounts. The Cheese sellers will be delighted, but you need a CRE and a staff of security mice. We are separate functions with the same goal: to save our Cheese from rats."

### Lessons Learned from Rats

- On average, "rats" employed by the company steal 6 percent of the company's annual revenue.[7]
- In more than 80 percent of all workplace fraud, cash is the target.[8]
- More than 5 percent of all applicants for entry-level employment have been rats.[9]
- Mice (security guards) do not want to be exterminators (fraud investigators), and exterminators do not want to be mice.

### Roles of Security and Fraud Prevention

As Exhibit 7.5 shows, several of the functions of the security department overlap with the role of the fraud prevention unit; the two functions should not be confused with each other. Fraud prevention is more closely aligned with finance and internal audit, whereas security is more aligned with operations. Security and fraud prevention units often do work together, as do the security and IT units.

## IT'S NOT ALL HERE

Although this chapter has covered internal fraud that companies will probably experience, it is by no means intended to be an all-inclusive encyclopedia of all of the various types of schemes and frauds. There are hundreds of ways employees can steal, and it is not practical to cover them all.

## ENDNOTES

1. Association of Certified Fraud Examiners, *2004 Report to the Nation on Occupational Fraud and Abuse* (Austin, TX: ACFE, 2004), 15.

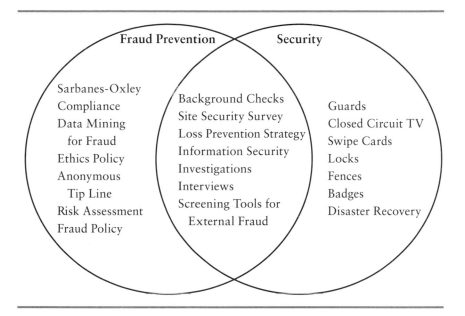

**EXHIBIT 7.5** Where Fraud Prevention and Security Meet

2. Joseph T. Wells, *Occupational Fraud and Abuse* (Austin, TX: Obsidian Publishing, 1997), 159.
3. Frank Abagnale, *The Art of the Steal* (New York: Broadway Books, 2001), 57.
4. Nicole Gull, "Taking the Pain out of Payday," *INC.*, January 2005, 36.
5. Association of Certified Fraud Examiners, *Fraud Examiners Manual,* (Austin, TX: ACFE, 2006), Section 1.530.
6. Jim Edwards, "Taken for a Ride," *Brandweek,* November 1, 2004, VNU Business Media, 24.
7. Joseph W. Koletar, *Fraud Exposed* (New York: John Wiley & Sons), 34.
8. Association of Certified Fraud Examiners, *2004 Report to the Nation on Occupational Fraud and Abuse* (Austin, TX: ACFE, 2004), 15.
9. According to Investigative Services & Technologies, Inc., Nashville, TN.

# CHAPTER 8

# Views from Both Sides of the Fence: Interviews with a Fraudster and a Fraud Investigator

## EXECUTIVE SUMMARY

There is much to be learned when one hears both sides of the story. Fraudsters and fraud investigators have different perspectives on the corporate fraud scandals. Corporate fraudster Walt Pavlo, who "cooked the books" and in the process defrauded a company out of almost $6 million, believes that employees are basically good but get corrupted by the system. A mixture of temptation, greed, and opportunity turned him to the dark side, and he paid a heavy price. Fraud prevention and internal controls were almost nonexistent at Pavlo's former company, with many temporary employees and manual transactions. The tone at the top was "meet the numbers."

The other part of the equation is the professional fraud investigators who are responsible for uncovering these massive frauds. Carl Pergola is a renowned Certified Fraud Examiner who is often called on by public and private companies to detect and prevent the financial schemes that victimize them. His insights into the current and future states of corporate crime form further proof that preventing fraud is paramount. Pergola believes that some employees have questionable moral characters and will steal if presented with an opportunity. Pergola talks about state-of-the art fraud prevention procedures: Employee and Vendor Screening, Ethics Policies, Fraud Awareness Training of Employees, Anonymous Hotlines, and Experienced Investigators.

## A FORMER FRAUDSTER AND NEW MAN: A CONVERSATION WITH WALT PAVLO

Much of what has been discussed in this book involves the criminal actions of corporate fraudsters. When the fraud is discovered, some deny any wrongdoing and, as is their legal and constitutional right, fight the government charges in court. Others take responsibility for their criminal acts, plead guilty, and face the consequences. The very act of admitting to oneself that the actions were wrong is but the first step in the redemption process.

Walt Pavlo is an example of such a person. He was a senior manager of credit and collections for telecom giant MCI in the mid-1990s before the company was bought by WorldCom. Pavlo directed the billing and collections process in their reseller division. His division was having a hard time collecting fees from resellers, but Pavlo came up with a unique approach to the problem. He turned to "cooking the books": between April 1996 and January 1997, he and others defrauded MCI of almost $6 million.

When the company became aware of the fraud, it launched an internal investigation that eventually involved the FBI and the IRS. As the pressure increased to a near breaking point, Pavlo turned himself in to the FBI and admitted his crimes. He pled guilty to wire fraud, money laundering, and obstruction of justice and received a nearly three and a half-year prison term in March 2001. He completed a drug and alcohol abuse program while in prison that reduced his sentence, as did good behavior. He was subsequently transferred to a half-way house for six months and was released in March 2003. Pavlo now travels the country lecturing at major university business schools, professional societies, corporations, and law enforcement agencies concerning the mistakes he made in his business career.

After graduating from West Virginia University in 1985, where he received an engineering degree, Pavlo joined Goodyear Aerospace as an estimator in its military defense division. There he designed and implemented computer estimating systems for complex military contracts. He left Goodyear in 1988 to work at GEC Avionics, Ltd. Pavlo was a senior contract administrator responsible for pricing and negotiations for military avionics equipment sold to countries around the world. While working at GEC Avionics, Pavlo completed an executive MBA program at Mercer University. After graduation in 1991, he began searching for a job more suited to his new degree in finance and accepted employment at MCI Telecommunications, Inc. in Atlanta, GA. He was given the title of manager of credit and collections and within three years was named senior manager of a $1 billion per month portfolio of clients. These clients represented wholesale carrier customers that bought long distance from MCI and resold it under their own brand name. Some of the clients were household names like Sprint and AT&T; many others were start-up long distance companies in the new world of deregulation.

When Pavlo was asked by the authors to submit to an interview for this book, he readily agreed and replied, "I truly appreciate the opportunity to express my opinions on the important subject of white-collar crime and its negative impacts to society, the victims, the convicted felon, and his/her family." The words in this interview are Pavlo's and whether one agrees or not with him, they provide much to think about.

Q: **Explain the fraud scheme you were involved in.**

A: A number of customers in MCI's reseller division began to default on payments during 1995. Frustrated by the fact that everybody (resellers of long distance service) seemed to be cheating, a person outside the company and I developed a scheme to enrich ourselves.

I would apply pressure to MCI's customers to pay up or be disconnected. I would institute a deadline with the customer that, if violated, would result in disconnection of service. The customer would then start a desperate search for funds to meet the demand for payment. These amounts were often in the millions of dollars. With what seemed like a stroke of good luck, my accomplice would show up at the MCI customer's doorstep within a day or two and portray himself as an investor looking to purchase telecommunications companies. The timing could not have been better.

My accomplice would send in accountants and scour the customer's finances. In the end, the angel investor would recommend that he pay off the debt to MCI for the customer so that they could begin their financial relationship. In return for paying off this debt, the angel investor would require a substantial fee, usually about $250,000, for putting the investment together and aggressive repayment of the loan amount in weekly payments to Cayman Island accounts.

The customer, desperate for money, quickly accepted. However, no money was ever sent by the angel investor to pay off the debt owed to MCI. Instead, I cooked the books at MCI to give the customer the impression that the outstanding balances had been paid by the angel investor. The customer believed the debt had been paid and began sending money to the Caymans. My accomplice and I did this with seven MCI customers and had $6 million in the Caymans within six months.

**Q: Were there internal controls in place that should have prevented your fraud?**

A: The biggest reason that my crime was not detected earlier is the simple fact that nobody questions good news. MCI had a number of customers that were not paying their invoices, so whenever I had a customer that suddenly paid $2 million as a result of my scheme, it was good news that nobody questioned. Everyone wanted to believe in the good news. My bosses believed, the internal auditors believed, and the customers even believed that an angel investor could come up with a few million dollars in a matter of days to pay off its debt to MCI. Good news is rarely criticized and rarely investigated. Had my bosses or an internal audit group asked me a simple question, Where's the check? I could not have provided one and was not prepared to invent one.

**Q: How did the internal controls at MCI break down to allow you and your co-conspirators to commit this fraud for so many months without detection?**

A: The first area of breakdown was the lack of control we had over temporary contractors. Of the 120 people in the department, nearly 50 percent were temporary contractors performing full-time roles for MCI. MCI, like many fast growing companies, hired temporary help to not only meet demand for increases in work load but to also reduce costs associated with the overhead of full-time, permanent employees. In this environment, turnover of employees exceeded 100 percent each year. With new employees came challenges of controlling passwords, training, and still having to meet the month-end results with whatever staff was available. The results were that passwords were routinely shared between employees, training was on the fly, and naïve staffers could be shown any transaction and would ask few questions about the legitimacy of the transaction.

There were also multiple billing platforms at MCI as a result of acquisitions over the years. This was common among many long distance carriers who consolidated with mergers and acquisitions in the late 1990s. To accommodate these different billing platforms, revenue was combined from them onto a personal computer. On a personal computer, an analyst would calculate the contractual rates and then manually post the appropriate credits, or debits, back to the main accounts receivable system. For some companies this may be manageable, but at MCI we had tens of millions of dollars each month that were being credited off of accounts by manual billing systems. Many companies face the challenge of auditing off-line billing systems to accommodate special pricing situations, and most use a manual database or spreadsheet program to accomplish their desired goal. There were just very few checks on the manual billing systems, and there were also major holes in the audit controls as a result.

If one were to combine high employee turnover, loose audit controls, and aggressive financial goals for the department, it may create a unique situation in which fraud could occur. MCI's goals for collections were very aggressive and measured in the amounts of bad debt written off each month as well as Days Sales Outstanding (days between invoice being sent to customer and invoice being paid). These absolute goals were measured, but the means by which they were attained were governed by weak internal controls. As was mentioned earlier, many of the staff were contractors, and they knew that the best way to get hired was to do a good job. A good job was measured in minimal amounts of bad debt and Days Sales Outstanding. This mentality was not unique to temporary employees but was merely a reflection of management and executives over them.

**Q: Did MCI have a formal fraud prevention program in place? If not, would that have made a difference?**

A: I assume that MCI had a fraud prevention program in place though I never heard of it. Being a Fortune 100 company, I would think that such a program was in place, but I had never attended a class on the program nor received any indoctrination on a fraud prevention or ethics program.

It is hard to say whether it would have made a difference in my crime or not. I think having a program would have been important, but if there was management that was more concerned with the result rather than the means of obtaining the result, I am not sure that any fraud prevention program would ever prevail in such an environment.

**Q: Can you explain your thoughts about the importance of appropriate internal controls and robust fraud prevention programs?**

A: Many who get involved in white-collar crime represent first-time offenders who were in a position of responsibility and abused it. Had the person known that the controls in place within the company would have detected his or her behavior, they most likely would not have attempted the crime. White-collar felons commit crimes because they do not believe they will get caught.

It is management's responsibility to provide a safe workplace, and that concept should be extended to the areas of temptation that are a part of human nature. We live in a materialistic society, with various financial pressures such as family, credit, home, etc., and then we put these same people at the cash registers of the company with loose financial controls. I believe management would have a better chance at having employees embrace new financial control policies when they are presented as a means to protect them and not to burden them.

**Q: If you had been in charge at MCI, knowing what you now know, what kind of internal controls and prevention efforts would you have installed?**

A: Audit should have concentrated on automation of billing systems and accounts receivable posting systems. The manual transactions that were being generated by over one hundred analysts were being manually audited by only a few. In this way the auditors were outnumbered and were never going to catch up. In this environment, finding a few million dollars in a pile of over a billion (MCI's monthly accounts receivable balance for the carrier division) is likened to the needle in the haystack.

**Q: My understanding is that you had never committed fraud before the crimes that you were charged with. What made you turn to fraud?**

A: While I take full responsibility for my crime, and have paid a significant price for it as well, I was frustrated by the unethical behavior of MCI's customers (resellers of long distance) and MCI executives who provided extreme performance measures for my department. A number of MCI customers ran up large invoices and never paid them, thereby leaving us with hundreds of millions in bad debt. However, rather than recognize this bad debt, I was encouraged to work with my peers in accounting to come up with creative solutions to this and other bad news financial situations. It seemed to me that everyone (MCI's customers) was cheating, and my efforts in canvassing the country to collect on deadbeat customers were all in vain.

At the height of my frustration, I met with someone who worked outside of MCI in order to look for a new job. However, when I told him of my frustration, the MCI customer behavior, and the creative bookkeeping that I was doing, he had an idea. After a number of meetings I was convinced that the only way to get ahead in telecommunications was to learn how to cheat. Clearly I was wrong, but the scorecard of now defunct telecommunications companies and exorbitant financial fraud in the industry illustrates the environment in which I found myself. Remember, my customers were the likes of Global Crossing, Winstar, Qwest, and WorldCom, all of whom went on to infamy for their creative business practices.

**Q: When you were doing the fraud, did you ever worry you would get caught?**

A: I worried but I did not feel that I would get caught. My own conscience was more of a problem than any internal controls. The ease with which we were able to move money internally at MCI to cover our fraud and the ease of convincing an MCI customer to go with the angel investor was remarkable. We stayed within the guidelines of our crime to keep the news good, and nobody would question how we were accomplishing what we did.

Having never committed a fraud before made for a new experience. It was exciting and not in a good way . . . exciting as in I want to throw up. Once the money started to flow, there were times that I felt that I deserved the money and the temporary excitement that it brought to my life. However, when I went to bed at night I found myself alone and felt sick at the person that I had become. Within eight months of committing the first act of fraud, I was near a nervous breakdown and could no longer function. I had not even been caught, but I wanted the madness of the crime to end.

**Q: Did a presence or absence of "tone at the top" at MCI impact what you did?**

A: MCI's tone was meet the numbers. When those numbers were not going to be made, then executives very high within MCI made some financial decisions that changed the way I thought about addressing difficult situations. Whether it was instructions to conduct creative accounting or the setting of unrealistic goals, it was clear to me that the only way to survive in this culture was to cheat. It was a very clear message.

**Q: All the money that you embezzled did not make your life better. Can you explain your descent into despair?**

A: I think that many may view participation in a white-collar crime as it is portrayed in a John Grisham novel. However, clarity of thought and self-control are not normal for someone who is in the midst of a complex crime involving millions of dollars in offshore accounts. It is frightening. Purchases at expensive stores and travel did little to erase guilt and fear. Someone once had asked me why I did not flee the country once I was found out, as if running would solve this problem. I did not have the mental wherewithal to comprehend a life on some secluded island. Neither the crime nor the money did anything for me except destroy my ability to think clearly.

**Q: Can you detail what went through your mind when you realized that the fraud had been discovered?**

A: I was tired of running, so when I knew that they knew (the authorities), it was a relief that I was not going to go on committing a crime that was driving me insane. Then I was sick at the thought of facing a punishment and being sought after for my actions. I don't want to sound like a coward, but I was frightened and not able to face the wrong that I had done or the associated punishment. Then finally I was mad. Why had I been singled out in this corrupt business to pay a price for wrongs that many others were doing? I am not justifying my actions with these statements but am only telling what I thought and felt at the time. I have learned that it is far better to be an honest convicted felon than it ever was to be a dishonest executive that everyone believes has the world on a string.

**Q: What was the hardest part about admitting your crimes, pleading guilty, and going to prison?**

A: The hardest part, by far, is the impact that this has had on my family. While I prefer to not go into details, one can only imagine the pain shared by all when visiting someone that they love in prison. We have all made mistakes in our lives, but, thankfully, those who know of them are few. My mistake was most public and most tragic. Prison was easy if you knew you went by yourself. But the truth is that you take along a number of loved ones in the process, and lives are changed forever. I am two years out of prison as I write this now, and the sorrow that I feel in writing these lines is overwhelming. I can only hope that two years from now it will be better, but the impact of the prison experience on all of my family will never go away. In that way, I received a life sentence.

**Q: When you were in prison, you met other corporate fraudsters. Was there anything that struck you from your interactions with them?**

A: I only hung out with the guys who could face their own failures and understood why they were in prison. There were a number of inmates who could not come to grips with their actions and felt that they were wrongly incarcerated. I had no time for these guys. However, I met with a few guys who genuinely regretted their actions and were trying, even in prison, to begin their recovery. We prayed together, cried together, provided each other support, and discussed current events. I was in prison while Enron, WorldCom, and the rest of the large corporate frauds were being uncovered, and it made for great talk around the dinner table. We did not condone the behavior of those involved, but we all certainly understood the pressure that may have led to their undoing.

**Q: How would you characterize prison life?**

A: The media has done an injustice to society by portraying prison for white-collar felons as a type of club fed, where there are swimming pools, golf courses, conjugal visits, and a life of relaxation. Nothing could be further from the truth. White-collar felons are housed with general population inmates in the same conditions. In the facility where I was located, Edgefield, South Carolina, there were roughly 500 inmates, and about 50 of those were white-collar offenders. The others were primarily drug offenders and counterfeiters who had either short sentences or had worked their way down through the prison system to end up in a prison camp with minimum security.

It is a difficult existence of missing home, family, and freedom. There is not one day from the prison experience that I would call a good day. They were all lonely and miserable, but somehow you learn to cope and survive. To do this, you must live a life that keeps you out of trouble, so I found comfort in writing, books, and meditation.

I hated prison, which is exactly what you are supposed to do. It is an unkind place with no love and none of the conveniences that make life worth living. Prison is meant as a punishment, and the media needs to get that fact out to the public, but that doesn't make for a good story.

**Q: You committed your fraud scheme in the years before the enactment of Sarbanes-Oxley. Would it have stopped you?**

A: I think that the unique thing about Sarbanes-Oxley is that it makes everyone responsible for ethical behavior. In the past, executives ignored unethical or illegal activities but no longer. Executives' treatment of offenders within the company is just as important as their own offenses. There is a punishment now if the watcher doesn't watch or react to violations. The chances of being caught for unethical behavior in this type of environment are very high, and with that the chances of testing the financial systems of the company would have been reduced. Would it have stopped me? I would like to think so, but even if it had not stopped me, it would have caught me sooner.

**Q: Do you think that Sarbanes-Oxley's increased criminal penalties for fraud will act as a deterrent?**

A: I don't think that increased prison sentences are the answer. While I do believe that prison is a punishment and can be effective in changing behavior, especially for white-collar criminals, there is no need for these long sentences. I think the answer lies in the area of addressing economic crimes with economic solutions. White-collar criminals should have their assets taken away. My approach would be that they would give up ALL of their assets and start life over again after a few years reflecting on their actions. The government allows a person to go to prison with millions still in the bank. It is a reflection that money is more important than a human life and that seems excessive for a society that values life as we do in America.

If prison sentences alone deterred crime, we would not need the procedures that are a part of the Sarbanes-Oxley legislation. Sarbanes-Oxley will not eliminate white-collar crime, but it does raise the bar for internal controls and oversight. Both of these should lead to an executive considering that the likelihood of being caught is high and therefore not worth the risk.

Sarbanes-Oxley and various internal controls should be viewed as a way to protect employees as much as they protect shareholders. Employees are constantly under pressure both professionally and personally. Under these pressures, employees must be provided a safe and ethical environment in which to work where temptations are limited and they can concentrate on the issues at hand. An unethical or loosely managed organization may provide what seems like an easy solution to the employee's problems or a quick way to feed the ego. Such an environment, I believe, can turn a good employee into a fraudster. I've seen it happen.

**Q: What message would you send to corporate executives and others in business to convince them to never commit fraud?**

A: Just as your family enjoys the riches associated with good and ethical decisions that you make, so they will also share in your unethical decisions. Many times those involved in white-collar crimes were thinking that their actions would only impact themselves, but this is far from the truth. It affects family, coworkers, subordinates, superiors (and we all have superiors, even CEOs), and friends. In the isolation of making a decision that may be unethical, let the pictures on your desk speak to you. How will your decision affect their lives? Will you sacrifice your integrity to meet financial goals at work? Would you do something that would also punish your family?

Q: **You are now a speaker on corporate fraud and conduct numerous presentations all over the world. How do audiences react to you when they learn what you did?**

A: Thus far my audiences have received my message favorably. I believe that most audience members have never met a convicted felon nor do they completely understand how that person's thought processes work. The truth is that they find out that the fraudster thinks, looks, and acts very much like they do. They develop an understanding for the pressures that I was under and can envision themselves in the same situation. It is very powerful to convince someone in the audience that they too could find themselves in a situation where they could resort to unethical behavior.

What is most important for me to get across to audiences is that I view them as victims of my crime. In some ways my crime represented greed and the loss of trust in our financial markets. As victims, the audience deserves to hear these four things from me:

1. I'm sorry and deeply regret what I have done and the people that I have hurt.
2. I understand my crime and have learned from it.
3. I was punished and suffered dire consequences for my crime.
4. I have found a way to give back to society through lecturing and sharing my story.

In this way the audience can see that the justice system works. This is something that I think the media misses in its coverage of the high-profile cases where there seems to be no real punishment.

## THE FRAUD INVESTIGATOR THAT CORPORATE AMERICA CALLS: INTERVIEW WITH CARL PERGOLA

Antifraud and investigative specialist Carl Pergola has a distinguished career in fraud investigations, forensic accounting, and fraud prevention that has spanned two decades. He is currently a partner with BDO Seidman, LLP, one of the nation's premier professional service organizations. He also serves as a member of BDO Seidman's board of directors. Pergola is the National Director of the Litigation & Fraud Investigation Practice at BDO Seidman where he leads a professional team of former federal law enforcement agents, Certified Fraud Examiners, licensed private investigators, forensic accountants, former bank and regulatory investigators, and technology consultants that provide a wide variety of complex financial analysis and forensic services on behalf of businesses and individuals.

Over the years, Pergola has conducted extensive investigations involving many different types of fraud including management fraud, employee embezzlement, and investor fraud, which have accounted for billions of dollars in losses to both individuals and businesses. Many of these investigations related to high-profile matters including massive financial statement, retail brokerage, and hedge fund frauds. He has been hired on behalf of boards of directors, senior officers, public and private companies, public accounting firms, professional athletes, professional sports leagues and franchise owners, and high net worth individuals in the investigation and evaluation of fraud-related issues.

Pergola is both a Certified Public Accountant and a Certified Fraud Examiner and is an outspoken advocate for the creation of a culture of fraud prevention throughout the corporate environment. Providing an investigator's point of view, here are the responses of Pergola to a series of fraud-related questions.

Q:  When we take a look at the recent corporate environment, sometimes it is hard to believe that these kinds of frauds took place. What happened in those companies?

A:  I think it's only hard to believe for the people who lack experience or don't study history. If you take a look back in history and understand human nature, you will find that if you put money together with people you wind up with fraud. Go back to the 1850s; go back to the robber baron days. Go back to any situation when individuals had virtually absolute power. They were able to withhold information from people who would otherwise have an interest in that information (i.e., the investors), and they had the means and motivation to do it. If you study history you will see an ebb and flow of opportunities for individuals to get control over organizations and loot those organizations; as a result, new legislation was enacted and then over the next few years, corporate practices loosened up again and the cycle continued. I don't think anything will be different in ten years. As long as there are money and people, there will be fraud.

**Q:** **With all the legislation now, isn't this enough? Is compliance with legislation enough to address companies' antifraud needs?**

**A:** I think there is an adequate amount of legislation right now. If you go back to the COSO Report and look at what was in there, there was an adequate amount of information out there. The challenges are in the actual implementation. At the board level, what you have typically is a lack of a genuine understanding of why fraud occurs and how to prevent it from occurring. What does a board do to ensure that the organization is implementing a genuine antifraud program? I don't think any of the legislation really has the prescription. Now if you look at the Sarbanes-Oxley Act of 2002, for the most part, it really is just more punitive than informative. It increased the pain without necessarily providing a clear solution. What you actually need is a very good understanding of genuine best practices. The most experienced people in fraud prevention are people who are involved in fraud investigations, and they can provide insights and effective solutions. Organizations that are forward thinking are going to make sure they are implementing the best practices, not necessarily to comply with Sarbanes-Oxley or COSO or the organizational sentencing guidelines, but rather to actually create an environment where fraud is significantly less likely to occur.

**Q:** **With all this effort being put into fraud prevention and new legislation that has been passed, do you think frauds will significantly diminish over the next decade?**

A: The short answer is no. The fraudsters aren't going away. The conditions, human behaviors, and human weaknesses that existed since the beginning of time will continue to exist in the next decade. People will find opportunities; certain people will probe for vulnerabilities; and there will continue to be fraud long after I am out of this business. Certainly, organizations that implement and stay vigilant about maintaining antifraud procedures will significantly diminish the likelihood of experiencing a major fraud. I think one of the best things to come out of the publicity of frauds in the past several years, however, is a greater willingness on the part of organizations to investigate fraud thoroughly and to assist in criminal prosecution of individuals who commit fraud. I can tell you, ten years ago, when I was called in to address an employee embezzlement-type case, or a vendor kickback scheme, or an employee expense account abuse case, typically the company wanted a limited investigation done mostly just to quantify the loss. They might seek an insurance recovery, but very rarely would they go much further in seeking prosecution of the individual who committed the fraud. These days, it is more of a "Let's leave no stone unturned" approach; let's understand everything that this individual did while he was in our organization; let's understand how it occurred; and let's seek to have him prosecuted. I think that's the proper mind-set. Executives who shy away from the realities of fraud are doing their organizations a disservice. It's important to recognize and publicize the fact that fraud exists and that the organization will not tolerate fraud. This should be part of the orientation of employees into an organization and become part of the overall culture. So while I don't think frauds will diminish significantly in the next decade (absent continuous vigilance), I do think some organizations are moving in the right direction by aggressively investigating fraud.

Q: **What are the essential components of an effective fraud prevention program?**

A: Effective fraud prevention is actually multifaceted and includes internal controls, external audit procedures, and various ongoing procedures specifically geared towards fraud prevention and detection. It is these ongoing procedures, which I am focused on professionally along with effective responses to suspected fraud. I refer to these as Critical Anti-Fraud Procedures or the CAP^sm program.

Q: **How did you identify these specific Critical Anti-Fraud Procedures? Was it a response to increased media attention to corporate fraud?**

A: In part, the immediate impetus was the wave of corporate misconduct in the 2000/2001 period. I recall thinking at the time that I had extensive experience investigating frauds that had already occurred and that there had to be a way to use that experience to help companies on a prospective basis. The key to identifying critical antifraud procedures was to reverse-engineer numerous investigations that I conducted and ask "what could this company have done differently to prevent fraud or detect it sooner?"

Candidly, purely from a business prospective, I did not initially have a great interest in providing a proactive antifraud program. Being in a reactive business is very profitable, much more so than selling proactive services. I actually felt morally obligated to provide consulting on proactive antifraud procedures.

Q: **BDO has developed the Critical Anti-Fraud Procedures or the CAP^sm program. What are the components of the BDO CAP^sm program?**

A: In the CAP^sm program, we perform a comprehensive initial scheme and scenario-based fraud risk assessment before we implement its components. For public companies, much of this should have been covered by the Sabanes-Oxley Section 404 compliance work, but we conduct a fraud risk assessment if it had not been done or, upon review, is deficient. The specific components include: (1) graduated levels of increasingly comprehensive background checks and screening for potential vendors, customers, and prospective or current employees—especially those who are considered for promotion or expanded financial responsibilities; (2) evaluation of current antifraud and ethics policies and recommendations for changes and communication strategies; (3) education of employees in fraud detection, prevention, and the personal impact of committing fraud; (4) implementation of an anonymous fraud hotline along with related communications and assessment tools to measure effectiveness;

and (5) best practices investigation of suspected fraud. Additionally, we perform program monitoring for adherence to the components of the CAP<sup>sm</sup> program and advise the company on updating its antifraud procedures as needed. While many companies have some form of these components, few have fully developed and integrated each into a genuinely effective program. Each of the components has an individual role in detecting and preventing fraud; however, when properly implemented, they work together to support each other so that companies gain much more by implementing all of the components of CAP<sup>sm</sup> rather than approaching fraud prevention in a piecemeal manner.

Q: **What do you mean when you say that the CAP<sup>sm</sup> components support each other? Are there synergies to be gained by implementing all of the components?**

A: Yes. For example, educating employees to be aware of activities that they may not think of as "fraud" is much more powerful when a company also gives a means to anonymously report those activities (and itself maintains effective monitoring systems).

Many employees who were involved in some type of embezzlement are also involved in some type of illicit behavior. Countless times as part of an investigation, one of the first things we do is computer forensics. We find that employees involved in fraud also visit gambling Web sites or continuously visit pornographic Web sites; they have in some way disconnected from reality. There are simple monitoring systems and programs that can be implemented to review activity and see if someone has gone off the deep end or is using these types of Web sites extensively. In addition, well-trained employees may recognize unusual behavior and report it in a timely manner. I have found that, as part of many investigations, employees often recall noting unusual behavior but failed to report it because they didn't understand its significance.

Q: **Is there a downside to an organization to inaugurating a hotline?**

A: Frauds are most often discovered in three ways: error by the fraudster (too random for comfort); because they become too large to conceal (the worst possible scenario); or as a result of a whistle-blower. A properly implemented and administered hotline can only be beneficial. It is the means that boards and senior management can control and use for the company's advantage.

Every effort should be made to implement an anonymous tip hotline, and every effort should be made to educate and encourage employees to call the hotline when they suspect fraud. Put that system in place because that's the way frauds will come to light, and that's something you have control over.

**Q:** **What proof can you offer that a fraud prevention program is good business?**

**A:** One of the challenges is that because fraud by nature is hidden, it is natural to assume that it is not happening at your organization because you believe you are a good person, you employ good people, and you run a good company. One of the difficulties in implementing fraud prevention programs is that its benefit cannot be measured. You may never have a massive fraud occur, but you will never know whether or not your antifraud program was the reason. Given the massive amount of fraud and abuse that is out there, it is reasonable to assume that, in a proper culture, you will see fewer employees who abuse expense accounts or employee benefit programs. I can assure you that the cost associated with putting in a genuine antifraud program is de minimis compared with the benefit to be derived. I think that innovative forward-thinking CEOs who seek to make their organizations known for integrity will ultimately achieve greater profitability, and as such, enhance shareholder value.

**Q:** **What have you seen in terms of the costs to companies of fraud?**

**A:** I have seen billions of dollars of losses over the years. I have seen elderly investors' entire pensions wiped out. I've seen thousands of employees lose their 401k value, and ordinary and institutional investors lose hundreds of millions of dollars as a result of fraud. I've seen tens of thousands of employees out of work as a result of bankruptcy filings. Yet, I often hear of concerns over the cost of prevention programs, and to me it's almost laughable. In fact, if effective preventive programs had been in place, corporate America would probably have avoided some of the requirements of the Sarbanes-Oxley Act.

Q: What about the ethics of the individuals involved in fraud? What is their mind-set?

A: I think that certain people are simply born bad. Their goal is to take advantage of and hurt other people. There are people who get up in the morning trying to figure out how to benefit at someone else's expense. These people are constantly looking for opportunities and new ways to defraud. When companies are going public quickly as in the dot.com era, fraudsters would create an entity that is fraudulent, then borrow or run up the stock, and then bust out. They will look for opportunities for kickback schemes and opportunities for identify theft. You name it; they will look for those opportunities. For that reason, companies need to constantly stay vigilant because there will always be people who will do bad things.

You also have people who generally don't have a strong moral background. They may not be inherently bad, but given an opportunity, they would cheat. For example, they may be in an environment where they find out that if they are injured at work they can get disability benefits. They collect the benefits and then they go out and get a second job. They may not think there is anything wrong with that because other people they know are doing it and that's all the rationalization they need to do it themselves. Again, this is why companies need to stay vigilant. If something in their organization suggests to employees that it's okay to cheat or that others are cheating, these people will cheat.

You also have people who are inherently good people, but certain pressures come on them, which cause them to go into a different mode. Those pressures could be real, like a very serious financial problem caused by the most understandable reasons, such as a sick family member, inadequate healthcare coverage, or some reason that they need to get money. Perceived financial need may stem from trying to live a lifestyle similar to what some of their friends are living, or they may be involved in other types of inappropriate behavior. Their marriage may be falling apart. They may have another relationship and, therefore, need to support their existing family at the same time they are supporting another relationship. Those people may find themselves in a position where they are under pressure to commit a fraud. Now all they need is to see an opportunity. This is another reason why companies need to be vigilant all the time.

It doesn't matter that new legislation has passed that requires officers to make disclosures or provides additional jail time in the event of a criminal conviction. Those factors do not change the fact that you have inherently bad people, people with minimal moral character, and people with some moral character who are going to break under pressure. I think there are a relatively small number of people who are of the highest moral character and even in the worst possible circumstances will not breach that moral character. If you think of things that way, then you start to understand why there is such a prevalence of fraud.

**Q: What has been the effect of recent frauds on board members?**

A: If you look at certain recent court cases, you are starting to see these issues touch the board. In most of the bigger cases, like WorldCom and Enron, not only did actual dollars come out of the pockets of the board members, but a significant amount of time was involved in defending themselves in these cases. I think it can no longer be business as usual at the board level. One of the provisions of the Sarbanes-Oxley Act requires disclosure of whether the audit committee is comprised of at least one individual who is deemed a financial expert. I can assure you that this individual will become the focus of more and more attention as problems arise within the organization. Investors and other interested parties are going to be looking to board members to ask what they did to ensure that the organization had a genuine antifraud program. If you want to avoid being exposed in litigation, you have to have 20/20 foresight, because prosecutors and plaintiffs attempt to hold companies to a standard of 20/20 hindsight. They look at everything you did and put it into a context of what you should have done at that time.

**Q: What are the future challenges? Do you think the use of computers by fraudsters has changed the types of frauds that are being committed?**

A: For the most part, the answer is no. Many of the frauds such as financial statement fraud, expense account abuse, kickback schemes, and embezzlement are the same. It is just that the computer provides an additional tool that the fraudster can use to commit a fraud. With that said, you are seeing certain new frauds and threats arise, which have come about through the use of computers and access to electronic information. In addition, theft of large volumes of personal data leads to various forms of credit-related fraud. In many respects, electronic information may make it easier for someone to commit a fraud, but it also leaves an incredibly useful trail for the investigators. Remember, most information on a computer is extremely difficult to actually delete. Unless the computer is destroyed completely and is unavailable, there is a very good chance that we will be able to retrieve the information. We found over the years from an investigative standpoint that securing e-mails and looking at information on hard drives and servers often lead us very quickly to incriminating evidence.

Q: **What message do you have for board members and chief executives?**

A: Most board members, and most CEOs, realize now that they are vulnerable and that there is a possibility, even a significant likelihood, that if a material fraud occurs in their organization, they are going to be held accountable. At the board level, this means reputational harm, disruption of normal personal and business activities, and potential financial damages, which may not be covered by insurance. Worse, at the CEO level, there is a possibility that they may be held criminally responsible. So keep this in mind, board members and CEOs should actively embrace fraud prevention within their organizations. I think it's their best line of defense in the event of a material fraud within their company.

A final bit of advice: when a company is implementing an antifraud environment, I think one of the first questions it should ask the service provider for antifraud services is: Can you provide a detailed discussion of the types of frauds you have actually investigated? There are many individuals and organizations out there talking about fraud prevention that have never actually investigated a fraud. Someone who has investigated fraud can give you some simple techniques that can be used to prevent fraud. So fraud prevention is cost effective, when the information you are getting comes from an experienced fraud investigator.

# CHAPTER 9

# External Fraud Schemes: The Rest of the Fraud Story

**EXECUTIVE SUMMARY**

To be fully protected, companies need to be concerned with more than just internal fraud schemes such as financial statement fraud and asset misappropriation. They can just as easily be victimized by external frauds such as the Ponzi, Pyramid, Advance Fee, and Bust-Out schemes. Credit card fraud is also a common fraud affecting companies who do business using credit cards. The losses from credit card fraud can be substantial. The potential impact from online frauds can damage both a business and its relationship of trust with its customers. Corporate fraud solutions must include proactive measures to be fully protected. The Address Verification System (AVS) and Card Security Value (CSV) are but two tools to prevent credit card fraud. These and other detection and prevention solutions must be used and improved for a successful fraud prevention program.

Many people consider fraud committed by nonemployees to be consumer fraud and therefore not a business issue to be addressed by a corporate fraud prevention program. This is a false assumption. Companies like the Cheese Company described in Chapter 7 that do not take proper steps to protect themselves from external fraud can find themselves with massive losses. Protecting the company from external crime is not a job for the security department alone.

This chapter examines some of the classic external fraud schemes as well as some of the newer developments that have occurred since the rise of the Internet.

## CLASSIC FRAUD SCHEMES

### THE PONZI SCHEME

Charles Ponzi came to America from Italy in the early twentieth century. He eventually turned to fraud. By 1920, Ponzi convinced many victims in Boston to invest in his "too good to be true" investment deal. It was a "robbing Peter to pay Paul" scheme. Using the money of new investors to pay high rates of return to the early investors, Ponzi soon got plenty of word-of-mouth publicity. Many of those who received 50 percent returns on their initial investments reinvested them with Ponzi. Soon, Ponzi was receiving hundreds of thousands of dollars per day from investors. Ponzi took in over $20 million and paid out $15 million in interest, spending the remaining $5 million on himself and his wife.

Authorities shut down the scheme and sent Ponzi to prison for 10 years. He died penniless in Brazil in 1949. Today, any fraudulent investment scheme that pays returns to the early investors with the money of later investors is called a Ponzi scheme. Unfortunately, we have not learned from the past as Ponzi schemes are still commonplace.

### THE PYRAMID SCHEME

This is a type of Ponzi scheme, but there are differences. Whereas true Ponzi schemes are marketed as investments, pyramid schemes are often actually marketed as pyramids and multilevel marketing opportunities. However, they are still fraudulent investments. Members benefit most, not by selling an investment opportunity, but by recruiting new "salespeople." The ruse is usually the sale of household products and services. There is an up-front charge to get started, which goes to pay those who got into the pyramid earlier. No one is really selling the products, just recruiting new members who will feed the pyramid. Like the Ponzi scheme, the money coming in from new recruits is used to pay off the early investors. The pyramid eventually collapses because there are not enough people to sustain the scheme.

## THE ADVANCE FEE SCHEME

This fraud has been made popular by millions of letters and e-mails (known as "419 letters" after the section of the Nigerian penal code that deals with this fraud) from Nigeria. Advance fee schemes advise the mark about winning a prize, or that help is needed to move a large sum of money out of a foreign country. All that is required is for the mark to send several thousand dollars to pay fees or taxes. Those who send the money never hear anything back.

Whereas the preceding three classic frauds target individuals and are classified as consumer fraud, there are many other frauds that are used by those posing as vendors or customers to steal from businesses.

## THE BUST-OUT SCAM

A "Bust-Out" refers to a fraud committed by a subject who establishes a pattern of prompt payment on small orders. After several small orders have been transacted with no problems, the mark is no longer suspicious. At this point, the large order is made. When the goods are delivered, the customer does not pay for the goods and moves away. This can also be done in reverse, with the subject being a supplier of goods. In these situations, the supplier offers a very good price but requires payment prior to delivery. After several small orders, the victim company gets comfortable with the idea that the supplier is legitimate. As soon as a large order is placed, the supplier takes the money and runs.

**EXECUTIVE INSIGHT 9.1: WENDY'S "FINGER HOAX" PROVES COSTLY**

External fraud schemes can impact an organization in a number of ways. The financial loss can pale in comparison with the reputational damage that occurs when fraud crosses the line and becomes a corporate and public relations nightmare. One example is the alleged product tampering that Wendy's International, Inc. faced in 2005. Wendy's is one of the world's largest restaurant operating and franchising companies, with over 9,700 worldwide locations. Their brand loyalty and reputation for quality food has been a mainstay of their success over the years, yet an incident on March 22, 2005, was about to bring all that success into question.

A woman dining at a San Jose, California, Wendy's restaurant claimed that she found a severed finger in a bowl of chili she had just purchased. The woman was repulsed by the experience. She hired an attorney who promptly filed a claim against Wendy's and threatened a damaging lawsuit. The story made national headlines and focused on Wendy's food-handling practices. The incident spawned jokes from late-night talk show hosts and others. Negative publicity was having an impact. Fewer customers ate at Wendy's. Sales for the first quarter of 2005 fell $1.5 million in part because of the woman's claim that she found a severed finger in her food. The western region of Wendy's was hit the hardest, with a decrease in same-store sales.[i]

Wendy's is to be applauded for what it did next. Rather than caving in and paying out millions of dollars just to make the troubling affair go away, Wendy's quickly started an internal investigation to learn the facts. They teamed with law enforcement officials in San Jose and elsewhere. Every restaurant employee was interviewed, as were food suppliers. A massive search was conducted for anyone who had lost a finger and who could have been the source. On April 7, 2005, Wendy's posted a $50,000 reward on their Web site "for the first person providing verifiable information leading to the positive identification of the origin of the foreign object found" at their San Jose restaurant. Wendy's President and Chief Operating Officer stated that "It's very important to our company to find out the truth in this incident."[ii] He also said, "Our brand reputation has been affected nationally." Wendy's then doubled the reward to $100,000, ran newspaper ads communicating the reward, and listed a toll-free information hotline for tips.[iii]

Authorities conducted an innovative "Ingredient Trace Back" investigation to determine whether "the finger specimen came from the production, transportation, and/or preparation of the Wendy's chili." The analysis found no evidence connecting the finger to the chili. The police were also able to disprove certain statements made by the woman. A search warrant was conducted at her residence. In addition, the police learned that the woman had a history of filing "nuisance" suits against corporations, and an unrelated criminal allegation surfaced. On April 21, 2005, the woman was arrested and charged with attempted grand theft.[iv]

As the police continued their investigation, they learned that the finger fragment allegedly in the chili was actually lost in an industrial accident by a friend of the woman's husband. The friend gave the severed finger to the woman's husband after the accident. Wendy's had always believed the woman's story was a hoax, and the investigation vindicated the company. On September 9, 2005, the woman and her husband plead guilty to the scheme to extort money from Wendy's. As Wendy's president publicly stated at the time, "We strongly defended our brand and paid a severe price."[v]

Wendy's crisis management program stopped what may have started out as an attempt to defraud the company that could have done far worse damage. Although it is rare for a company to do what Wendy's did in this case, it is a testament to its integrity and strength as a good corporate citizen. They conducted a thorough internal investigation, teamed with law enforcement authorities, and took a very public stance that their products and reputation were beyond reproach. Wendy's approach to this incident should be a roadmap for every organization facing a similar event.

---

[i] "Chili Finger Hurt Wendy's Profit," CNN Money online, April 28, 2005, http://money.com/2005/04/28/news/midcaps/wendys/index.htm.

[ii] "Wendy's Offers $50,000 Reward for Information in San Jose Incident," Wendy's Press Release, April 7, 2005. www.wendys-invest.com/ne/wen_reward040805.php.

[iii] "Wendy's President Comments on San Jose Incident," April 15, 2005, www.wendys-invest.com/ne/wen041505incident.php.

[iv] San Jose Police Department Press Release, April 22, 2005.

[v] "The Jig Is Up: Wendy's Finger-in-Chili Case Develops; Digit Belongs to Associate of Accuser's Husband," MSNBC.com, May 13, 2005, www.msnbc.msn.com/id/7844274.

## CREDIT CARD FRAUD

This is probably the fastest growing fraud in the world. It encompasses several different types:

- Stolen Cards: the card itself has been physically taken from the cardholder and used before it is reported stolen by the cardholder.
- Credit Card Identity Fraud: the card is not stolen, but the information is obtained through various methods (see the section Obtaining Credit Card Numbers below) and used by a fraudster to order items using the Internet. All that are needed are the card number and the expiration date. However, clever fraudsters have learned that they have a better chance of successfully completing the fraud if they use the real billing address of the cardholder and a different "ship to" address.
- Random Number Generators: software programs guess card numbers that are valid. Only valid credit card numbers will work, as virtually all credit card order systems screen out credit card numbers that have not actually been assigned. The fraudster then places large numbers of orders, each with a different credit card number. Merchants using "velocity" tables easily catch multiple orders on the same credit card number. Velocity tables look for multiple orders to one address in a short period.

- The False Credit or Return Scam: this is an internal credit card fraud. Customer service is important to all companies. When a customer is not happy, the policy of the company is usually to try to make things right. This often means refunding the money to the customer. Dishonest employees can enter a bogus refund into the system even though no merchandise was returned. Because there is no real customer asking for a credit, the employee credits the refund to his or her own credit card. Credit card refunds should be analyzed periodically to look for multiple refunds to the same credit card number or an unusual number of credits processed by the same employee.

## Obtaining Credit Card Numbers

Credit card fraudsters can obtain valid numbers in a variety of ways. One way is to buy these numbers from a "credit doctor." A credit doctor is well known in the criminal community as someone who can get stolen credit card numbers for those who are unable to get their own credit cards. The standard rate for a valid number and expiration date is about $3 per number. There are those who offer numbers for much less, but these are sucker numbers, which have already been fraudulently used. Those who purchase and use the sucker numbers are much more likely to be caught by authorities, since the cardholder will already have reported the first fraud on the card. Devious fraudsters use cards for themselves and then sell them to secondary fraudsters. These secondary fraudsters then become the targets of investigators, taking the heat off the first fraudster.

Common ways that fraudsters obtain "good" numbers are to bribe hotel desk clerks, call center agents, and gas station attendants. Organized credit card gangs actually send people to apply for jobs as hotel clerks or call center agents for the sole purpose of obtaining as many credit card numbers as possible.

## Credit Card Risk

Any company that uses the Internet or phones to take orders relies on credit card transactions, but these "card not present" transactions are risky. They require only a valid credit card number, the expiration date, and the name and address of the cardholder. The majority of all credit card transactions are in-person transactions, but a larger percentage of Internet credit card transactions are fraudulent. It has been estimated that more than 20 percent of all Internet orders on credit cards are fraud attempts.

Although credit card companies have consistently maintained that credit card fraud is no more prevalent online than in traditional forms of commerce, a number of experts are disputing the notion. Some estimates, like that of Alvin Cameron of Digital River, are that as many as 40 percent of online purchases are fraud attempts. Accordingly, Cameron says, e-tailers are now facing a do-or-die proposition: merchants who cannot control the flood of fraudulent purchase attempts will soon be out of business. According to Cameron, doing business on the Internet is the equivalent of having someone walk into a store wearing a ski mask without any identification and offering a bank counter check to purchase a $2,000 stereo system. Whereas no brick-and-mortar store would make such sale, Internet merchants do it all the time.[1]

Contrary to popular belief, it is the merchant, not the consumer, who has the most to lose from credit card fraud. Federal laws limit consumer liability to $50 for fraudulent use of a physically stolen credit card at a brick and mortar shop, but there is no consumer liablity for Internet fraud. Since brick and mortar shop merchants have a swipe reader, which requires the actual card to be present, and a signature, the credit card company absorbs any fraud losses. Internet and shop-by-phone merchants have no such protection. The credit card company accepts *no* responsibility for fraudulent transactions. The credit card company reimburses the cardholder for unauthorized purchases and deducts the amount from the merchant's credit card account. A fee is added, usually $15 per transaction. This process is called a "chargeback."

Credit card companies like MasterCard also impose fines on merchants if "chargeback" orders make up 1 percent or more of total dollar sales transactions, or 2.5 percent or higher of the total number of sales for more than two consecutive months. These rules could well force smaller e-tailers off the Web. However, many observers believe that MasterCard is merely trying to punish those merchants, which it sees as having lax credit card authorization policies.

Online merchants have been forced to develop sophisticated security protections that go far beyond the normal security approval process by the credit card companies. Customers have become accustomed to being able to bill the order to one address and ship the goods to another address. This is the weakness that credit card fraudsters exploit.

Credit card fraudsters make an order as the cardholder, entering the cardholder's name and address in the "bill to" field. They then put a temporary address in the "ship to" field. By the time the charge appears on the cardholder's bill, the orders have already been received and the fraudster is gone. Not all fraudsters use temporary addresses. Some cocky fraudsters have been known to use the same address for years to receive orders. Therefore, companies have to protect themselves by tracking addresses used to receive fraudulent orders. Denial tables (lists of known fraud addresses) can prevent subsequent orders from being shipped to a known fraud address. Denial tables are used to screen for any new orders to known fraud addresses. These denial tables should never try to match by the name of the customer, as false names are almost always used and are changed often. Fraudsters also have been known to alter the last digit in the delivery zip code to defeat denial tables. The local post office or the private delivery carrier will often correct the last digit.

A clever form of mail order credit card fraud has emerged thanks to eBay. Fraudsters can list an item for auction on eBay before the fraudster even has the item. When the winning bidder is determined, the fraudster orders the item using a stolen credit card number. If the stolen credit card is from John Smith in New York, that address is entered in the billing address; however, the winning bidder's home address is entered as the "ship to" address. This is why many mail order businesses will not ship to any address other than the billing address of record for the credit card being used.

## The Nigerian Forwarder Scam

Beginning in 2003, many Internet vendors saw a steady increase in the number of fraud attempts. Much of the increase in credit card fraud on the Internet can be directly attributed to a credit card scam from Nigeria known as the "Forwarder Scam."

Professional fraudsters in Africa surf Internet chat rooms looking for young marks. They give the young victim a story of how unfair the trade tariffs are in Africa on computer items. They ask the victim to accept orders from several merchants at the victim's home, and they ask the victim to forward the items to an address in Lagos, Nigeria. They offer to pay the forwarder $100 per package (which would be more than any tariff). The naïve victim agrees and begins to receive packages. All orders are on a different stolen credit card for an amount that is usually less than $500.00. This popular amount is frequently used as a limit for fraud screening on orders in the industry. Of course, the victim never gets paid for forwarding the goods.

Some victims have decided just to keep all the merchandise, which sometimes results in death threats over the telephone. The typical victim of the Nigerian scam is a male between the ages of 15 and 24, and the fraudsters often pose as young women. Some have even sent a photo of a pretty young blonde, who is supposed to be the person with whom the mark is chatting. Police all over the United States have been finding these mail drop forwarders, who have been duped into forwarding stolen merchandise. The more advanced scammers use accomplices in the United States, who rent warehouse space to use as a staging area for sending stolen goods overseas. Many such warehouses have been raided in Atlanta, Houston, Miami, and other cities, and authorities have found computer equipment and office supplies stacked to the ceiling, all bound for Nigeria.

## TOOLS TO STOP ONLINE FRAUD

Many companies use a "denied party list" to stop mail order fraud. If a fraud is discovered, the address is blocked to prevent any future orders. Although it is a good tool, a denied party list is not an effective protection against fraud by itself. There are too many ways for a fraudster to create address variations for a company to use denied party lists as the sole strategy to prevent mail order fraud.

The use of denied party lists along with velocity screening, Address Verification System (AVS) code blocking, and Card Security Value (CSV) or "V" code checking can greatly reduce fraud losses.

## Velocity

Velocity refers to the number of orders to one address in a short period. The order management system should be set to flag addresses that have more than three orders per week. "Forwarder Scams" usually employ the same address for a short period but use different credit card numbers. Most of the time the billing address is not the one on file with the credit card company. Velocity checks will be discussed again later in this chapter.

## AVS

AVS involves an authorization to compare the address provided by the online customer with the address of record for the credit card holder of that credit card number. There are three levels of address matching: (1) street number, (2) the first five digits of the zip code, and (3) the extra four digits of the zip code. The extra four digits of the zip code are not widely used, so there are only two levels that should be addressed, street number and five-digit zip code.

Credit card orders that have a customer-provided billing address that does not match the street number on the billing address on file with the credit card provider would result in a certain AVS code. These AVS codes identify whether the street address matches, if the zip matches, if both match, or if neither match.

Paymentech is an example of a middleman company that handles credit card payment verification for merchants using credit card merchant accounts. It generates AVS codes based on the information contained in online credit card transactions. Another such middleman is CyberSource. Many companies are setting their preset address verification programs to automatically cancel orders that are returned from the address authorization process with I-8 type AVS codes. An I-8 AVS code means that neither the street address number nor the zip code the customer has provided match the billing address of record for the credit card being used. Customers whose orders are coded as I-8 are notified by an e-mail message saying that the billing address provided on their recent order does not match the address of record with the credit card provider. Real customers, who may have moved without officially notifying the credit card provider, will simply reorder using the proper address of record, the address to which their credit card statement is mailed. Fraudsters are defeated unless they have the billing address of the person whose credit card number they stole. AVS blocking will not stop the small minority of fraudsters who know the actual billing address for the credit card number they are trying to use. Of course, all the fraudster needs is a credit card statement intercepted from the mailbox.

Many fraudsters still use randomly generated credit card numbers, hoping for a match to a valid card. Again, only valid card numbers will work, as virtually every order management system screens out credit card numbers that have not been assigned to a cardholder. See Exhibit 9.1 for sample AVS codes.

Orders with the proper billing street address will have an odd-numbered AVS code (I-1, I-3, I-5, I-7). System changes to cancel orders with I-8 AVS codes can save the company 10 percent of its total Internet business orders each year. There are too many innocent circumstances that generate codes I-2 or I-4 codes for these codes to be summarily blocked. For example, addresses that do not begin with a number, like One Rockefeller Plaza, will result in an I-4 code on many systems. This is because the whole address is not verified, only the numbers. If an address is 100 *Main* Street, Any Town, NY 10012, the AVS will see the address as 10010012. If it were typed as 100 *High* Street, Any Town, NY 10012, the AVS would see it as a matching 10010012. If the address does not have numbers (as in One Rockefeller Plaza), the number is an automatic no match. In short, order systems cannot be set to block all orders in which the street address does not match the AVS. At best, AVS stops fraudsters from using the credit cards of victims who live in different zip codes than they do. AVS is not an exact science. It is a tool that is best used in a system with other tools when one is developing a solid fraud prevention plan.

**EXHIBIT 9.1**   Address Verification System (AVS) Codes

| | |
|---|---|
| I-2 | Address no match, but 9-digit zip code matches |
| I-4 | Address no match, but 5-digit zip code matches |
| I-6 | Address no match, first 5 digits of zip code no match |
| I-8 | Address no match, no part of zip matches |

Fraudsters who have the proper billing address for the card number they are using will provide the correct billing address and get a valid AVS code and then enter a shipping address that is different from the billing address. This is an area in which company policy must come into play. Each company must decide whether to place limits on their customers' capability to send orders to addresses other than the one on their credit cards. The shortcomings of AVS were one of the reasons why the Card Security Value (CSV) was created.

## CSV

On a system using CSV, customers are prompted for the three-digit number on the back of a Visa or MasterCard or the four-digit number on the front of an American Express card. The small black numbers are located on the signature strip on the back of Visa and MasterCards. Supposedly, only a person with the card in hand can provide this number, as it is not allowed to be stored in any system. Companies have been found storing these codes in violation of payment card industry policy.

Many companies simply limit the dollar amount of an order that can be shipped to an address other than the billing address of record, or they call back the billing address to verify the order. Although this might be a grandparent sending birthday presents, it could be a fraudster looking to get free merchandise. The problem with call-back verification is that the callers often dial the billing phone number that was provided by the fraudster. The fraudster then verifies his own order. This is why CSV is becoming so popular.

Order screens that use CSV can be attacked by random number generators: The fraudster will use a computer to randomly attempt orders using every one of the 1,000 possible three-digit CSV codes. However, there are easier ways for the fraudster to steal than to try to defeat order systems protected by CSV. The most complete CSV protection includes a variable key word known as a "CAPTCHA" (Completely Automated Public Turing Test to Tell Computers and Humans Apart)[2] in a small picture on the order screen. The customer must read the key word and retype it. Since the word is a photo (not text) with lines, texture, and/or waves added, computers can't read it.

This prevents automated order attempts, so the fraudster would actually have to type the 1,000 possible CSV codes by hand one at a time.

CSV requires an additional field on the order screen that must be included in the data sent to a credit card verification company (like Paymentech and CyberSource). Although CSV is the best protection, most fraudulent online credit card order attempts can be stopped with AVS. Fraudsters are looking for companies that do not yet use the strategy of blocking invalid AVS and CSV codes. That being said, it is still recommended that all companies taking credit card orders over the Internet use the CSV technology.

Every year, CyberSource sponsors an annual Online Fraud Report, which is conducted by Mindwave Research. This survey of online merchants shows which credit card prevention methods are being used by the industry, and their increased usage[3] (see Exhibit 9.2).

In 2004, 73 percent of all online merchants were using some type of manual review of high-risk orders. Forty-five percent of all online merchants were using denial tables (also called negative files, or black address files), and 31 percent were using the newest technology, called geolocation.

### Geolocation

This is a tool that identifies the origin of an order based on the Internet Protocol (IP) address of the computer that generated the order. If an order is coming from an IP address in California, and the billing address of the credit card is in New York, there might be a problem. However, clever fraudsters can defeat geolocation by using anonymous

**EXHIBIT 9.2**  Percentage of Online Merchants Using Card Security Value (CSV) and Address Verification System (AVS)

| Tool | 2001 | 2002 | 2003 | 2004 |
|------|------|------|------|------|
| CSV  | 8    | 34   | 44   | 56   |
| AVS  | 46   | 71   | 75   | 82   |

*Source:* CyberSource *Annual Online Fraud Report,* www.cybersource.com, 2002 and 2004

proxy servers. Geolocation has not been very popular because it only works if the cardholder is using his or her home computer to place the order. This does not take into consideration business travel, college-aged children, or jet setters, who do not stay in one place all the time.

### Data Mining: Digging for Credit Card Fraud

There are many companies that take orders by mail, by phone, and by Internet and ship goods to their customers. Most orders involve customers using checks or credit card numbers. Sometimes, however, a problem arises with an order, and the customer deserves a free replacement. This is one of the most abused functions in a mail order business. Some companies do not require the customer to return the defective product in order to receive a new one. The companies' employees can send a free or "no charge" order to anyone, including themselves. A data mining operation would periodically query for any orders shipped "no charge" to any address in the same town as a company's order processing center. This is done by looking for orders with the same zip code as the business. The "no charge" orders are then sorted by which employee processed the orders. This process will identify all orders shipped to employees, their friends, or relatives who live in the same town.

Another data mining function looks at addresses with multiple no charge orders or with multiple paid orders where the credit card number is not the same on all orders. A company would establish a set policy of how many "no charge" orders a customer can receive before being flagged as a fraud suspect. Future orders to suspects can be placed on hold. This is known as a "Velocity" check.

Velocity tables look for multiple orders to one address in a short period. The order system should have preset rules that flag any customer who has ordered at least twice in the same week using a different credit card number on the orders. Fraudsters often try random credit card numbers in an attempt to obtain an order. Many rules engines are set to catch only more than one order in one day. Fraudsters have adapted to this and will often wait one day between orders. Many fraudsters also know that large dollar amounts are more likely to be verified prior to shipment. Therefore, they will try to place numerous small orders using different aliases. In most cases, however, the same address is used. Some fraudsters will attempt hundreds of orders in the hope that some will get through. They have all day to try to obtain free merchandise, because to them it is a full-time job. Simple rules engines created by an IT department to catch high-velocity order addresses can save thousands of dollars per day. If a company uses AVS and CSV, it can run velocity checks outside the order management system every week or so to screen for fraud that might have been missed by AVS and CSV.

### Useful Tips

- Use CSV.
- Review credit card orders going to or coming from Eastern Europe, Africa, or the Middle East (including Israel), as there is a particularly high rate of credit card fraud originating from these areas.
- Do not allow customers to make last minute alterations to their shipping addresses (after the AVS code has already been received).
- Deliver only to permanent addresses. Avoid shipping to hotels or mail drops.
- Consider calling to verify orders for high dollar amounts, but make sure the phone number area code matches the billing address of record. If the billing address is different from the shipping address, a company has no protection using AVS. It will lose any chargeback action by the cardholder.

### ENDNOTES

1. Stephen Caswell, "Credit Card Fraud Crippling Online Merchants" *E-Commerce Times*, March 20, 2000, www.ecommercetimes.com/story/2771.html.
2. Luis von Ahn, at Carnegie Mellon University, coined the acronym in 2000. See www.captcha.net.
3. See Annual Fraud Report at www.cybersource.com.

# Information Security and Fraud

**EXECUTIVE SUMMARY**

Everyone values computer security, but many businesses just do not have well-developed and efficient security systems. The best way to resolve the problem is with information security policies, which are really just good business rules to ensure that information systems are operated securely. Proper IT security can be a nightmare if systems are too old to allow efficient implementation of security policies. A project as simple as mandatory password changes can create a logjam on older systems. Sarbanes-Oxley requires accountability and documentation. Often, corporate financial documentation is in the form of electronic Excel spreadsheets stored on a server. Being able to document who has access to this valuable information is a significant issue. Policy always lags behind technology. Companies using wireless technology may not have security policies to protect business information on these devices.

One need look no further than the example of America Online (AOL) to show that the average consumer values information security. In 2003, AOL began marketing itself as a trustworthy Internet service provider offering antispyware and virus protection that automatically updates at no extra charge.[1] Because of this reputation, the company was able to continue selling its trusted, secure, Internet service at twice the price of some other providers. The best security is that which people do not have to think about.

The perception of security is not always the reality. AOL conducted an online safety study of dialup and broadband users. The results showed that 73 percent of the respondents thought their computer systems were safe from online threats. In reality, 67 percent did not have updated virus protection.[2]

## SARBANES-OXLEY AND INFORMATION SECURITY

Sarbanes-Oxley mandates IT process and security controls. A company has to have a formal information security policy that dictates such things as mandatory password changes, encryption of credit card numbers, and monitoring of security event logs. Information security policies are nothing more than documented business rules to ensure that information systems are operated in a secure manner and can be audited. Some of the factors to be covered in a formal written and distributed information security policy include the following:

- Nondisclosure agreements
- Access control
- Security event log monitoring
- Reporting mechanisms for incidents
- Inventory of information and computer assets
- Destruction procedures for confidential information
- Plans for training employees on the policy
- Password policy
- A business continuity plan.

The information security policy is an important document when audits are conducted. It can also provide evidence of a company's intention to protect proprietary information, which is important in legal protection of trade secrets. Business partners often rely on an information security policy when considering sharing confidential information with the partner. Although no real single authority has been recognized as having the "best practices" for information security, the most accepted standard for an information security policy is the International Standards Organization (ISO) document number 17799, or one of the newer American Institute of Certified Public Accountants (AICPA) assurance criteria like the SysTrust control model. SysTrust evaluates the reliability of a system objectively, looking at four essential principles: availability, security, integrity, and maintainability. Each of these principles is evaluated against four criteria: policies, communication, procedures, and monitoring.[3] One might think of a Statement on Auditing Standards Number 70 (SAS 70) audit, which is an in-depth audit of an organization's control activities including IT and security. In reality, SAS 70 was never really intended for compliance purposes although it is being used as such. SAS 70 certification may no longer be sufficient by itself for many companies to grant a contract to a services provider.

The old way of putting IT policies and procedures into a contract that is signed with "a wink and a promise" is long gone. IT compliance audits for Sarbanes-Oxley look deep into access controls and data integrity. Who can create a transaction? Who can alter a transaction? Who has access to the electronic files? What controls are in place to keep the output from being changed? It is not enough to audit documented IT procedures; the audit must look at what is actually done. Some companies have the process but do not have it documented. If done properly, IT audits not only uncover compliance gaps but also help a company get a better idea of how to direct IT resources. In reality, it often comes down more to dollars than sense.

In a 2004 survey of 241 senior finance executives, *CFO* magazine asked whether the demands of the Sarbanes-Oxley act fostered a closer working relationship between finance and IT. The results are shown in Exhibit 10.1.

Operating a business over the Internet without addressing information security is not exercising due care. Some experts think the absence of a well-defined information security policy is the most serious problem with security at companies today. The computer has become as much a tool for fraud as a tool for business.

**EXHIBIT 10.1**   Does SOX Compliance Foster a Closer Working
Relationship between Finance and IT?

|  |  |
|---|---|
| YES | 49% |
| NO | 31% |
| NOT SURE | 20% |

*Source:* Scott Leibs, "One Way, or Another," *CFO-IT,* Winter 2004, 19.

Mike Hager, the vice president of Security at Oppenheimer Funds
said, "Senior managers and CIOs can no longer sit back and assume
that computer security is being adequately addressed by someone
within their company. Senior managers need to assume an active
role in addressing the security on their systems. . . ."[4]

Fraud examination units will find themselves investigating login
records and IP addresses to determine who might have committed a
fraud. Having the proper rules and policies in place can ensure that
the computer audit trail is there when needed.

A business cannot protect its proprietary information if it does
not have a system in place to classify information. What are the procedures for the handling of confidential information? What systems
contain confidential information and who has access to them? These
questions are answered by a company's information security policy.
There is no question that the ability to use, and therefore also misuse,
computer systems is becoming widespread. How much computer
fraud is going on? How big is the problem?

## 2003 FBI SURVEY ON COMPUTER SECURITY

According to a 2003 survey on computer crime and security conducted by the Computer Security Institute and the FBI, 99 percent of
the responding organizations had experienced unauthorized use of
computer systems within the previous year. The survey also found
these weaknesses in the responding organizations:

- Forty-six percent reported outsider penetration of information
  systems.

- Forty-five percent reported unauthorized access incidents by insiders.
- Twenty-one percent reported theft of proprietary information.[5]

One of the problems is that some companies do not take information security seriously enough. Most companies leave the matter of information security to IT departments, which install firewalls and password protections. Many do not ever think about it again until there is a problem. Keeping business information safe from theft and fraud is not a one-time event. It is an ongoing commitment to stay up to date.

It is curious that when one is dealing with information, security and privacy are essentially synonymous. However, when one is talking about physical security, security and privacy are opposing interests.

## WHOSE JOB IS INFORMATION SECURITY ANYWAY?

The internal auditor needs to audit the information security of the company and be involved in organizing information security efforts to ensure auditability and compliance with Sarbanes-Oxley. During investigations, fraud examiners will use the audit trail created by an information security system, but they, like the auditor, will not be involved on a day-to-day basis. That leaves IT or the security function as the owner of information security. In companies that have a Chief Security Officer (CSO), the owner of information security is clear. However, many companies do not have a CSO. In most companies, the owner of information security is the Chief Information Officer (CIO), who often delegates the responsibility to an IT security manager. Information security is undoubtedly a risk management issue.

## THE ISSAC CONCEPT

What is really needed is an Information Security Steering and Audit Committee (ISSAC). An ISSAC includes the internal auditor, a loss prevention representative (security, fraud prevention, or both), the IT security manager, and someone from operations.

The ISSAC should meet on a monthly or quarterly basis and discuss the direction the company needs to go with respect to its protection of information assets; the Committee should also keep the executive team notified. The ISSAC can identify gaps in Sarbanes-Oxley compliance or ISO 17799 compliance and take steps to bring the company into compliance. The ISSAC monitors for training issues, as an information security policy is not effective if employees are not aware of it.

## PASSWORDS: ARE YOU WIDE OPEN TO FRAUD?

All companies have procedures for new employees to obtain passwords and logins for their computer systems. Far fewer companies have procedures to remove the login and password of an employee who leaves the company. Most employees have access to several systems once they log on to the main system. Since few companies track all the systems to which an employee has access, they only deactivate the main system login when an employee leaves. This leaves a large number of ways a fraudster can access systems without being identified by a login. Many companies delete logins that have not been used in 90 days. However, this leaves the fraudster 90 days to use the login and password of a departed coworker.

Another item an ISSAC might review is the problem a large company has with thousands of computer users and mandatory password changes. Employees forget their passwords. If there are 20,000 computer users in various locations and only a few IT administrators at headquarters, the need for password resets could cripple a company's productivity. The ISSAC would anticipate this problem and designate a password reset person for each work group in each location, so that employees forgetting passwords could be assisted quickly and efficiently. If the company were running on a system that did not allow for delegation of user administration rights (like NT 4.0), the ISSAC would consider recommending a system that does allow delegation of user administration rights (such as Windows 2003 Active Directory).

With the reset problem solved, companies can enforce mandatory changes of passwords every 60 days as well as the use of strong passwords. Strong passwords have the following characteristics:

- They use upper and lower case letters.
- They use letters, numbers, and symbols.
- They use at least 8 characters.
- They are not words.

The use of smart cards or token keys is improving the protection of key financial information. Instead of having to enter something that the user knows (password), the user must insert something the user has (key), in addition to the password. Biometric technology has improved to the point at which keyboards can be equipped with a fingerprint reader that will recognize the print of the individual user. Since fingerprint scans can be stored and copied, the use of fingerprint readers alone as a security device is not recommended.

Credit card information or any other confidential information requires encrypted storage. This is done with encryption software, which scrambles the information using a mathematical formula. Decryption is done using a unique key. Credit card information should never be stored in a nonencrypted state and should never be sent in nonencrypted e-mails.

E-mail can be encrypted using a public key granted by the recipient, company B, for example. Many users could have a public encryption key from company B, but only company B has the ability to decrypt e-mails that have been encrypted using their specific encryption key. Company B decrypts their e-mails using their private key, which is never shared publicly.

Passwords are a very important audit tool to ensure that key financial documents have not been altered. Many companies store financial data in Microsoft Excel format. These financial documents are almost always stored electronically and can, therefore, be tampered with. These financial documents have to be locked down in a secure data warehouse with auditable access logs that are saved for at least five years, according to Sarbanes-Oxley Section 802.

A company called Teradata, a division of NCR that provides data warehousing solutions, conducted a survey. Three hundred eighty-six top-level executives at public companies in the United States responded. Of all respondents, 90 percent said that they had purchased new technology to meet Sarbanes-Oxley requirements. Of all respondents, 66 percent are using data warehousing to meet Sarbanes-Oxley requirements.[6]

## EXECUTIVE INSIGHT 10.1 THE MOTHER OF ALL INFORMATION SYSTEMS

In May of 2001, the FBI contracted with DynCorp for networked personal computers, scanners, and printers. This constituted the first two parts of a project called Trilogy. The third part of Trilogy was a Virtual Case File (VCF) case management system. The FBI contracted with Science Applications International Corporation (SAIC) in June of 2001 for VCF, which would locate data within the FBI's various systems, analyze it, and make it available to all agents. VCF was to be a paperless and completely secure case management system that would make all criminal and antiterrorism information available to any agent. VCF was to be an information sharing system for a bureaucratic entity that was not very good at sharing information.

The FBI found, however, that the original software for VCF provided to them by SAIC at the end of 2003 did not work. SAIC agreed to work on the analytical software for another year. The project was abandoned in 2005 when it was determined that most of the code for VCF was not usable. Trilogy cost the FBI more than $500 million, which is more than $200 million over budget, and VCF was a complete waste. The Director of the FBI, Robert Mueller, and representatives of SAIC were called before Congress to explain how this disaster could have happened.

The FBI admitted that their VCF plan was too ambitious. Director Mueller confessed that they had been pushing too hard after September 11, 2001, to get the system in place. SAIC complained about the numerous changes and complexity of the project. Others pointed to the fact that five different CIOs had been at the FBI in less than two years. All this was the rhetoric of failure, however.

Michael Schrage, codirector of the eMarkets Initiative at the MIT Media Lab, has given us *Schrage's Law of Organizational Obviousness.* It states that "the smarter the organization thinks it is, the more complacently it manages the obvious" and "knowing, grasping, and even celebrating the obvious should be the single most important spec in every IT initiative."[i] Time and again basic functions within an organization are not understood. Schrage says that the obvious questions were not even asked, let alone answered before the FBI and SAIC started the VCF project. For example, how did FBI agents currently use technology to manage cases, and how would the new software modify and improve the process?[ii]

Schrage blames a "culture of complacency" as the greatest source of IT failures. The plan of the FBI was to build a tool to allow collaboration in an organization that has been known not to share information even from one squad to another in the same field office. Complacency, not complexity, explains the failure of the FBI's VCF.[iii]

---

[i] Michael Schrage, "Ignoring the Obvious," *CIO*, April 15, 2005, 36.
[ii] Ibid.
[iii] Ibid.

## SECURITY EVENT LOGS

Monitoring of IT security event logs and storing them provides more than an audit trail for Sarbanes-Oxley audits. One sees what is going on with the system, who is accessing what, or who has mistyped a password several times. Perhaps the person has forgotten the password, but maybe it is a hacking attempt. It is important to know whether the person is a financial manager. When anyone accesses data in financial folders, the event can generate a notification to the security manager. Failed login attempts by financial managers should raise a red flag and be investigated. Asking a network administrator or CSO to secure a network without monitoring its activity is like asking a mechanic to work on an automobile engine without opening the hood.[7]

After a fraud has been detected, it would be impossible to determine which employee accessed the system at the time of the fraud unless event logs are properly stored. Many companies do not monitor their logs or store security event logs beyond a few days, because they take up server space. After a short time, the logs are overwritten with new information. This practice can seriously impact a fraud investigation.

How do most companies stack up when it comes to protecting information? Five hundred thirty-nine respondents to a survey conducted by *CSO Magazine* in 2004 learned just that. Although a good majority of the respondents' companies regularly scanned for viruses (82 percent), only 48 percent could document that they had an established information security policy in place, and only 37 percent linked security policies to specific business objectives or areas of risk. Only 40 percent of the respondents' companies trained employees to identify suspicious events.[8]

Information security policies are only part of the issue. Enforcement of the policy, the development and delivery of training on the specific policy, and information security awareness in general are also part of the solution. What good does it do to have state-of-the-art firewalls, intrusion sensors, and password protection if executives are logging on to the system using a wireless network connection that is not operating special security technology? Wireless networks are simple and inexpensive to set up. When something is so easy that it can be set up by anyone, security is usually not considered. Many users do not realize that they are openly broadcasting their network address to anyone who also has a wireless laptop within range of the wireless signal.

A survey by RSA Security in 2002 recorded 328 wireless access points in the financial district of London; only one-third of them were protected by special security technology.[9] Securing the door means nothing if the windows are left open.

## THE TRANSPARENCY/GLOBALIZATION PARADOX

Whether the IT department is audited for Sarbanes-Oxley compliance or to satisfy a business partner that the data and network are secure, IT audits are now in vogue. IT audits can provide a snapshot or a footprint as to where a company is regarding compliance with ISO 17799 standards or Sarbanes-Oxley, both of which are now mainstream concerns. The term "IT audit" covers a great deal, but in general it can be thought of as a process by which organizations evaluate virtually any aspect of their technology controls, capabilities, and performance. They are moving into the mainstream as regulatory compliance, risk management, and information security become higher corporate priorities.[10]

As companies become global organizations, they also become more complex. This additional complexity makes it harder to document processes and measure risks. The primary reason for expanding to offshore locations is cost savings. At the same time, the main fear about this offshore expansion is the protection of proprietary information. This is the Transparency/Globalization Paradox[11] (see Exhibit 10.2).

The Transparency/Globalization Paradox is an extension of the opposing roles of finance and operations. It is the function of finance to be the control over risks taken by operations. In many cases in which there was a breakdown of governance that resulted in fraud, the line between finance and operations became blurred. An example of this is a company that is rapidly expanding offshore. Operations wants to get the business in place and meet deadlines. Finance cannot lose sight of its role of making sure that all payments are on the

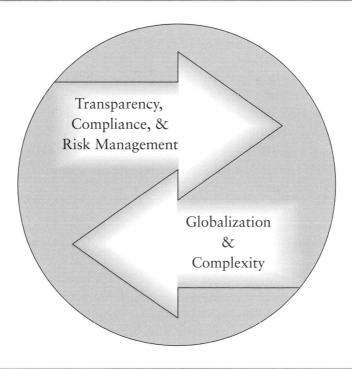

**EXHIBIT 10.2** The Transparency/Globilization Paradox

books and transparent. In Chapter 15 there will be specific examples of companies that were prosecuted for violating the Foreign Corrupt Practices Act.

## THE INFORMATION SECURITY POLICY

All information assets used to support business goals need to be subject to a regular risk assessment. Risk assessment (as discussed in Chapter 5) is about identifying and classifying the threats that could exist and the likelihood that they exploit a weakness or vulnerability that would result in an adverse impact on the business. Having identified the risks and the degree of each risk, the business must put appropriate mechanisms in place to mitigate and control risk to appropriate levels. Risk is ongoing and ever changing. Periodic reviews and reevaluations are necessary.

The ISSAC is responsible for ensuring that the information security policy remains practical and effective in support of the business goals and government regulations. All employees should be made aware of their responsibilities for appropriately protecting the business's critical information.

As a general rule, clear desk and blank screen policies are the best ways to protect information. A clear desk policy requires employees to have all papers with sensitive or "internal use only" information off their desks and put away before leaving their offices. A blank screen policy requires workers to log off their computers when leaving their desks. Some businesses have screens that autolock after five minutes of inactivity.

## THE TECHNOLOGY/POLICY GAP

Wireless technology has progressed enormously in the last few years. There are personal data assistants and cell phones that have amazing technological capabilities. Unfortunately, businesses have not kept pace with information security policies to cover these new devices. Often employees purchase a device and begin using it for business before the IT department knows about it. Even the IT department is not very good at updating the information security policy to include new technologies. Traditional information security policy models do not fit well with mobile communication and wireless access. Viruses can be transmitted from device to device just from being in close proximity. The Bluetooth program has a "discoverable" feature that will automatically communicate with other Bluetooth-enabled devices. A security policy might require that this feature remain off. It is another matter to communicate the issue to all employees and show them how to turn the feature off. Information security is about training. It does no good to spend millions of dollars on firewalls and antivirus programs if employees take their laptops home and surf the Web with them at night. This puts businesses at risk that their own workers will bring infected laptops back to the office the next morning.

Another technological advance that poses a huge risk to proprietary information is the thumb drive or USB drive. The USB drive is a portable storage device for electronic files. The USB drive is no bigger than a plastic cigarette lighter, yet it can hold 256 MB, 512 MB, 1 GB of information, or even more. Workers could conceivably copy their whole office C drives in less than two minutes, slip the USB drives into their pockets, and leave. Some companies have taken the drastic step to disable the USB drives on company computers in high security areas.

So what does it all mean? What does the future hold? The number of Net fraud incidents reported has been doubling every year. There were an estimated 10,000 complaints in 2000. By 2002, the complaints reached 48,000. In 2004, the number exceeded 200,000.[12]

## ENDNOTES

1. Briefing: "How AOL Earns Customer Trust," interview with Tatiana Platt, *CSO*, February 2005, 21.
2. Ibid.
3. Michael Cangemi and Tommie Singleton, *Managing the Audit Function*, 3rd ed. (Hoboken, NJ: John Wiley & Sons, 2003), 78.
4. Linda McCarthy, *IT Security: Risking the Corporation* (New Jersey: Prentice Hall PTR, 2003), 35.
5. Association of Certified Fraud Examiners, *The Computer and Internet Fraud*, (Austin, TX: ACFE, 2004), 4.

6. Elliot King, "Countdown to Compliance," *Windows IT Pro*, November 2004, 63.
7. Linda McCarthy, *IT Security: Risking the Corporation* (New Jersey: Prentice Hall PTR, 2003), 155.
8. Derek Slater, "A Long Way To Grow" *CSO Magazine*, January 2005, 46.
9. Malcolm Wheatley, "The Good, the Bad & the Internet," *CSO Magazine*, Special Issue Fall-2004, 23.
10. Bob Violino, "You Bought It, Now Audit," *CFO-IT*, Summer 2004, 17.
11. Steve Lindseth, "Operational Risk Management," *DM Review*, February 2005, 30.
12. Mara Der Hovanesian, "Hackers and Phisher and Frauds, Oh My!," *Business Week*, May 30, 2005, 81.

# CHAPTER 11

# Designing a Robust Fraud Prevention Program at Your Company

## EXECUTIVE SUMMARY

All entities need a robust fraud prevention program staffed with savvy and experienced fraud examiners. Certified Fraud Examiners (CFEs) are the gold standard in fraud detection and prevention, and the unit should have a requirement that all its investigators be so certified. A forensic accountant and forensic data analyst are also necessities. A financial integrity concept should be used in protecting the organization from all forms of fraud and abuse while reducing the risk of financial and reputational harm. The program should be based in internal audit, as there are great synergies to be achieved with such a partnership. Interaction with internal auditors will result in increased discovery of fraud and abuse issues. The fraud prevention program should include the detection, investigation, and prevention of all frauds including financial statement fraud, asset misappropriation, and corruption schemes. The investigative unit needs a wide variety of fraud detection software and technology solutions to combat fraud as well as excellent cross-group collaboration throughout the company.

In the aftermath of the corporate scandals that decimated a number of once prominent corporations, detecting and stopping fraud has become paramount. Fighting fraud is nothing new, yet, the risk to businesses and individuals, the current legal requirements for fraud risk assessment and mitigation, and the methods the government is using to attack fraud are all new. It is no longer an option to have a fraud prevention program at a company. It is now essential.

Companies face numerous risks. There are the financial risks from fraud losses, shareholders' lawsuits, federal prosecutions, convictions, and fines. Along with the financial risk goes the reputational risk. Vicarious liability, in which a company may be responsible for the actions of an employee even if those actions are unauthorized and contrary to company policy, stands out as another serious risk. Corporations and other organizations can be held liable for criminal acts committed as a matter of organizational policy. They may also be held liable for the criminal acts of their employees if those acts are done in the course and scope of their employment. Once well-respected companies have now been decimated by the impact of a fraud conviction. Consider the personal devastation to the thousands of innocent Enron employees who believed in their company but were deceived by their senior executives. They lost their jobs, their savings, and their pensions and will face years of emotional and financial issues.

## ONLY ROBUST WILL DO

Fraud prevention has come a long way in the last few years. Corporate executives are realizing that preventing fraud is critical to the long-term existence of a company. The concept of preventing fraud is more than just a good business practice; it is a requirement that is critical to proper company management. Building a state-of-the-art fraud prevention program requires effort to ensure integrity, transparency, honest reporting, and a culture of compliance. Only a robust fraud prevention program will do. Robust can be defined as having or exhibiting strength or vigorous health, firm in purpose or outlook, and strong. It is about being proactive rather than just reactive.[1] What makes a program robust are a number of elements. Highly experienced fraud examiners understand the reasons people commit fraud and then know how to detect it. They stay current with local, national, and world events related to fraud in order to integrate best practices into a company's program. It is about always adding new strategies to a fraud prevention tool chest. Most importantly, it is a commitment to excellence and innovation.

A robust fraud prevention program must build a predictable response model to allegations of fraud or financial improprieties, providing thorough and timely results in support of management action, including related business, legal, and human resources decisions. The primary focus should be on driving continuous improvement in policies, procedures, internal controls, and compliance, including the Sarbanes-Oxley Act certifications and whistle-blower provisions. Experience has shown that once a robust fraud prevention program is established, many instances of previously hidden frauds will be disclosed. The existence of a well-communicated reporting mechanism for employees and others to report allegations of fraud and noncompliance with company policy will lead to the identification and resolution of previously unresolved matters. See Executive Insight 6.2 in Chapter 6 for an example of how an anonymous letter resulted in the discovery of a huge accounting fraud. The types of fraud and abuse addressed will run the gamut of traditional financial fraud and abuse, ranging from low-risk areas such as expense reporting fraud and petty cash abuses, to higher risk areas including financial accounting issues, conflicts of interest, hidden business relationships, kickbacks, and bribes.

## THE FRAUD INVESTIGATION RESPONSE AND FINANCIAL INTEGRITY CONCEPT

Even the best prevention program will not stop all fraud. Therefore, an investigative response component through which company investigators can quickly respond to allegations of fraud is needed for all prevention programs. The fraud investigative unit must be responsible for the detection, investigation, and prevention of fraud and must have the strong support of senior management and the Audit Committee. The message that needs to be conveyed is that the company is ready, willing, and able to respond quickly and appropriately to allegations of fraud. Consider calling the fraud prevention unit something other than the "fraud investigation group" or a similar name. The unit could be called the financial integrity unit to emphasize the focus on the preservation of financial integrity, process improvements, and prevention rather than just reactive investigations. Using the term "financial integrity unit" sends a strong message that the overall mission is protecting the financial health and promoting the integrity of the organization.

A robust fraud prevention program is much more than a response to fraud. A vigorous and proactive program will include as much fraud risk assessment, detection, education, and awareness of fraud issues and prevention as responsive investigations. The term "financial integrity unit" also conveys a different and better message to employees. Incorporating the words "financial" and "integrity" sends a very positive message that the unit is protecting them as well as the company.

The fraud investigation unit should have a charter or mission that provides clear objectives and definitions of the organization-wide fraud prevention program. The charter or mission must be communicated to key stakeholders in the company. See Exhibit 11.1 for a sample financial integrity unit charter.

## KNOWING FRAUD

There is no substitute for experienced fraud investigators when one is staffing the financial integrity unit. Fraud investigation is a discipline that can take a number of years to master because of the many different types of fraud that can be committed. It is important to recruit a professionally trained and experienced financial fraud investigations team consisting of investigators, forensic data analysts, and forensic accountants. It is essential to have a forensic accountant on the team who can perform accounting and analysis to detect fraud, including accounting manipulations and revenue recognition issues. Successful fraud investigations start with the right people: those with experience and a thirst for innovation, learning, and making a positive impact. In fact, they must be agents of change and the voice of fraud prevention. At times, they may be the ones to convince upper management (and then all levels below) of the importance of fraud prevention. Corporate executives may have to change the corporate culture to one

The Financial Integrity Unit (FIU) is established as an integral element of Internal Audit to assist the General Auditor, Chief Financial Officer, General Counsel, Chief Compliance Officer, and other members of management and the Board of Directors in the effective discharge of their responsibilities over financial integrity. To this end, the FIU is authorized to respond to any reports or allegations of financial improprieties or violations of the company's code of conduct and other related code of conduct violations that could negatively impact the company's financial integrity. The FIU has a worldwide charter. The FIU's responsibilities include the following:

- Conducting timely and professional investigations into allegations of financial improprieties or violations of codes of conduct that could negatively impact on the company's financial integrity. Investigations will be conducted under the direction and supervision of the office of general counsel, and investigative reports will be issued to the office of general counsel and other members of management as appropriate for resolution.
- Identifying and making recommendations to correct control weaknesses and process deficiencies that increase the risk of financial improprieties; making recommendations to adopt industry best practices.
- Partnering with the controllers' community and other finance personnel to provide a proactive, comprehensive, and effective program aimed at preventing, detecting, and investigating incidents of fraud, waste, and abuse.
- Collaborating with business groups in their continuing efforts to improve finance-related processes and contribute to cost efficacy.

**EXHIBIT 11.1**　Sample Financial Integrity Unit Charter

of higher integrity in order to embrace a robust fraud prevention program. The investigators who are hired will help do this.

Investigators who have worked in fraud units for federal, state, and local law enforcement agencies or in the private sector come with the needed knowledge, skills, and abilities and should be sought to staff the unit. Fraud investigators must also stay current with developments in the world of fraud. They must be willing to continually learn new techniques for investigating and preventing fraud. That means continuing professional education courses in the field, especially to learn about new and evolving fraud schemes.

The financial integrity unit should have written polices and procedures and should work closely with other company departments. A needs and capabilities analysis should be conducted, which will identify a series of recommendations for key program elements, a proposed organizational structure, and team capabilities for the unit. A good start-up strategy includes the following factors:

- Program and process development, including a company-wide fraud risk profile
- Policy integration and close interaction with other company organizations, including senior executives, legal, office of compliance, human resources, internal audit and finance, procurement, and public relations
- Case management for event and trend tracking and reporting
- Development of technology solutions to identify fraud and abuse
- An investigative protocol for conducting investigations
- A company-wide communication program to disseminate fraud risk and prevention strategies.

Consideration should be given to hiring CFEs as well. The CFE certification has become the gold standard in fraud detection and prevention. CFEs are known the world over as fraud-fighting experts. To become a CFE, a fraud examiner must meet strict standards of education and experience in investigating fraudulent financial transactions and other fraud investigations and must also have knowledge of legal elements of fraud, accounting, criminology, and ethics. Thus they have extensive knowledge about investigating fraud and antifraud control measures. CFEs should be part of any robust fraud prevention program.

## TECHNOLOGY SOLUTIONS

Today's modern fraud prevention unit must have an extensive array of technology tools and solutions to conduct successful fraud investigations. Forensic data analysis tools must be used to identify anomalies or irregularities in electronic data that are indicative of fraud or abuse. The unit must be familiar with the fraud detection software on the market and must also have the technical expertise to develop in-house applications specific to particular fraud risk issues. It is recommended that each unit have a dedicated forensic data analyst to support complex investigations by identifying, designing, maintaining, and using appropriate technologies to mitigate fraud. Almost every case of fraud today has some connection to computers, e-mail, and the Internet. Thus, digital evidence recovery capabilities must exist for identifying, preserving, recovering, and examining electronic evidence. The unit needs to become competent in this area or, at the minimum, have access to skilled professionals who can examine digital evidence.

## BASE A FRAUD PREVENTION PROGRAM IN INTERNAL AUDIT

Many fraud investigation units are based within the corporate security department. This has been the traditional approach: The fraud response is aligned with physical security, theft investigation, workplace violence, and executive protection functions. Enhanced fraud prevention programs require a continuous interaction with a company's internal audit function. In today's world, "internal audit must have a solid understanding of measures intended to prevent and detect fraud and be able to evaluate and test antifraud control effectiveness."[2] More and more fraud prevention programs are now being placed within internal audit. As accounting firm PricewaterhouseCoopers states, "Some larger internal audit functions are creating internal units to address prevention, detection, investigation, and remediation of fraud and issues stemming from forensic investigations."[3] There are great synergies to be achieved with a partnership of fraud prevention and internal audit. The interaction with the internal auditors allows a free exchange of information and a quicker response to potential fraud matters for investigation. Professional fraud investigators can take the "red flags" found by auditors and determine whether there is a basis for them. A well-functioning financial integrity unit should be based within internal audit or at the very least have close interaction with that department.

The internal audit department is an independent appraisal function to examine and evaluate a company's activities as a service to management and the board of directors. To accomplish this, internal audit must be authorized to direct a broad, comprehensive program of internal auditing throughout the company. In carrying out their duties and responsibilities, members of internal audit will have full, free, and unrestricted access to all company activities, records, property, and personnel. This is also the function of a fraud prevention unit, so a close interaction of the two groups is beneficial to all.

Another positive benefit when the financial integrity unit is based within internal audit is ready access to the findings of both the internal and independent auditors. A member of the fraud investigative unit of a major technology company confided that his group has little if any interaction with the internal audit department. Furthermore, he wondered if having a closer interaction with internal audit would result in increased referrals regarding potential fraud issues arising from audits conducted. Effective fraud investigation units need to be proactive, and review of audit findings for the red flags of fraud is critical. Wherever the unit is based, it must be staffed with a sufficient number of experienced investigators who have extensive fraud detection experience and CFE certifications.

## WHERE FRAUD WILL BE FOUND

The types of fraud that a company may find are varied but generally can be broken down into three broad categories:

- **Fraudulent Financial Statements,** including fraudulent financial accounting, revenue recognition, improper asset valuations, abuse of accounting systems, and side letters (written or unwritten agreements not included in contracts).
- **Asset Misappropriation,** including fraudulent disbursements, larceny, and skimming. Common embezzlement schemes include contract fraud, false billing, fraudulent expense report submissions, relocation fraud, time and attendance fraud, and false disability claims.
- **Corruption,** including bribery, kickbacks, economic extortion and conflicts of interest, including insider trading, employees with hidden ownership of companies doing business with them, and spouses of employees with undisclosed ownership in vendor companies.

In the authors' experience, many companies will find that fraud involving expense reporting is the biggest fraud problem they have, followed by conflicts of interest and then vendor kickback schemes.

As much as a corporate executive may think a company has no fraud problem, it does. Once a fraud prevention program is up and running, it will uncover issues that have been ongoing for many months or years without discovery. In any population, including those within a company, a certain percentage will have their own agendas and will commit fraud when given the opportunity.

## ABUSE CANNOT BE IGNORED

Fraud is not the only problem facing an organization. As big a problem as fraud is, the issue with abuse is bigger. More importantly, whereas fraud is usually addressed, abuse is often ignored. Although fraud and abuse have two different meanings, abuse mitigation must be part of a robust fraud prevention program. Abuse can be defined as "improper use, misuse, to use wrongly, unjust or wrongful practice."[4] Abuse typically involves policy violations, such as the inappropriate use of corporate resources for personal reasons. It might involve taking home a box of company pens for personal use, consistently arriving at work late and going home early, using the photocopier to make personal copies, or using sick leave when one is not ill. Other examples are violating employee authorized purchase limits by splitting invoices to stay within the approved limits, excessive travel and entertainment spending such as $400 bottles of wine at a dinner, and first-class travel when coach is mandated. If abuse is not appropriately addressed, it can lead to fraud by giving the false impression that this behavior is condoned.

## EMPLOYEE COOPERATION WITH OFFICIAL INVESTIGATIONS

Internal employee investigations are a significant part of the investigative caseload of a financial integrity unit. In any allegation of fraud by employees, interviews will be conducted with potential witnesses and subjects. When people are confronted about possible fraudulent activities, admissions and truthfulness are paramount. It's all or nothing when it comes to being truthful; half-truths are not acceptable. Skill and experience play a key factor in obtaining the truth from employees when one is conducting interviews. Professional interviewing techniques and treating all people with dignity and respect go a long way in getting to the truth.

The cooperation of employees in internal investigations is critical to determination of the facts of the case and a successful outcome. Witnesses will provide great insight into and context for the allegations. The collection of documentary and supporting evidence along with witness interviews may help to prove or disprove the allegations before having to confront the subject employee. An interview with a subject is made easier with this approach, and when an employee is confronted with substantial evidence of wrongdoing, it is easier to obtain an admission. Therefore, the company code of conduct should include a statement that employees are required to cooperate fully and truthfully with any authorized company investigation. Employees who are subjects of investigations cannot be forced to speak with investigators, but the failure to meet and discuss the allegations can be used by human resources and management in a determination of final disciplinary action.

## INTERACTION WITH CORPORATE EXECUTIVES AND THE AUDIT COMMITTEE

A critical element for any financial integrity unit is acknowledgment and involvement at the executive level. CEOs and CFOs need not be subject matter experts in fraud detection and prevention, but they need employees who are. The executives also need to know what their fraud detection professionals are doing to protect the company's interests. The fraud prevention unit must have access to the top executives for the program to be successful. The leadership of the fraud prevention unit should meet regularly with the CFO, the Director of Compliance, the Audit Committee, internal auditors, and other appropriate personnel. There should be a discussion of the fraud and abuse issues investigated at the company as well as recommendations for improvements in process and internal controls.

A monthly meeting with the CFO or other appropriate corporate executive is recommended to discuss the work of the financial integrity unit including detection, investigation, prevention, and recovery. Included should be discussions of recent investigations conducted, how the issues were discovered, what internal control failures allowed the fraud to occur, employee terminations and other disciplinary actions, referrals for prosecution, recoveries and cost avoidance, and prevention and fraud awareness training of employees. Ongoing meetings with senior executives will open their eyes to the fraud risk and the importance of a robust program, as well as demonstrate their support of the program and tone at the top. This visibility within the highest reaches of the company will reinforce for all employees the commitment of the company to a culture of compliance and integrity. In addition to a close interaction with senior executives, the financial integrity unit must have key interactions with corporate security, legal counsel, public relations, human resources, and other corporate groups to ensure cross-group collaboration.

## ROLE OF HUMAN RESOURCES

Once an investigation has concluded that the subject employee has committed a fraud or other abuse against the company, management, legal counsel, and human resources must take appropriate disciplinary action. Assuming that the violation rises to the level requiring termination, the employee is removed from the company. Zero tolerance for fraud is the standard. Whether one dollar or one million is stolen, fraud in any form cannot be tolerated. A person with no integrity must be removed from the company. Although some might assume that the problem has been resolved with a termination, experience has shown that this may not be the case. It is not enough just to remove the fraudster from a company. The person responsible for the fraud should be prevented from returning to the company in another employment capacity.

If human resources does not list the employee as ineligible for rehire, it is quite possible that the terminated employee might apply for employment months or years later. In companies of significant size that have a high turnover in human resources departments, it is impossible to retain the institutional knowledge of who was fired and why without appropriate records being maintained. Employees terminated for fraudulent conduct may return to the company that fired them, as contingent staff or vendors. Although it is always possible that the terminated employee has reformed and will not commit a fraud ever again, one must always remember that the best indicator of future performance is past performance. Be on the safe side. If a worker was terminated for wrongdoing, a company would do well to place that employee on an ineligible for rehire list and always refer to it before hiring new employees.

## PROSECUTION AS A FRAUD DETERRENT

Companies should always consider referring internal and external fraud cases to law enforcement for prosecution. A certain percentage of the criminal element is deterred from committing fraud by knowing they may face a prison term for their actions. Holding a fraudster responsible is important in the pursuit of justice and the protection of the business. It can send a strong message to employees that the company is protecting their interests in a fraud-free environment and is willing to hold accountable those who break the law. A company's legal counsel should make the final determination for any prosecution referrals.

## RECOVERY OF DEFRAUDED ASSETS FROM FRAUDSTERS: MAKING FRAUD LESS PROFITABLE

A well-defined fraud prevention program must encompass recovery of defrauded assets to remove the financial gain from fraud. Fraud losses come out of the bottom line, so any recovery is beneficial. Recovery sends another strong message that not only will fraud not be tolerated, but also every effort will be made to recover the stolen assets. Consider civil actions, support and encourage criminal forfeiture in cases prosecuted, institute consent agreements to recover assets, and eliminate bonuses and other incentive compensation to employees who have defrauded the company.

Cost efficacy is about cost containment and reducing expenses while improving the bottom line. Equally important are measuring fraud losses, recovery, restitution, and cost avoidance. It is important to track losses and recoveries to know the full extent of the problem and the response. It is always hard to quantify fraud losses and the benefits of a fraud prevention program. One way to show the value of the program is through the amount of money recovered. Another way is by demonstrating the cost avoidance by early detection. When a fraud is discovered, consider extrapolating the losses over the next 12 months to show what the fraud amount might have been had it not been detected and stopped. Corporate executives are always concerned about the numbers, and recoveries and cost avoidance can demonstrate the benefit of a strong financial integrity program.

Another consideration in taking the profit out of fraud is the issuance of IRS Form 1099s to employees and others who have committed fraud or theft against the company either internally or externally. It is a given that fraudsters will not be declaring their ill-gotten earnings on their tax returns. The authors are aware of several companies that use this procedure, but it has not been universally accepted. It is quite possible that companies have never considered this possible course of action. There is no reason why it should not be at least considered and then possibly instituted. Issuing 1099s is an extension of good corporate governance and citizenship by reporting to the government the proceeds received by those who defrauded the company. It sends a strong message to those who commit fraud that the company will take strong measures including reporting the embezzled funds to the IRS for whatever action the IRS deems appropriate. It is important to let employees and others know that the company has this process of IRS reporting. It is quite conceivable that a person who has been discovered defrauding an organization will make restitution, knowing that he or she will ultimately have to deal with the IRS through the 1099 reporting procedure. That alone should strike fear into a fraudster and will add to cost efficacy and reimbursement of defrauded proceeds. Once this company policy is widely known, it should have a therapeutic effect and should increase fraud prevention. The resulting deterrence will add to an already effective culture of compliance. A sample company 1099 reporting policy is shown in Exhibit 11.2.

The company has initiated a policy in which income derived from illegal activity including fraud, embezzlement, and theft perpetrated against the company by an employee, former employee, vendor, contractor, partner, or any other person or persons will be reported to the IRS by the company's tax department via IRS Form 1099. The amount that will be reported is based on the actual loss amount suffered by the company as a result of the activity by the employee or others or, if actual numbers are not available, on a reasonable figure as determined by the legal department and the investigative group conducting the investigation. The amount reported to the IRS should be able to be justified in the event the amount is ever challenged by the former employee or other external persons. According to IRS regulations, income obtained from illegal means is taxable to the person who benefited.

The company's investigative group will maintain detailed records by case of each potential 1099 reporting. At the end of the calendar year, the head of the investigative group will report to the company's tax department the relevant information needed so a 1099 can be issued to the employee or others by the IRS notification deadline of January 31. Before the information is submitted to the IRS, the loss amounts will be carefully checked to ensure accuracy of reporting. Annual loss reports will be maintained by the investigative group, the legal department, and the tax department. These reports will contain the following:

- Name of employee or other person
- Title and work unit
- Mailing address
- Social Security number
- Amount to be reported to the IRS
- Case number
- Details of the violation of business conduct and how the amount was quantified.

The reported amount will appear on a 1099 Miscellaneous Form, Box 3 Other Income). Restitution of embezzled funds does not affect the reporting requirement. Income is recognized at the time the embezzler takes control of the funds and, is therefore, not affected by subsequent restitution.

**EXHIBIT 11.2** Sample Company 1099 Reporting Policy

## INTERNATIONAL INVESTIGATIONS

As corporate entities become more global, so will fraud investigations. Fraud is increasing throughout the world, and there is little chance that this trend will change. Companies with an international reach need investigative coverage in all countries of their operations. Fraud knows no borders or language differences. Accounting fraud, embezzlements, and bribes to government officials can and do occur everywhere in the world. If a company's operations are based in the United States, it needs a financial integrity unit presence at the headquarters office. If there are significant operations outside the United States, investigative units need to be in those regions too. Many companies are expanding into Europe, Asia, and Latin America; for full protection, financial integrity units need to be established in those regions to provide a quick response and resolution of fraud issues. It is important to remember that investigations conducted in one country may be conducted in an entirely different manner in another country, not only because of different cultures, but also because of different labor and employment laws, as well as business practices. Thus, the need for guidance from legal counsel is critical in protecting the interests of the company.

## QUARTERLY FRAUD DISCUSSIONS WITH EXECUTIVE LEADERSHIP

Fraud prevention and the reporting of fraud are critical to company management. With the enactment of Sarbanes-Oxley, CEOs and CFOs must now certify that their financial statements are truthful and free from misstatements and fraud. No more fuzzy financial accounting is allowed, unless that CEO and CFO want to land in jail. Section 302 of Sarbanes-Oxley requires certification by CEOs and CFOs that SEC Forms 10K (annual reports) and 10Q (quarterly reports) do not contain untrue statements, that financial information is fairly presented, and that disclosure controls and procedures are effective. Sarbanes-Oxley has a specific requirement that the company disclose "any fraud, whether or not material, that involves management or other employees who have a significant role in the company's internal controls."[5] Violation of this certification requirement is a federal felony punishable by up to 20 years in prison.

The fraud prevention unit has a key role in helping executives certify that their books and their companies are in compliance. In addition to quarterly meetings with the CEO, CFO, and other executives, the financial integrity unit needs to meet on a quarterly basis with other senior executives, General Counsel, the Chief Compliance Officer, the General Auditor, and others as appropriate to discuss the current fraud cases that may or may not need to be reported to the Disclosure Committee, the Audit Committee, the SEC, and/or the Department of Justice. Meetings may be more frequent if serious issues of fraud are disclosed that need to be reported. The financial integrity unit should prepare a report detailing all the various fraud and abuse cases, ranking them by risk level. This report should be presented at the quarterly fraud discussion meeting by the manager of the financial integrity unit, who will provide specific details on each case as well as answer any questions.

## QUARTERLY FRAUD DISCUSSIONS WITH THE EXTERNAL AUDITOR

An additional step to reduce the risk of fraud and promote transparency is to hold regular meetings with the company's external auditor. The American Institute of Certified Public Accountants' Statement on Auditing Standards (SAS) 99, Consideration of Fraud in a Financial Statement Audit, established standards and guidance for auditors in detecting fraud in the financial statements of companies. Because of SAS 99, auditors must look for fraud throughout the audit process. The auditors must ask probing questions and determine whether the company is in compliance with the requirements of SAS 99. The external auditor needs to work closely with the financial integrity unit to ensure that a robust fraud prevention program is in place.

It is recommended that the financial integrity unit meet on a quarterly basis with the external auditor to discuss the fraud prevention program in place at the company, including detection, investigation, recovery, and prevention aspects. In addition to the manager of the financial integrity unit, senior executives, General Counsel, the Chief Compliance Officer, the General Auditor, and others as appropriate should attend this meeting. The manager of the financial integrity unit should discuss relevant issues with the external auditor to demonstrate compliance and transparency. External auditors will be interested in the company's response to cases of fraud but will be just as interested in learning about what the company is doing proactively to identify fraud risk and communicate fraud prevention and a culture of compliance with policy, procedures, and laws.

## ENDNOTES

1. See, e.g., *Webster's Third New International Dictionary*, 1986 ed., s.v. "robust."
2. PricewaterhouseCoopers. *The Emerging Role of Internal Audit in Mitigating Fraud and Reputation Risks*, 2004, 15.
3. Ibid., 6.
4. See, e.g., *Webster's Third New International Dictionary*, 1986 ed., s.v. "abuse."
5. *Sarbanes-Oxley*, Section 302, codified in *U.S. Code* 15 (2005), § 7241(a)(4)(B).

# Whistle-Blowers and Hotlines

## EXECUTIVE SUMMARY

Whistle-blowers and hotlines are important elements in the detection and prevention of fraud. The Federal Sentencing Guidelines, Sarbanes-Oxley, and other corporate governance enhancements all discuss the importance of whistle-blowers and hotlines, as well as the standards to implement them. Tips from employees are the most common means of fraud detection, and a hotline is the reporting mechanism of choice. Creating a state-of-the-art reporting system and properly communicating its existence will allow employees and others to report violations of business conduct and other issues. In addition, legitimate whistle-blowers who have evidence of fraud must be confident that they will be protected from retaliation in reporting allegations. Failure to build this protection into a program will guarantee civil and criminal repercussions. Numerous requirements in setting up a successful hotline must be understood and carried out in protecting a company and all stakeholders. One major requirement is the use of a third-party provider for the hotline to ensure independence and transparency.

## WHAT ARE WHISTLE-BLOWERS?

Today's executive needs to have a greater understanding of potential risks than ever before, and few things are more important than knowledge of whistle-blowers and hotlines. If those entrusted with protecting their corporation's interests either intentionally hide the existence of fraud or fail to discover it, there are those who will assume that responsibility. They are the whistle-blowers, who risk their careers to expose significant allegations of financial fraud or other wrongdoing by public or private organizations.

Experience teaches that fraud is often uncovered and exposed by people with inside knowledge including employees, vendors, customers, and others. The long-time secretary or bookkeeper who has been with the company for ages may know where all the "bodies are buried" and if given the opportunity will give valuable information to an all-too-willing-to-listen federal agent, prosecutor, or news reporter. In addition to being referred to as whistle-blowers, these people are also called confidential informants (CIs), confidential sources, informed employees, or, as the Association of Certified Fraud Examiners (ACFE) calls them, sentinels, those citizens willing to come forward—regardless of personal or professional sacrifices or consequences—to expose corporate corruption at the highest levels.[1]

Some people think that whistle-blowers are simply disgruntled employees looking for an easy way to get back at their employers. In some cases this may be true, but clearly not all. This may have been the defense previously used by employers in dismissing a whistle-blower's allegations of corporate wrongdoing. Often it is easier to discredit the whistle-blower than to investigate thoroughly and determine whether the accusations are true. Being fired is sometimes not the worst consequence for a whistle-blower. Business and professional colleagues often turn against whistle-blowers rather than be identified with their cause. Whistle-blowers have lost friends and families, and some have turned to alcohol to ease their personal pain and depression.[2]

It is safe to say that no one ever aspires to be a whistle-blower. In fact, people usually do not use the term when referring to those who "blow the whistle" on fraud and abuse. They are often called rats, stool pigeons, snitches, betrayers, and much worse. All too often it is the whistle-blower standing alone against a rich and powerful corporation. "The lone wolf whistle-blower is often set up against a powerful corporate or government entity with more resources and power," says James E. Fisher, director of the Emerson Electric Center for Business Ethics at St. Louis University. He goes on to say, "From the get-go, you have the likelihood of retaliation."[3]

Retaliation is the big "R" word facing whistle-blowers. This fear has no doubt kept many a person with personal knowledge of corporate fraud from going public. Organizations that use retaliation as a weapon of silence may have succeeded in the past. There has been a steady attack on retaliation toward informers with the strengthening of the False Claims Act as a means to extract civil and criminal punishment in government fraud cases, the whistle-blower protection afforded by Sarbanes-Oxley, and the good press given to the role of whistle-blowers over the last few years.

## THE GOVERNMENT'S USE OF INFORMANTS AND WHISTLE-BLOWERS

It can be argued that the government's success against corporate fraud has been in large part because of the assistance of cooperating informants, cooperating defendants, and whistle-blowers. In the Arthur Andersen case, the government had a cooperating defendant, former Andersen partner David Duncan. He testified for the prosecution and helped convict Andersen of obstruction of justice for shredding documents and deleting computer files in order to protect its client, Enron. Although the conviction was overturned by the United States Supreme Court in May 2005, it was not because of Duncan's cooperation. In the prosecution of WorldCom CEO Bernard Ebbers, the government had cooperating defendant and former CFO Scott Sullivan testify, as well as other cooperating WorldCom defendants who helped convict Ebbers on all counts of corporate fraud. In countless other cases defendants decided to plead guilty and cooperate with the government in the hopes of receiving a lighter sentence.

A cooperating defendant is just that, a person who has committed a crime, pleads guilty to that crime, and agrees to cooperate with law enforcement authorities to provide evidence against co-conspirators in the hopes of receiving a reduced sentence. A whistle-blower "is someone in an organization who witnesses behavior by members that is either contrary to the mission of the organization, or threatening to the public interest, and who decides to speak out publicly about it."[4] Simply put, a whistle-blower is an informant who wants to expose and stop wrongdoing in an organization.

It has been said that if one wants information on crimes, it is more likely to come from criminals than from honest citizens. Every defense attorney will attack the credibility of a cooperating defendant, especially one who originally was part of the conspiracy and decided to break from his fellow criminals. The prosecution does not always have the luxury of using witnesses with high moral and ethical standards. Although one would prefer witnesses without "baggage" for the defense to attack, the fact is that prosecutors have to play the cards they are dealt and that includes using criminals to testify against other criminals. No one else has better knowledge of fraud than fellow fraudsters.

## WHISTLE-BLOWERS ARE CORPORATE SENTINELS

A number of well-publicized and lesser known whistle-blowers have been involved in the corporate scandals of the last few years. The best known of the group are Enron's Sherron Watkins and WorldCom's Cynthia Cooper, who exposed corporate fraud at their respective companies. Their actions gained new respectability for whistle-blowers and the gratitude of the investing public.

It is vital too for a company to foster a culture in which employees feel empowered to come forward to report allegations of wrongdoing. Watkins thought she was doing just that when, in August 2001, she sent a six-page letter to then Enron CEO Kenneth Lay detailing what she had uncovered about accounting abnormalities and possible fraud at the energy giant. She characterized it as "an elaborate accounting hoax."[5] She must have felt some level of trust and comfort in sending the letter to Lay rather than to an outside source such as law enforcement or the media. Obviously, she thought that Enron would take more action than it did because of her letter. A number of selected quotes from Watkins's letter to Lay are contained in Executive Insight 12.1

**EXECUTIVE INSIGHT 12.1: SELECTED QUOTES FROM ENRON WHISTLE-BLOWER SHERRON WATKINS'S AUGUST 2001 SIX-PAGE LETTER TO THEN ENRON CEO KEN LAY DETAILING "AN ELABORATE ACCOUNTING HOAX" AT THE COMPANY[i]**

---

*"Has Enron become a risky place to work? For those of us who didn't get rich over the last few years, can we afford to stay?"*

*"Skilling's abrupt departure will raise suspicions of accounting improprieties and valuation issues."*

*"I am incredibly nervous that we will implode in a wave of accounting scandals."*

*"Is there a way our accounting guru's [sic] can unwind these deals now? I have thought and thought about how to do this, but I keep bumping into one big problem—we booked Condor and Raptor deals in 1999 and 2000, we enjoyed a wonderfully high stock price, many executives sold stock, we then try and reverse or fix the deals in 2001, and it's a bit like robbing the bank in one year and trying to pay it back 2 years later. Nice try, but investors were hurt, they bought at $70 and $80/share looking for $120/share and now they're at $38 or worse. We are under too much scrutiny and there are probably one or two disgruntled 'redeployed' employees who know enough about the 'funny' accounting to get us in trouble."*

*"I realize that we have had a lot of smart people looking at this and a lot of accountants including AA&Co [Arthur Andersen] have blessed the accounting treatment. None of that will protect Enron if these transactions are ever disclosed in the bright light of day. (Please review the late 90's problems of Waste Management—where AA paid $130+MM in litigation re: questionable accounting practices)."*

*"The overriding basic principle of accounting is that if you explain the 'accounting treatment' to a man on the street, would you influence his investing decisions? Would he sell or buy the stock based on a thorough understanding of the facts?"*

> *"I firmly believe that executive management of the company must have a clear and precise knowledge of these transactions and they must have the transactions reviewed by objective experts in the fields of securities law and accounting."*
>
> *"I firmly believe that the probability of discovery significantly increased with Skilling's shocking departure. Too many people are looking for a smoking gun."*
>
> *"Cliff Baxter[ii] complained mightily to Skilling and all who would listen about the inappropriateness of our transactions with LJM."*
>
> *"I have heard one manager level employee from the principle [sic] investments group say 'I know it would be devastating to all of us, but I wish we would get caught. We're such a crooked company."*
>
> ---
>
> [i] Sherron Watkins' letter to Ken Lay, Enron CEO (August 24, 2001), http://energycommerce.house.gov/107/news/layletter.pdf.
> [ii] Cliff Baxter was an Enron executive who mysteriously committed suicide on January 25, 2002. CBS News reported that Baxter had agreed to testify before Congress in the Enron hearings. A congressional source told CBS News that Baxter was not a target but was going to provide evidence against others at the company.

The magnitude of Watkins's allegations greatly concerned her and was a harbinger of bad things to come for Enron. Watkins must be credited with having the courage to pen such a detailed letter of corporate wrongdoing and sending it to her CEO, yet, there are some who might question why she sent her whistle-blower letter only to Lay and not others outside the company. Why did she not also send the letter to the FBI, the Securities and Exchange Commission (SEC), or the media? The question will probably never be answered, but suffice it to say that whistle-blowers probably have their own level of risk tolerance.

Not all whistle-blowers gain notoriety. Some just come forward, do their duty, and try to go back to their prior lives. Most also do not write books capitalizing on their blowing the whistle on corporate fraud. Take the case of Maureen Castaneda, the director of foreign exchange and sovereign risk for Enron. When she was laid off by Enron in January 2002, she took home a box of paper shredding to use as packing material for a household move. She had no idea what the shredding contained until by accident she noticed a familiar name on a piece of paper. The shredded paper contained financial records of the fraudulent off-the-books partnerships that would result in indictments of many Enron executives.

Castaneda came to learn that the shredding continued long after the SEC had announced a formal investigation into Enron's finances. Castaneda told her lawyer about her discovery, and he promptly disclosed it to the government. The shredded documents were later used to verify that Enron employees were illegally destroying evidence. Castaneda told CNN's Jack Cafferty in an on-air interview that "There was a lot of arrogance at the company, I mean to the point where—an arrogance at the level where you think you can lie to Wall Street and get away with it. You can't get more arrogant than that."[6]

The ACFE has recognized the importance of the corporate sentinel who, without malice or a hidden agenda, wants to expose impropriety. In response, the ACFE has created an award called the Cliff Robertson Sentinel Award that is bestowed annually on a person who, "Without regard to personal or professional consequences, has publicly disclosed wrongdoing in business or government." The award is named for the Oscar-winning actor who blew the whistle on fraud in Hollywood in the 1970s and who was the first recipient of the award in 2003. The ACFE's Sentinel Award carries the inscription, "For Choosing Truth over Self." The award is significant because Robertson was a famous Hollywood actor who dared to come forward at great risk to his professional career to expose corporate corruption at the highest levels in Hollywood.

## SARBANES-OXLEY WHISTLE-BLOWER REQUIREMENTS AND PROTECTIONS

Sarbanes-Oxley's Title III (Corporate Responsibility), Section 301 (Public Company Audit Committees) requires that each Audit Committee establish procedures for "the receipt, retention, and treatment of complaints received by the issuer regarding accounting, internal accounting controls, or auditing matters; and the confidential, anonymous submission by employees of the issuers of concerns regarding questionable accounting or auditing matters."[7] This translates into the requirement for public companies to have a mechanism and process that provides confidentiality and anonymity for employees and others to report issues of financial impropriety. Clearly, the mechanism alluded to is a hotline.

Title IV (Enhanced Financial Disclosures), Section 404 (Management Assessment of Internal Controls) requires an annual assessment by the issuer and its external auditor "of the effectiveness of the internal control structure and procedures of the issuer for financial reporting."[8] This translates into the requirement of an assessment of the mechanism for receiving complaints and how they are investigated and resolved. Unless a company has set up an effective process from creating a hotline, to properly communicating its existence, to conducting professional and thorough inquiries, to taking appropriate action when necessary, to reporting the results to the Audit Committee, there will be no way that a company will be in compliance with Section 404.

Title VIII (Corporate and Criminal Fraud Accountability), Section 806 (Protection for Employees of Publicly Traded Companies Who Provide Evidence of Fraud) details the civil action that employee whistle-blowers can take to protect themselves against retaliation for reporting allegations of fraud at their companies.[9] Title XI (Corporate Fraud Accountability), Section 1107 (Retaliation against Informants) makes it a federal felony to retaliate against a whistle-blower who provides assistance to law enforcement. The penalties include up to 10 years in prison for managers and others who are convicted of retaliation.[10] The actual criminal penalties are detailed in the amended section of Title 18, United States Code, Section 1513, which reads, "Whoever knowingly, with the intent to retaliate, takes any action harmful to any person, including interference with the lawful employment or livelihood of any person, for providing to a law enforcement officer any truthful information relating to the commission or possible commission of any Federal offense, shall be fined under this title or imprisoned not more than 10 years or both."[11]

## Role of OSHA

The mission of the Occupational Safety and Health Administration (OSHA) of the Department of Labor's (DOL) is to ensure the safety and health of American workers by setting and enforcing standards and by working with employees and employers to create better working environments. The DOL (OSHA through inference) have been designated by Sarbanes-Oxley to enforce its whistle-blower protections. OSHA provides detailed information on the protection of whistle-blowers and reporting of possible retaliation against whistle-blowers.[12]

## Legal Protection When Reporting Corporate Fraud

People who work for a publicly traded company or brokerage firm, or their contractors, subcontractors, or agents, have special whistle-blower protection under Sarbanes-Oxley. All companies with a class of securities registered under Section 12 of the Securities Exchange Act or those that are required to file reports under Section 15(d) of the Act, or their contractors, subcontractors, or agents are covered. Although most companies are covered under this provision, it is important to check with the SEC at www.sec.gov and search the EDGAR database for the specific company, contractor, or agent.

Under Sarbanes-Oxley protections, a company may not discharge or discriminate in any manner against a person who has provided information, caused information to be provided, or assisted in an official government investigation including law enforcement, securities regulators, or Congress, or an internal company investigation relating to alleged violations of mail fraud, wire fraud, bank fraud, securities fraud, SEC rules or regulations, or other federal laws relating to fraud against shareholders. This also includes disclosing information to a supervisor or other person at the company. The protected employee must reasonably believe the misconduct is a violation of federal law or SEC rules. In addition, there is a ban on discharging or other discrimination for filing a complaint or otherwise assisting in a proceeding relating to a potential violation. There is a strict ban on any form of retaliation including the following:

- Discharge
- Demotion

- Suspension
- Threats
- Harassment
- Failure to hire or rehire
- Blacklisting
- Other discrimination or disciplinary action.

## Requirements for Filing Complaints

To be protected under OSHA, a person must file a complaint within 90 days of the alleged violation. OSHA will review the complaint and determine whether it will conduct an investigation into the allegation. OSHA will then issue findings and an order on the complaint. After OSHA issues its findings and order, either party may request a hearing before an administrative law judge of the DOL. There is an appeal process for any administrative law judge's decision and order. If a final agency order is not issued within 180 days of the date the complaint was first filed, the complainant can bring an action in the appropriate United States District Court.

## Whistle-Blower Relief

Whistle-blowers who prevail can expect to be made whole with compensatory damages providing:

- Reinstatement with the same seniority status
- Back pay with interest
- Compensation for special damages including litigation costs, reasonable attorney's fees, and expert witness fees.

There is always the possibility that a person will falsely allege wrongdoing on the part of company. An employee may have a personal agenda, anger, or resentment against a particular person such as a supervisor for any number of reasons. This may result in a false claim. OSHA recognizes this, and if a complaint is found to be frivolous or brought in bad faith, the false accuser may be held liable by both the government and the victim company.[13]

## HOTLINES: BUILD IT RIGHT AND THEY WILL CALL

"Build it right and they will call" should be the mantra for today's well-run employee hotlines. On the same day in January 2002, both Enron Vice-President Sherron Watkins and former CEO Jeff Skilling testified before Congress about the Enron implosion. They sat next to each other but gave opposite testimony. Skilling said that as far as he knew, everything was in compliance at Enron. Then Watkins detailed how she tried to "blow the whistle" to then CEO Kenneth Lay, but he would not listen. Watkins detailed to Lay an "elaborate accounting hoax." Instead of being hailed as a hero for reporting the fraud, she felt Enron's wrath. Her computer hard drive was confiscated; she was moved from her elaborate office; and Enron was considering firing her.[14]

All companies, public or private, benefit from hotlines. Confidential hotlines and business conduct lines are excellent ways to receive allegations of fraud and other wrongdoing. Hotlines allow employees and others outside the company to communicate compliance concerns to the company for appropriate action. Hotlines reveal hidden issues; company employees know that their financial futures are linked to the successful existence of their companies. If a company does not already have a hotline in place, it is putting itself at risk. Hotlines are here to stay. Whistle-blowers and hotlines together provide a potent mix that can protect a company significantly.

Other than the Sarbanes-Oxley requirement for having a hotline, some key statistics also support the benefit. The ACFE's *2004 Report to the Nation on Occupational Fraud and Abuse* found that tips were the most common way that frauds were detected. This occurred with a far greater frequency than through internal audit, internal controls, external audit, or even by accident. When one looks at the makeup of the tipsters, one sees that the greatest number came from employees, followed by customers, vendors, and then anonymous individuals.[15] As the graph in Exhibit 12.1 shows, the results were similar for both the 2004 and the 2002 surveys.

Based on the findings of the *2004 Report to the Nation*, it can be inferred quite reasonably that most tips about fraud have come from employees. Therefore, an organization needs the most appropriate

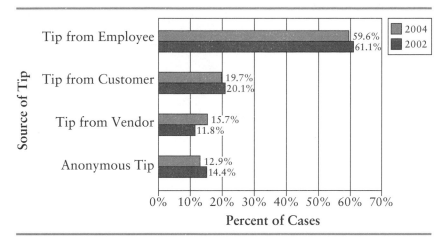

**Exhibit 12.1** Percent of Tips by Source[a]

*Source:* Reprinted with permission from the Association of Certified Fraud Examiners, Austin, Texas ©2005

[a] The sum of percentages in this chart exceeds 100% because in some cases the tips were received from more than one source.

mechanism to capture reporting of fraud from employees. That is through a hotline. The study's findings regarding reporting of fraud from people outside the company and through anonymous reporting also support the need for hotlines to capture information about fraud and other issues adequately. Some other findings from the *2004 Report to the Nation* also support the need for hotlines. When one reviews cases of fraud committed by owners and executives of organizations, again, most cases (51 percent) were detected through tips. Internal audit accounted for 24 percent, external audit accounted for 28 percent, by accident accounted for 12 percent, and internal controls only accounted for 6 percent of detection methods. When one looks at frauds in excess of $1 million, tips accounted for 42 percent of detection methods, internal audit accounted for 25 percent, by accident accounted for 18 percent, external audit accounted for 16 percent, and internal controls came in at 8 percent.[16]

## The Need for Hotlines

Another key statistic from the *2004 Report to the Nation* points to the beneficial aspects of having a hotline. Organizations that implemented hotlines and other confidential reporting mechanisms significantly reduced fraud losses. The median loss for organizations that had hotlines was $56,000. The median loss was more than twice that amount, $135,000, for organizations that did not have such confidential reporting mechanisms[17] (see Exhibit 12.2). The results were similar for the *2002 Report to the Nation*: The median loss for organizations that had hotlines was $77,500, whereas the median loss was $150,000 for organizations without them.[18] Tips from employees are the most common means of fraud detection; when tips are combined with an anonymous reporting mechanism such as a hotline, the detection and reporting of fraud greatly increases.

An interesting finding from the *2004 Report to the Nation* was that hotlines were the least common fraud detection and prevention method in place. Whereas 74 percent of survey respondents had external auditors and 57 percent had an internal audit department,

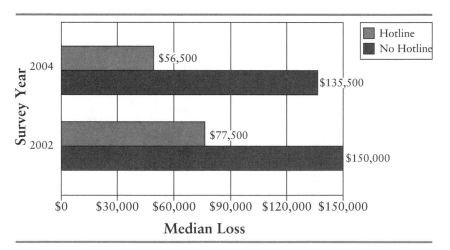

**Exhibit 12.2** Median Loss Based on Whether Organization Had Hotline
*Source:* Reprinted with permission from the Association of Certified Fraud Examiners, Austin, Texas ©2005

only 37 percent reported that they had instituted a hotline. The small number of hotlines in place at the time may seem remarkable; the fact is that many organizations do not realize the full potential of hotlines. Hotlines are nothing new, but they work. There is no reason for any company, no matter how small, not to have some manner of confidential and anonymous reporting such as a hotline. Now, with Sarbanes-Oxley, it is no longer an option.

One of the authors was involved in an investigation that started as a result of a hotline call. The caller stated that if the company had not had a hotline, the allegation would not have been reported. The caller wanted anonymity, and a hotline was the only mechanism that provided that level of comfort and trust. The whistle-blower used the hotline call to report a fraud scheme involving an employee and a vendor totaling thousands of dollars.

## Choose the Right Name

The term "hotline" is the common default for a confidential and anonymous reporting tool. Texas Instruments' *Accounting and Auditing Hotline*, Pepsico's *Speak Up Hotline*, and Citigroup's *Ethics Hotline* all use "hotline" in the name. Although the term conveys the idea of a quick and direct telephone line for information, it may also give a connotation that any call received may bring bad news. Callers will do more than just report fraud. They may inquire as to appropriate business practices, policy and procedure clarification, or matters totally unrelated to the mechanism's purpose. A company may consider using a term other than hotline that better signifies the intent. General Motor's *Awareline*, Merck's *Advice Line*, Altria's *Integrity HelpLine*, and Microsoft's *Business Conduct Line* all are "hotlines," but they use a more inclusive and less threatening title. The appropriate name sends a message to employees and others about the importance of the reporting mechanism.

Some companies' hotlines are not easy to find on the company Web site. If the intent is to provide a means to report violations of business conduct and foster good corporate governance, one can ask why the hotline is not in a prominent location on the home page. Build it right and they will call.

## Confidential versus Anonymous

Most hotlines say they are confidential and anonymous to provide a level of comfort to the caller. Maintaining the confidentiality and anonymity of hotline callers is absolutely critical to the success of the hotline. Violate the trust between the caller and the organization, and there is little chance of ever restoring confidence. If the caller's identity is not kept confidential and anonymous, it is a good bet that few people will call and report violations of business conduct. There is a difference between confidentiality and anonymity, however.

Confidentiality implies that the caller's identity and information will not be communicated broadly to those people without a need to know. If a person calls a hotline and provides a name along with the allegations, it must be understood that this information will be made known to officials at the company such as the legal department, the investigative unit, human resources, and other appropriate personnel. Confidentiality should ensure that the communication is only disclosed to the minimum number of authorized people in order to resolve the issue. If a person's name is provided, the organization has a duty to protect the confidentiality of that person. If it cannot do this, the organization may have far bigger problems than whatever the caller is reporting. There is an argument to be made that it might be better for a whistle-blower not to provide a name or other identifying information when reporting wrongdoing.

Anonymity provides secrecy and nondisclosure for the caller's identity but not the information provided. True anonymity involves the removal of any reference to a caller's gender or other identifying information, even if a name is not provided. Safeguards must be in place to protect the caller's identity in case certain personnel at the company attempt to determine it for any reason. Anonymity promised must be anonymity kept. It is important to always advise that the confidentiality of anyone reporting a possible violation will be maintained within the limits allowed by law.

## Hotline Basics

A number of basic rules apply when it comes to hotlines. The hotline number must be easily accessible. It must be available to callers in every country where the company operates. As globalization of business increases, it makes good sense to be able to receive calls from anywhere in the world. The number must be toll-free from within the United States and other countries where such a number can be dialed. In countries where a toll-free number is not available, there must be an international number that can be called collect. As previously stated, the hotline must be confidential and anonymous. It must be available 24 hours a day, seven days a week, to capture all possible calls. Employees may not want to call from work, where there is the chance they may be discovered, so a call at night from home is more likely. In fact, 40 percent of hotline calls are made outside of normal business hours.[19] In addition, with callers from other countries and time zone differences, round-the-clock availability is a must.

The hotline must be staffed by "live" people. The interaction with a live person cannot be duplicated in any other way. Having a telephone line with an answering machine to take calls after hours is not state-of-the-art compliance in today's world. The hotline must have language capability for all employees in all countries where the organization has operations. This means translators with excellent language skills must be available to speak to any caller. The caller should be advised that the calls are not recorded or traced. For callers who want to remain anonymous, any reports provided should be gender neutral to protect the caller's anonymity. Operators must be thoroughly screened and trained. The questioning of the callers must be professional in nature, focusing on the information or allegation provided. Callers should be provided a callback code word or number in case they want to call back and provide more information or ask about the status of any investigation resulting from their information. A good policy should be never to advise the caller of the details of any ongoing investigation. At the conclusion of any investigation, the organization's legal department should decide what information, if any, should be communicated to the caller.

## Types of Reporting Mechanisms

Potential reporters of fraud and abuse should have as many available means of communication as possible. This includes reporting by telephone, e-mail, letter, or fax. The more and varied types of reporting that a company has, the greater the chance that important information will be provided. When reporting is done by e-mail over the Internet, the third-party vendor should remove the header and other contact information before forwarding it to the organization. Anonymous e-mail accounts are easy to open for this purpose. When a number of different reporting systems are available, there is the potential for information to be missed or routed to the wrong person. Whoever maintains the hotline for an organization must have appropriate systems and safeguards in place to receive and respond to each type of report.

## Kinds of Calls the Hotline Should Take

An organization's hotline should take any and all kinds of calls. When calls are limited only to those related to financial accounting issues, as mandated by Sarbanes-Oxley, the hotline is not being used to the fullest extent possible. A hotline should take calls covering all kinds of wrongdoing, whether it is fraud, corruption, theft, sexual harassment, workplace violence, or other violations of business conduct. Hotlines should also take any other type of call even if it is not related to a wrongdoing. All reports from calls should be communicated to an appropriate official at the organization for further action.

## Questions to Ask of Callers

The operators of the hotline need to ask probing questions but not appear to be conducting an interrogation. Professionalism and experience play an important role in asking key questions and getting the answers without intimidating the caller. The tone and demeanor of the operator, the respect provided to the caller, and how the questions are asked will provide either a positive or negative result. The process to be completed and the information to be documented are as follows:

- Advise that the call is confidential and that nothing is provided to identify the caller unless the caller specifically requests to be identified.

- Record the time and date of the call.
- Record the operator's name, identification number, and location.
- Assign a specific caller identification code or number.
- Is the caller an employee, vendor, contractor or other?
- What is the business conduct violation or other wrongful act(s)?
- How is the caller aware of this information?
- Who are the people involved? In addition to the names, the operator should ask the caller to provide as much detailed information as possible such as titles, addresses, and other contact information.
- When did it occur?
- Where did it occur?
- How long has it been going on?
- It is still ongoing?
- How often has it been occurring?
- Does the caller have any physical evidence related to the allegation?
- Has the caller ever reported this before? If so, provide details.
- Have the caller provide as much information as possible, as there may be only one chance to capture it.

## Use Third-Party Vendors

Although some companies may feel it is more cost effective to maintain the reporting system in-house, this is improper and can lead to serious independence issues. To ensure transparency and a culture of compliance, there is nothing better than having an independent third-party vendor take hotline calls. In fact, it is highly recommended that a company's hotline be administered by an external third-party vendor to provide an increased level of trust and confidence and to avoid the "concern that 'anonymous calls' will go to a company person who will recognize the tipster's voice."[20] By outsourcing this function, the company is protected from accusations of covering up evidence of fraud. There is just too much risk if a company's in-house hotline receives an allegation of financial accounting fraud by a CEO or CFO and the company then finds the allegation without merit. There may always be that nagging feeling that a thorough and impartial investigation was not conducted and the matter was swept under the rug. Although this will not be true in most instances, it is not necessary to take the chance.

Third-party vendors of hotlines with many years of experience and many corporate clients are best able to receive and respond to all types of calls. They have trained professionals handling the calls, and they understand the importance of confidentiality and the reputational risk they face if the calls are not handled professionally. Hotlines can be built for the individual needs of each client. Of course, all hotline vendors may not have the same level of experience and skills. Before signing a contract, a careful vetting must be conducted. The vetting requires that the company obtain certain information and ask questions that must be appropriately answered, such as:

- How long has the company been in business?
- Who is (are) the principal owner(s)?
- Is there more than one physical office location?
- How many clients does the company have?
- Has the company received any complaints? If so, what are the details?
- Ask them to provide several references.
- Check the Better Business Bureau for complaints.
- Are there operators available around the clock to take calls?
- What is the experience level of the operators?
- What kind of educational requirements are needed to be an operator? All operators should at least have college degrees. Some vendors require postgraduate degrees in social work, psychology, or a related field.
- Are background checks including criminal checks and credit checks performed on all operators with periodic updates?
- Do all vendor employees (ownership and operators) sign nondisclosure agreements?
- What kind of training program do the operators complete?
- Is the training program general in nature or specific to the client's operation?
- How long are the operators trained before they can take calls?
- Is there an ongoing training program to keep the operators up to date on changes and process improvements?
- What is the operator turnover rate and why?
- How many languages are available and what is the proficiency level for each?

The third-party vendors should report allegations and other issues to several points of contact to ensure transparency and action. Among the people who should receive the information are the Chief Compliance Officer or Director of Compliance, the Ethics Officer, the Chair of the Audit Committee, the head of Internal Audit, and the Director of Corporate Security or Financial Integrity.

There are many experienced third-party providers of hotlines and related services. Because of space limitations, this book can discuss only two of the many quality providers available in the marketplace today. Potential clients of hotline services are encouraged to do their homework and find the most experienced provider that suits their needs. Global Compliance Services' AlertLine was founded in 1981 by a Secret Service investigator. Their related services include compliance audits, research, and employee education and awareness. They serve many of the Fortune 100 and Fortune 1000 companies but they do not advertise on their Web site the names of actual clients.

The Network, Inc. was founded in 1983 by a former FBI special agent. Their reporting mechanism is called ReportLine, and their other services include insurance claim reporting and employee education. Their Web site lists some of their clients, including General Electric, Citigroup, Starbucks, The Home Depot, Marriott Hotels, and Wendy's. Wendy's Web site actually advises that The Network is their third-party provider by stating, "If you do not want to discuss your questions through normal company channels, you may call The Network. The Network is an independent organization which helps businesses, like ours, maintain high ethical standards. The Network allows you to share questions or concerns with the company on an anonymous basis."[21] The Network also offers its customers access to strategic partners that provide investigative consultation services, fraud prevention training programs, and technology solutions.

## Communicating the Existence of the Hotline

A reporting system will not be successful unless all employees are aware of it and have a reasonable assurance that the company will act on allegations based on factual belief. A good test is for managers to ask employees about their knowledge of the hotline at one-on-one meetings and group training sessions. It might be surprising to find that a good number of employees are unaware that a reporting mechanism even exists in the organization. However, a company is only half protected unless the hotline is known by people outside the organization. People outside the company are as likely to call as those within, if they have knowledge of violations of business conduct. Thus, there is a constant need to communicate the existence of the hotline both inside and outside the company. There are a number of ways to do this, including the following:

- Prominently displaying information about the hotline on the organization's Web site
- Including hotline information in the company code of conduct as well as other codes used such as procurement, vendor, and finance
- Placing hotline information on the company Intranet, office bulletin boards, in newsletters, on posters, in break rooms, on table-tents in cafeterias, and other places where employees congregate
- Sending letters to all company employees at their homes announcing the hotline
- Communicating that the organization has an independent third-party vendor taking the calls
- Sending letters to all company vendors and partners announcing the hotline
- Printing the hotline number on all company checks paid to vendors; the benefit is that a supplier may call in and report a violation, as in the case of a company that received such a call after it printed its hotline number on its checks[22]
- Being sure to communicate that appropriate action will be taken against those who are found to have reported false allegations.

### Corporate Response to Hotline Calls

Responding to hotline calls must be a top priority for an organization. A quick response will build confidence and also remove potential doubts about the company's commitment to ethical behavior and a culture of compliance. The hotline provider should communicate all allegations and other reported information to appropriate officials at the organization. All reports should be immediately logged into a case management system for future reporting to the Chief Executive Officer, the Audit Committee, and, if necessary, external auditors and government regulators.

## Vetting the Hotline Calls

Third-party receivers of hotline calls will not normally test the validity of the information received or provide any commentary as to the legitimacy of the information. This is the organization's responsibility. Be aware that some people may use an anonymous reporting mechanism for their own sinister designs. Using live interviewers who can ask probing questions may lessen the possibility that a person will report false information. When the organization receives an allegation of fraud or other business conduct violation through a hotline, it is important to test and corroborate the allegations received. Detailed vetting for independent corroboration of allegations is critical. Financial integrity units are the logical choice to receive and investigate fraud allegations received through the hotline.

The content of calls that are received must undergo a further examination to corroborate the allegations. A number of questions need to be asked and answered, including the following:

- Is the allegation detailed and specific or just general, such as saying there is fraud at the company?
- Is the allegation reasonable or so outlandish that it may have no basis in fact?
- Is someone actually named in the allegation?
- If a person is named by the anonymous caller, is it even possible that the person could have committed the violation?
- Does the person named have the position and opportunity to commit the alleged fraud?
- Is evidence provided to substantiate the allegation or is information provided so as to find the evidence?
- Does it appear that the caller has a hidden agenda?
- Can a preliminary corroboration of the allegations be made?
- Does the caller make additional calls to the hotline providing additional information?

Another element needs to be added to this process. When a call is received and referred to an investigator for follow-up, advise the third-party vendor of the name and contact information for the investigator assigned to the matter. In case the whistle-blower calls back, the investigator's name can be provided to the whistle-blower, who may decide to contact the investigator directly to provide additional information. There is a great benefit when an experienced investigator has the opportunity to actually interview a hotline caller to learn more about the allegation and whether it has merit. Sometimes the whistle-blower then calls the investigator directly and provides even more useful information.

It is also important to test the effectiveness of the hotline when third-party vendors are used. A checks and balance approach will ensure that hotline calls are being routed by the vendor to the appropriate personnel at the company. An organization may consider having designated company personnel call the hotline and anonymously provide a specific but made-up allegation. Test how quickly and correctly the allegation is communicated to the company. In addition, make test calls on Sarbanes-Oxley-related issues and see whether they are referred to the Audit Committee by the hotline as they should be. Make these calls from the United States and various other countries where the company has offices. The calls outside the United States can be made by investigative or legal personnel while they are traveling to foreign countries on business.

## THE FEDERAL FALSE CLAIMS ACT

For whistle-blowers, possibly the best recourse for exposing fraud in government contracts has been the United States False Claims Act. The False Claims Act was enacted to encourage private citizen whistle-blowers to file lawsuits in the name of the United States Government charging false claim violations by government contractors, health care providers, and other businesses and persons who receive or use government funds. The greatest impact from False Claims Act whistle-blower actions has been in the health care industry. Physicians, hospitals, medical service and equipment providers, and pharmaceutical companies typically receive federal funds. Organizations and individuals who commit fraud involving federal funds face the possibility that employees or others who have knowledge of the fraud may use the False Claims Act not only to expose the criminal wrongdoing of the organization but also to reap huge monetary rewards from reporting it.

The False Claims Act was passed in 1863 after Congress uncovered widespread instances of fraud on the part of military contractors to the Union Army, resulting in defective weapons as well as price gouging during the Civil War. President Lincoln urged its passing to combat rampant fraud and restore needed funding for the war effort. In fact, it is often called the "Lincoln Law" because of the President's strong support of its enactment. The *qui tam* (is the short form in Latin meaning "who sues on behalf of the king as well as himself") Provision of the False Claims Act encourages private citizens to uncover and disclose fraud and as a result benefit financially. Although the Act was initially intended to fight military procurement fraud, it applies to all government contractors and federal programs when government funds are involved.

The original 1863 Act allowed a relator (plaintiff) to file a lawsuit, but there were a number of obstacles to overcome. The relator had to bear all the costs of the lawsuit, and the government could join the lawsuit at any time and completely take over the case. In later years, the government made it even harder for relators to prevail. The maximum monetary amount that could be awarded to a relator was reduced from 50 percent to 25 percent if the government did not join in the case with the relator. If the government entered the case, the maximum that a relator could receive was 10 percent. These restrictions resulted in little use of the False Claims Act.

That changed in 1986 with the emergence of new government contracting and procurement frauds. This long-forgotten Act gained new popularity when Congress reinforced it with strengthened amendments. Defendants now faced increased damages and penalties. The relator's share of recovered proceeds was now between 15 and 25 percent if the government joined the lawsuit. The maximum payout of 25 percent would be based on the whistle-blower's significant contribution to the case. If the government did not join the case, the whistle-blower could recover at least 25 percent but not more than 30 percent of what the government recovered. The amount awarded to the relator is based on the amount recovered and not the actual fraud loss. In addition, prior government knowledge of the fraud did not affect the ability of a relator to file a *qui tam* action and prevail.

## EXECUTIVE INSIGHT 12.2: A WHISTLE-BLOWER FINDS THE GOLDEN GOOSE

Whistle-blowers who utilize the False Claims Act not only find justice but often discover the Golden Goose along the way: The windfall can be huge for plaintiffs who prevail after blowing the whistle on fraud. "Since its inception, the False Claims Act has generated $12 billion for the federal treasury and more than $1 billion for hundreds of whistle-blowers."[iii] Jim Alderson is one who hit the jackpot after successfully filing whistle-blower claims. In one case, he received $20 million and in another, he split $100 million. In 1990, Alderson was employed as Chief Financial Officer at a hospital in Montana and was fired for refusing to maintain two sets of books. One set of books contained falsified numbers to be used for Medicare reimbursement and another set was only for the hospital's internal use, allegedly containing the true accounting numbers. Even though he was fired, Alderson continued digging and found massive fraud. He filed a wrongful termination lawsuit that eventually became *qui tam* actions against Quorum Health Group, Inc. and Columbia/HCA, two of the largest health care management companies in the United States. The Department of Justice joined Alderson's civil lawsuits in 1998, and the cases were eventually settled in the government's and Alderson's favor. He was richly rewarded for the heartache of 13 years of legal battles. Alderson now lives the good life knowing that he helped expose fraud and in the process took the defrauded proceeds from the offenders.[iv] As Senator Charles Grassley (R-Iowa), who helped enhance the act in 1986, said, "Whistle-blowers shed light on why something is wrong, and their insights can help hold the bad actors responsible, fix problems and achieve reforms."[v]

---

[iii] The Associated Press, "For Some Whistle-Blowers, Big Risk Pays Off," *New York Times.com*, November 28, 2004, A1.
[iv] Siobhan McDonough, "Whistle-Blowers Rake in the Dough," *Seattle Times*, November 27, 2004, A28.
[v] The Associated Press, "For Some Whistle-Blowers, Big Risk Pays Off," *New York Times.com*, November 28, 2004, A1.

Whistle-blowers can file civil actions under seal in district courts that will be reviewed by the local United States Attorney's Offices. If the prosecutors feel the cases have merit, the government can bring in federal agents to conduct a related criminal investigation. The addition of these resources would help to bring about a successful prosecution and greatly benefit a relator's civil case and subsequent monetary reward.

Whistle-blower protection is also included in the False Claims Act. The Act prohibits an employer from any form of retaliation against an employee who attempts to report allegations of fraud against the federal government. The retaliation protection covers discharge, demotion, suspension, threats, harassment, or other discrimination as a result of lawful acts by employees or employees on behalf of others in furtherance of a False Claims Act action. The affected party or parties "shall be entitled to all relief necessary to make the employee whole" and "shall include reinstatement with the same seniority status such employee would have had but for the discrimination, two times the amount of back pay, interest on the back pay, and compensation for any special damages sustained as a result of the discrimination, including litigation costs and reasonable attorneys' fees."[23]

As a result of the 1986 enhancements, the False Claims Act has become very popular with whistle-blowers by offering them significant financial incentives to expose wrongdoing. There has been a steady increase in the number of lawsuits filed and recoveries of funds. In 1987, 33 cases were filed; in 1995, 274 cases were filed. In one example, in fiscal year 2001 (October 1, 2000 to September 30, 2001), the Department of Justice recovered almost $1.2 billion from whistle-blower lawsuits; $210 million of that was paid to relators.[24]

A sampling of some recent settlements and relator's rewards are included in Exhibit 12.3. Fraud fighting tools such as *qui tam* allow whistle-blowers to team up with the federal government in a potent partnership to fight fraud. It is expected that the steady flow of *qui tam* cases will continue as people with knowledge of fraud become aware of the existence of this act. Organizations without fraud prevention and detection programs will find that whistle-blowers will do their work for them.

| Date | Company | Allegation | Settlement Amount | Relator's Reward |
|------|---------|-----------|-------------------|------------------|
| 4/17/03 | Bayer AG | Improper relabeling of drugs in order to avoid reporting and payment of Medicaid rebates as well as overbilling | $257 M | $34 M |
| 6/21/03 | AstraZeneca | Conspiring to encourage doctors to bill for a prostate cancer drug that the company distributed for free; kickbacks; inflating wholesale prices; and underpaying Medicaid rebates | $266 M | $47.5M |
| 6/26/03 | HCA, Inc. (formerly Columbia/HCA | A number of health-care fraud allegations including kickbacks to physicians | $631 M | $151 M |
| 3/15/04 | Fisher & Fisher, PC | False claims to federal agencies, including HUD and the VA for legal services related to mortgage foreclosures | $676.8 M | $169 M |
| 4/1/04 | CMC Electronics of Montreal | Charging inflated costs and delivering used and surplus parts instead of new equipment to the U.S. Army for its Patriot missile program | $9.6 | $1.5 M |
| 5/13/04 | Warner-Lambert (subsequently purchased by Pfizer) | Company's Parke-Davis division fraudulently promoted unapproved uses for its antiseizure drug Neurontin | $430 M | $24.6 M |
| 8/23/04 | Vortec Corp. | False claims for cost reimbursement sought in connection with a Department of Energy contract to recycle hazardous wastes | $4.5 M | $1.08 M |
| 10/4/04 | Photon Research Associates | Inflated bill submitted in connection with Department of Defense contracts | $1.9 M | $361,000 |

**Exhibit 12.3** Recent False Claims Act Settlements and Relator's Rewards
*Source:* Department of Justice False Claims Acts Recent Settlements found at the Web site of Fried, Frank, Harris, Shriver & Jacobson, LLP, www.ffhsj.com/quitam/recset.htm.

## ENDNOTES

1. "Awards and Special Recognition," Association of Certified Fraud Examiners, www.cfenet.com/membership/awards.asp.
2. Fred C. Alford, *Whistleblowers: Broken Lives and Organizational Power* (Ithaca, NY: Cornell University Press, 2001), 19–20.
3. Marci Alboher Nusbaum, "Blowing the Whistle: Not for the Fainthearted," *New York Times*, February 10, 2002, B10.

4. "Whistleblower Definition," www.definition-info.com/Whistle blower.html.

5. Charlene Oldham, "Diary of Deception," *Dallas Morning News*, February 3, 2002, 1H.

6. "Ex-Enron Exec: Shredding Went on after Probe Began," CNN.com, January 22, 2002, http://edition.cnn.com/2002/LAW/01/22/castaneda.cnna.cnna/.

7. *Sarbanes-Oxley Act* § 301.

8. *Sarbanes-Oxley Act* § 404.

9. *Sarbanes-Oxley Act* § 806.

10. *Sarbanes-Oxley Act* § 1107.

11. *U.S. Code* 18 (2005), § 1513.

12. "The Whistleblower Program," Occupational Safety and Health Administration, United States Department of Labor, www.osha.gov/dep/oia/whistleblower/index.html.

13. Ibid.

14. "Bitter Row Dominates Enron Hearing," *BBC News*, February 26, 2002, http://news.bbc.co.uk/1/hi/business/1841824.stm.

15. Association of Certified Fraud Examiners. *2004 Report to the Nation on Occupational Fraud and Abuse*, (Austin, TX, 2004).

16. Ibid.

17. Ibid.

18. Association of Certified Fraud Examiners, *2002 Report to the Nation on Occupational Fraud and Abuse*, (Austin, TX, 2002).

19. Timothy L. Mohr and Dave Slovin, "Making Tough Calls Easy," *Security Management*, March 2005, 51.

20. Ibid., 52.

21. Wendy's International, Inc. Standards of Business Practices, www.wendys-invest.com/corpgov/wenstandards.pdf, 43.

22. Timothy L. Mohr and Dave Slovin, "Making Tough Calls Easy," *Security Management*, March 2005, 52.

23. *Civil Actions for False Claims, U.S. Code* 31, § 3730 (h).

24. "Justice Recovers Record $1.6 Billion in Fraud Payments, Highest Ever for One Year Period," United States Department of Justice Press Release, November 14, 1001, http://usdoj.gov/opa/pr/2001/November/01_civ_591.htm.

# CHAPTER 13

# Time to Do Background Checks

## EXECUTIVE SUMMARY

It has often been said that the best indicator of future performance is past performance. Vetting all employees through background investigations is an absolute necessity today. The level of scrutiny should be commensurate with the employee's role and responsibilities. Background investigations cost money, but this is money well spent. Companies have been embarrassed and worse when the star CEO who was hired was found to have skeletons in the closet that could easily have been discovered through a simple public records search. Well-regarded CEOs have also had their reputations damaged when they joined startups without doing appropriate due diligence. Due diligence and background checks are also important in the world of mergers and acquisitions. Even the best background checks conducted at the time of hire will not help if there are no periodic updates to determine any arrests, civil actions, or adverse media reports regarding employees.

You have decided to adopt the recommendation of the Committee of Sponsoring Organizations (COSO), as well as other compliance initiatives, and start screening job applicants; you have taken a great first step. Now what? One of the easiest ways to establish a strong moral tone for an organization is to hire the right employees. Hiring the right employees not only reduces fraud but also reduces workplace violence. A startling 18 percent of all violent crimes happen at the victim's workplace.[1] Major corporations such as Wal-Mart, Ford, General Motors, and IBM conduct background checks on all job applicants.

Organizations should conduct thorough background checks on *all* employees, but especially managers. County-level criminal checks should be used in conjunction with statewide checks and national sex offender searches. For those in financially sensitive positions, credit checks are also recommended. Many studies have shown that those in financial difficulty are much more likely to commit workplace fraud.

## THE CHOICEPOINT DEBACLE

ChoicePoint is a leading broker of data collected on individuals, including names, addresses, Social Security numbers, and other personal information. It is almost a private intelligence database. In 2005, a Nigerian Criminal Enterprise (NCE) demonstrated that insufficient controls were in place to protect consumer data. Companies obtain background check information from vendors. These vendors have a relationship with ChoicePoint, from which they request background data on job applicants. Companies are required to have signed consent forms from every applicant for whom they request a background check. The vendor has to tell ChoicePoint (but not show ChoicePoint) that these consent forms actually exist. What the NCE did was set up at least 50 phony background check vendor companies. Since they did not have to show consent forms (just say they existed), the NCE was able to access records at will. ChoicePoint later notified over 100,000 people whose data had been compromised. This breach of information security should be a warning to the whole background check industry. Protection of privacy needs to be a prime concern.

The solution is to have stricter standards regarding approval of vendors, including background checks, licenses for vendors, and so on. Periodic audits should be conducted to verify the existence of consent forms (and actual clients for that matter).

The primary lesson to be taken away from the ChoicePoint case is that although checking employees is important, checking out customers is also important. Banks are required to know their customers. ChoicePoint published a statement on their Web site that said, "These criminals were able to pass our customer authentication due diligence processes by using stolen identities to create and produce documents needed to appear legitimate."[2] The statement did not elaborate how extensive the "customer authentication due diligence processes" actually are.

## THERE IS NO ONE-STOP SHOPPING FOR CRIMINAL RECORDS

"Wait a minute, isn't there a national criminal history search?" The answer is no, not for employment screening. The FBI's National Crime Information Center (NCIC) is for law enforcement use only. Companies that are conducting background checks for the first time have many decisions to make about how much checking they want to do and how much they want to spend. The fact is that more and more companies are conducting criminal checks on job applicants, with 80 percent of employers conducting checks in 2004, up from 56 percent in 1996.[3]

For employment purposes, each applicant should sign a consent form before any checks are done into criminal or credit histories. If derogatory information is found, applicants have the right to a copy of this information, so they may challenge any incorrect information from the actual consumer credit company or courthouse that is the official keeper of this information. Companies are encouraged to develop consent forms that authorize the search of criminal, civil, and credit histories of applicants.

Numerous firms offer background-screening services, and they make many claims about what kind of criminal checks can be done. Some companies claim they can do nationwide criminal checks on applicants. The only true database that tracks all criminal records from anywhere in the country is the NCIC. Although this same information is sometimes marketed as "National Wants and Warrants" by some background check vendors charging from $20 to $50, this information is not legally available, and the vendors are breaking the law. NCIC is accessible only by law enforcement and cannot be used to perform background checks. A national sex offender database exists, which is recommended for screening all applicants.

Many levels of criminal records are available for background check purposes, some automated and some not. Some states have statewide criminal check capabilities and some do not. States like Delaware have only three counties, whereas others have close to a hundred.

A United States federal criminal check will produce any records that the subject has nationwide but only for *federal* violations. This relates to crimes investigated by the FBI, the Drug Enforcement Administration (DEA), the United States Customs, and the United States Postal Inspection Service, and other federal law enforcement agencies. The results would not show all criminal records in the United States, only those from federal courts. Federal violations are a small minority of all convictions. When one is hiring for entry-level positions, which may be filled by high-school and college-aged applicants, it is very unlikely that the FBI or DEA has arrested any of these applicants or that the United States Attorney's office has convicted them. Federal criminal record searching is more suited for executive applicants.

State convictions are also a minority of all convictions. These are usually serious felonies like murder and rape. Many states maintain a database for all those convicted in the state. However, if a conviction occurred on the county level, which is the large majority, the conviction might not have been recorded in the statewide database. So, even if one were to pay for a U.S. federal criminal check and a statewide criminal check from each of the 50 states that had such a database, there would be no guarantee of finding all the convictions a person might have. The only way to ensure that all possible convictions that a subject has in one state are obtained is to check each county in the state one by one. Therefore, to do a real nationwide criminal check on one person would involve checking all counties in all states and would cost thousands of dollars.

To make the process workable, an initial search is run on the Social Security Account Number (SSAN) of the applicant. The SSAN is submitted for verification to the Social Security Administration. (Confirm with the background check provider that the verification is done from the Social Security Administration and not from a credit service.) Once verified, the SSAN can be linked to all the past addresses of the subject. This identifies which counties in which states to check for possible criminal records. Do not use the address history provided by the subject, as the subject may leave out any jurisdiction with a criminal conviction. If the subject has lived only in one county in one state for the previous ten years, only one county's records need to be checked

Any case in which an applicant is discovered to have more than one SSAN should be investigated. This is often caused by a mistake, or by a stolen identification. Advise the applicant of the issue and work together to solve it.

A check of the statewide database is a good idea if the state has one. However, a county check should also be done in the counties where the subject lived in the previous seven years. If the subject has lived in multiple counties, this could be expensive. Some background check firms offer to check all counties in which an applicant has lived in the previous seven years for a set price. What these firms lose monetarily on rare multiple-county checks is made up by the fact that most checks are on applicants who resided in just one county. The downside to this method is that convictions will not be found for areas in which the subject did not live. However, the vast majority of convictions are in the county of residence. As an example, suppose an applicant lives in Jefferson City, Missouri (Cole County) but holds season football tickets to the University of Missouri Tigers in Columbia, Missouri (Boone County). For the most part, the applicant is a law-abiding person. However, the applicant has a tendency to overindulge in beer and has been arrested a few times over the years at these football games. A background check that only examines county records where the applicant resides will not uncover this information. Furthermore, Boone County is not obligated to send conviction records to any state conviction repository. Even if Missouri has a state convictions list, the Boone county records might or might not be there.

The cost of county-level criminal checks averages about $10 per county, whereas the Social Security verification is usually done in conjunction with a credit check for about $7 or $8. Some states have free statewide criminal record databases on the Internet; however, let the buyer beware. Not all convictions are listed on the statewide databases. Especially suspect are those databases operated by the state Department of Corrections (DOC), rather than the state police. Some states have statewide databases that are very reliable but cost as much as $30 per check (Washington State, for example). Delaware, which has only three counties, does not have a statewide database. A check must be made of each of the three counties. There is a combined 38-state DOC database check that can be run for $15 to $20. This is the closest one can get to a nationwide search. Once again, some background check vendors offer "National Wants and Warrants." Beware! These data are taken from the NCIC, a national database for law enforcement use only. It is illegal to purchase this information.

There is a value in requesting criminal checks. Two suggestions are: not to be lured into a false sense of security and not to overspend doing unnecessary checks. Criminal checks are recommended for all employees. Credit checks are recommended for all employees who will handle large sums of money, credit card numbers, checking accounts, or valuable merchandise. This includes security guards. Any employee who has a problem with bad debt (written off by the creditor or turned over to collection) in the previous three years that cannot be appropriately explained should not be hired for these types of positions. Remember what Donald Cressey said about financial pressure and opportunity. An employee who is in a financial crisis is likely to steal from an employer when an opportunity presents itself and the employee can rationalize the action. (see Exhibit 13.1).

Credit checks usually cost about $7 or $8. It is possible to find a vendor that will do a Social Security verification, a one-county criminal check, and a credit check for about $20, depending on the volume. The price comes down as the number of checks per year

**EXHIBIT 13.1**   Percentage of Employers That Conduct Credit Checks

| 1996 | 2004 |
|------|------|
| 19%  | 35%  |

*Source:* Barbara Kiviat, "Watch Your Wallet," *Time,* January 17, 2005, 70.

requested by the company increases. The price for any applicants needing multiple county checks could be about $8 to $10 more per county. There are vendors that will include the national sex offenders search for free as a package deal. A statewide search is a good idea if that state has such a database, but do not use the state check to replace the county-level search! Including a check of federal criminal records could cost another $5. It is easy to spend $40 to $50 per applicant on background checks.

Remember that doing one background check at the time of hire is good, but follow-up checks are also important, especially for those employees in financially sensitive positions. It is recommended that follow-up checks be conducted every five years.

Additional questions may come to mind about drug screens, credit checks, and whether it is enough to do criminal checks alone. As there is no way to cover all the bases, a company does its best with the budget it has. Trying to keep convicted felons out of a company at all costs is not realistic.

---

### EXECUTIVE INSIGHT 13.1: JOHN SCULLEY AND A DEN OF THIEVES

The failure to conduct appropriate due diligence and background checks can result in serious financial and reputational issues whether a business is hiring an employee for an important role or considering a merger and acquisition. It is just as important for an employee to consider due diligence when deciding to join a new venture, as John Sculley unfortunately learned in 1993. Up to that point, Sculley was a renowned corporate executive with experience as the Chairman at Apple Computer and CEO at Pepsi-Cola.

Sculley shocked the technology world when he suddenly announced in October 1993 that he was joining a little-known company with no profits in the then emerging field of wireless communications. The company was Spectrum Information Technologies, Inc., headquartered in Manhasset, New York. Sculley had recently left Apple and was looking for new challenges. When Spectrum President Peter Caserta demonstrated the company's wireless technology for sending messages over cellular airwaves, Sculley was intrigued.[i] He decided to take Caserta's offer to be the new chairman and CEO of Spectrum. When Spectrum announced on October 18, 1993 that Sculley was joining the company, the stock jumped 46 percent.[ii]

However, all was not as it seemed. What Sculley did not know was that in May 1993, after signing a patent-licensing agreement with AT&T, Caserta had proclaimed that the deal would bring Spectrum "hundreds of millions of dollars" in royalties. Although this statement initially caused Spectrum shares to jump, they quickly fell the next day when AT&T publicly announced that the deal was actually worth only a few million dollars.[iii] This reckless assertion on the part of Caserta should have caused Sculley some concern had he known about it.

Caserta had claimed to be a "key management engineer on the Apollo space program," but he had no college degree and only a two-year certificate from a defunct training school.[iv] A resume claimed he was an electrical engineer.[v] A thorough background check of public information databases would have revealed that Caserta and the consulting companies he controlled had been the subject of litigation over the years from clients who sued, "for fees for services that the client companies claim were never rendered."[vi] Additionally, once Sculley joined Spectrum, Caserta and two other company executives exercised their stock options. The three made millions of dollars capitalizing on the soaring stock price that had benefited from Sculley's reputation and good name.[vii]

Within a few months of joining Spectrum, Sculley was starting to feel uneasy about the company's practices. In December 1993, he fired the company's external auditor, Arthur Andersen, and retained another. The new auditor quickly found that Spectrum's accounting practices were "overly aggressive in that they recognized revenue for license fees the company had not yet received."[viii] In addition, the SEC was conducting an investigation of Spectrum emanating from Caserta's comments about the AT&T deal of May 1993. Caserta never told Sculley until it became public in January 1994. This was unacceptable to Sculley, who felt that Caserta had lied to him. On February 7, 1994,

Sculley resigned from Spectrum and said, "recent events have made it clear that certain aspects of Spectrum's business are not what they were represented to be when I joined the company."[ix]

Sculley got out not a moment too soon. On March 22, 1994, 50 Postal Inspectors raided the offices of an investment firm that had been owned by Caserta and arrested five employees for mail fraud.[x] In April 1995, Caserta and nine others were indicted for operating an advance fee scheme whereby they allegedly "defrauded hundreds of companies around the country out of $6 million."[xi] Caserta eventually pled guilty to the fraud and in October 1996 was sentenced to 27 months in prison.[xii] Caserta was also charged by the SEC for "artificially boosting" Spectrum's stock price.[xiii]

Looking back, part of the problem was that Sculley trusted the word of Peter Caserta and failed to do his own due diligence. When Sculley was considering joining Spectrum, he asked Caserta whether there were any problems he should be concerned with and Caserta said no.[xiv] What he should have done was trust but verify.

---

[i] John J. Keller, "Sculley Suddenly Quits New Job and Accuses a Top Officers of a Plot," *Wall Street Journal*, February 8, 1994, A1.

[ii] James Bernstein, "Explosive Exit," *Newsday*, February 8, 1994, 3.

[iii] John J. Keller, "Sculley Suddenly Quits New Job and Accuses a Top Officers of a Plot," *Wall Street Journal*, February 8, 1994, A1.

[iv] Ibid.

[v] James Bernstein, "Just Who *Is* Peter Caserta?" *Newsday*, March 7, 1994, 31.

[vi] John J. Keller, "Sculley Suddenly Quits New Job and Accuses a Top Officer of a Plot," *Wall Street Journal*, February 8, 1994, A1.

[vii] Ibid.

[viii] James Bernstein, "Explosive Exit," *Newsday*, February 8, 1994, 3.

[ix] Ibid.

[x] Robert E. Kessler, "Investment Firm Raid," *Newsday*, March 23, 1994, 37.

[xi] Robert E. Kessler, "Caserta, Cronies Indicted: 10 Charged in Alleged Advance-Fee Loan Scam," *Newsday*, April 4, 1995, 35.

[xii] Robert E. Kessler, "Hi-Tech Con Man Sentenced," *Newsday*, October 1, 1996, 31.

[xiii] James Bernstein, "Feds Charge 3 in Spectrum Fraud," *Newsday*, December 5, 1997, A77.

[xiv] John J. Keller, "Sculley Suddenly Quits New Job and Accuses a Top Officer of a Plot," *Wall Street Journal*, February 8, 1994, A1.

## THE BEST INDICATOR OF FUTURE BEHAVIOR IS PAST BEHAVIOR

How a background check program is designed depends on what the goal is for conducting background checks. If the goal is to reduce fraud and workplace violence in general, there are several facts to consider:

- Those who have a record of stealing are likely to steal again.
- Those convicted of theft did it many times before getting caught and convicted.
- Drug abusers are more likely to steal than non–drug abusers.
- Those who have financial difficulties are more likely to steal than those who don't.
- Those who have been violent in the past are more likely than others to be violent.

Companies would do well to screen for drug use and for criminal convictions involving theft, drugs, or violence and also to check credit histories. County-level criminal checks are adequate for most entry-level positions, as federal convictions represent fewer than five percent of all convictions. (see Exhibit 13.2).

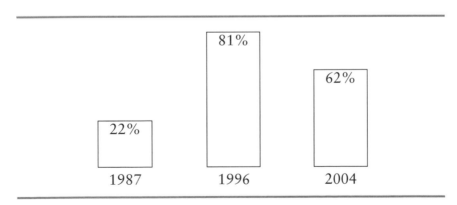

**EXHIBIT 13.2**  Percentage of Employers Using Drug Screening
Source: Dana Knight, "Employers' Negative Views of Drug Testing Growing," *The Indianapolis Star*, reprinted in *The Tennessean*, February 22, 2005, 4E.

The actions described earlier will reduce the risk of fraud, but they will not stop fraud from happening. Some people who steal from their employers never stole before, never used drugs, and always paid their bills on time. Background checks are a tool. A company does not need the best and most expensive tool, but one tool is not enough to do this job.

## IT IS NOT NECESSARY TO BE FORT KNOX

When John Stossel received the Cressy Award from the Association of Certified Fraud Examiners for his work exposing waste, fraud, and abuse in his "Give Me a Break!" segments on ABC's *20/20*, he spoke of the unreasonable amount of precaution in the world today.

There are companies that demand verification of military service, verification of high school and all college credits, a federal-level criminal check, a state-level criminal check, Social Security verification, reference checks with all former employers, and so on. This standard is applied to all positions no matter what level. Reason and logic may need to be applied here. If the position for which the organization is hiring does not require a college degree, and a high school diploma is sufficient, why verify college? If no preference is given for being a veteran, is it necessary to verify military service for this applicant? These companies may not be unreasonable in their background check requirements; they may just be using a little overkill for entry-level employees. Of course, this kind of intense background check is necessary when one is hiring auditors, accountants, investigators, and other financial managers, officers, and directors.

The companies mentioned in the preceding paragraph spend more than $100 on each background check. How does this apply to an industry in which a huge turnover in entry-level positions exists? Take ClientLogic, for example, where one of the authors is employed: ClientLogic has 20,000 employees, most of whom are in entry-level, call-center positions. There is a high turnover in the call-center industry. If ClientLogic has 20,000 call-center agents and the annual turnover is 50 percent, more than 10,000 agents a year are hired. If the background checks are $100 each, the cost would be $1 million a year just on background checks.

By doing those checks that give the most protection for the dollar, it is possible to cover most of the bases for less than $200,000 a year. Duplicating Fort Knox is not necessary, only the practice of reasonable due diligence. A good example of precaution run amok is the story of the Kinder Surprise chocolate eggs (with little toys inside). Kinder Surprise eggs were banned in Europe and the United States after two reported choking incidents.[4] Those incidents, although tragic, do not constitute an epidemic, especially with the billions of Kinder Surprise eggs sold around the world.[5] More children choke on hotdogs and bananas than that, and hotdogs and bananas are still on the market. It is more likely that a child will be struck by lightning (4.3 million to 1)[6] or bitten by a shark (6 million to 1)[7] than choke on a Kinder Surprise. John Stossel would be proud.

## ARE BACKGROUND CHECKS WORTH THE COST?

### STORY 1

A company decided to begin conducting criminal checks on its applicants and to track the results. In the first six months of checking, more than 60 applicants were found to have felony convictions: ten felons a month that the background checks kept out of the company. These were applicants who had claimed to have no convictions on their applications.

### STORY 2

One of the authors investigated bank fraud at one point in his career. He took a confession from a bank employee, and it was agreed to allow her to plead guilty to embezzlement, pay restitution, and serve a one-year probation. She still had a federal felony conviction on her record, but she didn't go to jail. The author had reason to contact her a few months later to get her to sign some documents regarding the restitution. When he called her home, her mother answered the phone and said that her daughter was at work. The mother provided the phone number. Imagine the author's surprise when the call went to a bank. It had hired a convicted bank embezzler who was still on probation!

## STORY 3

The State of Indiana discovered in 2002 that the person who was in charge of the state's $11 billion Public Employees' Retirement Fund had been convicted of bank fraud and mail fraud and had served time in prison. No federal-level criminal check was conducted, and the dates of former employment were not checked. He had lengthened the dates to fill in the period he was in prison.[8]

## STORY 4

"Chainsaw" Al Dunlap, the former CEO of Sunbeam Products Inc., got his nickname for cutting and slashing budgets. Also called "the butcher in a pinstriped suit," Al Dunlap was hired to turn around the slumping appliance company. "Chainsaw Al" began using accounting tricks to inflate the numbers, for which the Board of Directors fired him. The unfortunate news for Sunbeam came from the press, which discovered that Dunlap had been fired twice in the 1970s for questionable accounting practices. If only they had done a media search!

## STORY 5

The failure to conduct due diligence on a nominee can cause serious embarrassment to public figures. President Bush and former New York City mayor Rudy Giuliani were embarrassed when their nominee for Secretary of Homeland Security, Bernard Kerik, was found to have less integrity than originally thought. Bernard Kerik was a former New York Police Commissioner, proclaimed as a hero for his service on September 11, 2001. He had been advising on the effort to rebuild the police force in Iraq. He was billed as a symbol of accountability, the perfect choice to be Secretary of Homeland Security. Within a week of the nomination, Kerik was exposed as having questionable morals and ethics, with multiple reports of questionable ethical activities, conflicts of interest, and alleged mob ties. He withdrew his nomination.[9]

## THE ROLE OF HUMAN RESOURCES IN BACKGROUND CHECKS

Whereas it is the responsibility of the fraud prevention unit to strongly recommend the use of background checks, locate vendors, and even recommend policy, it is the responsibility of the Human Resources Department to make sure that a background check appropriate to the position is conducted on all applicants. Employment managers should handle the day-to-day implementation of the background check policy and have direct contact with the background check vendor.

## ENDNOTES

1. Occupational Safety and Health Administration, United State Department of Labor, OSHA Archive, Workplace Violence, 2001, www.osha.gov/sltc/workplaceviolence/.
2. "The ChoicePoint Heist," *PI Magazine*, June 2005, 65.
3. Ann Zimmerman and Kortney Stringer, "As Background Checks Proliferate, Ex-Cons Face Jobs Lock," *Wall Street Journal*, August 26, 2004, B-1.
4. Barbara Colton, "No Yolk: Smuggling of Chocolate Eggs is a Growth Industry," *Wall Street Journal*, June 24, 2002, A1.
5. British House of Commons, "Confectionary Safety," January 25, 2000, www.publications.parliament.uk/pa/cm199900/cmhansrd/vo000125/halltext/00125h04.htm, column 40WH.
6. National Safety Council, www.nsc.org.
7. MSN Encarta, "Shark Attack: What are the Odds?," http://encarta.msn.com/quiz_125/Shark_Attack_What_Are_the_Odds.html.
8. Gerard Zack, *Fraud and Abuse in Nonprofit Organizations* (Hoboken, NJ: John Wiley & Sons, 2003), 37.
9. "Homeland Security Nominee Withdraws, December 11, 2004, www.cnn.com/2004/ALLPOLITICS/12/10/kerik.withdraws/.

# CHAPTER 14

# Training, Training, and More Training

## EXECUTIVE SUMMARY

Training at all levels in an organization from the CEO down is an absolute requirement in preventing fraud and creating a culture of compliance. Training reinforces an entity's commitment to ethical conduct and compliance with company policies, as well as government laws and regulations. The training should encompass the code of conduct, the risk of fraud, the employees' role in preventing fraud, and the company's strong commitment to being a good corporate citizen. There are many ways to deliver quality training; all of them must be considered in designing an effective company-wide training program. An organization's fraud investigators should be involved in providing fraud prevention training. They are the ones involved with fraud on a daily basis and can provide context to the problem. Managers are role models for their direct reports and are the first line of defense in detecting and preventing fraud. Appropriate training of managers can provide great benefits to an organization.

*Excellence is an art won by training and habituation. We do not act rightly because we have virtue or excellence, but we rather have those because we have acted rightly. We are what we repeatedly do. Excellence, then, is not an act but a habit.*

Aristotle (384 BC to 322 BC)[1]


## BUILDING FRAUD AWARENESS THROUGH TRAINING

Fraud prevention begins with training. Education and awareness of the fraud risk, the types of fraud an organization may face, the impact on a business, how employees' lives are impacted by wrongful behavior, and what can be done to stop fraud are key elements in any fraud awareness and prevention program. Good companies recognize that fraud awareness and prevention training are essential for reducing the impact of fraud and abuse and for maintaining effective corporate governance. However, even good companies are limited in how much training they can provide, and the training budget is often the first to be cut in a downturn.

Training and reinforcement of policy and procedure should be required for all employees from the executive level on down. The difference will be in the type and length of a particular training. Training comes in many different forms; all forms can be effective if they are properly conceived and implemented. In-house training, seminars offered by professional organizations, Web-based interactive training modules, or college courses are possible avenues of training. The Committee of Sponsoring Organizations (COSO) recommends that "internal auditors and corporate accountants should study the forces and opportunities that contribute to fraudulent financial reporting, the risk factors that may indicate its occurrence, and the relevant ethical and technical standards."[2] Certified Public Accountants (CPAs), Certified Fraud Examiners (CFEs), and others with professional certification are required to complete a specific number of Continuing Professional Education (CPE) hours each year. It is recommended that all professionals in the organization, whether certified or not, receive a minimum of 40 CPEs per year, with at least four to eight hours related to fraud prevention.

Even a well-designed complaint procedure will fail without adequate training for employees. Companies must train employees on the reasons for the procedure, the type of complaints that may be reported, how to use the procedure, and how to maintain confidentiality. Without this type of training, the system will crumble.[3]

Effective fraud awareness training has four main parts:

1. Give a simple definition of fraud: fraud is lying, cheating, and stealing from the company.
2. Discuss how fraud negatively impacts a company's bottom line and reputation.
3. Give examples of various fraud schemes employees might discover, such as an offer for kickbacks or the illegal use of customers' credit card numbers by other employees.
4. Tell employees what they are supposed to do if they suspect a fraud.[4]

Obtaining employee buy-in for fraud training and then embracing the concept of fraud prevention is critical to success in training. The benefits of training need to be effectively communicated to all employees no matter where in the world they are located. "Education of employees should be factual rather than accusatory. Point out that fraud—in any form—is eventually very unhealthy for the organization and the people who work there. Fraud and abuse impact raises, jobs, benefits, morale, profits, and one's integrity. The fraud educated workforce is the fraud examiner's best weapon—by far."[5] The support of training for all employees by executive leadership sends a strong message about the tone at the top and throughout the organization.

Neither Sarbanes-Oxley nor the Securities and Exchange Commission (SEC) specifically mention education or training in conduct, ethics, and fraud prevention. However, both the New York Stock Exchange (NYSE) and NASDAQ have established training requirements. The corporate governance guidelines of the NYSE call for continuing education and training of directors, which the NYSE will help develop and sponsor. NASDAQ is calling for similar continuing education.[6]

## THE ROLE OF FRAUD INVESTIGATORS IN TRAINING

Any ongoing fraud prevention training should include presentations from the organization's fraud investigators. They have first-hand experience investigating various kinds of fraud and unique insights that are invaluable in educating employees. They can detail the elements of the fraud triangle for specific cases that were investigated; they can explain how frauds were detected through red flags, and they can outline the best practices to prevent them. Because of the nature of the fraud investigators' work, their experiences are of great interest to employees. Fraud investigators should make ongoing presentations to employees at all levels throughout a company. Depending on the size of the organization, the fraud prevention unit may spend a significant amount of their time in educating employees.

Informing employees that there is a professional investigative unit within the company that responds to allegations of fraud will send a strong preventative message. It also sends an important message that improper conduct has consequences and that fraud will not be tolerated. As a result of the training conducted by the fraud investigative unit, increased reporting of fraud allegations should be expected. Experience has shown that when employees are educated about the many kinds of fraud impacting a company and the associated red flags, they are much more likely to recognize possible wrongdoings and report them.

## TRAINING FOR CHIEF EXECUTIVES AND DIRECTORS

Although every public and private company has a responsibility to educate and train all its employees in ethics, compliance, and fraud prevention, no group is more in need of this training than chief executives and directors of boards. Even though the number of ethically challenged chief executives is small, there is always something new for CEOs and directors to learn because of ever-changing corporate compliance requirements. COSO recommends that "Participants in the financial reporting system must first understand the multidimensional nature of fraudulent financial reporting to be able to address it with appropriate responses."[7] COSO details how a public company needs to educate its directors, management, and employees about fraudulent financial reporting; it is especially important for the Audit Committee "to be alert to the risk of such fraud and to educate its members and the rest of the board about the forces and the opportunities" that can lead to fraud.[8] Executives and directors also need an understanding of other kinds of internal and external frauds that can attack a company. The Association of Certified Fraud Examiners presents a number of excellent fraud awareness and prevention training sessions. Their training can be customized to fit the needs of any organization. More information about custom antifraud training is included in Executive Insight 14.1.

---

### EXECUTIVE INSIGHT 14.1: CUSTOM ANTIFRAUD TRAINING

Custom-designed antifraud training taught by fraud examination professionals may be the ideal solution for businesses. Such training can be focused on the unique needs of a public or private company to improve fraud detection and prevention. A course on developing effective anti–money-laundering programs may be appropriate for a financial services organization. A course on conducting internal investigations might be perfect for a company starting up a fraud investigation unit. A course on the impact of the Foreign Corrupt Practices Act and detection and prevention strategies would be beneficial for a company doing business in high-risk countries where bribery and governmental corruption are common.

Bringing such training in-house has many advantages; it is convenient, comprehensive, motivating, and cost effective. The leader in antifraud training is the Association of Certified Fraud Examiners (ACFE; www.cfenet.com). The ACFE provides custom training to a wide variety of clients including corporations and government agencies. Courses are taught by Certified Fraud Examiners who are experts in fraud detection, investigation, and prevention and who provide practical training in an interactive learning environment.

The ACFE has a number of excellent training courses that are available to organizations worldwide including Principles of

Fraud Examination, Auditing for Internal Fraud, Professional Interviewing Skills, Conducting Internal Investigations, Contract and Procurement Fraud, Investigating by Computer, Investigating Conflicts of Interest, and Fraud Prevention. These courses and others offered by the ACFE can be adapted to any size audience and should be considered by any organization looking to improve its understanding of fraud and fraud prevention.

## NEW EMPLOYEE ORIENTATION

The first day of hire for a new employee is a perfect time to start developing a culture of compliance for that particular person. Typically, a company will have some form of introduction to the business for a new hire. Although the subjects covered in a new employee orientation may include general information about the company, employee benefits, policies and procedures, and compliance with the code of conduct, an introduction to the risk of fraud should be considered. A new employee will feel inundated with new information, and much of it may not be remembered, but a short and general introduction to the company's strong stand against fraud and abuse at any level is a good starting point. Consideration should be given to providing some key bullet points about how fraud can affect an organization. Some important messages can be highlighted including the types of fraud; key ACFE fraud statistics including how an average organization loses six percent of its annual revenue to fraud and abuse; how most frauds are discovered by tips or by accident; and how employees can report allegations of fraud and abuse.

## MANAGERS ARE ROLE MODELS

Good managers are role models to their employees. They provide guidance and mentoring. They show employees how to succeed, and they instill honesty and integrity by their actions. Managers who provide great oversight and lead by example can have a major impact in preventing fraud. "Trust but verify" should be every good manager's mantra. When employees see that their managers are following policy and procedure and are closely monitoring their group's operation, fraud is harder to commit and get away with. As an example, expense reporting fraud can be greatly reduced by increased manager scrutiny of expense claims and receipts. The credibility of "tone at the top" begins with a first-line manager.

On the other hand, poor managers can contribute to a fraudulent culture through a lack of engagement and leadership. Managers who are not well versed in an organization's policies and procedures or who fail to follow them can send the wrong message to their direct reports. A manager who is not engaged or committed to the company's code of conduct and who does not live it every day can do little to promote compliance by employees. The authors have seen numerous examples over the years of fraud occurring under the very noses of poor managers who never detect it.

Training of managers in fraud detection and prevention provides an opportunity for reinforcing and enhancing the skills of great managers while improving those of poor or uninformed managers. A unique approach to obtain manager buy-in is to appeal to career advancement. Provide examples of how managers had their careers derailed when fraud occurred on their watch and they failed to detect or report it. No one wants to have a career stopped dead in its tracks for failure to protect the organization from fraud. Good managers can stop fraud before it occurs.

## NEW MANAGER TRAINING

Many organizations provide training to new managers when they assume their new roles. There is no better way to start off new managers' careers than to educate them about the risk of fraud and their role in addressing that risk. Experience has shown that new managers often report allegations of fraud at a greater rate than existing managers. This is because new managers are learning their new roles, probing, asking questions, and often finding fraud and policy violations not detected by the managers who came before them. Fraud awareness and prevention training for new managers will yield unexpected benefits in protecting an organization.

## FRAUD TRAINING FOR FINANCE EMPLOYEES

It is recommended that all finance employees including internal audit personnel receive fraud prevention training. The recent improvements in corporate governance now require greater involvement and review by the finance function to protect an organization. An excellent training course is *Fraud and the CPA* created by the ACFE and the American Institute of Certified Public Accountants. This eight-hour computer self-study course provides an introduction to the problem of fraud; the CPA's fraud detection and reporting responsibilities; the basics of financial statement fraud, asset misappropriation, and corruption schemes; the reasons employees commit fraud; and methods for detecting and preventing fraud schemes. The course incorporates video clips of fraudsters detailing how they committed fraud and how they concealed it. Although this course is especially useful for CPAs, it is just as beneficial for any finance, procurement, or other employee within an organization. Because it is computer based, the course can be provided to large numbers of employees at an economical cost.

There are other opportunities for employees to receive fraud prevention knowledge through degree programs such as those offered in colleges and universities. Executive Insight 14.2 provides information about an excellent graduate program in economic crime management at Utica College.

---

### EXECUTIVE INSIGHT 14.2: BECOMING A MASTER IN ECONOMIC CRIME MANAGEMENT

Thanks to technology, experienced professionals can gain fraud prevention skills and knowledge and also earn an academic degree in the comfort of their homes or offices. Utica College, in Utica, New York, is the first college to offer a master's degree in Economic Crime Management (ECM) integrating online learning. Begun in 1999, the program is offered in a distance learning format, requiring students to be on campus for three four-day-long residencies a year for two years. The rest of the courses are presented online with faculty-directed study.

The ECM curriculum focuses on fraud and risk management strategies, current economic crime challenges, and applying innovative technological and analytical solutions to preventing fraud. The program has been designed to meet the growing security demands placed on experienced personnel in law enforcement, private corporations, government, and the military.

The ECM program's distance learning format allows full-time professionals to complete a master's degree without having to relocate and/or take a leave of absence from employment. Two courses are begun in each of the six residencies. The residencies provide an intensive learning experience (approximately 32 hours), which prepares the students to complete the courses on the Internet, using sophisticated learning software. The communication and discussion during the 14 weeks following each residency are crucial to the learning process. Students are given access to online library resources, including LexisNexis™, and applications such as i2 Inc.'s Analyst's Notebook, to provide them with the research tools necessary to advance their studies.

The two-year program is fully integrated, so the two courses that the students take each semester build on the courses they have completed. The curriculum, based on the four themes of management, technology, analytical methods, and economic crime, was developed in collaboration with experts in private industry, government, and law enforcement and is continually updated to meet societal changes. The 12 integrated courses (36 credit hours) cover organizational theory and management, research methods, economic crime, legal issues, Internet and computer security, and fraud analysis. Students are required to complete a professional project as a capstone to their academic experience. More information about the online Master's in Economic Crime Management can be found at www.ecii.edu.

## TRAIN YOUR ACCOUNTS PAYABLE DEPARTMENT: LOOKING FOR FRAUD ON THE FACE OF THE INVOICE

There are several strategies for searching payables proactively for fraud. An organization can ensure that its auditors are trained to conduct computerized data mining. It can also train accounts payable employees to look for clues to fraud on the invoices themselves. Making the accounts payable (AP) department "fraud aware" will result in increased detection of issues.

Many asset misappropriation schemes involve inserting a fraudulent invoice into the system. The AP clerk, not the auditor, is the one who will be in the best position to catch this fraud. For example, a false invoice from a known vendor has been placed into the AP system using an address that is different from the true address of this known vendor. This type of fraud will be caught if the addresses on vendor payments are always checked against the approved vendor file. A fraudster who inserts such a phony invoice will forget to fold the invoice—as it would have been had it actually arrived in the mail. An AP clerk should know to look for that clue (see Exhibits 14.1 and 14.2 for examples).

---

## INVOICE

International Enterprises
341 S 4th Street
Anytown, USA

March 25, 2006

Invoice #063511

For services rendered January 19, 2006  - PAST DUE..............$1,032
See invoice #063378
And February 20, 2006.................................................$1,300

Total due on receipt: $2,332

---

**EXHIBIT 14.1**   Invoice #1

---

INVOICE

International Enterprises
2503 West Linden
Anytown, USA

February 5, 2006

Invoice #064832

For services rendered January 19, 2006............................$7,580

Total due on receipt: $7,580

---

**EXHIBIT 14.2** Invoice #2

A March invoice has arrived from a known vendor with a past due notice for the February invoice. When the AP clerk pulls the February invoice, the clerk notices that the address on the February invoice is different from the "usual" address on the invoice from March. The February invoice that was paid is for much more ($7,580) than is usual from this vendor. The different address from the February invoice is the logical place to begin this fraud investigation. Someone, probably an employee, removed and discarded the real February invoice from International Enterprises and replaced it with one that was created—for much more money—to a different address. The fraudster hoped that AP would recognize the vendor as a valid one but would not notice the different address. Searching the records for payment of a February invoice numbered 063378 to International Enterprises for the amount past due will reveal no record that invoice #063378 was paid. Here is the critical moment. If the approving authority for this invoice does not recognize this for what it is, a fraud, there is a chance that the approving authority will assume that there were two invoices for February and that the one listed as past due has not been paid. If proper fraud awareness does not exist, this fraud might escape detection. What should an AP clerk do if the approving authority just authorizes the second payment for February? Should the clerk notify the fraud examiner? This is a prime example of the need to train AP clerks to be alert for anomalies like unusual addresses for known vendors. There is a possibility that the approving authority is the one who slipped this fake invoice into the system. Is the address on the February invoice for $7,580 the address of the person approving the invoice?

Here are other red flags that are best looked for on the face of the invoice by AP employees rather than auditors using data mining:

- Invoices with no telephone number
- Invoices with handwritten notes from the approver explaining unusual circumstances
- Any invoice that calls for rebates, retrofits, or refunds
- Invoices that mention delivery of goods to a site other than the company
- Invoices with large amounts just under the maximum approval authority of the approver
- Invoices with unusual lack of detail
- Invoices that have not been folded, since they were probably not mailed
- Invoices from a vendor that are a month apart but the invoice numbers are consecutive or close.

An invoice should show the name, address, and telephone number of each vendor. Vendors with a PO box for an address should be treated with suspicion. The telephone number should be called to verify the address. It is also a good idea to check Web sites for all vendors. Only after proper due diligence has been done should the vendor be added to an approved vendor list. Until a vendor is placed on this list, no payments should be sent. Each invoice should be compared with the vendor as listed on the approved vendor list.

## TRAIN THE AUDIT STAFF TO DATA MINE

Computerized data mining strategies can be used to look for disbursement amounts that do not fit the expected pattern. Benford's Law states that naturally occurring sets of data will have more small items than big items. Any deviation from this pattern raises a red flag.

Frank Benford was a physicist at GE Research Laboratories when he noticed that he used logarithms for numbers that began with low digits more often than he used logarithms for numbers that began with high digits. His log table book was much more worn in the beginning than it was at the back. Like any good physicist, he set out to find the law that made this so. He was able to find the specific formula that identifies these skewed frequencies of first-digit values.[9]

In any group of normal numbers (not assigned or having built-in maximum or minimum values), there is a greater probability that the first digits will be ones, and then twos and threes, all the way up to nines. The higher the number, the less probable it is that it will be the first digit in an amount. These skewed frequencies became known as Benford's Law.

If any group of amounts results in a positive spike of more than 5 percent out of this pattern, the figures should be reviewed in detail. There are systems and programs that are commercially available to run checks using Benford's Law (see Exhibit 14.3). One such product is the audit software available from ACL™ (www.acl.com).

Employees committing fraud inside an organization typically want to use figures that begin with nines. It is more efficient to steal $900 than $100 nine times. A common example is when an organization requires receipts for expenses over $75 and a fraud-minded employee submits phony expense claims for $74.99, just under the receipt threshold. Therefore, testing financial records using Benford's Law will expose fraudulent amounts. This type of data mining using Benford's Law can also be done by looking at the frequency of the first two digits.

The use of Benford's Law in an AP audit at one particular company showed an inordinate number of payments of $50. This caused an investigation into the $50 charges, most of which were for car batteries. However, the company had paid for twice as many car batteries in one year than they had cars. Someone was selling the car batteries.[10]

In addition to using ACL™ to apply Benford's Law, auditors can also look for red flags in payables using tools such as Business Objects™, Crystal Reports™, Microsoft Access™, ActiveData for Microsoft Excel™, and IDEA™. Fraud detection software is essential for any fraud prevention program. There are several obvious

**EXHIBIT 14.3**  Benford's Law[a]

| First Digit | Probability |
| --- | --- |
| 1 | .30103 |
| 2 | .176091 |
| 3 | .124939 |
| 4 | .09691 |
| 5 | .0791812 |
| 6 | .0669468 |
| 7 | .0579919 |
| 8 | .0511525 |
| 9 | .0457575 |

[a] http://mathworld.wolfram.com/BenfordsLaw.html.

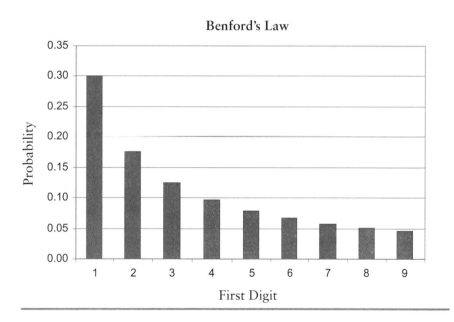

areas to keep in mind when looking for possible fraud inside an organization. The first places to look are in employee and vendor records. Employee records give the home addresses of employees. It is obviously a red flag if any of the vendors have the same address as an employee. A business can data mine using Microsoft Access to compare a table of employee addresses against a table of vendor addresses. This is called a "relational table query."

## Relational Table Query

Such comparison checks between vendor and employee addresses are not easy without Access, which has the ability to search not only for exact matches but also close matches. This is important, as vendor records are seldom in the same address format as employee records. Address information such as 200 1st Street might be in the address line in the employee records, but the address line in vendor records could show 200 1st STR. This will not be caught by an exact match check but would be caught by the close match relational table query in Access. Care must also be taken to cross-compare address lines one and two, as well as the telephone numbers (see Exhibit 14.4).

It is quite possible that a vendor and an employee could have the same address of 400 High Street, but one table could have that value in address line 1, whereas the other had that value in address line 2. Also causing problems are abbreviations for Street, which could be entered as St., ST, or Str. or written out as Street. These differences will foil a literal computer match. Fraudsters are known to misspell the name of their street intentionally for the sole purpose of defeating such exact searches and data comparisons.

## Find Duplicates Query

When an Access table titled "paid invoices" is created (Excel spreadsheets can be imported into Access format), duplicate payments can be found by running a "find duplicates query." Access has a query wizard that creates the query easily. Pick the table and the fields in that table to be searched for duplicates, and the results appear. Duplicate payments might be a mistake, but they could also be a red flag for kickbacks or other types of fraud such as interception of the duplicate payments by an insider, who then converts them for personal use.

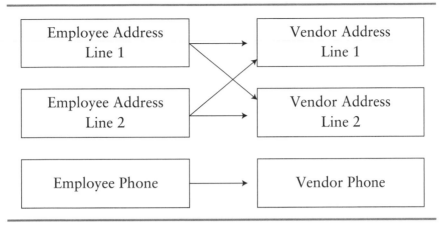

**EXHIBIT 14.4**   The Two-Line Address Problem

### Unmatched Query

In most payment systems, invoices associated with approved purchase orders will be paid with little question. Access can review all invoices paid on purchase orders to ensure that the approver of the invoice was an authorized approver. Therefore a master list of persons with authority to approve purchase orders should be maintained. This file can become an Access table called "PO Approvers" that is then compared with a "Purchase Order" table that has a field for "approver." This is an "unmatched query"—looking for any approver in the Purchase Order Table that does not appear on the PO Approver table.

The "unmatched query" can also determine whether any vendors have been paid who are not on the approved vendor list.

### Between Ranges Query

To find invoices that are just under the dollar limit of the approver, query using the "between" expression. If the approval authority is $10,000, query for all invoices approved when the amount is between $9,000 and $10,000. If fraud exists, it is very likely that there will be an inordinate number of invoices within this range. This red flag can also be uncovered using Benford's Law, as the frequency of invoices that begin with a 9 will be above the expected norm.

## Data Mining for Gold

Tammi Johnson, CFE, and Judd Hesselroth, CIA, CISA, both Microsoft employees, are experts on data mining and using Microsoft Access to detect fraud. Together, Johnson and Hesselroth summarized the value of data mining and the specific use of Microsoft Access in an article published in 2005 in the ACFE's *Fraud* magazine, from which some key points are reprinted here:

"Microsoft Access provides users with one of the simplest and most flexible database solutions on the market today. Regular users of Microsoft products will enjoy the familiar Windows 'look and feel' as well as the tight integration with other Microsoft products. An abundance of wizards lessens the complexity of administrative tasks. Access is inexpensive and is included in the MS Office suite. It allows analysis of data far beyond the 65,000-record limitation of MS Excel and does not require users to be familiar with SQL, the powerful and comprehensive data management and analysis software from Microsoft. Data mining can be used to find:

**Procurement Fraud:**
- Examine the data for same vendor, same amount, and same date (duplicate information to allow for vendor submitting the same invoice but changing the invoice number).
- Examine the data for split purchases (just under a dollar cut-off amount) and multiple transactions on the same day to the same vendor.
- For after-the-fact purchases, compare the purchase order date and the invoice date.

**Expense Report Fraud:**
- Import the list of expenditures that are within $1 of a key authorization threshold. (For example, if a receipt is required for all expenses over $30, import all transactions between $29.00 and $29.99.)

- Group by employee to see if certain employees routinely expense items just under the threshold.
- Investigate employees who have a significantly higher number of transactions that fall just under the limit. (A common one is taxi-cab rides.)

**Payroll Fraud:**

- Import a table of all employees receiving a salary and compare it with a table of authorized employees using the "Find Unmatched" functionality in the query wizard; follow the steps to find unauthorized employees receiving a salary.
- Annualize the salary payments for all employees (excluding expenses and bonuses). Compare the annualized salary calculation with the authorized salary amount.

### Dig for Gold but Withhold Quick Conclusions

Although taking the first steps to begin learning a new tool may be a bit daunting, if the staff starts with some simple scenarios they may quickly see the gold appear before their eyes. The data does not lie, although there is a chance that a misunderstanding can occur. Be careful not to jump to conclusions before verifying the results of data mining through additional investigation."[11]

## TRAIN VENDORS

A developing concern for compliance programs is how one mitigates possible fraud issues that may impact them through the many entities with which a company does business. Although a corporation may have a first-rate program in place, the program may not extend to the vendors and partners. Fraud losses incurred by a vendor will undoubtedly be passed on to customers. Fraud prevention results in decreased fraud losses and an increase in the bottom line of all involved. Thus, organizations with robust fraud prevention programs should consider offering their knowledge and best practices to their vendors and partners who may not have developed such programs.

Educating vendors about fraud risk and prevention will yield significant benefits. Vendors that develop sound detection and prevention programs will add greater value to the companies they do business with. These vendors can also use the existence of fraud prevention programs as a "value add" in developing new business.

## ENDNOTES

1. Aristotle, Greek critic, philosopher, physicist, and zoologist 384–322 BC.
2. The Committee of Sponsoring Organizations of the Treadway Commission, James C. Treadway, Jr., Chairman, *Report of the National Commission on Fraudulent Financial Reporting*, October 1987, ("The Treadway Report"), Chapter 5, Section V, www.coso.org/publications/NCFFR_Part_5.htm.
3. Marian Exall and Jack Capers Jr., "Establishing the New Complaint Procedures," *Fraud*, November/December 2004, 24.
4. Kenneth Dieffenbach, "Recruiting an Anti-Fraud Foot-Soldier Army," *The White Paper*, March/April 2004, 34.
5. Joseph T. Wells, *Corporate Fraud Handbook: Prevention and Detection* (Hoboken, NJ: John Wiley & Sons, Inc., 2004) 406.
6. Guy Lander, What Is Sarbanes-Oxley? (New York: McGraw Hill, 2004), 68.
7. The Committee of Sponsoring Organizations of the Treadway Commission, James C. Treadway, Jr., Chairman, *Report of the National Commission on Fraudulent Financial Reporting*, October 1987 ("The Treadway Report"), Chapter 5, Section I, www.coso.org/publications/NCFFR_Part_5.htm.
8. Ibid., Chapter 5, Section VI.
9. Mark Nigrini, "Digital Analysis: A Computer-Assisted Data Analysis Technology for Internal Auditors," *IT Audit*, Vol. 1, December 15, 1998, via www.theiia.org /itaudit/index.
10. Ibid.
11. Tammi Johnson and Judd Hesselroth, "Digging for Golden Evidence," *Fraud*, January/February 2005, 32. Selected content reprinted with permission from the Association of Certified Fraud Examiners, Austin, Texas © 2005.

# Fraud Risk outside the United States

## EXECUTIVE SUMMARY

An organization's fraud risk does not end at the border of the United States. In many ways, the fraud risk is even greater outside the country. This is especially true when a company has operations and employees based in foreign countries. The fraud prevention program must take this risk into consideration and institute internal controls, policy, training, and fraud prevention to mitigate the risk. Some countries pose a more serious risk of fraud and corruption than others. For example, fraud is more likely in the former Soviet Union, Nigeria, the Philippines, and Hong Kong than in Canada, France, Uruguay, and Australia. The three main differences that must be overcome when working in foreign countries are the language, the culture, and the legal system. The Foreign Corrupt Practices Act (FCPA) makes it a federal crime for a U.S. company to bribe foreign government officials. Penalties for noncompliance can be high for violators, both individuals and their companies.

## A WORLD OF DIFFERENCE

International business involves many different cultures. As corporate entities become more global, business leaders find themselves solving problems outside their home countries. Conducting business overseas is not the same as conducting business at home. The laws are different, the risks are different, and the solutions will be different. The three main differences that must be overcome, especially in developing countries, are the difference in the language, culture, and legal system. It would be a mistake to assume that things are comparable to the United States or to expect the same level of legal protection. Some countries have drastic differences even within their own borders.

Language differences cause more problems in remote areas, where English is not spoken and dialects are more unusual. Legal systems are less formal in developing countries. Fraud laws may not be well written, and employment laws differ widely. Sometimes the police or the courts choose not to enforce the law. Foreign businesses have economic influence and can usually get cooperation from local authorities.

### Offshoring

When Citibank made a business decision to outsource its customer service telephone operators to M Phasis BFL Ltd. and have the calls answered in India, the decision makers probably considered only cost savings. When several former M Phasis operators were found to be accessing Citibank customers' accounts and transferring money out, the security team had to try to get evidence from banks in India as well as action from Indian police.[1]

Business magazines published many articles about the blow this Citibank case dealt to offshoring in India. There have been steady complaints about United States jobs moving to India and the Philippines but not much complaining about United States customers' private banking information being available on computers in the third world. If 100 U.S. citizens were asked if they would give out their credit card numbers to someone in a foreign country, most would probably say "no," yet that is what they are doing every day. Companies like Citibank are not telling their customers where their information is going. Disclosure of the offshoring of customer personal identifiable information (PII) and other bank account information and obtaining customer consent is better than keeping it a secret from customers. There is legislation pending in several states to mandate customer notification of such offshore outsourcing of banking information without consent.

## Risk Index

Before a company expands operations to a foreign country, it is a good idea to conduct a risk assessment. Many countries present a significantly higher risk of fraud, corruption, terrorism, and natural disaster. Fraud is much more pervasive in Nigeria than in Sweden. Corruption is more commonplace in Indonesia than in Australia. The threat of terrorism is far greater in the Middle East although experience has shown that this threat can occur worldwide. Kidnappings are much more of a problem in Saudi Arabia and Mexico than in the United States.

The U.S. Department of State's Current Travel Warnings are issued when the State Department recommends that Americans avoid travel to a certain country (see http://travel.state.gov). Several nations present a significantly higher risk of violence, theft, and fraud. Conducting business in these countries should be done with a full understanding of the risk environment. Opening an office in Bogotá, Columbia is not like opening an office in Madison, Wisconsin.

Countries that present high or extreme risk tend to be located in the Middle East, Africa, Latin America, the Pacific islands north of Australia, and Eastern Europe. They include developing nations, those that have significant internal strife, and those with unstable economies. Some of these are Iraq, Israel, Zimbabwe, Nigeria, the Republic of Georgia, the former Yugoslavia, Nicaragua, the Philippines, Sri Lanka, and Haiti.[2]

One of the first things to be checked when one is conducting a pre-expansion risk assessment of another country should be that nation's legal protection of confidential and proprietary information. In some countries, information has no value under the law, and the theft of confidential or proprietary information is not a crime until the thief actually profits from the theft.

Another consideration when one is planning to do business in a foreign country is the culture of corruption that might exist in the country. In some nations, bribery is a way of life. The payment of bribes to facilitate business in foreign countries is specifically addressed in the United States Foreign Corrupt Practices Act.

## THE UNITED STATES FOREIGN CORRUPT PRACTICES ACT

Contrary to popular belief, Sarbanes-Oxley was not the first federal law to require strict internal controls within publicly traded United States companies to prevent fraud. In 1977, the Foreign Corrupt Practices Act (FCPA) mandated that corporate records contain accurate statements concerning the true purpose of all payments made by the company. The FCPA was passed after the Watergate investigation discovered that companies were paying bribes to foreign and domestic officials using funds maintained "off the books." The law makes it a crime for American companies, as well as individuals and organizations acting on their behalf, to bribe any foreign government official in return for assistance in:

■ Obtaining or retaining business
■ Directing business to any particular person
■ Influencing a foreign government official to do or to omit an act in violation of his or her duty
■ Influencing a foreign government official to affect an act or decision by a foreign government.[3]

However, the FCPA not only makes it a crime to pay bribes to foreign officials, it also makes it a crime for publicly traded United States companies to make payments of any kind that are not on the books. This reduces the burden of proof for the government. Government prosecutors do not have to prove a bribe, only that a payment was made and not recorded on the company's books.

In short, the FCPA makes it a crime for a company in the United States or for U.S. citizens or their agents to obtain business by bribery of a government official of another country (or even conspire to do so from the United States), or for a publicly traded United States company to fail to record such a payment on the company books.

While the U.S. Department of Justice handles bribery violations of the FCPA, the Securities and Exchange Commission (SEC) handles accounting violations of the FCPA. It is interesting to note that it is not a crime in the United States for an American company to pay bribes in a country where bribes are not illegal, as in several island financial havens. There are also specific exceptions granted in a 1988 amendment to the FCPA. American companies can pay facilitation fees to expedite permits, licenses, papers, visas, mail, and phone service and to expedite the movement of perishable cargo. Furthermore, it is not considered a bribe to reimburse public officials reasonably for expenses such as meals, travel, and lodging while the company is promoting or demonstrating a product or executing a contract. However, it must be kept in mind that these actions may still be illegal in the country where they occur.

The penalties for violating the FCPA can be high. Enterprises can be fined $2 million for each violation, and individuals face five years in prison and a $250,000 fine. In addition, the company can be forced to abandon the business won by bribery, be denied export licenses, or be disqualified from any U.S. government contracts.

U.S. companies can protect themselves with a compliance program ensuring that all employees are specifically aware of which actions are prohibited by the FCPA. Companies can also protect themselves by including special clauses in their contracts whereby local agents and partners confirm that they will not violate the FCPA. Many companies have tried to circumvent the FCPA by having local joint venture partners commit bribery, with the U.S. companies remaining willfully blind. The U.S. Department of Justice and the SEC expects U.S. companies to require their foreign subsidiaries to conform to the FCPA.

### FCPA Bribery Case Study

A Lockheed Corporation executive received the first prison sentence ever handed down for a violation of the FCPA.[4] He was sentenced to 18 months in prison for making illegal payments to a member of the Egyptian legislature in connection with the sale of three cargo planes to that country. Lockheed received $24.8 million in criminal and civil fines for the violation.[5]

## FCPA Accounting Case Study

The SEC charged that Banadex, a Colombian subsidiary of Chiquita, had bribed a local official to renew a customs license.[6] This facilitation payment to obtain a license is specifically exempted from the bribery violations of the FCPA. However, the payment had been falsely booked to an expense account, a violation of the accounting regulations of the FCPA. Chiquita paid a fine of $100,000.[7]

---

### EXECUTIVE INSIGHT 15.1: THE LONG REACH OF THE FCPA

The Foreign Corrupt Practices Act (FCPA) has a broad reach, far broader than most federal law enforcement statutes. It can be used to punish fraudulent and corrupt conduct that otherwise would be out of the federal government's jurisdiction.

For instance, in 2003 the U.S. government used the FCPA to go after James Giffen, the chief executive of Mercator, an investment bank in New York City, who had allegedly bribed senior officials in Kazakhstan to obtain lucrative oil contracts in the former Soviet Republic.[i] The indictment in this case, which has been called the most far-reaching use of FCPA in United States history, alleged that Giffen transferred more than $78 million in cash and gifts to the officials.[ii] The gifts allegedly included paying off $36,000 of the former Kazakh Prime Minister's debt, millions of dollars in jewelry and fur coats for the family of the Kazakh President, tuition for family members at exclusive private schools and colleges, and an $80,000 speedboat for the Kazakh President.[iii] Mercator allegedly then received access to the country's untapped oil deposits, the profits of which Giffen allegedly diverted from the company into his own pockets.

The legality of the payments under Kazakh law was questionable; however, the FCPA makes it illegal for a United States company to make payments to a foreign official to assist in obtaining or retaining business. The FCPA contains an exception to paying officials to perform routine transactions, such as licensing, document processing, or other basic government services. However, because these were facilitating payments, intended solely to influence the government to give Giffen's company new business, they were found to be beyond the exception.[iv]

The indictment alleged that the defendant routed the payments from the company in the United States to the officials' Swiss bank accounts. The FCPA applied, even though Giffen's conduct was beyond the reach of federal fraud statutes.

The original indictment alleged violations of the mail and wire fraud statutes, under the theory that he deprived the citizens of Kazakhstan of the honest services of their government. Although this theory is often used to attack domestic government corruption, it is too much of a stretch for these statutes to be applicable to foreign citizens.[v]

As of the writing of this book, this case has not gone to trial or reached a definitive conclusion; the court in *United States v. Giffen* has made it clear that foreign bribery is well within the government's law enforcement jurisdiction.[vi] This case should show the legal implications of the FCPA and also just how far the FCPA can reach.[vii]

---

[i] *United States v. Giffen*, 326 F. Supp. 2d 497, 499 (S.D.N.Y. 2004).

[ii] Marlena Telvick, Kazakstan: "United States v. James H. Giffen," available at: http://forumkz.addr.com/2004en/en_forum_03_06_04 (last visited May 17, 2005).

[iii] *Giffen*, 326 F. Supp. 2d. at 500; Telvick, Marlena, "Kazakstan: United States v. James H. Giffen," available at: http://forumkz.addr.com/2004en/en_forum_03_06_04 (last visited May 17, 2005).

[iv] *Giffen*, 326 F. Supp. 2d. at 501.

[v] *Giffen*, 326 F. Supp. 2d. at 504-6.

[vi] *Giffen*, 326 F. Supp. 2d. at 501.

[vii] Brad Hamilton, "Bribe 'Spy' Slick as Oil—Shadowy Saga of a Lexington Ave. Banker's Big-$$ Deals in Asian Despot's Exotic Realm," *New York Post*, March 6, 2005, 24.

## THE ORGANIZATION FOR ECONOMIC CO-OPERATION AND DEVELOPMENT AND OTHER INTERNATIONAL CONVENTIONS

As a result of pressure from the United States, other nations have also acted to make bribery illegal. In December of 1997, all members of the Organization for Economic Co-operation and Development (OECD), a group of 35 nations including Japan, Korea, Mexico, Canada, Australia, the United States, and most of Western Europe, signed the Convention on Combating Bribery of Foreign Public Officials in International Business. The signatory nations agreed to enact legislation similar to the FCPA and to create a legal basis for extradition and international cooperation. In 2000, the OECD amended its guidelines to broaden their scope, removing any reference to the identity of the bribe-taker. Therefore, payments made to anyone, regardless of status, to obtain or retain business in OECD nations constitute a violation. The point is that companies need to be aware of local bribery laws as well as the FCPA.

Twenty-two nations from the Organization of American States (OAS) have ratified the OAS Inter-American Convention against Corruption, which requires the criminalization of domestic and foreign bribery. Likewise, the Council of Europe held a Criminal Law Convention on Corruption in 1999. The Council of Europe Convention was the first to prohibit trading in influence specifically as well as the use of local agents specifically for their ability to influence public officials. In addition, more than 100 countries have also signed the United Nations Convention against Corruption, which requires parties to amend their domestic laws to prohibit private and public sector corruption.

Despite these international conventions, nations in Europe, Africa, Latin America, and Asia are still suffering from much more corruption than the United States or Canada. The problem is that laws are passed, but they are not enforced. The reasons could be indifference, lack of sophistication, incompetence, or corruption on the part of the police and government officials.

A headline in a German news weekly in 2002 read, "Help, we're living in a banana republic!"[8] Graft has long been accepted as a political reality in Europe. If anything, the problem is getting worse instead of better.[9] International contracts in Europe are often made through local agents or middlemen, who are nothing more than "bagmen" for local public officials selling their influence.

Africa too, has a corruption problem. In 2002, western businesses were abandoning Kenya because of what Transparency International, the leading nongovernmental organization fighting corruption worldwide, called "highly acute" corruption: 95 percent of all public officials in Kenya were "on the take." After a regime change, the percentage of corrupt officials dropped to below 90 percent in 2004. Transparency International dropped its description of Kenyan corruption from "highly acute" to only "rampant."[10]

Asia is not immune to corruption either. It is interesting that in supposedly Communist nations like China and Vietnam, golf courses are springing up for a new upper class. This upper class often includes local government officials whose meager government salaries could not support this lifestyle. According to Transparency International, corruption is widespread in China, Vietnam, India, Thailand, Pakistan, the Philippines, and South Korea.[11]

Obtaining business in Communist nations like China presents a problem for U.S. companies, because bribery is prevalent. The state owns many of the businesses, making those employees government officials. To illustrate the difference between China and the United States, perhaps as many as 200 public officials are prosecuted in the United States each year for demanding bribes. In a six-year period the total would be about 1,200 and perhaps as high as 2,000 U.S. prosecutions for public corruption. In China, between 1997 and 2003, more than 1 million Chinese officials were disciplined for violating anticorruption laws.[12] Still, compared with other nations on Transparency International's Corruption Perception Index, China is far from being the most corrupt country.

## TRANSPARENCY INTERNATIONAL'S CORRUPTION PERCEPTION INDEX

Transparency International's Corruption Perceptions Index (CPI) 2004 ranked a record 146 countries' perceptions of the degree of corruption as seen by business people and country analysts. The CPI score ranges from 10 (highly clean) to 0 (highly corrupt). At a press conference in October 2004, Transparency International Chairman Peter Eigen said, "Corruption in large-scale public projects is a daunting obstacle to sustainable development, and results in a major loss of public funds needed for education, healthcare, and poverty alleviation, both in developed and developing countries."[13] Transparency International estimates that the amount lost because of bribery in government procurement is at least US$400 billion per year worldwide.

A total of 106 of 146 countries score less than 5 against a clean score of 10, according to the 2004 index. Sixty countries score less than 3 of 10, indicating rampant corruption. Corruption is perceived to be most acute in Bangladesh, Haiti, Nigeria, Chad, Myanmar, Azerbaijan, and Paraguay, all of which have scores of less than 2.

Eigen pointed out that oil-rich Angola, Azerbaijan, Chad, Ecuador, Indonesia, Iran, Iraq, Kazakhstan, Libya, Nigeria, Russia, Sudan, Venezuela, and Yemen all have extremely low CPI scores. In these countries, public contracting revenues in the oil sector vanish into the pockets of middlemen and local officials.[14] Other business sectors in addition to oil that are particularly susceptible to bribery and corruption are construction and defense contracts.

It is interesting to note that the Scandinavian countries are perennially in the top ten least corrupt nations on the CPI. The United States ranked 17 on the list of 146 countries, with a CPI score of 7.5. China tied with Saudi Arabia and Syria at number 71 with a score of 3.4. Russia tied with India and several African nations at 90, with a 2.8. Kenya tied with Iraq and Pakistan at 129, with a 2.1. Nigeria was number 144, with a score of 1.6, ahead of only Bangladesh and Haiti, which were tied at 145 with scores of 1.5.[15] (See Exhibit 15.1.)

Several factors are present in all nations that have high CPI scores: accountability, political stability, effective government regulation, and rule of law. The fewer of these factors present, the lower the country's PCI score will be.

## OFFSHORE FINANCIAL SERVICES

Corruption often involves money laundering to conceal the illegal payments. Various offshore financial centers offer bank secrecy laws, which mask the payment transaction and the owner of the funds. Some of the most notorious offshore financial centers are Guatemala,

**EXHIBIT 15.1**  2004's Ten Least Corrupt Nations Ranked by Corruption Perception Index (CPI) Score[a]

| Country | CPI Score |
| --- | --- |
| Finland | 9.7 |
| New Zealand | 9.6 |
| Denmark | 9.5 |
| Iceland | 9.5 |
| Singapore | 9.3 |
| Sweden | 9.2 |
| Switzerland | 9.1 |
| Norway | 8.9 |
| Australia | 8.8 |
| Netherlands | 8.7 |

[a]Transparency International, www.transparency.org.

the Cook Islands, and Nauru, which is located near Australia and is the smallest nation in the world. The Financial Action Task Force (FATF), a group of 33 nations that have developed international standards and policies to combat money laundering, has listed these nations as Non-Cooperative Countries and Territories (NCCTs).

### Bribery Red Flags

Certain facts may indicate that bribery of foreign officials is going on, probably not in such an obvious fashion as a salesman saying, "I need $10,000 to get the business." Instances that should raise concern include the following:

- Lack of standard invoices. Agents who say that they do not use invoices should be told that they will use them in this case. It is critical to have a clear audit trail.
- Requests for funds to be routed to a bank in a different country, especially Switzerland, Hong Kong, Cyprus, or Caribbean nations. (Many officials have bribe payments sent to bank accounts outside their home countries to avoid detection by local authorities.)

- Requests for checks made payable to "cash" or "the bearer."
- Representations that a contract is not necessary. Again, it is essential to have a clear audit trail and clear direction as to the purpose of each payment.
- Commissions substantially higher than the going rate signal possible kickbacks.
- Requests for a large line of credit for the customer.
- Insistence by local government officials that a certain third-party agent or supplier be used. They will suggest their friends, who will then kick back funds to them. Conduct research and due diligence to find an agent independently.
- Lack of facilities or staff to actually perform any real service.
- Request by the local agent for a rate increase in the middle of negotiations.
- Suggested need to utilize more than one local agent. This should not be necessary.

### What Happens When Money Gets Sent to Latvia?

In 2004, a man was running a business in Miami. He went online to check his bank balance and found $90,000 missing. There was a record for a wire transfer of $90,000 to Latvia earlier that day. He made a quick call to the bank. The ensuing investigation showed that the customer had a computer infected with a Trojan Horse called Coreflood. Coreflood made it much easier for hackers to determine the customer's password. Since the customer did not have proper antivirus protection on his computer, the bank said it was not at fault. The U.S. Secret Service worked the case, but the fraudster was in Latvia.[16] There was no hope of extradition or restitution, or any help. The victim filed suit against the bank. Chasing stolen funds outside the United States is a whole new ballgame. Some countries simply do not cooperate with investigations or attempts to recover assets.

### ENDNOTES

1. J. Puliyenthuruthel, "The Soft Underbelly of Offshoring," *Business Week*, April 25, 2005, 52.

2. Daintry Duffy, "The Color of Risk," *CSO*, Fall 2004, Special Issue, 12.

3. *Foreign Corrupt Practices Act, U.S. Code* 15 (2005) § 78dd-2(a).

4. *United States v. Lockheed*, No. 1:94-CR-226 (N.D. GA 1994).

5. Ibid.

6. *SEC v. Chiquita Brands International*, Civil Action No. 1:01CV02079 U.S. (D.D.C. 2001).

7. Ibid.

8. Stefan Theil and Christopher Dickey, "Europe's Dirty Secret," *Newsweek International*, April, 29, 2002, 14.

9. Ibid.

10. "Where Graft Is Merely Rampant," *The Economist*, December 18, 2004. 65 US ed.

11. Nicole Strizzi and Gurprit Kindra, "Asian Influence," *Ivey Business Journal*, May 2000, 38.

12. Patrick M. Norton, "The Foreign Corrupt Practices Act: A Minefield for US Companies in China," *China Law & Practice*, November 2004, 15.

13. Transparency International, "Transparency International Corruption Perceptions Index 2004," www.transparency.org/cpi/2004/cpi2004.en.html#cpi2004.

14. Ibid.

15. Ibid.

16. K. Krebsbach, "Wire Transfer Brouhaha," April 2005, www.us-banker.com/article.html?id=20050401W0MNDYJG.

# CHAPTER 16

# The Feds Are Watching: What to Know and Do Now

## EXECUTIVE SUMMARY

The federal government has had a strong response to the many corporate frauds over the last few years. Using the full range of law enforcement actions and new laws, federal agents and prosecutors have used a "shock and awe" strategy against corporate fraudsters. "Flipping" lower level employees to testify against higher-ups, cooperation agreements, Grand Jury subpoenas, and search warrants are but a sampling of the weapons in the government's arsenal. Hopefully all businesses will embrace a culture of compliance; if not, the feds will be watching and will be ready to pounce. Organizations must also be prepared in the event the government makes them the focus of a fraud investigation. The right or wrong response at the beginning of the investigation may set the tone that follows. Entities that acknowledge wrongdoing early and "give up" their corrupt executives will do far better in surviving and emerging from a major fraud investigation. Companies must also have a policy as to legal recourse when it is discovered they have been the victims of fraud.

There is a new war on crime in America today, and it is being waged by the government to stop corporate fraud. Titans of industry are falling and in their wake are left the many victims of fraud. The government's attack has been unrelenting, and there is no reason to think that it will abate any time soon. This war is not being fought solely by the government, however. Businesses must now take appropriate action to detect and prosecute fraud of all kinds. Sarbanes-Oxley was enacted because some corporate executives failed to ensure ethical operations and the protection of shareholders and employees. Fraud prevention and enhanced internal controls help, but organizations must also know the strategies of law enforcement and be prepared to take action when allegations of fraud are discovered.

## ATTORNEY GENERAL ASHCROFT'S MARCHING ORDERS TO THE TROOPS

One day after President George W. Bush signed Sarbanes-Oxley into law, then Attorney General John Ashcroft issued a directive to begin the crusade against corporate fraud with great vigor. On July 31, 2004, he directed federal prosecutors to implement Title XI of Sarbanes-Oxley, the Corporate Fraud and Accountability Act of 2002. His message went out to all United States Attorneys in the country. It read:

> *Yesterday, President Bush signed the Act into law, giving federal prosecutors the ability to seek new criminal penalties for securities fraud, attempts to commit mail, wire, bank and health care fraud, certifying false financial statements, document destruction or tampering, and retaliating against whistleblowers.*
>
> *Today I directed our nation's federal prosecutors and investigators to utilize all of these new tools as they fight corporate crime. The Justice Department will do everything it can to protect the hard-earned savings and investments of the millions of Americans who have planned for their future, saved for their children's educations, and prepared for their retirement.*
>
> *These are the most significant and far reaching measures to reform corporate misconduct in decades. We will continue to investigate and prosecute vigorously corporate fraud—and we will bring to justice those who have abused the trust of investors and employees.*[1]

These were strong words and a public message never before heard. Fighting corporate fraud was a priority with the stated purpose of punishing those responsible, and in the process, restoring investor confidence in the stock market. The detection, investigation, and prosecution of corporate wrongdoing became a top priority, and the resources of the government would be applied in full measure. Assistant United States Attorneys, Securities and Exchange Commission (SEC) attorneys, FBI agents, postal inspectors, and others joined forces in a war on corporate crime never before seen.

## THE CORPORATE FRAUD TASK FORCE

In his introductory comments in the Corporate Fraud Task Force's First Year Report to the President in July 2003, then Task Force Chairman and former Deputy Attorney General Larry D. Thompson said, "When President Bush announced the formation of the Corporate Fraud Task Force in July 2001, I knew the Task Force had a tough job ahead of it. Our financial markets had been shaken by a series of episodes of significant criminal conduct at the highest levels of some American corporations. I emphasize *some* corporations. This aberrant business and corporate behavior has occurred in, I believe, a small minority of American businesses. Nevertheless, the problem is serious, and the criminal conduct of a few individuals has harmed the reputations of the majority of honest business people and corporations. Because the vitality of our increasingly complex economy rests on the free and fair exchange of accurate information, I strongly agreed with the President that these crimes were serious and deserved intense law and regulatory enforcement focus and action."[2]

In a very short period, the Corporate Fraud Task Force had an extraordinary impact on corporate crime. The members of the Task Force include the United States Department of Justice, the United States Attorneys' Offices in New York, Los Angeles, San Francisco, Chicago, Philadelphia, and Houston; and the FBI, Department of Treasury, Department of Labor, SEC, Commodity Futures Trading Commission, Federal Energy Regulatory Commission, Federal Communications Commission, and Postal Inspection Service. By May 31, 2003, the Task Force had conducted more than 320 criminal investigations involving more than 500 individual subjects. Charges had been filed against 354 defendants, and 250 individuals had been convicted.[3]

The results reported in the Task Force's Second Year Report to the President issued on July 20, 2004, were even more impressive. For the period ending May 31, 2004, more than 500 corporate fraud convictions had been obtained, double the number of convictions from the prior year. More than 900 defendants had been charged with crimes in more than 400 different cases, including more than 60 corporate CEOs and presidents. In the Enron case, 31 defendants were charged with corporate fraud, including 21 former Enron executives. The government also seized more than $161 million in defrauded funds, for restitution to Enron victims. In assessing the Task Force's work at the end of year two, Deputy Attorney General James B. Comey stated that the Task Force can "restore public confidence in our financial markets and in our criminal justice system—to make people know we will continue to work like crazy until we have brought all corporate crooks to justice."[4]

Whether the Corporate Fraud Task Force stays together in the form it is now or disbands at some point, there is no doubt that the various agencies and their dedicated personnel will continue to pursue corporate fraud. The public will demand and politicians will dictate that the war on corporate fraud continues. Organizations and executives who cross the line can expect no let-up in the aggressive government approach.

## THE GOVERNMENT'S "SHOCK AND AWE" STRATEGY

In years past, it often took a lengthy period to investigate white-collar crime cases thoroughly. Considering the complexity of sophisticated corporate fraud, the vast numbers of documents to be obtained and analyzed, the numerous interviews to be conducted, the resource constraints, the court proceedings, and the legal maneuvering, it was not uncommon for investigations to continue for years. All that has changed, however, as a result of the corporate scandals. The government and the public have little sympathy or patience for corporate fraudsters, and justice demands quick resolution to allegations.

As a result, federal law enforcement has also changed its modus operandi for investigating white-collar criminals. In the past, the FBI and other federal investigative agencies often spent years developing every possible criminal violation against a subject or subjects of an investigation. The purpose was to make an airtight case, but valuable resources were often not available for similar investigations. The new approach is "deterrence" rather than the development of every possible criminal charge. In the investigation of HealthSouth Corporation for a massive accounting fraud, the government adopted a "shock and awe" strategy against corporate fraud. Federal prosecutors and the FBI in Birmingham, Alabama used new levels of cooperation among various federal agencies, search warrants, the new laws from Sarbanes-Oxley, strong court maneuvers, a push for plea bargains, and cooperation against other fraudsters not yet charged. In a matter of weeks after first announcing the investigation against HealthSouth in March 2003, the government had obtained 12 guilty pleas from company officials, and this was just the beginning.[5]

The cooperating defendants provided evidence against other corporate officials, who also pled guilty and agreed to work with the government. They provided even more significant evidence of the fraud, which allowed the case to progress rapidly and, most importantly, pointed directly to CEO Richard Scrushy. Alice H. Martin, the United States Attorney in Birmingham, whose office prosecuted HealthSouth said, "Your case doesn't have to be perfect. You don't have to prove every crime. If you've got enough evidence to back up a few good charges, don't work for another year nailing down every shred of evidence for every possible charge that might be there."[6] She added that the Department of Justice sent out a strong message to prosecutors and federal agents that they "wanted real-time prosecution of corporate crime."[7]

Unfortunately, this approach did not work in the government's trial of Scrushy. The Scrushy jury bought the "Mr. Magoo Defense" of the CEO who has no idea that a massive fraud is occurring inside the company. Clearly, the government was at a disadvantage. The trial was held on Scrushy's home turf of Birmingham, where he had strong support from religious groups and others in the community. The defense team did an amazing job of portraying the defendant as the only innocent person in a den of thieves and created reasonable doubt. The fact that Scrushy did not take the stand and face cross-examination also helped in his acquittal. Even though the CEO was not convicted, there is no denying the depth and breath of the accounting fraud at HealthSouth. Exhibit 16.1 gives a list of the many HealthSouth employees who were charged by the government for this fraud and the prosecution results.

Part of the government's strong approach in fighting corporate fraud has been to treat corporate fraudsters no differently with the media than organized crime figures. "Perp walks" are now routinely used to showcase white-collar defendants. Federal agents are going to fraudsters' homes and arresting them, rather than allowing them to surrender. Handcuffing is not optional. Defendants are being charged with more than just typical fraud and securities violations. Although some prosecutors are using the "quick hit" approach, others are using all the weapons in their arsenal when necessary. Money laundering,

**EXHIBIT 16.1**   HealthSouth Prosecution Results[a]

| Date Charged | Defendant | Title | Status |
| --- | --- | --- | --- |
| March 19, 2003 | Weston Smith | CFO | Convicted |
| March 26, 2003 | William T. Owens | CFO | Convicted |
| March 31, 2003 | Emery Harris | VP, Finance and Assistant Controller | Convicted |
| April 3, 2003 | Rebecca Kay Morgan | Assistant Controller | Convicted |
| April 3, 2003 | Cathy C. Edwards | VP | Convicted |
| April 3, 2003 | Ken Livesay | Chief Information Officer and Assistant Controller | Convicted |
| April 23, 2003 | Michael Martin | CFO | Convicted |
| April 23, 2003 | Virginia B. Valentine | Assistant VP | Convicted |
| April 23, 2003 | Angela C. Ayers | VP | Convicted |
| April 23, 2003 | Malcolm McVay | CFO | Convicted |
| April 24, 2003 | Aaron Beam | CFO | Convicted |
| July 9, 2003 | Jason Brown | VP, Finance | Convicted |
| July 31, 2003 | Richard Botts | Senior VP, Tax | Convicted |
| July 31, 2003 | Will Hicks | VP, Investments | Convicted |
| September 26, 2003 | Catherine Fowler | VP, Treasury and Cash Manager | Convicted |
| November 4, 2003 | Richard Scrushy | CEO | Acquitted |

[a] HealthSouth Criminal Investigation prosecutions, United States Attorney, Northern District of Alabama, www.usdoj.gov/usao/aln/Pages/HSdefendantmainwithform.htm.

conspiracy, and racketeering, as well as the new criminal charges resulting from Sarbanes-Oxley are also being used. Federal prosecutors are using asset forfeiture statutes to take back the ill-gotten gains of corporate criminals. A defense attorney who has represented both organized crime figures and corporate executives explains that the government's strong approach is a result of "the public demanding that white-collar criminals be sent to prison, and prosecutors are playing tough....There's no more white-glove treatment."[8]

Prosecutors are asking for bail in the millions of dollars to ensure that defendants appear for court proceedings. In the case of former Tyco CEO Dennis Kozlowski, the New York County District Attorney's Office obtained a $10 million bail on the indicted executive, causing his defense attorney to utter incredulously, "This is not a narcotics case."[9] Prosecutors are using every possible advantage to get defendants to plead guilty and cooperate against other defendants, even using a loved one as leverage. The Enron Task Force charged former Enron CFO Andrew Fastow with fraud, money laundering, and conspiracy. This was not enough to get him to cooperate. Fastow was then indicted on new charges, but this time his wife, Lea Fastow, was also charged. Lea Fastow had been a former assistant treasurer at Enron and was charged with helping her husband and other executives perpetrate the massive fraud at Enron. She was arrested, handcuffed, and given her perp walk. Clearly, the intention was to put pressure on the husband to cooperate now that his wife and the mother of his children was facing many years in jail if convicted. After lengthy negotiations, both Andrew and Lea Fastow agreed to plead guilty. Andrew agreed to a ten-year prison term, forfeiture of $24 million in cash and property, and cooperation with the government in the continuing case. Lea received a misdemeanor charge of filing a false tax return and was sentenced to one year in prison.

There was a time when a corporate plea was more acceptable than having a corporate executive take a fall for fraud. In the late 1980s, one of the authors investigated a security guard services company in a scheme to defraud commercial airlines operating out of John F. Kennedy Airport in New York by overbilling for guard services and other crimes. More than 20 lower level employees were convicted. When the investigation began to focus on higher level executives, the company wanted to take a corporate plea rather than have any of their top executives prosecuted. The government went along with this approach. The company pled guilty to wire fraud and paid a $1M fine. This would not happen today; corporate executives are now being held accountable and businesses are doing everything they can to avoid criminal convictions.

---

### EXECUTIVE INSIGHT 16.1: COMPUTER ASSOCIATES AND THE "35-DAY MONTH"

In today's world, protecting the viability of a business is paramount. Computer Associates is another example of a company that has learned from the past and has taken strong steps to promote good corporate governance while protecting its investors and employees. Computer Associates is one of the world's largest management software companies. It was founded in 1976 and is a global business leader with operations in more than 100 countries. It is listed on the New York Stock Exchange with a market capitalization of $16.45 billion.

What is remarkable about what Computer Associates did lies not in the fraud committed by senior executives, although securities fraud and obstruction of justice charges are not to be taken lightly, but in the fact that the company's board took charge and put the interests of shareholders over those of corporate executives.

In 2002, the SEC and the United States Attorney in Brooklyn, New York started a probe into accounting practices at Computer Associates. The government felt that the company was not being totally cooperative in producing documentary evidence and asked the Board of Directors to start its own investigation, which it did. Computer Associates' Audit Committee Chair drove the internal investigation.

In October 2003, the company announced that it "found improper booking of sales."[i] Investigators working for the Board turned over evidence including e-mails, documents, and results of internal interviews in which executives had lied. The Board fired or forced out numerous employees including top finance people and the General Counsel. Computer Associates knew that the

level of cooperation, the replacement of "responsible management," and the "pervasiveness of the criminal conduct" were all
factors that the government used in determining whether to
charge the company criminally.[ii]

The SEC investigation found that employees conducted a
fraudulent accounting practice known internally as the "35-day
month" because company accountants would extend the booking of revenues in the final month of a fiscal quarter several days
beyond the actual end of the month."[iii] In Fiscal Year 2000 alone,
Computer Associates prematurely recognized more than $1.4
billion in revenue.[iv] The internal investigation conducted by
Computer Associates discovered that corporate executives
"snipped date-stamps off faxed documents and added fake dates
to contracts" to hide the fraud from outside auditors.[v]

In January and April 2004, four former senior executives
including the CFO pled guilty to securities fraud and obstruction
of justice charges. The securities fraud charges involved "a long-
running, company-wide scheme to backdate and forge licensing
agreements in order to allow the company to meet or exceed its
quarterly earnings projections during multiple fiscal quarters."[vi]
The obstruction of justice charges related to "the defendants'
lying to the government investigators and concealing evidence of
the securities fraud."[vii] The United States Attorney for the
Eastern District of New York who was prosecuting the case
stated that the guilty pleas of executives and their allocutions to
their crimes "demonstrate the corrupt culture in Computer
Associates' management."[viii]

On September 22, 2004, former CEO Sanjay Kumar was
indicted for his "alleged participation in a long-running, company-wide accounting fraud scheme and subsequent efforts to
obstruct the government's investigation."[ix] On the same day,
Computer Associates agreed to pay the government $225 million
to settle the SEC lawsuit and avoid criminal prosecution. The
company's agreement with the government included accepting
responsibility for its criminal conduct and continued cooperation
with the government. Computer Associates also agreed to the

appointment of new management, the addition of independent members to the Board of Directors, and the appointment of an independent examiner to review compliance with the terms and conditions of the agreement with the government. In short, it would continue implementing remedial steps throughout the organization to ensure that fraud does not recur. In return, Computer Associates would receive a deferred prosecution for the criminal conduct of its former officers, executives, and employees. It does face possible prosecution if it violates the terms of the agreement or commits any other crimes.[x]

Computer Associates posted details of the deferred prosecution agreement and related information at the Investor Relations section of its Web site. The posting states that the resolution of the government investigation "marked the end of a troubling period" for the company and that it "has agreed to implement controls and governance measures to ensure that such past practices are never repeated."[xi]

[i] Steve Hamm, "A Probe—and a Bitter Feud," *Business Week*, April 12, 2004, 78.

[ii] Charles Forelle and Joann S. Lublin, "Kumar Gives up Leadership Posts under Pressure," *Wall Street Journal*, April 22, 2004, A1.

[iii] Charles Forelle, "Ex-CFO at Computer Associates to Enter Plea in Accounting Probe," *Wall Street Journal*, April 8, 2004, A1.

[iv] Charles Forelle, "CA Ex-Executives Plead Guilty, Call Fraud Pervasive," *Wall Street Journal*, April 9, 2004, A3.

[v] Ibid.

[vi] "Second Year Report to the President," Corporate Fraud Task Force, July 20, 2004, www.usdoj.gov/dag/cftf/2nd_yr_fraud_report.pdf.

[vii] Ibid.

[viii] Charles Forelle, "CA Ex-Executives Plead Guilty, Call Fraud Pervasive," *Wall Street Journal*, April 9, 2004, A3.

[ix] Press Release issued by the United States Attorney's Office, Eastern District of New York, September 22, 2004, www.usdoj.gov/usao/nye/pr/2004oct06a.htm.

[x] Ibid.

[xi] Deferred Prosecution Agreement between the Government and Computer Associates posted on the Computer Associates Investor Relations Web site, September 22, 2004, http://investor.ca.com/phoenix.zhtml?c=83100&p=irol-govdeferred.

## SNAPPING THE BONDS OF LOYALTY: JOINING TEAM AMERICA

An attorney with a white-collar defense practice in New York was once fond of giving federal prosecutors and agents baseball hats with the words "Team America 5K1.1" emblazoned on the cap. "5K1.1" refers to the Federal Sentencing Guidelines Section 5K1.1 that pertains to a possible reduction in the criminal sentence for a defendant who has provided substantial assistance in the investigation or prosecution of another person who has committed an offense. This usually means becoming a federal informant and witness. This attorney represented many fraudsters who, because of the enormity of the evidence against them, decided to cooperate with the government in the hope of receiving a reduced sentence. The defense attorney would joke that since he and his client had joined the "team" and were now working on behalf of the "red, white and blue," it was only proper that everyone have some kind of uniform accoutrement. Although many thought this was humorous, in reality the practice of defendants "joining Team America" to help prosecute other fraudsters is quite common and is a very useful weapon in the government's war on corporate fraud.

The government uses the power of prosecution and long prison terms as a strong inducement to plead guilty and cooperate against other defendants. As the United States Court of Appeals for the Second Circuit stated so well in the case of *U.S. v. Rosner* in 1973, "in human experience, the pressure of imminent incarceration tends to snap the bonds of loyalty."[10] The possibility of long periods of incarceration has been known to convince even the most hardened individual to cooperate with the government in the hope of a reduced sentence. White-collar criminals are usually not in the same league as organized crime figures, who subscribe to the code of "omerta" or the vow of silence. For fraudsters, prison is something to be feared. Fraudsters are not used to prison life and all the harshness and violence associated with it. Factor in the increased penalties that translate to much longer jail time, and one can see how cooperation with the government begins to look appealing.

A former federal prosecutor, who is now in a white-collar defense practice and represents a number of the corporations under investigation, had some interesting things to say about the new compliance environment. A number of his clients are well-known public companies, and their corporate executives are under investigation for fraud involving revenue recognition and other issues. His view is that executives are now facing what amounts to life sentences if convicted for corporate fraud, and they are fearful. As a result of the new landscape, executives need to understand that willful blindness + conscious avoidance = knowledge under the law. Prosecutors are using this threat to obtain cooperation. Now it is how quickly one can get to the prosecutor's office to cooperate and tell all. "Take five" as this defense attorney calls invoking the Fifth Amendment right against self-incrimination, is no longer an option. The attorney said that the SEC is telling corporations not to assist corporate executives under investigation and not to provide them with any of their e-mails, files, or records for review prior to government interviews. Corporate boards are no longer protecting the chief executives and are the ones now turning them in to the government when wrongdoing is discovered. The attorney's advice to clients is to question every deal and every accounting procedure in which they are involved, to ensure that everything is above board, and to blow the whistle early and often when fraud is found.

## THE FBI'S STRATEGIC PLAN FOR COMBATING CORPORATE CRIME

Historically, the FBI has been committed to fighting all forms of fraud and economic crime. The war on terror has caused a rebalancing of investigative resources from areas such as white-collar crime to antiterrorism efforts. Since September 11, 2001, the FBI's major focus has been to defend the security of the United States and protect against terrorist attacks. The FBI Strategic Plan 2004–2009 "serves as a high-level road map...with strategic goals and objectives that address the mission of the FBI."[11] Of the eight investigative priorities in the Strategic Plan, combating major white-collar crime including corporate fraud ranks number seven. Only combating violent crime was lower, at number eight. Although it is now a lower priority than previously, fighting fraud is still an important issue for the FBI.

The Strategic Plan's long-term forecasting section for white-collar crime states that "Corporate fraud has undermined the public's confidence in American business institutions, and the aggressive investigation and prosecution of major corporate fraud will be a key factor in restoring long-term confidence in our business leaders."[12]

---

### EXECUTIVE INSIGHT 16.2: FBI STRATEGIC PLAN 2004–2009: STRATEGIC OBJECTIVES TO REDUCE CORPORATE FRAUD

Strategic Objective: Reduce levels of corporate fraud by targeting those groups or individuals engaged in major corporate fraud schemes that significantly impact the investing public and financial markets.

Fraud by company executives and those in positions of trust not only damages stockholders, but also erodes public confidence in the corporate community at large. The FBI will continue increasing its efforts in this area by using agents and analysts with high degrees of expertise in financial investigations. The sheer complexity of illegal corporate transactions requires extraordinary time and commitment to investigate.

#### Priority Actions

- Expand the intelligence base through private sector and community outreach specifically focused on private industry personnel, government regulators, and all levels of law enforcement.
- Initiate major investigations on all aspects of corporate fraud.
- Incorporate aggressive asset forfeiture actions in every criminal case to strip violators of their ill-gotten gains.
- Develop human sources that can substantially reduce the time and resources dedicated to complex investigations.[xii]

---

[xii] FBI Strategic Plan 2004–2009, www.fbi.gov/publications/strategicplan/strategic planfull.pdf,59.

## THE CHALLENGES OF RUNNING A BUSINESS WHILE ATTEMPTING TO PROSECUTE A COMPLICATED CIVIL FRAUD CASE

For a business, there may be no more disruptive and challenging event than prosecuting a civil fraud claim against former officers and directors who have defrauded the company. The challenges are numerous and substantial. First, the company must conduct an internal investigation to determine what occurred and decide what, if any, communication must be made to governmental agencies, including law enforcement agencies, about the relevant events. Then the leadership of the company must decide what steps are to be taken to pursue compensation from those former insiders who committed fraud. Although the principal decision-maker will almost certainly want to pursue recovery of any funds that the wrongdoer may have stolen, executing that decision can be difficult and disruptive to ongoing business.

This section provides some guidance into what a lawyer retained to pursue civil insider fraud for a business will consider to prosecute the case successfully. It also provides some insight into how long it will take to pursue a successful action as a plaintiff. The section's main themes can be summed up in four words: capture, cooperation, cost, and patience.

### Capture

It is axiomatic that prosecution of any case requires evidence. White-collar cases may require the production of thousands of documents. Document control is both expensive and time consuming. Moreover, all this production must occur while management simultaneously rebuilds its reputation and remains profitable.

"Capture" refers to preserving the record that will prove the fraudulent actions by the former employee. The less complete the documentary trail, the more difficult prosecution becomes. If documentation is lost or destroyed, then the case against the wrongdoer is jeopardized through the legal doctrine of "spoliation." "Elements of a spoliation claim are (1) the existence of a potential civil action; (2) a legal or contractual duty to preserve evidence which is relevant to the potential civil action; (3) destruction of that evidence; (4) significant impairment in the ability to prove the lawsuit; (5) a causal relationship between the evidence destruction and the inability to prove the lawsuit; and (6) damages."[13] Moreover, the negligent destruction of relevant evidence can be sufficient to give rise to the spoliation inference, allowing a jury to conclude that the destroyed evidence would have been unfavorable to the offending party.[14]

Consequently, a business must capture the record as quickly and as thoroughly as possible. This process is complicated by the fact that critical databases change literally every second of every day at some businesses. Therefore, it is important for a business to have in place a procedure for capturing data as soon as it discovers a fraudulent act. Taking that data "snapshot" will immensely assist the prosecution of litigation, and failing to take this "snapshot" jeopardizes the case.

Document capture is a highly involved process. It should involve employees from a company's technology, accounting, and legal departments. The process will need to be closely managed and may require that specific personnel be dedicated solely to this task. It will probably also require the retention of outside consultants and attorneys. For example, a forensic accountant can assist with the reconstruction of illicit insider transactions, whereas an investigator can interview employee witnesses who may have knowledge about events.

No matter how prevalent or outlandish the fraud, nothing can be proved without capturing the record. Capture is critical.


### Cooperation

Personnel of a business that has become the victim of internal fraud may be uncomfortable and reluctant to cooperate with any external entity, including outside counsel or investigators retained to assist with an internal investigation. Therefore, cooperation with these entities must be a priority of top management, and top management must emphasize this to all employees. Cooperation should extend to governmental agencies, including law enforcement. The business will be far better served by quickly disclosing to law enforcement any fraudulent acts that may qualify as crimes. The top management of public corporations faces additional disclosure obligations as set forth by Sarbanes-Oxley.

Informing counsel for the company about the problems that confront it will probably be the most effective strategy for successful prosecution against any wrongdoer. First, adept counsel will be able to focus on the most salient issues. Counsel will also be able to temper the impractical emotions of righteous indignation that executives may be feeling toward those suspected of defrauding the company. Finally, fully informed counsel should be able to be the leader of the team charged with performing any internal investigation, shaping that investigation toward the goal of prosecuting those who have breached their fiduciary duties.

Failure to make substantive disclosures both inside and outside the company jeopardizes any civil action that management may pursue against former employees, officers, and directors who have defrauded the company. Moreover, a failure to cooperate in an attempt to protect the company's "dirty laundry" is unlikely to be successful. In most cases, there are simply too many individuals who have knowledge of what has occurred for the salient facts to remain secret. Any party attempting to maintain the secret is probably spending entirely too much time on the ultimately fruitless task of protecting that secret.

## Cost

Pursuing a fraud case is expensive. Understanding the economic factors associated with the prosecution of a civil fraud claim is critical to successful resolution of that claim. Unfortunately, a company's motivation in pursuing a wrongdoer for fraudulent acts often exceeds its litigation budget. Sometimes the company has lost so much money to the wrongdoer that scarce resources must be devoted to getting the business back on track rather than spending big to pursue a Pyrrhic victory. Spending $1 million to recoup $100,000 is not fiscally prudent. Additionally, the target of the investigation may have become "judgment proof," meaning that any monetary judgment against the wrongdoer may not be collectable if the wrongdoer has few assets.

The biggest expense to a company pursuing an action against a wrongdoer is the retention of experts needed to assist with the investigation and prosecution efforts. From the start, the company will probably need to retain forensic accounting experts to reconstruct suspicious transactions. The company will also need to hire attorneys with experience in white-collar crime issues to prosecute any action and to interact with governmental authorities, including law enforcement personnel. Investigators may be needed to interview witnesses and to conduct background checks on suspects. Additionally, the company may need to retain technology consultants to comb through data housed on its computer networks. The lawyers will insist on placing any and all documentation that the company has captured in its "snapshot" on an independent database under their control for purposes of doing their own review and assisting with the production of documents when discovery in any litigation commences.

One constant is that costs to prosecute the case will exceed all initial expectations. It is incumbent on the executive charged with litigation management to understand the rationale for all services that its experts believe necessary to do their respective jobs. This does not mean that the professionals retained are attempting to exploit the company's predicament. It rather means that virtually every professional services firm can name a product, piece of software, or employee that can assist with the prosecution of the case; however, simply because the item may assist marginally with the task at hand does not mean that it is in the economic interest of the company to possess that tool.

One way to control costs is to appoint a company manager who does not have a vested interest in the outcome of the litigation. In other words, the individual who feels most "wronged" by the fraudulent acts should not also be the point person for litigation management. The likelihood of conflicts of interest for that individual are simply too great. The "wronged" party may be too willing to spend freely on the prosecution, feeling a need to recoup the company's losses. Such individuals may also be unwilling to divulge all they know to those they have retained, in an attempt to protect their reputations. The task of litigation management is thus best left to an independent manager who had little, if anything, to do with the original problem.

### Patience

In addition to being expensive, the pursuit of a fraud case is time consuming. Reconstructing the transactions that resulted in the fraudulent acts is time consuming. Witness interviews are time consuming.

Moreover, managers and employees will be compelled to spend time on nonproductive activities, such as document review. This consumption of time represents a significant opportunity cost to the company.

In addition, the entire judicial system is designed to be time consuming. In the federal courts, it is not uncommon for civil cases to continue on for three to five years from the filing of the first complaint. Therefore, the time from initial discovery of the fraudulent acts to the successful conclusion of a trial can represent a multiyear project for a company, with the company lacking control over much of that timeline. Collection of any judgment will take additional time. Appeals are also a possibility. Any company contemplating the prosecution of a fraud claim must therefore guard against "claim exhaustion." It is difficult to have the same feelings of righteous indignation after two years of investigation and civil discovery that one had when initially discovering the fraudulent act. Personnel often leave the company, and memories lapse. Consequently, as with the cost factor, it is valuable to have someone in place who can objectively balance the benefits of pursuing claims against the time that will be needed to prosecute the case successfully.

## Staying the Civil Proceeding

It is quite possible that in today's compliance-driven climate, a business will self-report significant fraud to the government as soon as it was reasonably certain of the crime. At this point, the government might ask the entity to stop any further investigation while the government put its own investigation into gear. It is also possible that the courts might intervene during a civil prosecution if a conflict with the government's criminal proceedings appeared to be a possibility.

There is a test regarding whether to stay a civil proceeding when there is a criminal proceeding. "The court has the inherent power to stay civil proceedings, postpone civil discovery, or impose protective orders when the interests of justice so dictate. In determining whether a stay should be granted in a civil trial based on the existence or potential existence of a criminal proceeding, the court considers six factors: (1) whether the two actions involved the same subject matter, (2) whether the two actions are brought by the government, (3) the posture of the criminal proceeding, (4) the public interests at stake,

(5) the plaintiff's interests and possible prejudice to the plaintiff, and (6) the burden that any particular aspect of the proceedings may impose on the defendants."[15]

"The decision to grant or deny a stay is within the court's broad range of discretionary powers."[16] "The similarity of the issues underlying the civil and criminal actions is considered the most important threshold issue in determining whether or not to grant a stay. The strongest case for deferring civil proceedings until after completion of criminal proceedings is where a party under indictment for a serious offense is required to defend a civil action involving the same matter."[17]

### Making a Business Decision

Although corporate fraud is often perceived as a victimless crime, it most emphatically is not. The corporation itself loses greatly. It loses fiscally. It may experience productivity losses and may have its public reputation besmirched. Ultimately, investors and shareholders lose. Once the fraud is discovered, management's immediate reaction may be to launch a lawsuit to get the "bad guys." Often this is the proper, although not always effective, approach, but sometimes it is not. If the fraud is significant, the government may launch its own criminal prosecution. In fact, the government may or may not request the company to hold off on any civil prosecution until completion of the criminal case. Like virtually every business decision, only after a rational analysis of the "capture, cooperation, cost, and patience" factors should the decision be made as to whether to pursue justice through the initiation of a civil suit.

## BLAKELY AND BOOKER IMPLICATIONS FOR SENTENCING

The government has promised to prosecute white-collar offenders to the fullest extent of the law and impose heavy sentences in accord with the Federal Sentencing Guidelines. The Guidelines used various factors, to be determined by the judge after the verdict, to determine the defendant's sentence in a sort of mathematical formula. Sarbanes-Oxley amended the Guidelines, adding stricter terms for white-collar crime defendants. However, two recent Supreme Court cases have dramatically altered the federal prosecution landscape by calling into question the validity of the Guidelines. In *United States v. Blakely*, the Supreme Court held that a judge cannot determine any factors that would increase a defendant's sentence.[18] In other words, any factors that would enhance sentencing must be found by a jury. Although the *Blakely* decision applied to Washington State's sentencing guidelines, the question that immediately arose was whether the federal Guidelines would be struck down on the same basis.

The Supreme Court answered this question with *United States v. Booker*. *Booker* was an unusual decision, both for its dual opinions and for the fact that the Guidelines survived. *Booker* held that the Sixth Amendment prohibits federal judges from using factors not found by a jury to increase a defendant's sentence. The Court also found that the Guidelines should be applied in an advisory, rather than mandatory fashion, sparing them from being overturned. Thus, judges must consult the Guidelines during the sentencing phase of a trial but are not required to follow them.[19]

What effect does this have on white-collar crime defendants? In reality, it will only have a limited effect. Acts that were illegal before, such as fraudulent accounting practices or making false statements to the SEC, remain illegal, and federal prosecutors will pursue the offenders to the fullest extent of the law. Since the Guidelines are no longer mandatory, this may encourage defense lawyers to "judge shop" to find judges who are willing to depart downward from the advisory guidelines.[20] It may also lead to more cases going to trial, since prosecutors may lack as much leverage to strike a plea bargain as under the mandatory Guidelines, and defense attorneys might be more willing to try their luck at trial—they may be able to receive a lesser sentence from the judge. Nevertheless, prosecutors will continue to operate as they have before. Many defendants will probably still receive sentences within the Guidelines range, as judges continue to give out sentences similar to those they gave before *Blakely and Booker*.[21]

## MAKING THE BEST OF A BAD SITUATION: WHAT TO DO IF THE FEDS SHOW UP AT THE DOOR

Hopefully this day will never come, but a company must be prepared for the eventuality of federal agents showing up asking questions, with subpoenas, or, worse yet, with search and arrest warrants. In years past, businesses generally reacted with anything but full cooperation with the government. At the first sign of a federal agent attempting to interview a company employee, the company would hire the best attorney money could buy to represent that employee before any questioning. The rest of the company would typically "lawyer-up" and either refuse to answer questions or at least make it as hard as possible to obtain information. In the past, it was rare for a company to provide the government with the results of an internal investigation, disclose wrongdoing on the part of employees, or waive attorney-client privilege.

Federal agents and prosecutors have a powerful set of tools when they are conducting fraud investigations. They use Grand Juries, subpoenas, confidential informants, and undercover operations. They also use proffer agreements, euphemistically referred to as "Queen for a Day Letters" to learn what a cooperating defendant can offer in a criminal investigation, "flip" defendants into cooperators, and have them "wear a wire" to get evidence that moves up the corporate ladder. Federal authorities use a little fish to get the bigger fish, and even use a big fish such as former WorldCom CFO Scott Sullivan to flip, plead guilty, and testify against an even bigger fish, former WorldCom CEO Bernard Ebbers. The government knows how to use the domino effect in investigating and prosecuting corporate crime.

As federal agents, the authors have investigated fraudulent employee conduct and tried to obtain assistance from companies in corroborating the fraud. Employees under investigation would refuse to be interviewed, and the companies did nothing to make them comply. One attorney hired by the company would typically represent all other potential witnesses. That attorney would be present during all interviews and would report back to the company what transpired in every meeting. There was no doubt that the government would be getting little help from the company, and there was no incentive or requirement to do anything different.

In the post-Sarbanes-Oxley and enhanced Federal Sentencing Guidelines world, everything has changed. Cooperation with government investigations is now a requirement. CEOs, CFOs, and Board Members face civil and criminal risk for not being compliant and truthful. It is therefore necessary to have a plan in place whenever federal, state, or local authorities approach an organization and ask for information. Businesses have contingency plans for business interruption, natural disasters, strikes, and other possible risks. A contingency plan and response to a government investigation is just as appropriate.

In developing a response plan, an organization's legal department should take the lead role. Assistance from experienced outside counsel should be considered in designing the plan. Former federal prosecutors and agents with extensive experience conducting corporate investigations can work with a company to design and then implement a robust response. They can also brief appropriate company personnel from their experience on what to expect during a government investigation. The following factors should be considered in particular:

- A written company policy requiring cooperation with any government investigation and possible ramifications for not cooperating fully with the government
- Awareness of this policy by corporate executives, the board of directors, and all employees
- Assignment of specific legal department personnel to have ownership of the program and be an initial point of contact for law enforcement conducting an investigation related to the company
- The role of corporate security during any law enforcement action
- The response when government investigators ask to interview a specific employee or employees, including determination of whether outside counsel will be retained to represent them
- The response when government agents serve subpoenas on the company and referral to appropriate legal counsel
- The response when government agents conduct search warrants, including a policy of noninterference with the search
- A decision about whether designated company personnel should monitor any search being conducted, including videotaping the actual search by law enforcement

- The response when agents take privileged material and proprietary information
- Follow-up with the government to obtain copies of important documents taken as a result of a search warrant
- The response when agents announce they have an arrest warrant for an employee, including whether the employee should be arrested at this work location or should be asked to report to a private area and then be arrested.

What a company does at the beginning of a government inquiry can set the tone for all further interactions and outcomes. Cooperation is key throughout the process. There must be an appropriate response and compliance with subpoenas, search warrants, and requests for employee interviews. At the first knowledge of an allegation of fraud or wrongdoing, an organization should conduct an unbiased and impartial internal investigation to determine the facts. The results of such an investigation may very well be provided to the government at some point. In fact, releasing the internal investigation reports, findings, and evidence goes a long way in demonstrating cooperation with a government investigation. In addition, government investigators may require a waiver of attorney-client privilege, and this should also be considered in any contingency plan.

## ENDNOTES

1. "Attorney General Ashcroft Directs Federal Prosecutors to Implement the Corporate Fraud and Accountability Act of 2002," News Release of the United States Department of Justice, Washington, DC, July 31, 2002, www.usdoj.gov/opa/pr/2002/July/02_ag_443.htm.
2. "First Year Report to the President," Corporate Fraud Task Force, July 22, 2003, www.usdoj.gov/dag/cftf/first_year_report.pdf.
3. Ibid.
4. "Second Year Report to the President," Corporate Fraud Task Force, July 20, 2004, www.usdoj.gov/dag/cftf/2nd_yr_fraud_report.pdf.

5. Ann Carrns, Carrick Mollenkamp, Deborah Solomon, and John R. Wilke, "HealthSouth Case Unveils a Shock Strategy," *Wall Street Journal,* April 4, 2003, C1.

6. Ibid.

7. Ibid.

8. Edward Iwata, "Prosecutors Give CEOs the Mobster Treatment," *USA Today,* October 4, 2002, 1B

9. Ibid.

10. *U.S. v. Rosner,* 485 F.2d. 1213 (2d Cir. 1973).

11. The FBI Strategic Plan 2004–2009, www.fbi.gov/publications/strategicplan/stategicplantext.htm.

12. Ibid.

13. *Florida Evergreen Foliage v. E.I. DuPont De Nemours and Co.,* 336 F.Supp.2d 1239 (S.D. Fla. 2004).

14. *Mosaid Tech. Inc. v. Samsung Electronics Co., Ltd.,* 348 F.Supp.2d 332 (D. N.J. 2004).

15. *Doe v. City of Chicago,* 2005 WL 503733 (N.D. Ill., Jan. 18, 2005).

16. *Maloney v. Gordon,* 328 F.Supp.2d 508 (D. Del. 2004).

17. Ibid.

18. *Blakely v. Washington,* 124 S. Ct. 2531 (2004).

19. *United States v. Booker,* 125 S. Ct. 738 (2005).

20. "Supreme Court's Recent Landmark '*Sentencing Guidelines'* Decision Will Affect in Various Ways the Investigation and Prosecution of Business Crimes," *White Collar Criminal and Regulatory Enforcement Bulletin,* publication of the law firm of Baker & McKenzie, www.bakernet.com, February 2005.

21. Ibid.

# CHAPTER 17

# Beyond Compliance: A Fraud Prevention Culture That Works

**EXECUTIVE SUMMARY**

Building a fraud prevention culture that works is no longer an option in today's business world. It is a requirement for survival. Sarbanes-Oxley, the Federal Sentencing Guidelines for Organizations, and other corporate governance enhancements require accountability and oversight. As expected, not every corporate executive has embraced the idea that Sarbanes-Oxley is necessary. In a 2005 survey of 186 corporate executives, 34 percent said that Sarbanes-Oxley should be repealed. However, this will not happen any time soon. Fraud prevention was a requirement before Sarbanes-Oxley, and embedding that concept within the framework of an organization makes even better business sense now. This means that every organization, public or private, must have a zero tolerance for fraud of any kind. Fraud risk management based on a "checklist" mentality is not conducive to success in fighting fraud. Outstanding companies view compliance enhancements as opportunities to create a stronger fraud prevention program and an internal control system that ultimately give them a competitive advantage.

## FRAUD PREVENTION DOES NOT BEGIN OR END WITH SARBANES-OXLEY

By now, it should come as no surprise to executives or those in business that a heightened awareness of fraud and fraud prevention is critical to an organization's success. Implementing the new and enhanced corporate governance requirements is just the beginning of a culture of compliance. Having a checklist mentality is clearly not enough, no matter how many internal control mechanisms one has. Fraud can invade any organization, be it large or small, new or old. There was corporate fraud long before Sarbanes-Oxley was ever conceived. Unfortunately, there will be fraud no matter how many compliance requirements are enacted. However, with a true culture of compliance, fraud can be greatly lessened and even prevented.

As expected, not every executive has embraced the idea that Sarbanes-Oxley is necessary. In a 2005 survey of 186 corporate executives, 34 percent said that Sarbanes-Oxley should be repealed.[1] Businesses may be resistant when new and possibly onerous government regulations are enacted. An almost universal complaint from businesses has been the huge expense related to compliance with the various sections of Sarbanes-Oxley, especially Section 404, with its strong requirements for reviews of internal controls. Companies have complained that in addition to the high costs for compliance, the expensive procedures have failed to detect significant material weaknesses in internal controls. Only eight percent of companies reported material weaknesses as a result of Section 404, but these are companies with market capitalizations of more than $75 million.[2] Investors are jittery after their huge losses in the stock market, so even eight percent is still more than might have been publicly reported before Sarbanes-Oxley. Then Public Company Accounting Oversight Board (PCAOB) Chairman William J. McDonough stated that investors strongly support these improved financial controls because they "make financial statements more believable and more reliable."[3]

Government regulators understand that the cost of compliance can be burdensome and must be balanced to protect the interests and investments of shareholders. On May 16, 2005, the Securities and Exchange Commission (SEC) released its "Commission Statement on Implementation of Internal Control Reporting Requirements." This statement commented on issues that were noted during the first year of experience with implementation of Sarbanes-Oxley's Section 404. Two central themes came out of the feedback the SEC received from public companies. The first is that "compliance with Section 404 is producing benefits, including a heightened focus on internal controls at the top levels of public companies," and the second is that costs are significant and some may be unnecessary or excessive.[4]

The SEC has indicated that it is willing to be flexible in issuing clarifications for Section 404 implementation. It has further stated that common sense and open communication are necessary for both government regulators and corporate executives to improve internal controls and ultimately fraud prevention.[5] The message is clear that the SEC, PCAOB, and other government regulators are willing to work with corporations to ensure compliance. Expect this trend to continue, as Sarbanes-Oxley is relatively new legislation and some issues still need to be worked out. However, do not expect to see Sarbanes-Oxley overturned or significantly weakened. Representative Oxley opposes any suggestions of changes to the act he coauthored. "Most CFOs I talk to can quote [the Act's] cost down to the dollar," said Oxley. "Actually, they'll quote it down to the dime." He argued that the cost of compliance with Sarbanes-Oxley "is an investment in the strength of the United States capital markets."[6] The investing public has a long memory, and Congress, who heard the outcry, has an even better memory. As stated earlier in this book, the Mail Fraud Statute was enacted in 1872 to prosecute various schemes that used the mail to defraud. The Mail Fraud Statute is still in use today and in fact has been strengthened by Congress over the years. Expect the same for Sarbanes-Oxley in the years to come.

Federal Reserve Chairman Alan Greenspan is a strong supporter of Sarbanes-Oxley and its effectiveness in attacking corporate fraud over the short period of its existence. He also believes that Sarbanes-Oxley will be "fine-tuned" to make for improved compliance.[7] He reinforces the simple truth that "shareholders own our corporations and that corporate management should be working on behalf of shareholders to allocate business resources to their optimum use."[8] Greenspan emphasizes the importance of tone at the top for chief executives and the very positive effect it can have for employees and others outside the company. His hope is that if officers and directors have highly ethical behavior, they will, "not need detailed rules on how to act."[9] Just in case, there are always the strengthened antifraud measures to fall back on. Greenspan also made another insightful comment about the importance of ethical conduct when he stated that "material success is possible in this world, and far more satisfying when it comes without exploiting others."[10]

Some storm clouds may be on the horizon for aggressive SEC enforcement actions in the future. On June 1, 2005, SEC Chairman William Donaldson announced he was stepping down. Donaldson played a significant role in restoring credibility and trust to the financial markets. His replacement, Representative Christopher Cox (R-California), has been critical of the SEC's aggressive market regulation and has a reputation for protecting business. He was the main sponsor of the Private Securities Litigation Reform Act of 1995, which created obstacles for investors who wished to file civil actions against those who had defrauded them.[11] Under Cox, the SEC may not pursue multimillion dollar fines for corporate wrongdoing but may instead focus on the actions of individual executives and in addition may only litigate clear-cut violations.[12] Still, Cox will not want to incur the wrath of the voting public by not remembering their financial pain as a result of the corporate scandals. If the SEC does not remain a strong protector of investors, others will step in. The New York State Attorney General's office will no doubt keep up its fight against corporate fraud and will surely take action in any area in which the SEC fails to protect investors.[13]

## HAVE A ZERO TOLERANCE FOR FRAUD AND MEAN IT

Jack Welch, the legendary former CEO of General Electric, appeared on *The Tonight Show* on April 25, 2005. Host Jay Leno asked him why the general public had such a poor opinion of CEOs. In his inimitable fashion, Welch said, "Because so many of them were skunks." Indeed, a number of corporate executive "skunks" succumbed to greed and fraud and put their personal interests above those of investors and employees. The many "perp walks" and convictions show that executives are now being held accountable. All corporations and employees must be responsible for both the spirit and the letter of the law at all levels of the organization. No executive today will ever say that fraud is a good thing. However, if there are different standards of disciplinary action for executives and employees, the message is that fraud is condoned for some and not for others.

Corporate codes of conduct should address the problem of fraud by clearly stating that there is a zero tolerance for fraud of any kind. Whether it is a $50 inflated expense report or a $50 million revenue recognition issue, an organization must take appropriate action against all fraud. A good rule to follow is that the amount of the fraud is immaterial and any fraudulent activity that is disclosed and proved through professional investigation should result in termination of the employee. In addition, organizations should consider referring fraud by employees, vendors, and others to the appropriate law enforcement agency for criminal prosecution. The general counsel should be the focal point for final decisions as to criminal referrals. Companies should also consider publicizing prosecutions of employee fraudsters to reinforce a culture of compliance and a zero tolerance for fraud.

John McDermott is an expert in the investigation of corporate fraudsters. He has been a United States Postal Inspector for more than 22 years and is the team leader of the Fraud Investigations Team covering Brooklyn, Queens, and Long Island, New York. Over the years, he has conducted and supervised high-profile fraud cases in New York including Symbol Technologies, Spectrum Technologies, and Hanover Sterling, a huge stock fraud case that resulted in more than 60 convictions of brokers, stock promoters, and company executives. McDermott is a strong believer in criminal prosecution and punishment as a driving force for fraud prevention and compliance. He has said, "If the threat of doing twenty years, or life in jail doesn't scare anybody straight, I don't know what would. I certainly wouldn't take any risk by signing 10K's or 10Q's that I knew were fraudulent, when I knew the risk was going to jail."[14]

McDermott also hopes "that the corporate executives reading this book would have learned these lessons from those who were foolish enough to commit crimes" and do a "better job of self-policing."[15] His experience in investigating corporate fraud has led him to believe that corporations must improve "teaching ethics and morals to their corporate executives" and also do "a better job of listening to their internal and external auditors" when compliance issues are raised.[16]

Organizations can also send a great signal to employees, shareholders, and the government that they take fraud detection and prevention very seriously by hiring former federal agents and prosecutors with experience investigating and prosecuting fraud and white-collar crime for their internal investigation and legal departments. Smart companies know that by bringing in fraud detection talent, they are improving their compliance programs and lessening their fraud risk.

Probably the biggest sea change for corporations has been how they deal with the government in cases of fraud. Gone are the days of "us versus them" when business would hire the best defense attorneys money could buy and fight the government at every turn. Today, fighting the government means losing if the allegations of fraud are true. The age of "dinosaur" CEOs who ran their public companies their way with little concern for transparency is over. The tone at the top must be one of compliance and collaboration with government investigators, or ultimately the company will suffer.

During the New York State Attorney General's investigation of Marsh and McLennan for allegedly cheating clients by bid-rigging and collusion with other insurance companies, Eliot Spitzer made it clear that he was not happy with the lack of cooperation his office was receiving from Marsh executive leadership. In announcing a civil lawsuit against Marsh in October 2004, Spitzer said publicly to the Marsh directors that they "should think long and hard, very long and hard, about the leadership of your company."[17] Shortly after this strong message from a prosecutor questioning the tone at the top at Marsh, CEO Jeffrey Greenberg was forced out by the company's Board of Directors.[18] Greenberg's replacement was Michael Cherkasky, a former prosecutor and CEO of a corporate investigative firm with a reputation for integrity.[19] Marsh acted quickly to save the company at the expense of its CEO. Interestingly, Greenberg's father, Maurice "Hank" Greenberg, former President, Chairman, and CEO of American International Group, was an insurance industry legend who faced his own problems. For more on the elder Greenberg, see Executive Insight 17.1.

## EXECUTIVE INSIGHT 17.1: A CHANGE IN CULTURE AT AIG

In October 2004, New York State Attorney General Eliot Spitzer announced a far-ranging investigation of bid-rigging in the insurance industry. Spitzer alleged that Marsh & McLennan, the largest insurance broker in the world, "cheated corporate clients by rigging bids and collecting huge fees from major insurance companies for throwing business their way."[i] Among the major insurance companies also named as being involved was American International Group (AIG), the nation's largest business insurance company. In announcing the civil complaint filed against Marsh, Spitzer also revealed that two AIG executives had pled guilty to felony charges of fraud for their involvement with the scheme.[ii] At the time, Spitzer described an industry wrought with corruption.

In the months to come, Spitzer's investigation would grow and focus more on AIG and its long-reigning CEO, Maurice "Hank" Greenberg. Greenberg had been CEO since 1967 and Chairman since 1989. Greenberg had a reputation for running the company his way and "brushed off investors' desires for more disclosure and better governance."[iii] There were also concerns about the independence of AIG's Board of Directors. As one reporter stated, "Contrary to the tide of corporate behavior, AIG seems to operate as if it is accountable only to Mr. Greenberg and its insiders."[iv]

A new culture was coming to AIG. Spurred on by an aggressive prosecutor and a changing landscape of vastly improved corporate governance, AIG decided that nothing was more important than the interests of investors. Greenberg resigned as AIG President and CEO on March 14, 2005 but stayed on as Chairman. Possibly in a move to shield his assets from the government, on March 11, he transferred 41.4 million shares of company stock worth $2.2 billion to his wife.[v]

AIG then enforced its policy that all employees cooperate fully in any government investigation. When two top executives, CFO Howard I. Smith and Vice-President Christian M. Milton, signaled their intent to use their Fifth Amendment rights against self-incrimination and not talk to Spitzer's investigators, they were fired by AIG.[vi]

On March 28, 2005, Greenberg announced that he was retiring from the company. Two days later, AIG advised that it had identified eight accounting issues that "could reduce shareholder equity by $1.1 billion."[vii] After an extensive internal review of its books and records, AIG announced on May 1, 2005, that it would restate its financial statements for calendar years 2000 through 2003.[viii] In addition, AIG stated that shareholder equity as of December 31, 2004, would be reduced by approximately $2.7 billion.[ix]

On May 26, 2005, Spitzer and the New York State Insurance Department filed a civil lawsuit alleging that AIG's former top management, including former Chairman Maurice R. Greenberg and former Chief Financial Officer Howard I. Smith, "engaged in numerous fraudulent business transactions that exaggerated the strength of the company's core underwriting business to prop up its stock price."[x]

"The irony of this case is that AIG was a well-run and profitable company that didn't need to cheat," Spitzer said in the press release, "and yet, the former top management routinely and persistently resorted to deception and fraud in an apparent effort to improve the company's financial results."[xi]

There were some interesting statements in the civil complaint, for example, "four days after AIG publicly announced its receipt of a subpoena from this office [Spitzer's office], Greenberg called the AIG trading desk from his private jet. AIG's shares were down, and Greenberg told the trader to buy up to 250,000 shares." He made several more calls asking the trader to be more aggressive in buying the stock in order to push up its price.[xii]

The civil complaint also alleged that an assistant to Greenberg ordered the destruction of company documents related to an offshore affiliate reinsurer that was related to the investigation.[xiii]

The press release stated that AIG was taking steps to restore the company's credibility and reputation and that it was cooperating with the investigation. The press release went on to say that AIG "admitted that many of the transactions were improper, has terminated implicated personnel, and has announced plans to restate its earnings."[xiv] There was definitely a culture change at AIG but at a significant price for shareholders and employees.

In a postscript, on November 3, 2004, a *Wall Street Journal* reporter devoted a column to how AIG needed a new "playbook," as "AIG seems determined to follow the [Arthur] Andersen playbook, and if it doesn't stop soon, I predict the consequences will be dire."[xv] The reporter suggested that AIG needed to do several things.

- Stop asserting its innocence
- Take the allegations very seriously, conduct an internal investigation, and then publicly announce the results
- Cooperate fully with the government, find evidence of wrongdoing, and turn it over to the government before they find it
- Don't destroy anything
- Confess.[xvi]

Although AIG eventually put most of these recommendations into place, it did not follow all of them. On June 1, 2005, AIG further announced in a filing with the SEC that accounting irregularities had resulted in a restatement lowering five years of results by $3.9 billion.[xvii]

---

[i] Theo Francis, "Spitzer Charges Bid-Rigging in Insurance," *Wall Street Journal*, October 15, 2004, A1.

[ii] Ibid.

[iii] Jesse Eisinger, "AIG's Chief Shows Signs of Humility As Spitzer Probe Rattles Industry," *Wall Street Journal*, October 20, 2004, C1.

[iv] Ibid.

[v] Theo Francis and Ian McDonald, "Greenberg Move May Not Shield Assets," *Wall Street Journal*, April 14, 2005, C1.

[vi] Theo Francis and Ian McDonald, "AIG Fires Two Top Executives As Probe Intensifies," *Wall Street Journal*, March 22, 2005, A1

[vii] Brooke A. Masters, "Breadth of AIG's Problems Stands Out," MSNBC.com, April 1, 2005, www.msnbc.com/id/7355730.

[viii] "AIG Nears Completion of Internal Review: Will Restate Results, Provides Update on Internal Review and Timing of Form 10-K," AIG Press Release, May 1, 2005, http://ir.aigcorporate.com/phoenix.zhtml?c=76115&p=irol-newsArticle&ID=703645&highlight=.

[ix] Ibid.

[x1] "State Suit Cites Pattern of Fraud at AIG," Press Release of the Office of New York State Attorney General Eliot Spitzer, May 26, 2005, www.oag.state.ny.us/press/2005/may/may26a_05.html.

[xi] Ibid.

[xii] The People of the State of New York by Eliot Spitzer, Attorney General of the State of New York, and Howard Mills, Superintendent of Insurance of the State of New York, Plaintiffs, against American International Group, Inc., Maurice R. Greenberg and Howard I. Smith, Complaint, Supreme Court of the State of New York, County of New York, filed May 26, 2005, New York, New York.

[xiii] Ibid.

[xiv] Ibid.

[xv] James B. Stewart, "AIG May Need a New Playbook," *Wall Street Journal*, November 3, 2004, D2.

[xvi] Ibid.

[xvii] James B. Bernstein, "AIG Restates Results by Nearly $4 Billion," *Seattle Times*, June 1, 2005, E3.

## THE *WALL STREET JOURNAL* RULE

What should keep an executive up at night? One big worry is the possibility of fraud occurring at the company, whether potentially fatal fraudulent financial accounting or other asset misappropriation fraud. Once detected, how a fraud is communicated to investors, employees, government authorities, and the press can make a big difference in the final resolution. Today, it is harder than ever before to contain the existence of a fraud quietly. With the abundance of whistle-blowers and self-reporting requirements for companies and corporate executives, it is extremely difficult to hide fraud. It is also foolhardy even to consider any form of concealment. Bad news always seems to be made public. How would one react if an act by a company were published on page one of the *Wall Street Journal*? A good rule to follow is to always think of this worst-case scenario and do everything possible to prevent it from happening.

# A FRAUD PREVENTION VISIONARY: INTERVIEW WITH JOSEPH T. WELLS ON THE FUTURE OF FRAUD AND FRAUD PREVENTION

Joseph T. Wells is the founder and Chairman of the Board of the Association of Certified Fraud Examiners (ACFE), the world's largest antifraud organization, with 33,000 members in more than 125 nations. A CPA, Certified Fraud Examiner, and former FBI agent, Mr. Wells founded the ACFE in 1988. In addition to his administrative duties as Chairman, Mr. Wells researches, writes, and lectures to business and professional groups on white-collar crime issues. He is also an Adjunct Professor of Fraud Examination at the University of Texas in Austin. Mr. Wells has received numerous honors for his teaching and writing. In 2002, the American Accounting Association named him the Accounting Education Innovator of the Year. He has received the top writing awards from both the Journal of Accountancy and Internal Auditor Magazine, and for the last seven years, Mr. Wells has been named to *Accounting Today* magazine's annual list of America's "Top 100 Most Influential People" in accounting.

Mr. Wells is truly a fraud prevention visionary. He was promoting the professionalism of fraud examination and education as fraud deterrence long before it was fashionable. In the following wide-ranging interview, Mr. Wells provides insightful comments on the future of Sarbanes-Oxley, corporate crime, fraud prevention, and compliance.

Q: Do you think Congress will blink and reverse some of the regulations resulting from Sarbanes-Oxley?

A: As we know, Sarbanes-Oxley was passed in a flurry of activity resulting from some of the large accounting frauds. The pressure for Congress to act at that time was tremendous. Generally, these "hurry-up" laws are seriously flawed and overreaching. As just one example, the penalties for mail fraud have been quadrupled from five to twenty years. I term this "feel-good legislation." Although the penalties have been quadrupled, the resources devoted to the criminal justice system that would implement these laws have not. As a result, fewer people—not more—will likely find themselves in our crowded prisons. Besides, volumes of research by criminologists have failed to document a connection between lengthy prison terms and deterrence.

Some aspects of Sarbanes-Oxley are good and overdue. The accounting profession—of which I have been a member for nearly four decades——has historically shown that it is unable or unwilling to regulate itself. Switching the regulatory authority to the Public Company Accounting Oversight Board (PCAOB) will probably turn out to be a good thing. Additional protection for whistle-blowers may prove useful. Financial statement certifications by executives won't deter those who are hell-bent on cooking the books, but overall, this procedure can't really hurt, either. Board members of public companies who are completely independent are a step in the right direction, too.

It seems that passing a law in the first place is much easier than getting bad legislation repealed. So I am not expecting Congress to blink any time soon. But my guess is that whether or not Sarbanes-Oxley is a good law won't be known for at least ten years. It will take that long to see if it really reduces the incidence of financial statement frauds.

Q: In the 1980s we had the savings and loan frauds, in the early 1990s we had insider trading, and in this decade we had the massive financial statement frauds. What's next?

A: First, we have not seen the end of massive financial statement frauds, regardless of Sarbanes-Oxley. The law does nothing to remove the root cause of the problem, which is caused by companies under great pressure to perform in the short term. Fifty years ago, investors bought stock to see it grow over the long haul. That simply isn't the case any more. Now, in part because of the speed of the Internet, investors and day traders will turn stock over in a matter of hours. They aren't concerned about what a company makes or its long-term innovation; it's more like playing corporate poker using company management as the chips. Unless and until we can change the investing mentality, we will continue to see executives pressured to cross the line.

Second, because of the aging baby-boomers (like me) I am seriously concerned with our pension funds. We've already seen cracks in the dike; many companies are filing bankruptcy in order to avoid their pension fund obligations. Other companies have simply spent the money reserved for their retirees on other things. Only one underfunded quasi-government organization, the Pension Benefit Guaranty Corporation, is chartered to protect our pensions. But, it must keep track of 32,000 separate pension plans. And, it currently has $65 billion in liabilities versus only $39 billion in assets. And of course, those assets are primarily invested in the stock market. So, I am concerned that the net effect of stock market manipulations and pension plan frauds could have a devastating economic impact.

Third, because of the increased globalization of business, I think that transnational investment swindles are likely to increase. This is exacerbated by the fact that there are not uniform accounting standards worldwide. China, for example, is likely to be a major economic force in the 21st century. But currently its economy, because of pyramiding growth, has a "wild west" aura. As financial opportunities there (and in other emerging economies) increase, can investors trust the numbers? We'll just have to wait and see.

**Q: What do you think is the best way to convince corporate executives to allocate more resources to fighting fraud?**

A: I think the best way is to appeal to their sense of profit. Currently, the approach is to teach ethics, as if ethics really needs to be taught. Don't misunderstand; we all need to be reminded of what ethical conduct is all about. But, normally socialized individuals know right from wrong. And if they don't, all of the ethical training in the world is not going to fix that. What seems to get lost in the shuffle is that fraud prevention is one of the best investments that a business can make. I've seen studies that suggest the return on fraud prevention programs can be 50:1. So, I think that executives should be told, "Fraud prevention doesn't cost much money at all, and it pays huge dividends." I think that they should also be reminded that so-called "immaterial" frauds could have very material consequences. One example is the former investment firm of E.F. Hutton. You may recall that the corporate "money management" strategy was actually to kite checks. Now, the kiting itself was immaterial to the financial statements as a whole. But the reputational damage drove E.F. Hutton out of business. There are many more examples like that. So the simple message to management is that tolerating fraud, in any form and at any level, is bad business; nothing good can come from it.

**Q: What more must corporate executives do that they are not doing now to prevent fraud and abuse?**

A: Once you get down from the executive level, two things become critically important. The first is the well-used phrase, "tone at the top." Should executives not walk the talk, then the people below them won't. If mid-level managers are dishonest, so too will be the employees. It is necessary, indeed vital, to lead by example. Second, there is a perception that occupational fraud can be prevented with adequate internal control. Controls are a necessary part of any fraud prevention effort, but control is not the root cause of fraud; it is dissatisfaction with the company or with workplace conditions. A number of landmark research projects, including one by Hollinger and Clark, clearly document that workers who are well treated, respected, and adequately compensated are much less likely to take out their hostility on the company. Executives need to understand that.

**Q: How do we move compliance from an initiative to a cultural mind-set?**

A: Regrettably, our society seems to have adopted a "get rich quick" mentality. In part, we can thank the mass media for that. By featuring the lifestyles of the rich and famous, people—quite naturally—are convinced that they deserve the same things and they become dissatisfied with what they already have. Sociologist Robert Merton developed an anomie theory to explain the disconnect between what we have and what we want. And in his view, this dissatisfaction is at the root of much crime.

Many compliance laws are enacted to protect us from ourselves. But that is not really a fix; it is the equivalent of trying to put out the forest fire with a garden hose. What is needed is a realignment of society's priorities, where honesty and integrity are more important than fame and fortune. However, that becomes extremely difficult when we see our leaders and role models lie, cheat, and steal. Psychologists tell us that our values are formed very early in life. And if they are not instilled in us by our parents at an early age, we'll never adopt them. So, the only true—and permanent—solution is to teach the right things to our children and they to theirs.

**Q: How is fraud prevention being instituted outside the United States?**

A: According to the saying, "when America sneezes, the world catches cold." Our European and Canadian neighbors often look to us for guidance and have similar programs to prevent fraud. Although there are no concrete studies, my suspicion is that Europe has less fraud overall because the gap between the "haves" and "have nots" is generally smaller. European society tends to take better care of its underprivileged than we do in the United States. In Eastern Europe, where they are still recovering from the Soviet era, fraud and corruption are rampant. I suspect it will take them at least another decade or two to get where we are. In Japan and much of Asia (excluding China), cultural prohibitions against dishonesty probably equate to less fraud than in America. In Latin America, especially in Mexico and Columbia, the dependence on the drug trade to help fuel the economic system has created a huge underground economy. The efforts of the United States to control illicit narcotics through interdiction, as well-meaning as it might be, has actually worsened the drug problem by driving up prices.

Worldwide, I don't see fraud coming down until around the mid-21st century. Fraud is the crime of the older and better educated perpetrator. Street crimes are for the young and dumb. Society is aging, and it's more educated; that is one of the reasons we see less violent crime today than at any time in the last 30 years. Technology may offer some solutions, but it is not a panacea. Without being an alarmist, I think fraud is going to get worse before we see it get better.

**Q: What is your vision of the future for the fraud prevention field?**

A: The study of fraud prevention is in its infancy. For example, we can take two companies or individuals with indistinguishable characteristics. One will experience fraud while the other will not. We really don't know why. The only hope is that additional research may provide some of the answers. But, we do know what doesn't work: punishment after the fact. As we say here in Texas, that is like closing the barn door after the horses are gone. That's not to imply that people who commit crimes shouldn't be punished; it's something that must be done in a civilized society. However, we didn't experience a rise in fraud overnight, and this seemingly intractable problem won't be solved quickly.

## MOVING FROM A COMPLIANCE INITIATIVE TO A CULTURAL MIND-SET

As stated by the SEC regarding internal controls, "A one-size fits all, bottom-up, check-the-box approach that treats all internal controls equally is less likely to improve internal controls and financial reporting than reasoned, good faith exercise of professional judgment focused on reasonable, as opposed to absolute, assurance."[20] Fraud risk management based on a "checklist" approach is not conducive to success in fraud prevention because fraudsters are very adaptive and imaginative in their schemes. What is better is a principle-based system because "it is impossible to develop comprehensive rules for every situation."[21] Truly world-class companies understand that fraud prevention and enhanced internal controls are not achieved by just checking off a list. The "initiative" idea that compliance is just a project or a one-time idea must be replaced with embedding sound principles of fraud prevention into the "cultural mind-set" of all employees.

In announcing its intent to amend existing organizational sentencing guidelines on April 13, 2004, the United State Sentencing Commission strongly stated the importance of effective compliance and ethics programs for an organization. The Commission's "focus on ethical corporate behavior is a unique development in the 13-year history of the organizational sentencing guidelines," but it is altogether not surprising given the magnitude of recent corporate crime.[22] The message they sent to all corporate executives is as follows:

*A fundamental component of the organizational sentencing guidelines, promulgated by the Commission in 1991, is the effective compliance and ethics program. Last week, the Commission made the standards for the compliance and ethics program more rigorous and put greater responsibility on boards of directors and executives for the oversight and management of compliance programs. In particular, directors and executives now must take an active leadership role for the content and operation of compliance and ethics programs. Companies that seek reduced criminal fines now must demonstrate that they have identified areas of risk where criminal violations may occur, trained high-level officials as well as employees in relevant legal standards and obligations, and given their compliance officers sufficient authority and resources to carry out their responsibilities. Under the revised guidelines, if companies hope to mitigate criminal fines and penalties, they must also promote an organizational culture that encourages a commitment to compliance with the law and ethical conduct by exercising due diligence in meeting the criteria.*[23]

To ensure a cultural mind-set of fraud prevention, the following key elements must be in place in an organization and must stay in place.

### Tone at the Top

Chief executives, officers, and directors set an important tone with every word and action they take. Their accountability and responsibility and how they push the message down to the lowest level employee may be the single most important aspect of building a fraud prevention culture that actually works. No employee can be expected to follow company policy or obey laws if their leaders are not doing the same.

### The "Policing" Role of the Board of Directors and the Audit Committee

Along with the entire Board of Directors, Audit Committee members are truly the "police officers" of an organization; they ensure compliance with company rules and policy, as well as laws and regulations. Sarbanes-Oxley requires that boards take an active role in corporate governance, acting as "checks and balances" to executive leadership. Strong and independent Audit Committees ensure compliance, whereas weak and ineffectual ones foster the criminal behavior seen at disgraced companies. Directors who abdicate their important roles will be held accountable both civilly and criminally.

## The Challenge to Internal Audit

Internal audit departments must accept the challenge to take a leadership role in fraud prevention. The importance of internal audit departments has been reinforced with the enactment of Sarbanes-Oxley and the overall climate of enhanced fraud prevention and detection. In a perfect world, internal audit should uncover issues before they become headlines in the *Wall Street Journal*. The fraud detection, investigation, and prevention component must be added to internal audit to ensure linkage and continuous interaction with the auditing function. Adding needed professionals to the internal audit team, training and empowering them, giving them direct reporting to executive leadership, and providing high visibility to the Audit Committee are steps that should be considered.

## The Important Role of Managers in Fraud Prevention

Managers must provide oversight to their employees and be held accountable for preventing and reporting fraud. Managers are role models in developing their direct reports and ensuring compliance with both company policies and governmental regulations and laws. Managers must know how fraud can infect an organization and how to detect the warning signs. Understanding how to report potential violations of standards of business conduct is paramount for any manager. Strong and committed managers are an important element in a compliance program that is effective overall.

## Integrity and Honesty for All

Integrity and honesty are core values for all employees, and there can be no exceptions. A successful fraud prevention program must constantly reinforce these values among all employees at all levels wherever the organization operates. Having a zero tolerance for fraud goes hand in hand with integrity and honesty at an organization.

## A Well-Communicated and Responsive Reporting System

Every organization, public or private, large or small, must have an effective reporting mechanism such as a hotline to allow employees and others outside the company to report financial fraud or other violations of standards of business conduct. People must feel confident that they can anonymously and confidentially report issues and that whistle-blowers will be protected from retaliation. Whatever the form of the reporting mechanism, it must be well communicated and accessible to ensure full reporting of all issues.

## Cross-Group Collaboration

Consistency and linkage of all components within an organization are essential and translate to effective cross-group collaboration among Chief Executives, Officers, Directors, and the various legal, compliance, internal audit, finance, human resources, investigative, and corporate security functions.

## Embracing a Culture of Compliance

Truly outstanding companies view Sarbanes-Oxley and the other compliance enhancements as an opportunity for improved corporate governance. They understand and embrace the importance of creating a stronger fraud prevention program and internal control system that ultimately give them a competitive advantage.

## THE ROAD AHEAD

The purpose of this book is to provide a roadmap for reaching the highest levels of compliance in fraud prevention and internal control. The trip is not always easy and there can be many roadblocks and detours—but stay the course. The route can be successfully navigated with the many tools, programs, and insights provided by the authors. Building a fraud prevention culture that works is no longer an option in today's business world. It is a requirement for survival. Sarbanes-Oxley, the Federal Sentencing Guidelines for Organizations, and other corporate governance enhancements require accountability and oversight on an ongoing basis. However, there is another simple and straightforward reason for compliance and that is because it is the right thing to do.

It is unfortunate that so many people had their first experience with fraud as a result of the corporate scandals, large and small, resulting in billions of dollars of investor losses. Shareholders and others came to learn first-hand what professional fraud investigators have long known. Fraud can happen anywhere, and its damaging effects go far beyond the financial loss. The impact to reputation can be long lasting and often fatal. Fraud is really simple when one gets right down to it. The definition is clear. It is lying, cheating, and stealing. It is motive, opportunity, and rationalization. What is far more important than the definition is how to prevent it. "The potential of being caught most often persuades likely perpetrators not to commit the fraud. Because of this principle, the existence of a thorough control system is essential to fraud prevention."[24] Fraud prevention is about being proactive rather than reactive. Accountability and integrity stop fraud.

## ENDNOTES

1. 2005 Christian & Timbers survey of 186 United States executives, *Business Week,* May 23, 2005, 16.
2. Floyd Norris, "Regulators Seek to Trim Cost of Rules on Auditing," *New York Times,* May 17, 2005, C6.
3. Ibid.
4. United States Securities and Exchange Commission, "Commission Statement on Implementation of Internal Control Reporting Requirements, May 16, 2005, 2005-74, , www.sec.gov/news/press/2005-74.htm.
5. Ibid.
6. Tim Reason, "Feeling the Pain: Are the Benefits of Sarbanes-Oxley Worth the Cost?," CFO, cfo.com, May 1, 2005, www.cfo.com/printable/article.cfm/3909558?f.
7. Byron Acohido, "Greenspan Marvels at How Effective Sarbanes-Oxley Has Been So Far," *USA Today,* May 16, 2005, 3B.

8. Ibid.
9. Ibid.
10. Ibid.
11. Robert Kuttner, "Cox's SEC: Investor Beware," *Business Week,* June 27, 2005, 134.
12. Amy Borrus, "What to Expect from Chris Cox," *Business Week,* June 20, 2005, 42.
13. Ibid.
14. Statement to the authors on April 22, 2005.
15. Ibid.
16. Ibid.
17. Monica Langley and Ian McDonald, "Marsh Directors Consider Having CEO Step Aside," *Wall Street Journal,* October 22, 2004, A1.
18. Thor Valdmanis, "Spitzer Backs Down a Bit after Marsh CEO Resigns," *USA Today,* October 26, 2004, A1.
19. Ian McDonald, "The New Sheriff at Marsh," *Wall Street Journal,* October 26, 2004, C1.
20. United States Securities and Exchange Commission, "Commission Statement on Implementation of Internal Control Reporting Requirements, May 16, 2005, 2005-74, www.sec.gov/news/press/2005-74.htm.
21. Peter Morton, "Risky Business," *camagazine.com,* May 2005, www.camagazine.com/index.cfm/ci_id/26177/la_id/1.htm.
22. "Sentencing Commission Toughens Requirements for Corporate Compliance Programs," News Release of the United States Sentencing Commission, Washington, DC, April 13, 2004, www.ussc.gov/PRESS/rel0404.htm.
23. Ibid.
24. Association of Certified Fraud Examiners. *Fraud Examiners Manual,* (Austin, TX: ACFE, 2006), 4.601.

# Key Sections of the Sarbanes-Oxley Act of 2002

| | |
|---|---|
| Sec 101-107 | Establishes a new regulatory agency, a five-member Public Company Accounting Oversight Board, to register and oversee public accounting firms |
| Sec 201 | Prohibits auditor from providing certain specific services to audit clients |
| Sec 202 | Requires Audit Committee to approve all audit and nonaudit services provided by independent auditor |
| Sec 204 | Requires independent auditor to report certain matters to the Audit Committee, including critical accounting policies and alternative accounting treatments of financial matters discussed with management, as well as the treatment preferred by the accounting firm |
| Sec 204 | Requires one-year cooling-off period before client can hire audit engagement team members |
| Sec 204 | Modifies disclosure of total fees paid to independent auditors |
| Sec 301 | Requires that all Audit Committee members be independent and that the Committee establish procedures for processing complaints and anonymous employee submissions regarding the company's accounting, accounting controls, or auditing matters |
| Sec 302 | Requires certification by CEO and CFO that Forms 10K and 10Q do not contain untrue statements, that financial information is fairly presented, and that disclosure controls and procedures are effective |
| Sec 304 | Requires CEO and CFO to forfeit bonus and options if financial statements are restated due to noncompliance with securities law |
| Sec 306 | Prohibits officers, directors, and other insiders from trading stock during pension-fund blackout periods |
| Sec 307 | Prescribes minimum standards of professional conduct for corporate attorneys |

| | |
|---|---|
| Sec 401 | Requires financial statements to reflect all material correcting adjustments identified by auditor |
| Sec 401(a) | Requires certification by CEO and CFO that financial statements fully comply with SEC Act of 1934 and fairly present in all material respects the financial condition and results of the operations of the company |
| Sec 401(b) | Requires auditor to retain records relevant to audit for seven years |
| Sec 402 | Requires disclosure of Audit Committee financial expert |
| Sec 403 | Requires disclosure of Code of Ethics for CEO, CFO, and Controller |
| Sec 404 | Requires an annual evaluation and report by management on the effectiveness of internal controls and procedures for financial reporting, as well as a report by the independent auditor attesting to management's assertions |
| Sec 406 | Accelerates reporting of sale and purchase of stock by directors and executive officers. |
| Sec 406 | Accelerates filing of Forms 10K (60 days) and 10Q (35 days) |
| Sec 407 | Prohibits personal loans to directors and executive officers. |
| Sec 802 | Requires that non-GAAP (i.e., pro-forma) financial measures be reconciled to GAAP and explained. |
| Sec 906 | Requires disclosure of all material off-balance sheet transactions. |

# Fraud Risk Factors Related to Misstatements Arising from Fraudulent Financial Reporting

The following are examples of risk factors relating to misstatements arising from fraudulent financial reporting.

### Incentives/Pressures

A. Financial stability or profitability is threatened by economic, industry, or entity operating conditions, such as (or as indicated by):

- High degree of competition or market saturation, accompanied by declining margins
- High vulnerability to rapid changes in technology, product obsolescence, or interest rates
- Significant declines in customer demand and increasing business failures in either the industry or overall economy
- Operating losses making the threat of bankruptcy, foreclosure, or hostile takeover imminent
- Recurring negative cash flows from operations or an inability to generate cash flows from operations while reporting earnings and earnings growth
- Rapid growth or unused profitability, especially compared to that of other companies in the same industry
- New accounting, statutory, or regulatory requirements.

B. Excessive pressure exists for management to meet the requirements or expectations of third parties due to the following:
- Profitability or trend level expectations of investment analysts, institutional investors, significant creditors, or other external parties (particularly expectations that are unduly aggressive or unrealistic), including expectations created by management in, for example, overly optimistic press releases or annual report messages
- Need to obtain additional debt or equity financing to stay competitive including financing of major research and development or capital expenditures
- Marginal ability to meet exchange listing requirements or debt repayment or other debt covenant requirements
- Perceived or real adverse effects of reporting poor financial results on significant pending transactions, such as business combinations or contract awards

C. Information available indicates that management or the board of directors' personal financial situation is threatened by the entity's financial performance arising from the following:
- Significant financial interests in the entity
- Significant portions of their compensation (for example, bonuses, stock options, and earn-out arrangements) being contingent upon achieving aggressive targets for stock price, operating results, financial position, or cash flow[1]
- Personal guarantees of debts of the entity.

D. There is excessive pressure on management or operating personnel to meet financial targets set up by the board of directors or management, including sales or profitability incentive goals.

### Opportunities

A. The nature of the industry or the entity's operations provides opportunities to engage in fraudulent financial reporting that can arise from the following:
- Significant related-party transactions not in the ordinary course of business or with related entities not audited or audited by another firm.
- A strong financial presence or ability to dominate a certain industry sector that allows the entity to dictate terms or

conditions to suppliers or customers that may result in inappropriate or non–arm's-length transactions
- Assets, liabilities, revenues, or expenses based on significant estimates that involve subjective judgments or uncertainties that are difficult to corroborate
- Significant, unusual, or highly complex transactions, especially those close to period end that pose difficult "substance over form" questions
- Significant operations located or conducted across international borders in jurisdictions where differing business environments and culture exist
- Significant bank accounts or subsidiary or branch operations in tax-haven jurisdictions for which there appears to be no clear business justification.

B. There is ineffective monitoring of management as a result of the following:
- Domination of management by a single person or small group (in a nonowner-managed business) without compensating controls
- Ineffective board of directors or audit committee oversight over the financial reporting process and internal control.

C. There is a complex or unstable organizational structure, as evidenced by the following:
- Difficulty in determining the organization or individuals that have controlling interest in the entity
- Overly complex organizational structure involving unusual legal entities or management lines of authority
- High turnover of senior management, counsel, or board members.

D. Internal control components are deficient as a result of the following:
- Inadequate monitoring of controls, including automated controls and controls over the interim financial reporting (where external reporting is required)
- High turnover rates or employment of ineffective accounting, internal audit, or information technology staff
- Ineffective accounting and information systems, including situations involving reportable conditions.

### Attitudes/Rationalization

Risk factors reflective of attitudes/rationalizations by board members, management, or employees, that allow them to engage in and/or justify fraudulent financial reporting, may not be susceptible to observation by the auditor. Nevertheless, the auditor who becomes aware of the existence of such information should consider it in identifying the risks of material misstatement arising from fraudulent financial reporting. For example, auditors may become aware of the following information that may indicate a risk factor:

- Ineffective communication, implementation, support, or enforcement of the entity's values or ethical standards by management or the communication of inappropriate values or ethical standards
- Non-financial management's excessive participation in or preoccupation with the selection of accounting principles or the determination of significant estimates
- Known history of violations of securities laws or other laws and regulations, or claims against the entity, its senior management, or board members alleging fraud or violations of laws and regulations
- Excessive interest by management in maintaining or increasing the entity's stock price or earnings trend
- A practice by management of committing to analysts, creditors, and other third parties to achieve aggressive or unrealistic forecasts
- Management failing to correct known reportable conditions on a timely basis
- An interest by management in employing inappropriate means to minimize reported earnings for tax-motivated reasons
- Recurring attempts by management to justify marginal or inappropriate accounting on the basis of materiality
- The relationship between management and the current or predecessor auditor is strained, as exhibited by the following:
  - Frequent disputes with the current or predecessor auditors on accounting, auditing, or reporting matters
  - Unreasonable demands on the auditor, such as unreasonable time constraints regarding the completion of the audit or the issuance of the auditor's report

- Formal or informal restrictions on the auditor that inappropriately limit access to people or information or the ability to communicate effectively with the board of directors or audit committee
- Domineering management behavior in dealing with the auditor, especially involving attempts to influence the scope of the auditor's work or the selection or continuance of personnel assigned to or consulted on the audit engagement.

Source: Reprinted with permission from AICPA; Copyright © 2002 by American Institute of Certified Public Accountants

---

[1] Management incentive plans may be contingent upon achieving targets relating only to certain accounts or selected activities of the entity, even though the related accounts or activities may not be material to the entity as a whole.

# Fraud Risk Factors Related to Misstatements Arising from Misappropriation of Assets

**R**isk factors that relate to misstatements arising from misappropriation of assets are also classified according to the three conditions generally present when fraud exists: incentives/pressures, opportunities, and attitudes/rationalizations. Some of the risk factors related to misstatements arising from fraudulent financial reporting also may be present when misstatements arising from misappropriation of assets occur. For example, ineffective monitoring of management and weaknesses in internal control may be present when misstatements due to either fraudulent financial reporting or misappropriation of assets exist. The following are examples of risk factors related to misstatements arising from misappropriation of assets.

### Incentives/Pressures
A. Personal financial obligations may create pressure on management or employees with access to cash or other assets susceptible to theft to misappropriate those assets.
B. Adverse relationships between the entity and employees with access to cash or other assets susceptible to theft may motivate

those employees to misappropriate those assets. For example, adverse relationships may be created by the following:

- Known or anticipated future employee layoffs
- Recent or anticipated changes to employee compensation or benefit plans
- Promotions, compensation, or other rewards inconsistent with expectations.

### Opportunities

A. Certain characteristics or circumstances may increase the susceptibility of assets to misappropriation. For example, opportunities to misappropriate assets increase when there are the following:

- Large amounts of cash on hand or processed
- Inventory items that are small in size, of high value, or in high demand
- Easily convertible assets, such as bearer bonds, diamonds, or computer chips
- Fixed assets that are small in size, marketable, or lacking observable identification of ownership.

B. Inadequate internal control over assets may increase the susceptibility of misappropriation of those assets. For example, misappropriation of assets may occur because there is the following:

- Inadequate segregation of duties or independent checks
- Inadequate management oversight of employees responsible for assets, for example, inadequate supervision or monitoring of remote locations
- Inadequate job applicant screening of employees with access to assets
- Inadequate recordkeeping with respect to assets
- Inadequate system of authorization and approval of transactions (for example, in purchasing)
- Inadequate physical safeguards over cash, investments, inventory, or fixed assets
- Lack of complete and timely reconciliations of assets
- Lack of timely and appropriate documentation of transactions, for example, credits for merchandise returns

- Lack of mandatory vacations for employees performing key control functions
- Inadequate management understanding of information technology, which enables information technology employees to perpetrate a misappropriation
- Inadequate access controls over automated records, including controls over and review of computer systems event logs.

## Attitudes/Rationalization

Risk factors reflective of employee attitudes/rationalizations that allow them to justify misappropriations of assets are generally not susceptible to observation by the auditor. Nevertheless, the auditor who becomes aware of the existence of such information should consider it in identifying the risks of material misstatement arising from misappropriation of assets. For example, auditors may become aware of the following attitudes or behavior of employees who have access to assets susceptible to misappropriation:

- Disregard for the need for monitoring or reducing risk related to misappropriation of assets
- Disregard for internal control over misappropriation of assets by overriding existing controls or by failing to correct known internal control deficiencies
- Behavior indicating displeasure with the company or its treatments of the employee
- Changes in behavior or lifestyle that may indicate assets have been misappropriated.

Source: Reprinted with permission from AICPA; Copyright © 2002 by American Institute of Certified Public Accountants

# Index